Ambiance, Tourism and the City

Ambiance, Tourism and the City considers how tourism and urban development affect the lived ambiances of contemporary cities around the world. As most of the existing literature on sensory atmospheres says little about the intersection between tourism and atmospheric production, this book affirms the centrality of the notion of ambiance as a mode of inquiry into the making and remaking of urban places for tourist consumption.

The book takes the reader into the sensory worlds of a traditional Italian marketplace, a jungle park in Kuala Lumpur, a slum in the Colombian city of Medellín, or the "sun and sand" tourism destinations in Southern Spain, among other case studies. It offers new insights into the impact of tourism on the urban environment from multidisciplinary perspectives and a wide range of geographical regions across Europe, North America, Asia, and South America. Through these contemporary case studies, the book further deepens our understanding of the ways in which "ambiances" and "atmospheres" pervade the physical regeneration and sensory transformation of contemporary tourist destinations. Conversely, this book offers insights on the effects of tourism on everyday urban experience.

By bringing together a diverse group of scholars and case studies to present a global perspective on the atmospheric production of the tourist city, this book is to serve as a valuable reference tool for researchers and undergraduate and postgraduate students with an interest in urban ambiances, tourism, cultural geography, and urban planning.

Iñigo Sánchez-Fuarros is Ramón y Cajal senior postdoctoral researcher at the Institute of Heritage Sciences (INCIPIT-CSIC) in Santiago de Compostela (Spain). He holds a PhD in Anthropology (University of Barcelona). Previously, he worked as a postdoctoral researcher at NOVA University (Lisbon, Portugal) and Queen's University Belfast (UK). He is the author of Cubaneando en Barcelona: música, migración y experiencia urbana (2012). His research interests cover urban sound and music cultures, tourism and urban transformation, critical heritage studies, and the relationship between materiality and expressive cultures.

Daniel Paiva is Human Geographer interested in the experience of urban space in consumption and touristic areas. He holds a European PhD (2019) in Geography by the Universidade de Lisboa. In 2019, he was awarded a postdoctoral research fellowship to undertake a six-year research project at the Centre for Geographical Studies of the Universidade de Lisboa to explore the integration of art, urban design, and geotechnologies to create more sustainable human–nature interactions in urban public space. His research has been published in several geography and social science journals, including but not limited to Progress in Human Geography, Transactions of the Institute of British Geographers, Annals of the American Association of Geographers, Geography Compass, and Urban Geography.

Daniel Malet Calvo is Assistant Researcher at the Centre for Research and Studies in Sociology (CIES) at ISCTE – the University Institute of Lisbon (Portugal). He is also guest lecturer at different undergraduate and PhD programmes at ICSTE-IUL. As a trained anthropologist and historian specialized in urban studies and ethnography, his research interests cover international students and student migration (youth cultures, social class, and lifestyle mobility), urban transformation (nightlife gentrification, heritage, touristification, and social movements), urban infrastructures (daily mobility, urban planning, and public space), and race and ethnicity in urban contexts.

Ambiances, Atmospheres and Sensory Experiences of Spaces
Series Editors:
Rainer Kazig
CNRS Research Laboratory Ambiances – Architectures –
Urbanités, Grenoble, France
Damien Masson
Université de Cergy-Pontoise, France
Paul Simpson
Plymouth University, UK

Research on ambiances and atmospheres has grown significantly in recent years in a range of disciplines, including Francophone architecture and urban studies, German research related to philosophy and aesthetics, and a growing range of Anglophone research on affective atmospheres within human geography and sociology.

This series offers a forum for research that engages with questions around ambiances and atmospheres in exploring their significances in understanding social life. Each book in the series advances some combination of theoretical understandings, practical knowledges and methodological approaches. More specifically, a range of key questions which contributions to the series seek to address includes:

- In what ways do ambiances and atmospheres play a part in the unfolding of social life in a variety of settings?
- What kinds of ethical, aesthetic, and political possibilities might be opened up and cultivated through a focus on atmospheres/ambiances?
- How do actors such as planners, architects, managers, commercial interests and public authorities actively engage with ambiances and atmospheres or seek to shape them? How might these ambiances and atmospheres be reshaped towards critical ends?
- What original forms of representations can be found today to (re)present the sensory, the atmospheric, the experiential? What sort of writing, modes of expression, or vocabulary is required? What research methodologies and practices might we employ in engaging with ambiances and atmospheres?

Sensory Transformations
Environments, Technologies, Sensobiographies
Helmi Järviluoma and Lesley Murray

Ambiance, Tourism and the City
Edited by Iñigo Sánchez-Fuarros, Daniel Paiva and Daniel Malet Calvo

For more information about this series, please visit: www.routledge.com/
Ambiances-Atmospheres-and-Sensory-Experiences-of-Spaces/book-series/AMB

Ambiance, Tourism and the City

**Edited by Iñigo Sánchez-Fuarros,
Daniel Paiva and Daniel Malet Calvo**

LONDON AND NEW YORK

First published 2023
by Routledge
4 Park Square, Milton Park, Abingdon, Oxon OX14 4RN

and by Routledge
605 Third Avenue, New York, NY 10158

Routledge is an imprint of the Taylor & Francis Group, an informa business

British Library Cataloguing-in-Publication Data
A catalogue record for this book is available from the British Library

ISBN: 978-1-032-07497-9 (hbk)
ISBN: 978-1-032-07499-3 (pbk)
ISBN: 978-1-003-20720-7 (ebk)

DOI: 10.4324/9781003207207

Typeset in Times New Roman
by Apex CoVantage, LLC

Contents

Figures

Maps

Tables

Contributors

Sandi Abram holds a PhD in Social and Cultural Anthropology from the University of Eastern Finland. Between 2017 and 2021, he participated as Doctoral Researcher in the ERC-funded project SENSOTRA – Sensory Transformations and Transgenerational Environmental Relationships in Europe and currently works as Postdoctoral Researcher at the Peace Institute, Ljubljana, and at Department of Ethnology and Cultural Anthropology, University of Ljubljana. His main research interests are aestheticization, sensory and urban studies, non-institutional creative practices, multimodal and collaborative ethnography.

Panizza Allmark is Professor of Visual and Cultural Studies, in the School of Arts and Humanities at Edith Cowan University, Perth, Australia, and Adjunct Professor at the Universitas Airlangga, Surabaya, Indonesia. Panizza is the long-standing chief editor of Continuum: Journal of Media and Cultural Studies, published by Taylor and Francis. Her research is in the field of visual culture, media, identity, feminism, and urban space. As a photographer, she has had solo exhibitions in New York, London, Italy, and Australia.

Pablo Arboleda is "Juan de la Cierva-Incorporación" Postdoctoral Researcher at the Department of Anthropology of the Spanish National Research Council (CSIC). His interdisciplinary focus to the study of modern ruins combines critical discourses and aesthetical approaches, and it is informed by urban studies, heritage, cultural geography, contemporary archaeology, social anthropology, and visual arts. Experimental methods are at the heart of Pablo's work, including film-making, photo-essay, photo-comic, and multivariate forms of creative writing. For him, boundaries between academic and artistic practices are blurred, or even non-existent.

Lisa Marie Beiswenger received her PhD in Anthropology from The Ohio State University. Her training includes advanced degrees in Literature, Media, and Cultural Studies, as well as a graduate interdisciplinary specialization in Folklore. She studies public markets, food culture, laborlore, folkcraft, and commodity fetishism. She is currently Assistant Professor of English at Saint Francis University in Loretto, PA.

Natalia Bieletto Bueno works at the Research Center of Arts and Humanities of the Universidad Mayor (Chile). She is an author and investigator in Latin American popular music, voice, noise, audible cultures, and sensory studies, and is interested in the role of music making and listening in processing conflict and socio-cultural difference, in urban contexts. She has studied the role of street music in the making of the urban experience and in notions of citizenship. Recipient of the Samuel Claro International Prize of Latin American Musicology (2018) for her article "De incultos y escandalosos: Noise and Social Classification in Post-revolutionary Mexico". Editor of *Ciudades Vibrantes: Sonido y Experiencia Aural Urbana en América Latina.*

Rachel Brahy is a PhD in political and social sciences. She is Lecturer at the Faculty of Social Sciences of ULiège. Her research is rooted in a socio-anthropology of human action, with a particular focus on sensitive/aesthetic experience and how (social, cultural, and city) policies enable (or not) such experiences. In 2019, she published: *S'engager dans un atelier-théâtre. À la recherche du sens de l'expérience* (Ed. Du Cerisier). In this book, Rachel Brahy offers an in-depth examination of the creative stages in workshop theatre and thus questions the contemporary political dimension of action theatre.

Elisa Bruttomesso holds a PhD in Cultural Geography from the University of Padua (Italy) and in Social Anthropology from the University of Barcelona (Spain). Her research interests include creative forms of protest against touristification processes, with a focus on urban tourism and anthropology of tourism, visual and creative research methods.

Yonatan Collier is currently working towards a practice-based PhD, an examination of how location-based recording, musical performance, and production can be used as tools for examining artistic practice, landscape, and history. Alongside a written thesis, Yonatan is composing and producing immersive, interactive musical pieces that are laid over specific landscapes and "performed" through location-aware Smartphone apps. Yonatan holds a BA in Popular and World Musics from the University of Leeds and an MSc in Sound Design from Leeds Beckett University. Alongside his research, he continues to work as a freelance producer, composer, and performer.

Manuel Delgado is Professor of Urban Anthropology in the Universitat de Barcelona. He is a member of the research groups GRECS (Grup de Recerca en Exclusió i Control Socials) at the UB, and OACU (Observatori d'Antropologia del Conflicte Urbà). He has worked especially on social appropriations and forms of exclusion in urban spaces. On these subjects he is the author of the books *Ciudad líquida, ciudad interrumpida* (1999), *El animal público* (Anagrama Essay Award 1999), *Disoluciones urbanas* (2002), *Sociedades movedizas* (2007), *La ciudad mentirosa* (2007), *L'espace public comme ideologie* (2016), and *Ciudadanismo* (2017).

Nicola Di Croce is an architect, musician, sound artist, and researcher. He holds a PhD in Regional Planning and Public Policies from Università Iuav di Venezia,

Italy. and is currently Marie Sklodowska-Curie Fellow at Iuav and McGill University's School of Information Studies, Montreal. His research deals with the relationship between Urban Studies and Sound Studies; he is interested in collaborative and participatory approaches to urban policy analysis and design. Sound is central to his artistic and academic activities.

Aileen Dillane is Senior Lecturer in Music and Ethnomusicologist at the Irish World Academy, University of Limerick. She has co-edited seven books, written over 40 articles and book chapters, and is currently working on a monograph, *Irish American Musical Imaginaries*. Aileen is Series Editor of *Discourse, Power and Society* and *Popular Musics Matter: Social, Political, and Cultural Interventions*, both with Rowman & Littlefield.

Gustavo Galván Cázares holds a BA degree in Music Education and a Master's degree in Habitat Sciences. He is currently a PhD candidate in Latin American Studies at the Universidad Autónoma de San Luis Potosí, where he develops the dissertation "Processes of transformation of listening practices, from the patrimonialization of the territory in the historical downtowns of San Luis Potosí and Guanajuato". He has been the recipient of several scholarships related to sound heritage. He is the author of three publications concerned with sound and listening in urban spaces and the notion of sound heritage through ethnography.

Ofer Gazit is a lecturer in ethnomusicology at Tel Aviv University, Israel. He teaches and writes about issues of migration, borders, and citizenship from a musical perspective. He has contributed articles and chapters to publications in sound and media studies, ethnomusicology, and jazz studies. His book *Jazz Migrations* is forthcoming.

Anthony Kwame Harrison is the Edward S. Diggs Professor in Humanities and Professor of Sociology, with a joint appointment in Africana Studies, at Virginia Tech. His areas of research include popular music studies, Black creative practice, qualitative research methodologies, and the racialized construction of social space. He is author of two books – *Hip Hop Underground* (2009) and *Ethnography* (2018) – and co-edited *Race in the Marketplace: Crossing Critical Boundaries* (2019).

Andrew S. Hoffman, Ph.D. is a Data Steward in the Faculty of Social Sciences at Leiden University in the Netherlands. In this capacity, he supports the research data management needs of social scientists working across the methodological spectrum, and contributes to the development of data management policy and tooling that is responsive to diverse epistemic cultures.

William Trevor Jamerson is Collegiate Assistant Professor of Sociology at Virginia Tech and teaches Sociological Theory and Sociology Senior Seminar. He is author of "Race and Critical Tourism Studies: An Analytical Literature Review" in Sociology Compass (2016) concerning theoretical links between fields of race and tourism studies. His research involves intersections of race, tourism, digital technology, and critical theory – particularly in the Harlem context.

Maria Lindmäe is a social and cultural geographer with a background in humanities. She is most fascinated by sonic geographies and how sound(making) produces places. Her research has focused on the production of public space through music making in Medellín, Colombia, and through the sonic presence of traders in different parts of Catalonia, Spain.

Plácido Muñoz Morán holds a PhD in Social Anthropology with Visual Media at the University of Manchester. He has extensive experience in qualitative research and the use of audio visual media. Looking at the transformation of cities through sensory approaches, he has participated in interdisciplinary and community-based research projects across fields such as art, environmental studies, and architecture. He collaborates with the multidisciplinary research group Aedificatio at the University of Alicante and is currently based in Berlin, where he has been involved in projects linked to the Berlin Opera Academy and the creation of the ElisaBeet community garden.

Luca Pattaroni holds a PhD in Sociology and is a senior scientist at the Laboratory of Urban Sociology of EPFL where he leads the research group "Urban Hospitalities". His work is concerned with the expression of differences and the making of the common in contemporary cities. Among his last publications is the edited book *Politics of Urban Planning: Making and Unmaking of the Mumbai Development Plan 2014–2034* (2022).

Sarah Raine is a Postdoctoral Researcher in Ethnomusicology at the Irish World Academy of Music and Dance at the University of Limerick, Ireland. She is the author of *Authenticity and Belonging in the Northern Soul Scene* (2020) and the co-editor of *Towards Gender Equality in the Music Industry* (with Catherine Strong, 2019) and *The Northern Soul Scene* (with Tim Wall and Nicola Watchman Smith, 2019). Sarah is also Co-Managing Editor of *Riffs*, Book Series Editor for Equinox Publishing (*Music Industry Studies/Icons of Pop Music*), and Editor for *Jazz Research Journal*.

Sebastián Wanumen Jiménez (he/him/his) is a PhD candidate in Musicology and Ethnomusicology at Boston University. He received his BA in musicology in Colombia (Corpas University) and earned an MA in Musicology from Cardiff University. Sebastian has lectured at Corpas University, National Pedagogic University, and Universidad del Norte in Colombia and at Boston University. His research has been supported by the Colombian Ministry of Culture and the BU Arts Initiative and the Associate Provost for Graduate Affairs. He is the official program annotator of the Colombian National Symphony Orchestra. He is currently exploring the Barranquilla's queer music and sound.

Preface

This book results from an interdisciplinary research project in which, over the last four years and with a pandemic in-between, we strived to study the impact of tourism on Lisbon's sonic urban ambiances. The project was called "Sounds of Tourism" (https://soundsoftourism.pt) and involved an interdisciplinary team of geographers, ethnomusicologists, sociologists, anthropologists, and sound artists. Although the project's initial focus was to explore the changes in the sound environment of a city going through an accelerated process of touristification, we quickly realized that, in order to account for the complexity of these changes, we needed to incorporate other dimensions of the sensory experience into the analysis. That is how we arrived at the notion of "ambiance" as a means of interrogating the contemporary tourist city.

The idea behind this edited volume arose out of a session organized by Iñigo Sánchez-Fuarros, Daniel Malet Calvo, and Salwa El-Shawan Castelo-Branco at the 14th Conference of the Société Internationale d´Ethnologie et de Folklore (SIEF) in Santiago de Compostela (Spain) in April 2019. The panel focused on the relationship between heritage and tourism as drivers of change in urban settings, placing the notions of ambiances and urban atmospheres at the centre of the discussion. The session drew a variety of proposals that problematized the sensory transformation of touristic urban spaces (from Viennese coffeehouses to vacant industrial sites or affluent shopping districts), some of which were finally included in this volume. The remaining contributions were selected from an open call distributed through different mailing lists and professional networks shortly thereafter.

This edited collection is the product of a collective effort of productive discussion and academic exchange between editors and authors which culminated in a small hybrid symposium that took place in Lisbon in February 2022. The aim of the symposium was to collectively discuss the individual chapters and the volume as a whole. Thus, prior to the meeting, each chapter's final draft was carefully read by a fellow author and an editor so that, on finally meeting, all authors and editors were uniquely aware of the strengths and flaws of each other's work. For two days, we had the opportunity to meet, eat and drink together (those physically present at the symposium), and discuss our work in an enriching process that not only resulted in more polished and compelling contributions but also demonstrated that every intellectual journey is – or should be – a collective endeavour.

We would like to thank the Centro de Informação Urbana de Lisboa (CIUL) and all its staff for welcoming us and hosting the event. We also wish to thank the contributors of the book for the work they have put into their chapters, their cooperation, and their patience throughout the long process of making this edited collection a reality. We would also like to give special thanks to our colleague and friend Prof. Manuel Delgado, an influential figure in Ibero-American urban anthropology, who kindly agreed to write the afterword to this book.

Our institutions provided the material and intellectual infrastructures that allowed us to devote research time to this book. In particular, we wish to thank the Institute of Ethnomusicology – Centre of Studies in Music and Dance (INET-md) at Nova University of Lisbon, the Centre of Geographical Studies and Institute of Geography and Spatial Planning (CEG-IGOT) at the University of Lisbon, the Centre for Research and Studies in Sociology (CIES) at ISCTE – the University Institute of Lisbon, and the Institute of Heritage Sciences (INCIPIT) at the Spanish National Research Council (CSIC).

We would like to thank Faye Leerink, Commissioning Editor for the *Geography, Urban Studies and Tourism* series, for the interest shown in our project, and Prachi Priyanka, editorial assistant, whose care, attention, and patience with inexperienced editors like ourselves made our job very easy.

Finally, we would like to acknowledge the financial support received from various funding bodies in Portugal and Spain, starting with the Foundation for Science and Technology of Portugal (FCT) which, through a SR&TD Project Grant (PTDC/ART-PER/32417/2017), funded the original research on which this book is based and also supported numerous scientific meetings at which we were able to discuss the issues raised in this book. Daniel Paiva and Daniel Malet Calvo were also funded by FCT, through the program Estímulo ao Emprego Científico (CEECIND/03528/2018 and CEECIND/01345/2018). In the case of Iñigo Sánchez-Fuarros, the final stages of writing the introduction, revising chapters, and editing the definitive manuscript were also made possible thanks to the support of a Ramón & Cajal grant (RYC2018–026083-I) funded by the Spanish Ministry of Science and Innovation (MICIN), the State Research Agency (AEI/10.13039/501100011033) and by ESF "Investing in your Future". This publication is part of the project "HabitPAT. Caring and Dwelling Intangible Heritage" (PID2020-118696RB-I00) funded by MCIN/AEI/10.13039/501100011033. Daniel Paiva also wishes to thank the Foundation for Science and Technology of Portugal (EXPL/GES-URB/0273/2021), the Centre for Geographical Studies (UIDP/00295/2020 and UIDB/00295/2020), and the Associated Lab TERRA (LA/P/0092/2020) for their support to his research.

Introduction

1 Ambiance, tourism, and the city: An introduction

Iñigo Sánchez-Fuarros, Daniel Paiva, and Daniel Malet Calvo

Cruise passengers arriving in Lisbon enjoy a privileged sight of the city's urban layout. Observed from the viewpoint of the Tagus River, the city – magnified and vibrant as the vessel slowly approaches the docking area – reveals its unique orography, covered by a mixture of different architectural styles punctuated by contemporary flagship buildings and new open public spaces along the riverside. A popular cruise destination on the rise before the pandemic, around 300 vessels dock in the Portuguese capital city each year (Kovačić and Silveira 2020). Cruise ships have thus correspondingly become a frequent feature on the historic city's skyline. Their presence in the old port area all year around embodies the success story of Lisbon as a thriving tourist destination.

In 2019, the year before the outbreak of the COVID-19 pandemic, the city received almost five million tourists – a new yearly record – of which more than 600,000 were cruise passengers.[1] For several consecutive years (2017–2020), Lisbon was elected as the Best City Break Destination in the World, boosting its popularity as a tourist destination. The rapid transformation of Portugal's capital city into a "tourist city" (Judd 2003) also stemmed from the stimulus policies that led to economic recovery in the years after the harsh austerity that followed the Portuguese financial crisis (2010–2015), a narrative shared by other tourism-dependent economies in Southern Europe (Malet Calvo and Ramos 2018). The combination of real estate development and tourism emerged as apparent solutions for the recession (Cócola-Gant and Gago 2019). This exponential growth in foreign visitors was abruptly broken off by the pandemic (Sánchez-Fuarros and Paiva 2021), although at the time of writing this introduction (September 2022) Lisbon's tourism market appears to have recovered its pre-pandemic momentum.

Cruise passengers arriving at the gates of the historic city centre quickly join the other crowds of tourists on foot, in tuk-tuks, on scooters, on bicycles, or driving all sorts of the personal transporters that flood through the narrow streets and alleyways of the historical neighbourhoods. In addition to such saturation, an increasing number of public spaces have been privatized and with others turned into tourist attractions (Gomes 2019). Furthermore, souvenir shops, convenience stores, nightlife venues, international restaurant chains, and automatic laundries have rapidly taken over from traditional shops and spaces of local conviviality (Guimarães 2021), boosting "tourism gentrification" (Cócola-Gant 2018) and

DOI: 10.4324/9781003207207-2

Figure 1.1 Cruise ship docked at the gates of the historic neighbourhood of Alfama, Lisbon.

Photo: Iñigo Sánchez-Fuarros

altering the look and feel of these areas. In addition, hotels, Airbnb apartments, and other lucrative short-term accommodation markets have mushroomed in Lisbon's central areas, displacing local residents and escalating property prices (Cócola-Gant and Gago 2019; Montezuma and McGarrigle 2019). Over the course of less than a decade, the pressure of (over)tourism has generated a lasting impact on the city's social, economic, and physical environments. For instance, that "the city [of Lisbon] is losing its soul" (Borges 2016) was the motto of a campaign that gained notoriety in the media and in local political circles around 2016–2018 as a response to the transformation of the city centre into a "theme park" for tourists (Lovell and Bull 2017). As any theme park worthy of its name, Lisbon's city centre has become "no longer a physical space to be inhabited but instead a cultural frame to be experienced" (Muñoz 2010, 81). In this context, the vindication of the "soul" of Lisbon may be read as a poetic gesture tinged with nostalgic overtones while also highlighting the gradual loss of individual and collective urban landmarks – which provide local residents with "a sense of origins" (Zukin 2010) – as a result of the rapid changes experienced by the city. What is the soul of a city if not the everyday ambiances to which its inhabitants feel attuned?

This process – which some authors refer to as touristification (Sequera and Nofre 2018) – is far from exclusive to Lisbon. As the different contributions to this book demonstrate, it is repeated, with subtle variations and different intensities, in cities all over the world. Indeed, as we shall see in the next section, critical research on tourism has long been warning about the negative effects on the everyday life of city dwellers of an industry aligned with the processes of accumulation by dispossession (Harvey 2003) so characteristic of financial capitalism (Milano and Mansilla 2018). It is not by chance, therefore, that the ideas that inspired this collection have arisen amidst the growing unease of Lisbon residents about the negative impact of tourism on their daily lives. Indeed, this introductory chapter – written from a small capital city in the European South which has recently entered the academic debates about touristification and its discontents – is intended as a critical contribution to these debates.

However, this collection seeks to approach this issue from a slightly different angle. Whereas the existing literature has focused mainly on tourism as a powerful force of urban change and as a source of contention (see e.g. Colomb and Novy 2016), the book advocates a critical approach to the notion of urban ambiances as a means to interrogate the contemporary tourist city. Through a series of case studies, this volume approaches the impact of tourism on the urban environment with an emphasis on the notions of "ambiance" and "atmosphere" as tools to explore the physical regeneration and sensory transformation of contemporary tourist sites (Degen 2008). How do tourism and city development affect the ambiances lived in the urban context? How do sensory experiences participate in creating particular urban ambiances and sites for tourist consumption? Furthermore, what is the role of atmospheric production in relation to the marketing of contemporary tourist destinations?

This introductory chapter aims to introduce some of the key themes that inform the different case studies developed in the chapters that collectively form this volume. The first section provides a brief overview of the critical traditions studying global tourism within the scope of neoliberal capitalism. Rather than an isolated system, global tourism is a hybrid and complex economic and socio-cultural process that, as Marc Morell argues, "needs society to work as a whole" (Morell 2018, 43). As such, "it implies processes of change in the socio-economic dynamics and the components of the landscape and environment of a territory" (Ojeda and Kieffer 2020, 143) and with these transformations generating deeper impacts on tourist cities.

The centrality of tourism to the urban economies of cities is, indeed, the focus of the next section. As privileged spaces for capital accumulation, the development of cities as urban tourist destinations has exacerbated the dynamics of inequality, exclusion, and discrimination as over-tourism exerts excessive pressures on urban infrastructures with negative consequences for the quality of life of local residents. Thus, touristification is often contemporaneous to other urban processes such as gentrification, urbanalisation (Muñoz 2010), or the displacement of local population. As such, we contend that touristification cannot be dissociated from urban capitalism's own development and contradictions and therefore requires studying within this framework.

The third section introduces the notion of "ambiance" and argues about its relevance as a lens through which to study the impact of tourism on the urban environment. Although there has been a growing interest in the study of ambiances within tourism research, there is surprisingly little interest in the articulation between tourism, ambiances, and the city. Thus, this collective volume aims to fill this gap by focusing on the relationship between the ambiances of tourism and the liveability and cohesion of local communities. This relationship most frequently takes on the form of a vicious circle: Tourism activities depend on the unique character of local cultures to compete on the "global catwalk" (Degen 2003), while these very same local cultures are threatened by the growth of tourism, and therefore the very atmosphere that made them special might eventually fade away. This paradox is explored in the following section, approaching the notion of authenticity and its atmospheric resonances as an example. In fact, no discussion of the ambiances of tourism can ignore the issue of authenticity as most of the chapters in this volume demonstrate. Authenticity is not only a driver for urban renewal and branding but also a catalyst of tourism experiences. The sixth and final section then introduces the rationale and chapters of the book.

Critical approaches to global tourism and neoliberalism

The global industry of travel, tourism, and hospitality has grown exponentially over the last four decades whether accounted for in terms of recorded arrivals, accommodation capacity, revenues earned, or the geographic distribution of new destinations (Scott and Gössling 2015). The global tourist system accounted for 10.4% of global GDP in 2019 and was responsible for 1.4 billion international visitors travelling to which we must also add many more billions of domestic tourists (JLL and WTTC 2019). These figures fell away dramatically during the pandemic years of 2020 and 2021 but are currently heading swiftly back to recovery, especially in regions highly dependent on tourism such as Mediterranean Europe and the Caribbean (UNWTO 2022). The success and growth of the global tourist system have been sustained by specific material conditions: The massive expansion of transportation technologies, the reduction in border travel restrictions, and Information and Communication Technology (ICT) developments with software and apps facilitating travel planning and marketing. These infrastructures also changed the meaning of travelling and prompted the formation of new subjectivities around mobility, reinforcing materially and morally differentiated (although interdependent) transnational circuits of travel (Amit 2015). In our contemporary hyperconnected world, the allure of other places, cultures, and opportunities shapes individualistic and collective mobility projects, including workers, international students, tourists, and lifestyle migrants (Hayes 2021). Consequently, new "regimes of mobility" arose (Glick Schiller and Salazar 2013), redefining human border-crossing fluidity while still reproducing global inequalities, privileges of circulation, and colonial imaginaries. The current consensual devotion to the tourism industry and its "benefits", simultaneous to the continued perception of labour migration and refugees as a threat, especially in the Global North, provides a good example of the contemporary (and contradictory) politics of global mobility (Bianchi et al. 2020). Moreover, this entire global framework structurally connects to the consolidation of the post-industrial, neoliberal agenda (Harvey 2007), a global formula for economic development (free trade, institutional restructuring, financialization, service economy) that enshrined the tourism industry as the cherry on top of the global capitalism cake. In this sense, in accordance with this hegemonic cosmovision, governments, international organizations, and the private sector unanimously insist that tourism creates jobs, boosts trade, facilitates investments, and generates prosperity to the host countries (see for instance Mastercard's Global Destination Cities Index 2019).

In contrast with this triumphant narrative, broadly trumpeting the interests of the industry, a tradition of critical studies on tourism has flourished since the decade of 1970s, following classic works such as Turner and Ash's *The Golden Hordes* (1975), MacCannell's *The Tourist: A New Theory of the Leisure Class* (1976) or Valene Smith's *Hosts and Guests* (1978). However, it was not until the 1990s that the critical production on tourism studies multiplied and experienced consolidation by the development of two different approaches. On the one hand, there was the "cultural turn" in tourism studies (Bianchi 2009) nourished by post-structuralism's emphasis on power, discourse, performativity, and identities, which draws upon the seminal work by Urry in *The Tourist Gaze* (1990). On the other hand, the return of a structural critique of the global tourist system from a political economy perspective, which recovered Marxist approaches to working conditions, capital accumulation and material inequalities (Ioannides and Debbage 1998; Fletcher 2011). Both of these critical traditions evolved in tandem with the boundless expansion of mass tourism and global touristification, returning an integrated understanding and revealing, among other aspects, the huge levels of job precarity in the sector (Cañada 2018; Robinson et al. 2019), the sociocultural and heritage dispossession felt in destinations (Devine and Ojeda 2017; Morell 2018), and the substantial interlinkage between the tourism industry and climate change (Gössling and Peeters 2015; Lenzen et al. 2018). Therefore, contemporary critical scholars have unveiled the ubiquitous presence of global tourism in neoliberal capitalism (Mosedale 2016; Cañada and Murray 2019), identifying it as an ominous, holistic device that extends beyond being some discreet sector of economic activity. In their article about tourism and its forms of structural violence, Büscher and Fletcher wrote that tourism is "not merely a capitalist practice but a central practice through which capitalism sustains itself" (2017, 651). Within the same line of thought, Nogués-Pedregal, when summarizing the anthropological contributions to tourism studies, suggested that tourism is "capitalism's most perfect and sophisticated creation" (2019, 230). Whatever the case may be, it would seem clear that the global touristic system and its proficiency in framing and commodifying social relationships, landscapes and territories, global imaginaries and transnational mobility, represents not only a portion of the global economy but rather the very form adopted by capitalism as a means of extracting economic value from human and non-human natural resources in post-industrial conditions. It is precisely due to the particular nature of tourism as a hybrid and complex economic and socio-cultural process involving images, technology, practices, infrastructures, meanings, and textuality that the developments of the Actor-Network

Theory, the methods, and theoretical insights of anthropology and, in general, qualitative approaches to particular tourist sites (such as those contained in this book) have proven to be fruitfully applicable to tourism studies (van der Duim et al. 2017; Salazar 2017).

City tourism, urban change, and social contestation

Almost half of the 1.4 billion international tourists who travelled in 2019 did so with the purpose of visiting cities and with the majority of the rest spending at least one night in cities while travelling to another destination (JLL and WTTC 2019). Indeed, tourism has become a central component of the urban economies of many cities worldwide, playing its role in the complex transformations of their morphologies, institutional structures, and social lives. Even though cities under capitalism have always been privileged spaces for capital accumulation and centralization (Harvey 1978; Brenner and Theodore 2002), the advent of mass tourism and global touristification increased and accelerated many processes inherent to urban capitalism. From the 1980s onwards, many global cities launched post-industrial city marketing campaigns aimed at attracting capital investments, wealthy residents, and businesses, developing specialized tertiary districts and leisure sites for visitors, in a neoliberal urban governance shift towards entrepreneurialism (Harvey 1989). In parallel, the growing presence of tourists and the dynamics of the industry in cities further encouraged urban renewal operations and the attraction of real estate investment, opening new areas and spaces to commercialization and consumption. The subsequent expansion of global mobility deepened the effects of gentrification on a transnational scale (Hayes and Zaban 2020) changing the demographic composition and class structure in many global cities and increasing urban polarization and inequalities. These processes have been threatening not only sociocultural and class heterogeneity (the very fabric that renders cities unique and appealing) but also the social life of neighbourhoods, including the lack of access to housing, health, and mobility for low-income communities (Musterd and Ostendorf 1998). In fact, tourism seems not only to intensify previously existing gentrification processes but also to trigger new ones (Cócola-Gant 2018; Cocola-Gant et al. 2020), which bring about different forms of displacement, especially through successive waves of evictions. The impact of tourism accommodation digital platforms (such as Airbnb) provides one of the most obvious interconnections between tourism and gentrification, with house owners and real estate investors putting their properties into the much more profitable (and liberalized) short-term tourist market. Consequently, cities have experienced house scarcity, huge increases in rental prices, the displacement of residents to suburban areas, and the proliferation of evictions in an exclusionary process now spread throughout many urban areas and regions around the world (Valente et al. 2022).

Apart from the central problem of housing, many other issues have been impacting on the sustainability of urban destinations and disturbing their inhabitants, a varied array of grievances which have recently been portrayed and discussed under the label of "overtourism" (Milano et al. 2019; Mihalic 2020; Wall 2020). First, everyday mobility and accessibility for residents may become compromised due to the overcrowding of touristic sites and the saturation of public transportation services, potentially occurring commonly during the peak season, especially in cities with historical, usually narrow, central districts. Second, residents often suffer from excess noise levels caused by the presence of large groups of tourists, music festivals in towns, public entertainment shows, open markets, and nightlife venues (such as bars and clubs), places that may also motivate drunkenness and other impactful, annoying or even dangerous behaviours. Third, the monoculture of tourism has led to the spread of tourist-oriented shops and facilities, frequently as franchises displaying a considerable level of uniformity, that substituted the previous local retail outlets in a process sensed by the inhabitants as a loss of local identity and sense of community. Fourth, the presence of tourists stimulates the privatization of public spaces (terraces, fairs, markets, and festivals) and the commercialization of private property through the utilization of applications (from housing to meals), activities connected with precariousness, the informal economy, and the lowering of employment standards. And last, but not the least, the ecological pressures on destinations are huge, with rising levels of air pollution in cities (planes, cruisers, more vehicles circulating), the difficulties of managing the additional waste produced by visitors, and the challenges of providing a water supply in many urban destinations located on islands or in desert/arid environments.

Over the last decade, the growth of mass tourism and its pressures on urban infrastructures and inhabitant quality of live have led to the multiplication of local conflicts, political struggles, and forms of contestation against that perceived as "overtourism" in many cities worldwide (Colomb and Novy 2016). While reactions to mass tourism are not a new phenomenon (Boissevain 1996), this new cycle of protests and tensions has connected with people's contemporary awareness of their own weakened, disempowered citizenship, a lack of urban governance to tackle urgent questions such as housing access, and the widespread sense of navigating through a permanent economic crisis. Neighbourhood groups, left-wing political parties, and grassroots social movements have identified the excesses of mass tourism, pointing at its negative consequences both for residents and the sustainability of urban environments and demanding social justice and their "right to the city" (Purcell 2002). However, the boundaries between tourist and non-tourist, locals and foreigners, are more blurred than ever before, defying the former borders between travel, migration, work, and leisure. Frequent travellers, international students, digital nomads, retired foreigners, tourists, and the local middle and upper class often circulate through the same places and infrastructures, consume similar urban experiences, and share interchangeable narratives about their practices and lifestyles in the convoluted settings of global cities. Therefore, the problems often identified as *touristic* (such as gentrification) actually intersect and overlap with the ordinary developments and contradictions of urban capitalism, which themselves only serve to reproduce previously existing situations of exclusion, inequality, and discrimination. Moreover, given that the strategy of many cities has been for decades to entrust their economies to tourism monocultures, global organizations and with political parties only presenting mitigating solutions and "greenifying" measures to calm down urban inhabitants (see for instance UNWTO 2018). In any case, challenging the limits of tourism expansion and its consequences for the populations, whether by critical scholars or by grassroots movements, involves questioning the core neoliberal restructuring of cities as theatres of leisure and consumption, reaching beyond tourism as a discrete economic activity.

Ambiance and tourism. And the city?

One of the most relevant (and intangible) facets enacted, manipulated, and marketed by the economic actors responsible for the touristic exploitation of the world's cities is that of ambiance. We may describe "ambiance" as the unified perception of the sensory emanation of places. Thinking about ambiances draws our attention to the affective power of the sensory factors that compose places and how people sense, feel, and think about them (Sumartojo and Pink 2018). The concept of ambiance is akin to atmosphere, a term which is more often used in the Anglophone and Germanophone context (for the conceptual differences between ambiance and atmosphere, see Adey et al. 2013; Paiva 2022). In this book, we prefer to adopt the term "ambiance" due to its longer history in the field of tourism studies (Volgger and Pfister, 2020).

Indeed, ambiance has long since been considered fundamental by the tourism industry. This interest of the tourism industry in ambiance stems from the longer history of atmospheric production in retail and services in which spatial design and the introduction of affective sensorial features, such as music or fragrances, have been recurrent tools to draw customers into immersive and pleasurable consumption experiences (Bitner 1992; Goss 1993; Howes 2004; LaBelle 2010). Tourism service providers have appropriated these tools to create more satisfying experiences for tourists, and the production of ambiances is now central to the design of many tourism-oriented facilities. Hotels rely on architecture, spatial design, and management to provide positive experiences for tourists (Heide et al. 2007). Spas design ambiances to suggest quietness, wellness, and relaxation (Manhas et al. 2019). Airplanes focus on air quality, temperature, layout, and amenities to provide a satisfactory flight experience (Han 2013) and deploy music and video to generate an in-flight atmospheric identity (Vanspauwen and Sánchez-Fuarros 2023). Airports rely on spatial design and ambient music to enact safe and tranquil spaces for travellers (Adey 2009, 2014; Adey et al. 2013).

The widespread interest in the production of ambiances by tourism service providers is hardly surprising when considering the amount of evidence produced by tourism studies demonstrating their efficacy. These studies argue that perceptions and acknowledgement of ambiances of place interrelated with strong emotional experiences (Lu et al. 2017). For this very reason, ambiance plays a fundamental role in the formation of memorable experiences (Kim 2014; Coelho et al. 2018), and with the literature reporting that tourists having positive atmospheric experiences attain higher levels of satisfaction and are more willing to recommend the destination (Jani and Han 2014). Consequently, ambiance is perceived as fundamental to the development of destination loyalty (Wang et al. 2021).

It has been noted that the production of ambiances entails the mobilization of several fields of knowledge, including architecture, urban design, business management, marketing, and UX design, among others (Heide et al. 2007; Paiva and Sánchez-Fuarros 2021). In this sense, there are also different approaches to producing ambiances. At the level of architecture, ambiances can be designed to create spaces that direct subjects towards practices of consumption, promoting interactivity and immersive multisensory experiences (Heide et al. 2007; Adey 2008, 2014). At the level of design, ambiances can be staged by introducing elements such as light, music, or food, which provide novel or distinct sensory experiences in a given place (Bille et al. 2015; Bjerregaard 2015; Bille 2019). At the level of performance, producing ambiances involves the organizing of events that engage consumers in affective practices with special sensory experiences (Sumartojo 2016; Michels and Steyaert 2017; Paiva and Cachinho 2018).

One interesting aspect of tourism studies is that ambiance is considered not only in terms of an embodied, site-specific multisensory experience but also in terms of the indirect experiences mediated by media and the imagination (Coelho et al. 2018).

Despite the tourism industry's interest in ambiance, and the burgeoning literature on urban atmospheres, strikingly few studies have approached the relationship between ambiance, tourism, and the city. While the role urban ambiance plays in tourism experiences has been thoroughly explored, there has been far less attention to how the ambiance of tourism destinations sustain liveability and social cohesion for local communities. According to Wheeler and Laing (2008), the well-being of local communities in tourism destinations depends on the existence of vibrant ambiances for both residents and tourists. Such balances are difficult to achieve. Places with vibrant ambiances that stem from the effervescence of the local community's social life often become the key attractions for tourists seeking that same vibrancy (Zhang et al. 2016), leading to touristification processes that degrade local resident quality of life (Paiva and Sánchez-Fuarros 2021). Over time, this not only harms local communities but also negatively impacts on the quality of tourism experiences.

Such issues highlight the intimate relationship between tourism and local cultures. The ambiances of tourism draw upon the facets of local cultures that endow identity and a sense of belonging to communities alongside a sense of uniqueness to each place (Volgger and Pfister 2020). For instance, the power of the ambiance of historical architecture and urban heritage over creating unique and distinct experiences, especially for tourists, has been underlined (Berman 2006). On the other hand, increasing attention is now paid to intangible heritage, such as music and food (Sánchez-Fuarros 2016).

In this sense, tourism activities depend on local cultures to sustain them and compete with other unique products in a competitive international market. Paradoxically, local cultures are nevertheless under threat from the growth of tourism in many different ways. On the one hand, the touristification of urban places often leads to processes of transnational gentrification that displace local residents from those neighbourhoods becoming tourism hotspots (Sequera and Nofre 2018, 2019; Malet Calvo and Ramos 2018). On the other hand, the success of tourism-oriented businesses often leads to the decline of resident-oriented stores and services, leading to the loss of important community hangouts (Guimarães 2021, 2022). More importantly, the ambiances of touristified places are themselves subject to change as the tourism activities go about introducing their own sensescapes, commonly leading to increases in noise and litter (Shaw 2014; Paiva and Sánchez-Fuarros 2021).

Tourism, ambiance, and authenticity

Urban ambiances for tourism consumption depend on the production and performance of various sensorial elements to be experienced by visitors. One of the most valued and relevant depends on the (re)production and enactment of what is perceived as the local culture's "authenticity". Indeed, authenticity has become a major force in shaping contemporary urban life (Tate and Shannon 2018). As a place-making strategy (Cao 2022), different ideas of authenticity are mobilized as discursive devices with real and practical effects on enhancing the heritage value in the rehabilitation and preservation of historic centres (Barnes et al. 2006) or on rendering the unique characteristics of a location into a commodity as is often the case in top-down revitalization projects of ethnic and deprived urban areas (see e.g. Sánchez-Fuarros 2017). In her book *Naked City: The Death and Life of Authentic Urban Places* (2010), sociologist Sharon Zukin explores the powerful paradox at the root of this phenomenon: how the pervasive demand for experiences of authenticity, mostly by educated urbanites and tourists, is destroying the local uniqueness of the very urban places they seem to venerate. Zukin maintains that authenticity refers to a sense of origins linked to a feeling of community rooted in a particular territory – or, as she puts it, to "the social connectedness that place inspires" (Zukin 2010, 220). In Zukin's view, urban authenticity retains certain atmospheric overtones as the authenticity of a place leads us back to its vibes or feeling. As seen earlier, processes of urban change such as gentrification and touristification threaten those vernacular ways of inhabiting the city which, in Zukin's words, "create the distinctive character of the streets (Zukin 2010, x). This is especially the case in (over)touristified urban centres, where the introduction of new consumption practices, tourist attractions, and global lifestyles disrupt traditional everyday urban ambiances (see Di Croce in this volume).

An elusive concept, authenticity is embedded not only in the vocabulary of urban preservation (Salah Ouf 2001) and revitalization (Waitt 2000) but also in that of the tourism industry.[2] As Sine Heitmann argues, authenticity "is one of the key drivers for most tourism experiences" (Heitmann 2011, 45). Whether searching for obscure graffiti through the back alleys of the city (see Lindmäe and/or Muñoz Morán in this volume), finding that restaurant frequented by local patrons, or discovering that music bar off the beaten tourist track, tourists constantly search for experiences of authenticity (MacCannell 1976). The idea of authenticity has been conceptualized in different categories within tourism research, with the objective, constructive, and existential approaches the most prominent in recent scholarship (Wang 1999; Rickly 2022; Knudsen and Waade 2010). While the first approach equates authenticity with the notions of originality and uniqueness related to the typical objects of tourist desire (heritage sites, museums, cultural events), the constructivist approach focuses on the socially constructed nature of authenticity. On the other hand, the category of existential authenticity aims to capture precisely the experiential dimension of authenticity, which is mobilized through interactions of its objective and constructed components (Rickly-Boyd 2013).

Tourism authenticity is, in short, a hard to define, multi-faceted concept (Rickly-Boyd 2012). An authentic tourist experience does not mean the same to every tourist: This correspondingly involves a combination of the expectations of tourists, their prior understandings and knowledge of local/foreign values, and the nature of the tourist encounter itself (Larsen 2010). David Grazian's work on the Chicago blues scene brilliantly illustrates this idea (Grazian 2003). In his book, Grazian explores how the values attached to a certain idea of music authenticity mediate the relationship between tourists arriving in Chicago in search of an "authentic" blues performance and the surrounding urban environment and how the latter is transformed to accommodate (or resist) foreign values and expectations.

In this sense, tourism authenticity advances along a continuum ranging from displays of "staged authenticity" (MacCannell 1976) for mass tourism consumption to tailor-made, individualized, and exclusive tourism experiences. While the former is often associated with theme parks, cultural events, or historical re-enactments of heritage sites, the contemporary embodiment of the latter would be the economies of authenticity that circulate within the sharing and experience economies (Lalicic and Weismayer 2017; Andersson 2007; Paulauskaite et al. 2017; Pine and Gilmore 2013). In the latter scenario, the tourist moves from being a more or less passive spectator to becoming a performer or producer of these experiences. In both cases and along the continuum, the creation of particular atmospheres that evoke the sense of an "authentic past", uniqueness, wonder, or truth – all attributes associated to a certain idea of authenticity – is required. In this sense, pre-existing atmospheres are often modified, adapted, or recreated for the tourist audience to deepen their attractiveness and to better align them with tourist expectations. For instance, shops selling traditional products in tourist areas often adopt a fake vintage aesthetic in which the patina of tradition is replaced by scenarios in papier-mâché, carefully groomed sale assistants and photo-friendly backgrounds. By the same token, eating and drinking spaces in tourist districts also perform and stage atmospheres of authenticity attuned with the "real" dining experience they intend to convey to their diners (Cuthill 2007). For instance, Bryce Peake explores how ambient sounds and music contribute to the production of "authentic" eating experiences in restaurants on the Maltese island of Gozo (Peake 2008).

The paradox underlying the production of authentic ambiances for tourist consumption evokes the figure of the "innocent vandals" referred to by Bruno Latour in the introduction to the exhibition catalogue for *Iconoclash* (Latour et al. 2002). Through this figure, Latour refers to a type of iconoclast that destroys images "unintentionally", almost with kindness. The French anthropologist sets the example of restoration and architecture as two activities that, in their eagerness to protect and idolize images – to restore works of art in the first case and to embellish cities in the second – they end up destroying them. The desire for authenticity can generate the same outcome. Indeed, Francesc Muñoz suggests the concept of "urbanalisation" to account for a process of city simplification in which urban diversity and complexity are reduced to fit into a common visual order (Muñoz 2010). The production of *banalscapes*, according to Muñoz, is the result of processes of imitation and selection in which certain vernacular elements of the past are emphasized over others.

Following Muñoz and expanding this idea to other domains of the sensorial, we propose the concept of "sonic touristification" to account for the dynamic and contested process through which the sound environment of a place, that is collectively recognized and valued as distinctive, is progressively affected by other sonorities associated with – or directly produced by – tourist activities. For instance, the increased demand from tourists visiting Lisbon to listen to live fado in traditional neighbourhoods such as Alfama has led to a proliferation of fado venues that cater mostly for a tourist audience, at the expense of other types of establishments (Sánchez-Fuarros and Lacerda 2022). As a result, the sound of fado – Portugal's quintessential form of urban popular song – pervades the streets of Alfama as the evening draws in, masking other sonorities and becoming the prevailing "soundmark" of the territory. On the other hand, sonic touristification also manifests itself through the implementation of noise ordinances and the control of certain practices in public spaces that are considered inappropriate (Sánchez-Fuarros 2017). Thus, sonic touristification implies significant – and sometimes irreversible – changes in the local sound environment through processes of equalization and filtering that result, in most cases, in the banalisation and homogenization of its sonic diversity.

Hence, any study about the production of atmospheres for tourist consumption cannot avoid discussing authenticity. This represents a theme that, to a greater or lesser extent, cuts across all of the chapters in this book. Both ambiance and authenticity are relational concepts. While the former "foreground the interaction between the properties of the built environment and the lived experience of city dwellers" (Thibaud 2011, 204), in the case of authenticity, its meaning and value emanate from the interplay between objects, sites, and experiences (Rickly-Boyd 2012). In this sense, we argue that the conceptual framework of atmospheric studies provides the potential to extend the studies of authenticity within tourism research to incorporate the sensuous production of authentic experiences for the consumption of tourists.

The contents of this book

The book is divided into five sections covering a wide range of case studies spanning different geographic locations and fields of study. These contributions explore how atmospheres for touristic consumption are designed, staged, and performed in different social and cultural contexts, including Spain, Ireland, Colombia, the United States, Italy, Slovenia, Mexico, France, Puerto Rico, Jamaica, and Malaysia. The book extends to a companion web page that includes various audiovisual materials that complement the content of the individual chapters.[3]

The first section contains a strong musical emphasis as two of the three contributions included explore the role of music in the affective enactment of urban public spaces. In their chapter, Ofer Gazit and Elisa Bruttomesso discuss the problematic contributions of music tourism to the social and economic development of impoverished tourism destinations in the Caribbean. By analysing the return of viral YouTube videos to the locales in which they were filmed, in this case San Juan's La Perla neighbourhood and Kingston's Fleet Street, Gazit and Bruttomesso suggest the need to rethink the obligations of big tech companies to the cultural places that generate so much of their revenues due to the disproportionate financial gains of data mining companies as compared to those of local musicians, venues, and producers. The next chapter further explores the role of music in the construction of sonic urban imageries. Natalia Bieletto Bueno and Gustavo Galván Cázares set out comprehensive analysis of the *estudiantinas* phenomenon in Guanajuato (Mexico) and how public performances affect the experience of the surrounding built environment. At the core of this chapter is the delicate balance between urban planning, cultural legacies, cultural policies, and tourism, with the presence of the *estudiantinas* in the narrow streets of Guanajuato's colonial city centre raising timely questions about the usage and control of public space, the reproduction of colonial legacies, and the monoculture of certain musical expressions oriented towards tourist consumption. The third and last chapter of this section takes a critical look at the metamorphosis of one of Medellín's evil districts into a tourist destination. In particular, Maria Lindmäe examines this transformation on two, closely intertwined, levels: the design of urban ambiances through urban planning, and the staging and performing of such ambiances via walking tours (see also the Trevor Jamerson and Kwame Harrison chapter for an interesting comparison). Lindmäe's chapter resonates with Gazit and Bruttomesso's in the sense that both contributions raise critical awareness about the dangers of commodifying underrepresented and impoverished local communities, and the ways in which the production of atmospheres for tourist consumption can contribute to such fetishization.

The second section is dedicated to the ambiances of the built environment. Panizza Allmark draws on her own photographic research in shopping malls across the globe to reflect upon the social representations embedded in the consumption-oriented ambiances of shopping malls. Her reflection examines how representations of hegemonic gender and racial ideals are built into the aesthetics of shopping malls, creating spaces of Debordian spectacle that simultaneously attract and fetichize. Allmark's reflection leads us to think about the production of spaces of consumption under capitalism, and how they interweave aesthetics and politics. While shopping malls have long since been understood as the most iconic materialization of consumption culture, Allmark highlights how they are now also advertised as "shopping destinations" across the globe, creating a new social and economic role for these kinds of spaces. Pablo Arboleda, on the other hand, provides a novel perspective on sun and sand tourism facilities by exploring these spaces during the low season in Spain. Arboleda draws upon a creative ethnographic excursion during wintertime, which resulted in the making of a videopoem about the ambiances of abandoned tourism facilities, to discuss their liminality and spectrality. Arboleda's discussion raises important questions about how the rhythms and cycles of tourism interact with the material landscape, and how the architecture of tourism facilities encapsulates ambiguous emotions and senses of place over time. The reflections by Allmark and Arboleda unveil the cultural complexity of the ambiances of tourism – and consumption – oriented architecture and offer significant examples of how researching ambiances can unveil the nuances and contradictions of wider social and economic processes.

In the third section, we turn to the moving experience of ambiances. Here, the understanding of movement spans two different dimensions. On the one hand, these chapters explore walking through ambiances as a specific mode of relating to the environment, and perhaps one of the most important in everyday life. On the other hand, they also unveil how ambiances move us, changing our knowledge of the city, our sense of place, and our connection to the environment. First, Brahy, Pattaroni, and Hoffman investigate La Ligne Verte, an urban pedestrian route in Nantes, France. The authors are concerned with understanding how the route is perceived by pedestrians, and how it orients and frames their experience of the city. They question the sensory experience of the route, looking at how it paves the way for a specific version of the city, which in turn raises the question of what kinds of city are under creation through contemporary urban projects and for whom. In this sense, Brahy, Pattaroni, and Hoffman also unveil how the construction of urban materiality and ambiance also builds up what they call the "common of the city". Second, Sandi Abram approaches the impact of the touristification of Ljubljana, Slovenia, on the sensory organization of public space. Abram applies a sensobiographic walking method with old and young residents in the city to understand how they perceive the changes in the city's public space from the material and sensorial perspectives. His study conveys how residents respond cognitively and emotionally to what Abram describes as the hyperaestheticization and spectacularization of public space that aims to create sensory-affective enticement for tourism consumption. Third, Yonatan Collier reflects on the outcomes of his own creative practice through describing the making of "Taman Tugu: Interference/Resistance", an interactive musical work developed for the Taman Tugu jungle park in Kuala Lumpur, Malaysia. The musical work is mapped into the jungle park through an augmented reality (AR) audio app, allowing visitors to explore the work while walking through the park, providing interesting interactions between the park's ambiance and Collier's atmospheric musical work. While the Brahy, Pattaroni, and Abram studies lead us to question the ambiances created for tourism and consumption, Collier's work provides a hopeful inspiration to think about ways to create more sustainable and ecologically aware experiences in tourism cities.

The fourth section shifts the focus to local spaces of sociability in which identities and a sense of belonging are negotiated and affirmed. The section's three chapters explore how tourism threatens the sustainability of these local environments. Muñoz Morán's chapter navigates through different scenarios and urban environments in which graffiti images interface urban tourism, creating "textures" that extend beyond the visual and material dimensions of an artwork. Taking the relational features of ethnographic research as both a method and a metaphor, the author details how graffiti combine the past, present, and future of cities, participating in urban meta-pictures that connect different worlds while transmitting meanings and generating urban ambiances. From the geodesic domes of a listening spy station in West Berlin to the abandoned buildings and empty walls of Barcelona's Vallcarca neighbourhood, this chapter collected different examples of how the material features of urban environments are active and political non-human entities that enable and facilitate the interface between people, images, and meanings. In this sense, the author proposes the academia to take seriously not only the discourses and practices of graffiti artists but also the way materials, images, and environments – that function as their canvas – impact (and transform) artists and artworks. The article also identifies how many of the images and narratives that facilitate individual and collective political struggles have ended up engulfed by the demands and presence of the power dynamics of mass tourism.

The next chapter places its focus on the many changes experienced in Cincinnati's Findlay Market (Ohio), the only surviving public market in the city that daily receives many locals and a growing number of tourists and visitors. Lisa Marie Beiswenger presents us with the history of this market, that went through many difficult episodes from cleansing reforms in the nineteenth and twentieth centuries to the current modern logistic difficulties. Based upon surveys and participant observation, the article presents three major changes experienced in the market during the last decades, which relate to the sociocultural transformations of American cities in the twenty-first century. First, the market evolved from being a place where people come to purchase cooking ingredients to a space full of shops selling prepared food and beverages. Second, the market expanded its opening hours and days from just three to six days (closing only on Mondays), which attracted new types of visitors from outside the area. Third, vendors depended traditionally on food stamp purchases from poor people (mostly Afro-American) while now most of their customers are urban professionals looking for more gourmet and sophisticated foods and ingredients. In sum, gentrification processes in the area changed the socioeconomic status of visitors who, in turn, demanded the new products that continue to transform the Market.

Meanwhile, Wanumen's chapter presents the promotion and marketization of Barranquilla's Gay Carnival by the local and national authorities to project the city as a modern and cosmopolitan destination, especially aimed at attracting LGBTIQ+ niche tourism. However, the author demonstrates the many ways heteronormativity (and homonormative neoliberalism) appropriate and dominate queer bodies to produce a profitable, touristified carnival while disregarding the violence and discrimination these same bodies suffer not only during the carnival but also in their everyday lives. On the one hand, carnival's promotional videos manipulate the soundtrack to conceal people's disapproval and reactions of mockery towards LGBTIQ+ parade participants, trying to dispel the tensions, discrimination, and violence that still prevail in Barranquilla's public space. On the other hand, queer bodies are only allowed and accepted in the carnival as artistically productive in specific roles (dancers, producers, choreographers, directors) but are excluded from music making, which is an integral part of the heteronormative core of Caribbean identity and politics. While the carnival creates some free space-times for gender and sexual diversity, these are totally intersected by everyday violence and discrimination, including homophobic and transphobic shouts during the carnival's parade.

The articles included in the fifth and final section explore the mechanisms through which atmospheric production participates in the creation of experiences of tourism authenticity. It is not by chance that the three articles in this section focus on different aspects of the urban sonic environment, for sound, through the "anamnesis effect", possesses a unique power to "revive a situation or an atmosphere of the past" (Augoyard et al. 2006, 21), merging sound, perception, and memory. In his chapter, Nicola Di Croce examines the changes in the acoustic environment of traditional markets in the Italian city of Palermo as they become tourist attractions. In particular, he analyses the survival of traditional sonic practices such as the trader's everyday cries and sales pitches that reflect a line of continuity with a past that is now fading due to the decline in traders and local consumers and the homogenizing forces inherent to the very process of touristification. Drawing from the findings of two creative and research led projects, Di Croce argues that a critical listening culture is key to attuning to the affective tonalities that endow urban public spaces with their unique characters. The urban sound environment is also the focus of the next chapter. William Trevor Jamerson and Anthony Kwame Harrison explore the way different types of sound (musical, verbal, and ambient) create an immersive sensuous experience of Blackness for tourists who participate in community-based walking tours in Harlem, what they refer to as a "moving tourist bubble". Connecting critical race theory with sound studies, Jamerson and Harrison's contribution unveils a powerful paradox at the core of the touristification of deprived urban areas: Tourism operates simultaneously as an agent of gentrification and, in the particular case of Harlem, all the while supporting a claim that it remains, essentially, a space for – and belonging to – African American Blackness.

Finally, Aileen Dillane and Sarah Raine's chapter draws us into TradFest, an annual music festival that is held at Temple Bar, Dublin's iconic cultural district famous for its traditional pub culture and association to traditional Irish music. Their contribution problematizes the authenticity/inauthenticity dichotomy that is frequently implied in tourism discourses and practices by exploring the distinctive atmosphere of Temple Bar's traditional Irish pubs as a complex interaction between the built environment, the materiality of objects, people, and music, in which tourists and locals confront their own expectations. Aileen and Raine depart from the assumption that equates the authentic with the "real", and instead propose an approach to the study of authenticity that privileges the performative, conjunctural, and relational aspects of the tourist encounter.

The book closes with an afterword written by Manuel Delgado entitled "Urban correspondences" in which the author draws a fine line connecting the urban theory implicit in Charles Baudelaire's work with the revolutionary sensory ecology proposed by the CRESSON researchers in France to which this volume is greatly indebted. The author firmly rejects the temptation to read the city as a text and, instead, views it as

> an order of profound coincidences, at once clear and lush, in which colours, smells, patterns . . . and sounds dialogue and merge with each other until engendering something we are unable to either define or describe. (p. 258)

To deepen the understanding of the ways in which these elusive entities that we call "ambiances" or "atmospheres" pervade the physical regeneration and sensory transformation of contemporary tourist destinations is the ultimate aim of this edited collection.

Notes

1 *Source*: TourMIS (www.tourmis.info).
2 Urban revitalization and tourism development are, in fact, mutually dependent.
3 The multimedia and audiovisual documents may be consulted at the following URL address: https://soundsoftourism.pt/ambiance-tourism-and-the-city/.

References

Adey, P. 2008. "Airports, Mobility and the Calculative Architecture of Affective Control." *Geoforum* 39: 438–451. https://doi.org/10.1016/j.geof orum.2007.09.001

Adey, P. 2009. "Facing Airport Security: Affect, Biopolitics, and the Preemptive Securitisation of the Mobile Body." *Environment and Planning D: Society and Space* 27: 274–295. https://doi.org/10.1068/d0208

Adey, P. 2014. "Security Atmospheres or the Crystallisation of Worlds." *Environment and Planning D: Society and Space* 32: 834–851. https://doi.org/10.1068/d21312

Adey, P., L. Brayer, D. Masson, P. Murphy, P. Simpson, and N. Tixier. 2013. "'Pour votre tranquillité': Ambiance, Atmosphere, and Surveillance." *Geoforum* 49: 299–309. https://doi.org/10.1016/j.geoforum.2013.04.028

Amit, V. 2015. "Circumscribed Cosmopolitanism: Travel Aspirations and Experiences." *Identities* 22 (5): 551–568.

Andersson, T. D. 2007. "The Tourist in the Experience Economy." *Scandinavian Journal of Hospitality and Tourism* 7 (1): 46–58. https://doi.org/10.1080/15022250701224035.

Augoyard, J. F., and H. Torgue. 2006. *Sonic Experience: A Guide to Everyday Sounds*. Montreal and Ithaca: McGill-Queen's University Press.

Barnes, K., G. Waitt, N. Gill, and C. Gibson. 2006. "Community and Nostalgia in Urban Revitalisation: A Critique of Urban Village and Creative Class Strategies as Remedies for Social 'Problems'." *Australian Geographer* 37 (3): 335–354. https://doi.org/10.1080/00049180600954773.

Berman, R. 2006. *Assessing Urban Design: Historical Ambience on the Waterfront.* Lanham: Lexington.

Bianchi, R. V. 2009. "The 'Critical Turn' in Tourism Studies: A Radical Critique." *Tourism Geographies* 11 (4): 484–504.

Bianchi, R. V., M. L. Stephenson, and K. Hannam. 2020. "The Contradictory Politics of the Right to Travel: Mobilities, Borders & Tourism." *Mobilities* 15 (2): 290–306.

Bille, M. 2019. *Homely Atmospheres and Lighting Technologies in Denmark: Living with Light.* London: Bloomsbury.

Bille, M., P. Bjerregaard, and T. F. Sørensen. 2015. "Staging Atmospheres: Materiality, Culture, and the Texture of the In-between." *Emotion, Space and Society* 15: 31–38.

Bitner, M. J. 1992. "Servicescapes: The Impact of Physical Surroundings on Customers and Employees." *Journal of Marketing* 56 (2): 57–71. https://doi.org/10.2307/1252042

Bjerregaard, P. 2015. "Dissolving Objects: Museums, Atmosphere and the Creation of Presence." *Emotion, Space and Society* 15: 74–81. https://doi.org/10.1016/j.emospa.2014.05.002

Boissevain, J., ed. 1996. *Coping with Tourists: European Reactions to Mass Tourism.* Oxford: Berghahn Books.

Borges, L. 2016. "Alfama quer manter a alma lisboeta livre da invasão de casas para turistas." *Público.* www.publico.pt/2016/09/13/local/noticia/alfama-quer-manter-a-alma-lisboeta-segura-da-invasao-de-casas-para-turistas-1743983.

Brenner, N., and N. Theodore. 2002. "Cities and the Geographies of 'Actually Existing Neoliberalism'." *Antipode* 34 (3): 349–379.

Büscher, B., and R. Fletcher. 2017. "Destructive Creation: Capital Accumulation and the Structural Violence of Tourism." *Journal of Sustainable Tourism* 25 (5): 651–667.

Cañada, E. 2018. "Too Precarious to Be Inclusive? Hotel Maid Employment in Spain." *Tourism Geographies* 20 (4): 653–674.

Cañada, E., and I. Murray, eds. 2019. *Turistificación Global. Perspectivas críticas en turismo.* Barcelona: Icaria Antrazyt.

Cao, L. 2022. "Consuming 'Authenticity'? Reinterpreting the 'New Middle Class' in China through the Lens of Retailing Changes." *Urban Studies.* https://doi.org/10.1177/00420980221107318.

Cócola-Gant, A. 2018. "Tourism Gentrification." In *Handbook of Gentrification Studies,* edited by L. Lees and M. Phillips, 281–293. Cheltenham: Edward Elgar Publishing.

Cócola-Gant, A., and A. Gago. 2019. "Airbnb, Buy-to-let Investment and Tourism-driven Displacement: A Case Study in Lisbon." *Environment and Planning A: Economy and Space* 53 (7). https://doi.org/10.1177/0308518X19869012

Cocola-Gant, A., A. Gago, and J. Jover. 2020. "Tourism, Gentrification and Neighbourhood Change: An Analytical Framework – Reflections from Southern European Cities." In *The Overtourism Debate,* edited by J. Oskam, 121–135. Bingley: Emerald.

Coelho, M., M. Gosling and A. Almeida. 2018. "Tourism Experiences: Core Processes of Memorable Trips." *Journal of Hospitality and Tourism Management* 37: 11–22

Colomb, C., and J. Novy, eds. 2016. *Protest and Resistance in the Tourist City.* New York: Routledge.

Cuthill, V. 2007. "Consuming Harrogate. Performing Betty's Café and Revolution Vodka Bar." *Space and Culture* 10 (1): 64–76.

Degen, M. 2003. "Fighting for the Global Catwalk: Formalizing Public Life in Castlefield (Manchester) and Diluting Public Life in El Raval (Barcelona)." *International Journal of Urban and Regional Research* 27 (4): 867–880. https://doi.org/10.1111/j.0309-1317.2003.00488.x.

Degen, M. 2008. *Sensing Cities: Regenerating Public Life in Barcelona and Manchester.* New York: Routledge.

Devine, J., and D. Ojeda. 2017. "Violence and Dispossession in Tourism Development: A Critical Geographical Approach." *Journal of Sustainable Tourism* 25 (5): 605–617.

Fletcher, R. 2011. "Sustaining Tourism, Sustaining Capitalism? The Tourism Industry's Role in Global Capitalist Expansion." *Tourism Geographies* 13 (3): 443–461.

Glick Schiller, N., and N. B. Salazar. 2013. "Regimes of Mobility across the Globe." *Journal of Ethnic and Migration Studies* 39 (2): 183–200.

Gomes, P. 2019. "The Birth of Public Space Privatization: How Entrepreneurialism, Convivial Urbanism and Stakeholder Interactions Made the Martim Moniz Square, in Lisbon, 'Privatization-Ready'." *European Urban and Regional Studies.* 27 (1) https://doi.org/10.1177/0969776418823052

Goss, J. 1993. "The 'Magic of the Mall': An Analysis of Form, Function, and Meaning in the Contemporary Retail Built Environment." *Annals of the Association of American Geographers* 83 (1): 18–47.

Gössling, S., and P. Peeters. 2015. "Assessing Tourism's Global Environmental Impact 1900–2050." *Journal of Sustainable Tourism* 23 (5): 639–659.

Grazian, David. 2003. *Blue Chicago: The Search for Authenticity in Urban Blues Clubs.* Chicago: University of Chicago Press.

Guimarães, P. 2021. "Retail Change in a Context of an Overtourism City. The Case of Lisbon." *International Journal of Tourism Cities* 7 (2): 547–564. https://doi.org/10.1108/IJTC-11-2020-0258

Guimarães, P. 2022. "Unfolding Authenticity within Retail Gentrification in Mouraria. Lisbon." *Journal of Tourism and Cultural Change* 20 (1–2): 221–240. https://doi.org/10.1080/14766825.2021.1876079

Han, H. 2013. "Effects of In-flight Ambience and Space/Function on Air Travelers' Decision to Select a Low-Cost Airline." *Tourism Management* 37: 125–135. https://doi.org/10.1016/j.tourman.2013.01.008

Harvey, D. 1978. "The Urban Process under Capitalism: A Framework for Analysis." *International Journal of Urban and Regional Research* 2 (1–3): 101–131.

Harvey, D. 1989. "From Managerialism to Entrepreneurialism: The Transformation in Urban Governance in Late Capitalism." *Geografiska Annaler: Series B, Human Geography* 71 (1): 3–17.

Harvey, D. 2003. *The New Imperialism.* Oxford: Oxford University Press.

Harvey, D. 2007. *A Brief History of Neoliberalism.* Oxford: Oxford University Press.

Hayes, M. 2021. "A Global Sociology on Lifestyle Migrations." In *International Residential Mobilities,* edited by J. Domínguez-Mujica, J. McGarrigle, and J. M. Parreño-Castellano, 3–18. Cham: Springer International.

Hayes, M., and H. Zaban. 2020. "Transnational Gentrification: The Crossroads of Transnational Mobility and Urban Research." *Urban Studies* 57 (15): 3009–3024.

Heide, M., K. Lærdal, and K. Grønhaug. 2007. "The Design and Management of Ambience – Implications for Hotel Architecture and Service." *Tourism Management* 28 (5): 1315–1325. https://doi.org/10.1016/j.tourman.2007.01.011

Heitmann, S. 2011. "Authenticity in Tourism." In *Research Themes for Tourism,* edited by P. Robinson, S. Heitmann, and P. U. Dieke, 45–58. Wallingford: CABI.

Howes, D. 2004. *Empire of the Senses. The Sensual Culture Reader.* London: Routledge.

Ioannides, D., and K. G. Debbage, eds. 1998. *The Economic Geography of the Tourist Industry: A Supply-Side Analysis.* London: Routledge.

Jani, D., and H. Han. 2014. "Testing the Moderation Effect of Hotel Ambience on the Relationships Among Social Comparison, Affect, Satisfaction, and Behavioral Intentions." *Journal of Travel & Tourism Marketing* 31 (6): 731–746. https://doi.org/10.1080/1054 8408.2014.888967

JLL & WTTC. 2019. *Destination 2030. Global Cities' Readiness for Tourism Growth*. London: JLL and World Travel Tourism Council.

Judd, D. 2003. *The Infrastructure of Play: Building the Tourist City*. New York: Routledge.

Kim, J.-H. 2014. "The Antecedents of Memorable Tourism Experiences: The Development of a Scale to Measure the Destination Attributes Associated with Memorable Experiences." *Tourism Management* 44: 34–45. http://doi.org/10.1016/j.tourman.2014.02.007

Knudsen, B. T., and A. M. Waade. 2010. *Re-Investing Authenticity: Tourism, Place and Emotions*. Bristol: Channel View Publications.

Kovačić, M., and L. Silveira. 2020. "Cruise Tourism: Implications and Impacts on the Destinations of Croatia and Portugal." *Pomorstvo* 34 (1): 40–47. https://doi.org/10.31217/p.34.1.5.

LaBelle, B. 2010. *Acoustic Territories. Sound Culture and Everyday Life*. London: Bloomsbury.

Lalicic, L., and C. Weismayer. 2017. "The Role of Authenticity in Airbnb Experiences." In *Information and Communication Technologies in Tourism 2017*, edited by R. Schegg and B. Stangl, 781–794. Cham: Springer International Publishing. https://doi.org/10.1007/978-3-319-51168-9_56.

Larsen, J. 2010. "Goffman and the Tourist Gaze: A Performative Perspective on Tourism Mobilities." In *The Contemporary Goffman*, edited by M. H. Jacobsen, 313–332. New York: Routledge.

Latour, B., et al. 2002. *Iconoclash*. Cambridge, MA: MIT Press.

Lenzen, M., Y. Y. Sun, F. Faturay, Y. P. Ting, A. Geschke, and A. Malik. 2018. "The Carbon Footprint of Global Tourism." *Nature Climate Change* 8: 522–528.

Lovell, J., and C. Bull, eds. 2017. *Authentic and Inauthentic Places in Tourism: From Heritage Sites to Theme Parks*. London and New York: Routledge.

Lu, D., Y. Liu, I. Lai, and L. Yang. 2017. "Awe: An Important Emotional Experience in Sustainable Tourism." *Sustainability* 9 (12): 2189. http://dx.doi.org/10.3390/su9122189

MacCannell, D. 1976. *The Tourist: A new Theory of the Leisure Class*. New York: Schocken Books.

Malet Calvo, D., and M. J. Ramos. 2018. "Suddenly Last Summer: How the Tourist Tsunami Hit Lisbon." *Revista Andaluza de Antropología* 15: 47–73. https://doi.org/10.12795/RAA.2018.15.03.

Manhas, P., N. Charak, and P. Sharma. 2019. "Wellness and Spa Tourism: Finding Space for Indian Himalayan Spa Resorts." *International Journal of Spa and Wellness* 2 (3): 135–153. https://doi.org/10.1080/24721735.2020.1819705

Mastercard. 2019. "Global Destination Cities Index 2019." https://newsroom.mastercard.com/wp-content/uploads/2019/09/GDCI-Global-Report-FINAL-1.pdf

Michels, C., and C. Steyaert. 2017. "By Accident and by Design: Composing Affective Atmospheres in an Urban Art Intervention." *Organization* 24: 79–104. https://doi.org/10.1177/1350508416668190

Mihalic, T. 2020. "Conceptualising Overtourism: A Sustainability Approach." *Annals of Tourism Research* 84. https://doi.org/10.1016/j.annals.2020.103025

Milano, C., J. M. Cheer, and M. Novelli, eds. 2019. *Overtourism: Excesses, Discontents and Measures in Travel and Tourism*. Oxfordshire and Boston: CAB International.

Milano, C., and J. A. Mansilla, eds. 2018. *Ciudad de vacaciones. Conflictos urbanos en espacios turísticos*. Barcelona: Pollen Edicions.

Montezuma, J., and J. McGarrigle. 2019. "What Motivates International Homebuyers? Investor to Lifestyle 'Migrants' in a Tourist City." *Tourism Geographies* 21 (2): 214–234. https://doi.org/10.1080/14616688.2018.1470196

Morell, M. 2018. "Urban Tourism via Dispossession of Oeuvres: Labor as a Common Denominator." *Focaal* 82: 35–48. https://doi.org/10.3167/fcl.2018.820103.

Mosedale, J., ed. 2016. *Neoliberalism and the Political Economy of Tourism*. New York: Routledge.

Muñoz, F. 2010. "Urbanalisation: Common Landscapes, Global Places." *The Open Urban Studies Journal* 3 (1): 78–88. https://doi.org/10.2174/1874942901003010078.

Musterd, S., and W. Ostendorf, eds. 1998. *Urban Segregation and the Welfare State: Inequality and Exclusion in Western Cities*. New York: Routledge.

Nogués-Pedregal, A. M. 2019. "Anthropological Contributions to Tourism Studies." *Annals of Tourism Research* 75: 227–237.

Ojeda, A. B., and M. Kieffer. 2020. "Touristification. Empty Concept or Element of Analysis in Tourism Geography?" *Geoforum* 115: 143–145. https://doi.org/10.1016/j.geoforum.2020.06.021.

Paiva, D. 2022. "Ambiance." In *Encyclopedia of Tourism Management and Marketing*, edited by D. Buhalis, 145–148. Cheltenham: Edward Elgar. https://doi.org/10.4337/9781800377486.ambiance

Paiva, D., and H. Cachinho. 2018. "Artistic Practices and the Redistribution of the Sensible in Largo do Chiado: Attention, Corporeal Isles, Visceral Politics." *Tijdschrift Voor Economische En Sociale Geografie* 109: 597–612. https://doi.org/10.1111/tesg.12312

Paiva, D., and I. Sánchez-Fuarros. 2021. "The Territoriality of Atmosphere: Rethinking Affective Urbanism through The Collateral Atmospheres of Lisbon's Tourism." *Transactions of the Institute of British Geographers* 46 (2): 392–405.

Paulauskaite, D., J. Raymond Powell, A. Coca-Stefaniak, and A. M. Morrison. 2017. "Living Like a Local: Authentic Tourism Experiences and the Sharing Economy." *International Journal of Tourism Research* 19 (6): 619–628. https://doi.org/10.1002/jtr.2134.

Peake, B. 2008. "Eating in the Real Gozo: Sound, Authenticity, and Identity in Gozitan Restaurants." *Omertaa, Journal for Applied Anthropology*, 235–242.

Pine, B. J., and J. H. Gilmore. 2013. "The Experience Economy: Past, Present and Future." In *Handbook on the Experience Economy*, edited by J. Sundbo and F. Sørensen, 21–44. Edward Elgar Publishing. https://doi.org/10.4337/9781781004227.00007.

Purcell, M. 2002. "Excavating Lefebvre: The Right to the City and its Urban Politics of the Inhabitant." *GeoJournal* 58 (2): 99–108.

Rickly, J. M. 2022. "A Review of Authenticity Research in Tourism: Launching the Annals of Tourism Research Curated Collection on Authenticity." *Annals of Tourism Research* 92: 103349. https://doi.org/10.1016/j.annals.2021.103349.

Rickly-Boyd, J. M. 2012. "Authenticity & Aura." *Annals of Tourism Research* 39 (1): 269–289. https://doi.org/10.1016/j.annals.2011.05.003.

Rickly-Boyd, J. M. 2013. "Existential Authenticity: Place Matters." *Tourism Geographies* 15 (4): 680–686. https://doi.org/10.1080/14616688.2012.762691.

Robinson, R. N., A. Martins, D. Solnet, and T. Baum. 2019. "Sustaining Precarity: Critically Examining Tourism and Employment." *Journal of Sustainable Tourism* 27 (7): 1008–1025.

Salah Ouf, A. M. 2001. "Authenticity and the Sense of Place in Urban Design." *Journal of Urban Design* 6 (1): 73–86. https://doi.org/10.1080/13574800120032914.

Salazar, N. B. 2017. "Anthropologies of Tourism." *American Anthropologist* 119 (4): 723–747.

Sánchez-Fuarros, I. 2016. "'Ai, Mouraria!' Music, Tourism, and Urban Renewal in a Historic Lisbon Neighbourhood." *MUSICultures* 43 (2). https://journals.lib.unb.ca/index.php/MC/article/view/25475

Sánchez-Fuarros, I. 2017. "Mapping Out the Sounds of Urban Transformation. The Renewal of Lisbon's Mouraria Quarter." In *Toward an Anthropology of Ambient Sound*, edited by Christine Guillebaud, 153–167. New York: Routledge https://doi.org/10.4324/9781315755045.

Sánchez-Fuarros, I., and M. T. Lacerda. 2022. "Tourism-Dependent Local Music Ecosystems under COVID-19: The Case of Lisbon's Fado Music Scene." *Journal of World Popular Music* 9 (1–2). https://doi.org/10.1558/jwpm.23350.

Sánchez-Fuarros, I., and D. Paiva. 2021. "Postales sonoras de una ciudad turística confinada: Lisboa y la resonancia del turismo como híper-objeto." In *Sé lo que hicisteis el último verano". Crisis, Covid-19 y turismo*, edited by Jorge Sequera, 171–200. Barcelona: Bellaterra.

Scott, D., and S. Gössling. 2015. "What Could the Next 40 Years Hold for Global Tourism?" *Tourism Recreation Research* 40 (3): 269–285.

Sequera, J., and J. Nofre. 2018. "Shaken, not Stirred. New Debates on Touristification and the Limits of Gentrification." *City* 22: 843–855. https://doi.org/10.1080/13604813.2018.1548819

Sequera, J., and J. Nofre. 2019. "Touristification, Transnational Gentrification and Urban Change in Lisbon: The Neighbourhood of Alfama." *Urban Studies* 57: 3169–3189. https://doi.org/10.1177/0042098019883734

Shaw, R. 2014. "Beyond Night-Time Economy: Affective Atmospheres of the Urban Night." *Geoforum* 51: 87–95. https://doi.org/10.1016/j.geoforum.2013.10.005

Smith, V. 1978. *Hosts and Guests: The Anthropology of Tourism*. Philadelphia: University of Pennsylvania Press.

Sumartojo, S. 2016. "Commemorative Atmospheres: Memorial Sites, Collective Events and the Experience of National Identity." *Transactions of the Institute of British Geographers* 41: 541–553. https://doi.org/10.1111/tran.12144

Sumartojo, S., and S. Pink. 2018. *Atmospheres and the Experiential World: Theory and Methods*. Oxon: Routledge.

Tate, L. E., and B. Shannon. eds. 2018. *Planning for Authenticities*. New York: Routledge, Taylor & Francis Group.

Thibaud, J. P. 2011. "The Sensory Fabric of Urban Ambiances." *The Senses and Society* 6 (2): 203–215. https://doi.org/10.2752/174589311X12961584845846.

Turner, L., and J. Ash. 1975. *The Golden Hordes: International Tourism and the Pleasure Periphery*. New York: St. Martin's Press.

UNWTO. 2018. "Overtourism? Understanding and Managing Urban Tourism Growth beyond Perceptions." https://doi.org/10.18111/9789284419999.

UNWTO. 2022. *International Tourism and Covid-19* (UNWTO Tourism Data Dashboard). United Nations World Tourism Organization. www.unwto.org/tourism-data/unwto-tourism-dashboard.

Urry, J. 1990. *The Tourist Gaze*. London: Sage.

Valente, R., A. P. Russo, S. Vermeulen and F. L. Milone. 2022. "Tourism Pressure as a Driver of Social Inequalities: A BSEM Estimation of Housing Instability in European Urban Areas." *European Urban and Regional Studies* 29 (3): 332–349.

van der Duim, R., C. Ren, and G. T. Jóhannesson. 2017. "ANT: A Decade of Interfering with Tourism." *Annals of Tourism Research* 64: 139–149.

Vanspauwen, B., and I. Sánchez-Fuarros. 2023. "Embracing postcolonial diversity? Music selection and affective formation in TAP Air Portugal's in-flight entertainment system". In *Legacies of The Portuguese Colonial Empire: Nationalism, Multiculturalism and Citizenship*, edited by E. Peralta and N. Domingo, 199–217. London: Bloomsbury.

Volgger, M., and D. Pfister. 2020. *Atmospheric Turn in Culture and Tourism: Place, Design and Process Impacts*. Bingley: Emerald.

Waitt, G. 2000. "Consuming Heritage." *Annals of Tourism Research* 27 (4): 835–862. https://doi.org/10.1016/S0160-7383(99)00115-2.

Wall, G. 2020. "From Carrying Capacity to Overtourism: A Perspective Article." *Tourism Review* 75 (1): 212–215

Wang, D., F. Kotsi, S. Pike, and J. Yao. 2021. "Stopover Destination Loyalty: The Influence of Perceived Ambience and Sensation Seeking Tendency." *Journal of Hospitality and Tourism Management* 47: 159–166. https://doi.org/10.1016/j.jhtm.2021.03.015

Wang, N. 1999. "Rethinking Authenticity in Tourism Experience." *Annals of Tourism Research* 26 (2): 349–370. https://doi.org/10.1016/S0160-7383(98)00103-0.

Wheeler, F., and J. Laing. 2008. "Tourism as a Vehicle for Liveable Communities: Case Studies from Regional Victoria, Australia." *Annals of Leisure Research* 11 (1–2): 242–263. https://doi.org/10.1080/11745398.2008.9686795

Zhang, X., C. Ryan, and J. Cave. 2016. "Residents, Their Use of a Tourist Facility and Contribution to Tourist Ambience: Narratives from a Film Tourism Site in Beijing." *Tourism Management* 52: 416–429. https://doi.org/10.1016/j.tourman.2015.07.006

Zukin, S. 2010. *Naked City: The Death and Life of Authentic Urban Places*. Oxford: Oxford University Press.

Part I

Music, ambiance, and affective enactments of public space

2 Musical extractivism and the commercial after-life of San Juan's (PR) La Perla and Kingston's (JM) Fleet Street

Ofer Gazit and Elisa Bruttomesso

In the Caribbean, music is a crucial part of the tourism industry (Guilbault and Rommen 2019; Rommen and Neely 2014).[1] Music tourism is promoted through government and municipal sponsored initiatives such as religious events, carnivals, and saints' days and through private enterprises, genre themed cruises and music festivals (Ballico and Watson 2020). Over the last decade, YouTube has brought unprecedented visibility to Caribbean music and musicians, with Reggaeton and Reggae reclaiming long lost mainstream attention in US American and European media (Marshall 2017). While some research has dealt with the impact of YouTube videos on tourism in K-pop contexts (e.g. Oh 2015), the impact of high visibility videos on Caribbean tourism has not been studied directly. Here we focus on one such potential impact, namely how the economic logics of YouTube, and the conditions under which such Caribbean music achieves visibility are transferred vis-à-vis tourism onto the "live" music scenes in San Juan, Puerto Rico, and Kingston, Jamaica. We use Puerto Rican singer Luis Fonsi's video 'Despacito' ft. Daddy Yankee (dir. Carlos Perez, 2017) and Jamaican singer Koffee's video 'Toast' (dir. Xavier Damase, 2018) as indicators of this impact.

Sounds of tourism

In a recent book on the impact of tourism on music in the Caribbean, Guilbault and Rommen (2019, 13) write that

> [O]ne cannot consider the Caribbean tourism industry without foregrounding specifically the historical relationship of human labor – the labor of the slaves and of the colonized marshaled by the colonizers to reproduce the structure of wealth abroad and poverty at home.

In the case studies we explore below – where poverty itself becomes a site of commercialized tourism – such considerations become ever more pertinent. While Guilbault and Rommen point to cruise ships and resorts as sites of neocolonial encounters, grounded in unequal and exploitative political economies, we seek to decentre the discussion to contexts that have been seen as informal and unofficial

DOI: 10.4324/9781003207207-4

tourist sites: the streets, bars, and public art projects in historically low-income Caribbean neighbourhoods.

Low-income neighbourhoods, particularly those that maintain public arts projects through murals and community-based art, are crucially important sites of Caribbean tourism, as they signify prized "authentic" and "uncommercial" locales to those tourists that seek them (Skinner and Jolliffe 2017). Low-income neighbourhoods are equally important sites of "uncommercial" musical performances. In many Caribbean cities, both live and recorded music are performed in public, making DJs, selectors, performing musicians, and perhaps most importantly local dancers and listeners sites of tourist "imperial gaze" and "imperial audition" (Guilbault and Rommen 2019, 11). If low-income urban environments, public arts projects, and the visual and sonic dimensions of Caribbean musicking are crucial sites of Caribbean tourism, the neocolonial political economies they reproduce are never more present than in their online manifestations as highly visible YouTube videos.

From plantation to YouTube logics

In order to examine the impact of hyper visibility on Jamaican and Puerto Rican music scenes, we developed the notion of "YouTube logics", which connects Surveillance Capitalism (Zuboff 2018) with what Donna Haraway and Anna Tsing referred to as "Plantation Logics". According to Tsing, Plantation Logics are characterized by scalability and interchangeability: Scalability refers to the proficiency through which the plantation was able to expand using an established programme, decimating the existing indigenous population and replacing it with a coercive economic system based on slavery and foreign crops. The notion of interchangeability refers to the ability to exchange one species for another, for example, exchanging sugar canes for enslaved people as an integral part of the plantation system (Tsing 2015, 38–39).

The image of the planation system was further reinscribed in the 1920s, when live radio broadcasts from Harlem nightclubs, such as The Plantation Club and The Cotton Club, offered white middle-class households having a radio a theatrical, musical and at time comical representation of plantation slavery. These live radio transmissions were laden with commercials, adding a stream of income to the radio station and the club itself (Wall 2012).

YouTube videos similarly monetize fantasies of Caribbean urban poverty, using the scenery of neocolonial inequalities as a foil on which to play out and project exoticized images of Caribbean dancers and musicians.

Plantation Logics aim at maximizing the potential profits of the plantation system. This extends beyond the plantation system itself to the exploitation of racialized bodies not only through forced labour, but also through theatrical, musical, and choreographed representations of the plantation. Indeed, as we later discuss, the possibility to benefit both from the trauma of the plantation and from stylized, musical representations of that trauma is an important antecedent to contemporary depictions of recent Caribbean disasters and the recovery efforts of local residents circulated through YouTube videos.

Because YouTube's revenue is dependent on increasing its scale, that is, the number of users, the company provides incentives only to those who prove most efficient in generating social connections. The nature, content, and quality of such social relations may impact the type of advertisement a user may see, but any and all communications are valuable – they are therefore interchangeable (Hesmond-halgh 2017). As we show next, the interchangeability and scalability of plantation are similarly properties of YouTube logics.

Music videos as promoters of tourism

Research on the impact of YouTube videos – specifically music videos on tourism, is only taking its first steps. South Korea in particular has been a crucial centre for research on the impact of YouTube videos on tourism. Writing about the impact of K-Pop tourism Oh et al. (2015) have argued that videos by some of Korea's most popular bands have propelled a wave of tourism to destinations where music videos by these groups have been shot. The writers further argue that the choice of filming location for a music video can function as a predictor of tourism activity and as an indicator of economic vitality following the success of the video. While several studies discuss the potential future benefits of music videos on local tourism destinations, such research is grounded in data from focus group surveys (Lee and Bai 2016) or overall increase in incoming tourists to South Korea in relation to growing popularity of Korean popular culture abroad (Hur and Kim 2020). However, the impact on specific tourism destinations and the performative and economic role local residents play in such destinations remains under-explored.

Who participates in participatory culture?

Researchers dealing with marketing strategies have argued that YouTube videos serve as an important tool for creating "participatory culture" within the tourism industry. While sharing vacation photos and videos among friends has long been an implicit promoter of tourism, the mass broadcasting capabilities available to social media users and the ability to harness these videos and photos by tourism companies have had a drastic effect on tourism marketing. Examining the case of YouTube videos and video sharing among Spanish tourists, Huertas et al. (2017) argued that tourism agencies (whether private or public) can harness personal videos shot by travellers to promote particular destinations. The authors argue that modelling commercial advertisements on YouTube videos made by tourists themselves will enhance the relatability of advertisements to potential viewers. With the pervasiveness of mobile phone cameras, this created a two-way influence, where the visual language of amateur "homemade" films is transferred to the commercial arena while tourists themselves make videos to mimic commercial videos.

This visual exchange or mimicry is further highlighted by Briciu and Briciu (2020). Examining YouTube videos made by travellers in Transylvania, the authors emphasize the notion that personal videos encourage duplication or recreation of previous videos (sometimes referred to as "challenges" in YouTubers terminology). By recreating and personalizing videos created by other travellers in the same locations or destinations, video makers engage in a participatory exchange with other viewers (and potential re-makers), through comments, criticisms, and other forms of social media engagement. "Participatory culture" thus includes the perspective of tourism agencies (who mimic these privately made videos) or other private viewers (who also mimic and react to these videos). Importantly, "participation" is considered solely from the perspective of viewers, who identify themselves as potential targets of marketing through their engagement with these videos and marketing agencies. It excludes from participation those who appear in the video but are not part of the social media exchange – particularly local residents during their everyday engagement with tourists. As we show in the following case studies, the degree to which local residents stand to benefit from the production of music videos in tourism sites greatly depends on their ability to insert themselves into this social and economic exchange.

Considering the case of two low-income Caribbean neighbourhoods, La Perla in San Juan PR, and Fleet Street in Kingston Jamaica, and the respective commercial videos that were made in them, we ask: How do YouTube logics manifest in "off-line" socio-economic relations? To what extent can local residents in "music video tourism sites" participate in the political economies of "participatory culture"? What is the effect of high visibility YouTube videos on the neighbourhood in which they were shot? In other words, what does it mean to be "seen" according to YouTube logics? What are the social implications of the ambiences created by music videos on the different locations and their inhabitants?

Situating "Despacito"

"Despacito" is a song and music video written by Luis Fonsi, Daddy Yankee, and Erica Ender. Since its online release in January 2017, "Despacito" has accumulated more than seven billion views on YouTube (7.6 billion at the time of writing). It is extremely difficult to give an accurate assessment of the profits YouTube has made through advertisement revenue attached to the video, nor is it possible to know the precise payouts YouTube made to Universal Music Group, the label that owns the majority share of the song's recording and publishing rights. It is also impossible to know the division of rights and revenue between the label and Fonsi, Daddy Yankee and Ender who have songwriting credits for the song. A careful estimate, based on YouTube's own advertised price for an ad of $0.1 per view (it can be as high as $0.3), is that YouTube made roughly 760 million dollars in advertisement revenue since "Despacito" was aired. It is important to note, however, that YouTube's payout contracts are not public, and are highly divergent between different content producers. Content produced under contract with a multinational corporation like Universal Music is likely to be more lucrative for the label than content produced by a private individual with a standard contract.

The video for "Despacito" was shot in one 14-hour workday, both in La Perla and in the nearby bar named La Factoria. Carlos Perez, The director of "Despacito" who is based in Miami, explained the concept of the video: "We decided that the video would be like a day in a life inside the culture of Puerto Rico" (Perez, cited in Courtens 2017). In order to capture the collaboration between Fonsi, a Puerto Rican born, Miami-based star of Latin pop, and Daddy Yankee, the reggaeton pioneer still living on the island, Perez wanted a place that was both romantic and urban and chose an area of social housing that contrasts sharply with the rest of Old San Juan's hotel-studded coastline. "We knew the textures of the barrio that we wanted would be there", he explains: "Also, the Malecon in La Perla is very unique. It's the only place where public housing is literally on the water" (Perez, cited in Courtens 2017). The video highlights the juxtapositions between San Juan's poorly maintained but vibrantly coloured public housing with the beauty of the Caribbean Sea throughout, as shots move from the coastal path to its urban interior, before finally coming to rest in a bar where the track succumbs to the (apparently) diegetic sounds of the singers and percussion.[2]

Figure 2.1 La Perla's Malecón in San Juan (Puerto Rico). Screenshot from Luis Fonsi's "Despacito" video.

Source: https://youtu.be/kJQP7kiw5Fk

The success of "Despacito" was instant, reaching 5.4 million YouTube views within 24 hours (Flores 2017). By July 2017, it had become the most watched YouTube video ever, and La Perla the world's most viewed neighbourhood. This quickly drew the attention of businessmen and politicians; just eight months after the release of the video, in August 2017, the then governor of Puerto Rico, Ricardo Rosselló, declared Luis Fonsi a Tourism Ambassador. Jose Izquierdo, the director of the Puerto Rican Tourism Company (PRTC), said in a press statement, "We will unveil the land of 'Despacito'" (Fernandez 2017). Online news outlets reported an increase of 45% in Puerto Rico Google searches, while others report an actual 45% rise in tourism itself (Draper 2017) (see Figure 2.2). However, these headlines remained unconfirmed and appear to have been boosted by a misleading but arguably understandable campaign by the PRTC. Despite the unprecedented success of "Despacito", tourism in Puerto Rico did not increase dramatically between January and August 2017. In fact, a report by the *Washington Post* shows that hotel occupancy and income from tourist taxes actually decreased slightly compared to previous years, while traffic to online travel sites also remained constant: There does not appear to have been a clear "Despacito" effect (Friedman 2017).

What did create a clear and significant rise in interest in Puerto Rico was not "Despacito" but a catastrophe of historic proportions, one which decimated its tourism industry. Just three weeks after Luis Fonsi was appointed Tourism Ambassador by the PRTC, the island was hit by hurricanes Irma and Maria, leaving La Perla and countless other neighbourhoods in ruins and without electricity and running water for months. A comparison between the Google search numbers for "Despacito" and "Puerto Rico" reveals that, for a brief moment in the weeks following the Hurricanes, the term "Despacito" was surpassed by searches

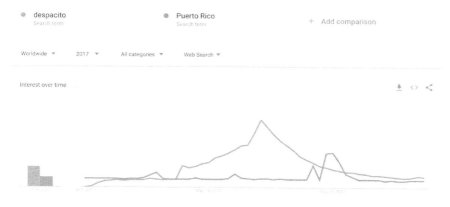

Figure 2.2   Google searches for "Despacito" versus "Puerto Rico" in 2017.

Source: Google Trends (https://trends.google.com/trends/explore?date=2017-01-01%202017-12-31&q=despacito,puerto%20rico)

for "Puerto Rico". When these search numbers began to decrease by early October, it became clear that neither the international success of "Despacito" nor the heightened news visibility in the wake of Hurricane Maria had done much to help the island's ailing economy, the dire humanitarian crisis, or the devastated infrastructure in any tangible way. Rather, these increased hits appeared to enrich various media companies who used the island's theatre of poverty and distraction as a backdrop for advertisements. Mass global visibility, in other words, did not translate into tangible benefits for the local population.

La Factoria

The second scene of "Despacito" was shot at La Factoria, a bar and live music venue above La Perla on Calle San Sebastian. It depicts a crowd dancing to live music at the packed nightclub. The scene's gendered, sexualized, and racialized representations of dancers (what Perez referred to as "dirty dancing, Latin style") are transferred onto the lived reality of La Factoria's weekly live salsa dance floor, which is now advertised as the "Despacito bar" in travel guides and websites (Cobo 2020; Hernández-Acosta 2020, 139). Although the entire video serves as an invitation to Puerto Rico, the second half of the video is particularly pointed in communicating this to the viewer. The scene depicts a crowd dancing at the packed nightclub, with a group of musicians playing instruments associated with Puerto Rico, including the cuatro, a four double-string instrument used in the intro to the song, a string bass (which is not heard in the recording at all), and three drummers, playing a common Bomba pattern call in the last seconds of the song.[3] Perhaps most significant to the video's success in generating social connections are several dance sequences, featuring former Miss Universe Zuleyka Rivera and staged by Puerto Rican choreographer Danny Lugo. Similar to the La Perla waterfront shots, the choreography marks the collaboration between Fonsi and Daddy Yankee by combining the synchronized dance of Latin pop with couples dancing associated with Reggaeton, particularly the *perreo*. "Despacito" then capitalizes on the juxtaposition of contradictions: public housing on prime real estate, a poor neighbourhood with an upscale nightclub, reggaeton played with acoustic instruments, and *perreo* danced within choreographed sequences. As we discuss next, such juxtaposed contradictions are reproduced in San Juan's live music scene.

To understand how YouTube logics have been "scaled" down into the local music scene in San Juan, it is important to untangle the relationship between locals and tourists, salsa dancing and live music. When one of the authors of this chapter (Gazit) visited Puerto Rico in the summer of 2018, several months after the onset of Maria, much of the renovations at La Factoria had been completed, and the bar was working at full capacity. In one of the back rooms, Tempo Alomar's salsa band was playing, preferring salsa adaptations of jazz standards to salsa songs, with the PA system barely holding over the chatter of the crowd. Several couples were dancing salsa, but the majority of people were crowded against the bar, observing the dancers while attempting to grab the bartender's attention.

Pablo Rodríguez, one of the co-owners of the bar, explained that since it opened in 2013, having a live salsa band was crucial to the bar's success. "The Factoria always has locals *and* tourists" he says,

> I think it's very important to have places with live music, and that's what I try to do. Before Covid, I was having live music every Friday, Saturday, Sunday and Monday, and on Mondays and Sundays I was doing double set. It was a total success for us, like breaking all the records since we opened seven years ago.
>
> (Rodriguez 2020)

The dynamics of mimicry work on multiple levels in Rodríguez's telling. First, the bar's success is dependent on the presence of locals, who perform authenticity and "un-commerciality" of the venue to tourists. By dancing salsa, locals perform the experience of Puerto Rico as presented in the dance scene in "Despacito", albeit to very different music. The fact that music is played live, rather than from recordings, makes for an additional marker of "authenticity"[4] (Grazian 2004) between the imaginary experience of La Factoria presented in "Despacito", and the experience tourists observing and participating in salsa dancing at La Factoria. Juan Botta, a local radio broadcaster, told Gazit that many of the live salsa bands in the city play primarily as part of hotels and resorts' entertainment programs, or in the case of famous salsa bands like Gran Combo in large concert halls. La Factoria is the only place in Old San Juan where local residents can hear and dance live salsa (Botta 2020). Because of the limited options, and thanks to the reputation created by "Despacito", La Factoria became both a tourist attraction and local hang for salsa dancers.

"I like to keep it accessible for people that want to see good salsa, but can't afford to pay for expensive drinks, so we do it for free", Rodriguez (2020) says. "They come in, and it doesn't matter if they can spend too much money because, for me, honestly the assistance, just to have them there . . . then you have the tourists that like to see the locals, and maybe learn how to dance". In La Factoria, the social relations created by local dancers are used to advertise and sell drinks and food to tourists. Local dancers at La Factoria are markers of cultural authenticity, performing "a day in the life of Puerto Rican culture" in exchange for a free "service" of live music. They are neither the customer (those would be the tourists) nor the product (food and drinks) but rather employees whose embodied knowledge of dance and racialized bodies help sell a product. This in itself may seem innocuous enough; La Factoria simply offers free admission while hotels and resorts that offer live music are largely closed to local residents. One might say that local residents are simply voting with their feet. But it is important to recall that, for local residents, just like YouTube videos, there is no alternative for listening to music for free. Since YouTube logics are scalable, one might ask: What about access to local music styles that do not satisfy tourists' fantasy of Puerto Rico?

As Rodríguez acknowledges, other scenes in San Juan are suffering.

> [I]f you pay or even if it's free sometimes, it's complicated to bring people to see live music, especially if you try to do something different. For the tourists, it's easier . . . they can go to La Factoria, on Monday we have always music, but it's not the best for the music scene in PR, people don't want to pay. Especially salsa dancers, there are always just 6–7 people, and if you want to do something good you have to bring the whole band, not only the keyboard guy playing the songs – you want the real thing.
>
> (Rodriguez 2020)

As Rodríguez makes clear, although La Factoria is packed – local salsa dancers make up only a small fracture of the audience attending. This small group of dancers is essential for the marketing of La Factoria as "everyday life" "Despacito".

Reliance on tourism can thus be problematic for musical genres that do not adhere to YouTube logic, or those that are not associated with Puerto Rican culture. As Rodríguez explains,

> [I]t's complicated here, especially with rock and roll, if you want to have something every weekend, it's very hard . . . sometimes bands want to get paid too much money to play. . . . For example, I tried to bring people from outside of Puerto Rico, like I brought the band Television, it was a complete disaster economically.

As Rodríguez explains, the music scene in San Juan became dependent on the tastes and imaginations of tourists and the music they associate with Puerto Rico, primarily Salsa and Reggaeton. Music scenes that are not played as a "free" service, struggle to sustain themselves.

Koffee, "Toast", and Fleet Street

While "Despacito" holds a problematic relationship with the location of its shoot, "Toast" has had a more favourable impact. Several recent studies have pointed to the relationship between the Jamaican music industry, what Spence (2021, 148) calls "the platform economy", and tourism development in downtown Jamaica. Grammy award winning reggae singer Koffee has been particularly celebrated for the ways in which she challenges gender norms and the representation of women in the reggae industry, and shines a positive light on the low-income neighbourhoods of Downtown Kinston (Chevy 2019). "Toast", the video responsible for Koffee's reputation and Downtown Kingston's massive global visibility, was produced by IzyBeats and Walshy Fire and filmed by London-based director Xavier Damase. It was uploaded to Vevo and YouTube on 16 November 2018. Since its release, the song has been viewed approximately 195 million times on YouTube alone. The video was shot on Fleet and Orange streets, often celebrated for their importance in Jamaican music history (Samuels 2022). Like "Despacito", "Toast" represents a fictional "day in a life" of the locale, but rather than feature a catalogue of "Jamaicanisms", it focuses on a series of youth activities, including playing football on a flooded concrete field, doing wheelies on a motorbike, bleaching dreadlocks, and boxing. Most prominently, it features Koffee herself, singing about the importance of gratitude and riding her bicycle in red work overalls around Paint Jamaica, a community street art initiative featuring elaborate colourful murals. This focus on the local urban community and simple youth past times positions "Toast" against the sexualized constructions of women in many Caribbean YouTube videos geared towards the "touristic imperial gaze". Instead, it seeks to represent (and commodify nonetheless) a positive image of women and a safe and welcoming image of downtown Kingston.

Created in 2014, Paint Jamaica has since become a popular site for shooting video clips in a city with a storied musical legacy but few available locations. The growing popularity of "Toast" and other videos shot on Fleet Street gave the Paint Jamaica increased visibility, and it began to attract tourists. Rafael Ruiz, a Spanish videographer who works mainly in the Reggae music industry, explains Fleet's Street draw: "In Fleet Street", he says,

> [W]hat is happening is clear: foreign people started to go there as, normally, people who shoot videos come from abroad. The artists (musicians) are from here (Jamaica), but those who make the videos are from abroad. Well, this attracts people from the outside.
>
> (Ruiz 2020)

In the case of "Toast", the video was filmed by London-based director Xavier Damase.

With the increased number of foreign film crews coming to Paint Jamaica, local residents decided to open a small co-op run restaurant. Rafael recalled "those that live there, the Rastafari people that live in front of the murals, figured this out and opened a vegetarian restaurant" (Ruiz 2020). With the help of Paint Jamaica, the Life Yard collective was established. They transformed an area just in front of the murals area at Fleet Street 41–44 into a community vegetable garden, built a small restaurant that hosts tourists, and supplies the community with affordable food.

Ruiz (2020) explains the economic dynamics around the project:

> Those people realized that, if they have the restaurant and all of this well arranged, . . . people can come, have a juice, take some photos and then leave. And this [has] benefits. The restaurant charges a certain money to those who live there, and twice as much to those who come from abroad, which I don't see as a bad action as it keeps on being cheap for tourists.

Ruiz does not consider what is happening in Fleet Street touristification. "What I see in Fleet Street is a worthy project, it ensures the attractiveness of the space, without changing it and its surroundings and basically with no capital investments.

It turned it attractive for young reggae tourists". For him, one of the crucial points is that the place grew organically, from the shared needs of the residents.

By focusing on positive representation, community art projects, and social issues, "Toast" offers a digital version of a fairly recent kind of niche tourism, one which caters specifically to politically and ideologically minded viewers (Luh et al. 2015). Yard Life similarly seeks to attract a new kind of social and politically conscious tourists. To what extent then does Life Yard follow YouTube Logics? While the murals and street art made Fleet Street into a site of increased social media visibility, the murals themselves are not dependent on tourists for their existence, nor are they framed as a "service" given for "free" in order to sell food or juice. Instead, local residents provide food to both locals and tourists at a price that is proportional to their economic abilities and relationship to the place. In addition to the community garden and restaurant Life Yard also provides afternoon daycare and school tutoring for the children of the neighbourhood. For tourists, Life Yard leads tours through the community and hosts the Paint Jamaica Open Air Gallery. In 2017, Life Yard has been selected to receive the inaugural Caribbean Heritage award from Marley Family foundation.

In seeking to commodify representations of positive social actions, and to a degree actually promoting positive social change, both "Toast" and Life Yard can be seen as related manifestations of a growing market-driven, (often) platform based, social justice economy (Spence 2021, 119).[5] As our conversation with Ruiz makes clear, the mass circulation of YouTube videos filmed at Paint Jamaica does not benefit the local residents directly, but the online touristification of social action that stands at the base of their mass visibility became its own source of income for local residents, selling a worthy "cause" to politically minded tourists.

Conclusion

Thinking through the case studies of La Perla and Fleet street, in two former (and we might say contemporary) plantation colonies, one cannot help but wonder if Puerto Rico and Jamaica continue to hold the position of musical plantations, where poverty is transformed into tourist attractions, and YouTube videos further monetize neocolonial relations in an unequal data and streaming industry. What then is the obligation of YouTube to the places whose colourful scenery and depleted infrastructures generate hundreds of millions of dollars in revenue as a site of online poverty tourism? That the scenes of the destruction of Puerto Rico by rainfall and wind the year after the release of "Despacito" grossed even more money into its accounts?

As Ballico and Watson convincingly show (2020), music tourism can make an important contribution to the economic fabric of a city, but as we sought to highlight with the two case studies, direct economic benefits are not likely to reach local residents without a concerted effort and intervention on their part. Life Yard's collaborative model offer's one such intervention, but many other exist. Hernández-Acosta (2020), for example, argues that the emphasis should be on a long-term strategy in which international actors and online media companies coordinate with local stakeholders, such as universities, venues, foundations, and government agencies to recognize the crucial and unpaid labour of local residents in cultural tourism.

This reflects an additional point with regard to Caribbean music scenes. At a time where musicians are facing restrictions from travel, and indoor performances are limited, what is our responsibility as audiences and scholars to making sure YouTube Logics do not decimate the diversity and mere existence of our live music scenes? How can we make sure that cultural labour is properly compensated, and the social relations are not commodified? To quote Rommen and Neely, "What would happen if the twentieth-century 'tourist Other' and the historicized and already-complex character of the 'Caribbean local' were described as co-present and co-producers of contemporary musical practices?" (2014, 314) Far from being autonomous from the virtual world, the Life Yard project provides for us an initial indication that participatory culture can be shaped by the collective agency of local residents. Rather than a comparative research, we consider the analysis of tourist ambiences in La Perla and Fleet Street as an attempt to make explicit the fact that online visibility is not synonymous with political or economic agency. The locales and communities that serve as background to hyper-visible online products must be recognized not only in relation to the unpaid labour of contemporary cultural tourism and the spectacle of the "Caribbean every day". They must also be historicized in relation to centuries-long legacy of the unpaid labour in the plantation system and in relation to the theatrical, advertisement-sponsored radio transmissions of Harlem's Plantation club. YouTube did not invent this logic; it merely exploits it on a new, global scale.

Notes

1 Dr. Ofer Gazit conducted the interviews with Pablo Rodriguez and Juan Botta, conducted fieldwork in Puerto Rico, conducted the analysis of Despacito, and wrote the full and final draft of the chapter. Dr. Elisa Bruttomesso, conducted and translated the interview with Rafael Ruiz, conducted the literature review on music and tourism, and conducted the research on Fleet Street and Life Yard. The conclusion was written together. The authors would like to thank Pablo, Juan, and Rafael for their time during the uncertainty of the COVID-19 pandemic.
2 See later for an analysis of the video's second scene.
3 Each of the instruments displayed stands for another genre (jibaro, salsa, and bomba, respectively), visually mapping Puerto Rican music. Importantly these instruments are rarely played together.
4 The literature on the production of authenticity in tourist contexts is vast, beginning with MacCannell's landmark work from the 1970s. We refer the reader to MacCannell (1973), and Jillian (2022) for a recent review on this topic.
5 Koffee's recent contract as "Brand Ambassador" for Mastercard is part of this growing trend.

References

Ballico, C., and A. Watson, eds. 2020. *Music Cities, Evaluating a Global Cultural Policy Concept*. London: Palgrave Macmillan.
Botta, J. 2020. Interview with the authors, Online, May 8.

Briciu, A., and V. A. Briciu. 2020. "Participatory Culture and Tourist Experience: Promoting Destinations Through YouTube." In *Strategic Innovative Marketing and Tourism*, edited by A. Kavoura, E. Kefallonitis and P. Theodoridis, 425–433. Cham: Springer International.

Chevy, R. J. E. 2019. "Towards a Framework for Caribbean Reparations." *Journal of Eastern Caribbean Studies* 44 (3): 54–77.

Cobo, L. 2020. *Decoding Despacito: An Oral History of Latin Music*. New York: Vintage.

Courtens, R. 2017. "Cut With FCP X: 'Despacito' Gets Over 4 Billion Views on YouTube and is Nominated for Best Music Video in the 2017 Latin Grammy Awards." Last modified October 23, 2017. Accessed June 10, 2020. https://fcp.co/final-cut-pro/articles/2008-cut-with-fcp-x-despacito-gets-over-4-billion-views-on-youtube-and-is-nominated-for-best-music-video-in-the-2017-latin-grammy-awards.

Draper, J. 2017. "Despacito Boosts Puerto Rico Tourism by 45 Per Cent." *Daily Mail Online*, August 29, 2017. www.dailymail.co.uk/travel/travel_news/article-4833254/Despacito-boosts-Puerto-Rico-tourism-45-cent.html

Fernandez, S. 2017. "Luis Fonsi Named Puerto Rico's Tourism Ambassador." *Billboard*, August 15, 2017. www.billboard.com/articles/columns/latin/7905040/luis-fonsi-puerto-rico-tourism-ambassador-despacito.

Flores, G. 2017. "Luis Fonsi Talks Anatomy of 'Despacito'." *Billboard*, January 18, 2017. www.billboard.com/music/latin/luis-fonsi-despacito-daddy-yankee-interview-7661716/.

Friedman, M. 2017. "No, 'Despacito' Is Not Actually Driving a Boom in Tourism to Puerto Rico." *Washington Post*, July 17, 2017. www.washingtonpost.com/news/posteverything/wp/2017/07/18/no-despacito-is-not-actually-driving-a-boom-in-tourism-to-puerto-rico/.

Grazian, D. 2004. "The Symbolic Economy of Authenticity in the Chicago Blues Scene." In *Music Scenes: Local, Translocal, and Virtual*, edited by A. Bennet and R. A. Peterson, 31–47. Nashville: Vanderbilt University Press.

Guilbault, J., and T. Rommen. 2019. *Sounds of Vacation: Political Economies of Caribbean Tourism*. Durham: Duke University Press.

Hernández-Acosta, J. 2020. "A Bottom-up Strategy for Music Cities: The Case of San Juan, Puerto Rico." In *Music Cities, Evaluating a Global Cultural Policy Concept*, edited by C. Ballico and A. Watson, 127–143. London: Palgrave Macmillan.

Hesmondhalgh, D. 2017. *The Cultural Industries*. London: Routledge.

Huertas, A., M. I. Míguez-González, and N. Lozano-Monterrubio. 2017. "YouTube Usage by Spanish Tourist Destinations as a Tool to Communicate Their Identities and Brands." *Journal of Brand Management* 24 (3): 211–229.

Hur, J. Y., and T. Kim. 2020. "Understanding Contraflow Pop-Culture Tourism: The Case of Transnational Fandom of South Korean Pop-Culture and the 'Hallyu' Tourism." *Journal of Tourism Insights* 10 (1): 4.

Jillian, M. R. 2022. "A Review of Authenticity Research in Tourism: Launching the Annals of Tourism Research Curated Collection on Authenticity." *Annals of Tourism Research* 92: 103349.

Lee, S., and B. Bai. 2016. "Influence of Popular Culture on Special Interest Tourists' Destination Image." *Tourism Management* 52: 161–169.

Luh Sin, H., T. Oakes, and M. Mostafanezhad. 2015. "Traveling for a Cause: Critical Examinations of Volunteer Tourism and Social Justice." *Tourist Studies* 15 (2): 119–131.

MacCannell, D. 1973. "Staged Authenticity: Arrangements of Social Space in Tourist Settings." *American Journal of Sociology* 79 (3): 589–603.

Marshall, W. 2017. "Everything You Ever Wanted to Know about 'Despacito'." *Vulture*, August 22, 2017. www.vulture.com/2017/08/everything-you-ever-wanted-to-know-about-despacito.html

Oh, S., J. Ahn, and H. Baek. 2015. "The Effects of Social Media on Music-induced Tourism: A Case of Korean Pop Music and Inbound Tourism to Korea." *Asia Pacific Journal of Information Systems* 25 (1): 119–141.

Rommen, T., and D. T. Neely. 2014. *Sun, Sea and Sound: Music and Tourism in the Circum-Caribbean*. New York: Oxford University Press.

Rodriguez, P. 2020. Interview with the authors, Online, April 14.

Ruiz, R. 2020. Interview with the authors. Online, April 1.

Samuels, R. 2022. "Downtown Kingston to Become Music and Tourism Mecca in Jamaica." *Caribbean National Weekly*, January 3, 2022. www.caribbeannationalweekly.com/entertainment/downtown-kingston-to-become-music-and-tourism-mecca-in-jamaica/.

Skinner, J., and L. Jolliffe, L. 2017. *Murals and Tourism, Heritage, Politics and Identity*. London: Routledge.

Spence, K. M. 2021. "Caribbean Creatives and the Intelligent Economy." In *Intelligent Economies: Developments in the Caribbean*, edited by S. A. Wilson, 145–186. Santa Rosa, CA: Informing Science Press.

Tsing, A. 2015. *The Mushroom at the End of the World*. Princeton: Princeton University Press.

Wall, T. 2012. "Duke Ellington, Radio Remotes, and the Mediation of Big City Nightlife, 1927 to 1933." *Jazz Perspectives* 6 (1–2): 197–222.

Zuboff, S. 2018. *The Age of Surveillance Capitalism: The Fight for a Human Future at the New Frontier of Power*. London: Profile Books.

3 Estudiantinas in Guanajuato

Street music, architectural heritage, and the making of space hierarchies

Natalia Bieletto Bueno and Gustavo Galván Cázares

Introduction

As a country, Mexico has had an important trajectory of touristic exploitation, but since the beginning of the twenty-first century, cultural tourism has been promoted as an important economic motor. This cultural policy has particularly impacted colonial towns. Guanajuato is a case in point, with its colonial downtown area defined as "heritage site" by the UNESCO in 1988 (see Álvarez de la Torre and Zubia 2017). As a result, official strategies of touristic promotion have clearly affected public policy concerning the use of public spaces. Furthermore, to reinforce Guanajuato's cultural identity, performing arts such as theater and music have been extolled among its most relevant assets of cultural interest. The *estudiantinas* – also called *tunas* or *rondallas* – are musical ensembles based on a sort of music-based fraternity of Spanish origins, whereby students sing and play string instruments while telling jokes. In the Mexican city of Guanajuato, they are closely linked to the imaginaries that connect this colonial city with seventeenth-century Spanish literature; therefore, they have been presented by touristic agents as the musical embodiment of the Golden Age of Spanish literature. The "sonic ambiance" they provide enhances the architectural appeal of the city, complementing the touristic experience of the space and are thus a powerful product by which Guanajuato has been marketed to tourists (see Guilbault 2017; Guilbault and Rommen 2019). Concordant with the touristic display of Guanajuato as a vestigial treasure of the Hispanic Golden Age, the estudiantinas have created both narratives of the city and a sonic ambiance that galvanizes the sensorial experience of Guanajuato at large. The performing traditions of these musical ensembles, and most particularly the events known as *callejoneadas* – singing tours across the streets of the city – have been instrumentalized to sell Guanajuato urban space. But while the estudiantinas and their callejoneadas are inextricably linked to the accompaniment of the touristic experience in Guanajuato, they have also had a negative impact on local people's opportunities to spontaneously use the urban space.

Taking as a premise that music making is a spatialized activity, this chapter participates in the broader question of how music transforms specific cities into touristic hotspots. Specifically it inquires how street music in Guanajuato contributes

DOI: 10.4324/9781003207207-5

to commodify the public space, thus transforming the urban experience of both visitors and locals and the relationships between and among the city and its dwellers. It engages with intersecting areas of scholarly interest, being among the most obvious of them: the study of sound and/or music in space, and the role of street music in the making of the urban experience (Truax 2001; LaBelle 2010; Born 2013; Bennett and Rogers 2014; Herschmann and Fernandes 2014; Doughty and Lagerqvist 2016; Bieletto-Bueno 2017, 2019, 2021; Argüello González 2018; Bennett and Mckay 2019; Bieletto-Bueno 2021). As a working thesis, we sustain that touristic agents have used Guanajuato's colonial architecture to build heritage discourses that have caused a profound impact of the city's identity construction and space management. Such heritage discourses have played a crucial role in determining the course of public life in general, and of music-making in particular. The problem of using public space in Guanajuato prompted us to consider as a secondary research question how the commodification of music for touristic purposes can "reproduce the inequalities and struggles of the late modern world" in this case by creating urban hierarchies and by assigning them different uses, even if such allocation may work against the desires of local inhabitants (Lashua et al. 2014, 3). Because tourism has converted the estudiantinas in the most dominant instantiation of street music, we examine how street musicians not working in or for these ensembles have relocated their musical activities in places considered "peripheral", thus challenging the local social hierarchies of the city. As a result, street music has expanded to spaces that re-signify the musical life of Guanajuato in the benefit of larger sectors of the local population. As we demonstrate, street music reveals issues of larger social import; including the role of music in place branding a city, surely, but also its impact on the urban subjectivities of its dwellers in a historical moment when open, and once public spaces are being increasingly privatized.

The study of the connections between music-making and the promotion of a city was pioneered by the work of Sarah Cohen for the case of the city of Liverpool with the music of The Beatles (1997, 2017); it has since been followed by authors who have interpreted the utility of various musical activities or genres in place branding a city (Wynn and Yetis-Bayraktar 2016; Klett 2017; Sakakeeny 2006, 2013; Bevan-Baker 2016). However, and in contrast with cities such as Liverpool, in Guanajuato music has not been singled out as the main touristic attraction. In that sense, the music of the estudiantinas has not activated "musical tourism" in the sense proposed by Lashua et al. (2014) and which means that tourists visit the city motivated by its musical interest. By contrast, in Guanajuato, these ensembles are considered an important aspect of the touristic themes, thus assisting its place branding strategies. This entails the construction of distinctive cultural features *vis-à-vis* other neighbouring cities as well as the marketing of particular cultural products and experiences (e.g. Barrera-Fernández and Arista Castillo 2016).

The area connecting music and tourism studies is now vast and growing (Cohen 2017; Vargas-Cetina 2009; Fuarros 2013, 2016; Le Menestrel and Henry 2010; Sakakeeny 2006, 2013; Lashua et al. 2014; Flores-Mercado et al. 2016; Guilbault

2017; Guilbault and Rommen 2019; Connell and Gibson 2017). Our inquiry is invested in similar attempts to connect music's role in place marketing for touristic purposes. But beside the touristic aspect, the interrelatedness of music and sound in the public space, the materiality of the city, and people's agency in the making or contesting of the neoliberal city are also interpreted (Holt and Wergin 2013; Connell and Gibson 2002; Gibson and Connell 2007; Bieletto-Bueno 2021). This responds to previous invitations to take seriously the studies of music and tourism insofar as they contribute to understand the complex political economies of places whose subsistence depends on tourism, as well as the role of sound and music in creating what Steven Feld refereed as "sound emplaced subjectivities" (Feld in prologue to Guilbault and Rommen 2019). Along with other authors in this volume, our query "move[s] beyond the discourse of the negative impact of tourism and urban regeneration projects on the everyday life and local identity . . . to emphasize the tensions and ambivalence inherent to any process of urban change" (Sánchez-Fuarros 2016, 68).

Our focus on street music rather than on established musical scenes or on a particular musical genre responds to a previous and prevailing interest on the question of the public spaces and of the role that street musicians play as agents in the making of the aural urban experience (Bieletto-Bueno 2017, 2019, 2021, 2022). As discussed in previous articles, street music is a cultural practice that is dependent upon a city's cultural legacies and its urban structures. The everyday practices of street musicians reveal the tensions between institutionalized and quotidian practices of music and their impact in both, cultural identity building and place marketing. Particularly, when music is performed in the so-called historical downtown areas, the battles over the use of public space become more intense. More than any other musical practice, street music reveals the tensions and conflicts that arise when certain social groups feel more entitled than others to use the public space. Furthermore, it allows observing people's making of the urban experience, for as Bennet and Rogers (2014, 457) state: "[since] music acts on and influences phenomenological perceptions of space and place . . . the [street] musician performance is part of the everyday narrative of the urban setting and the collective production of the cultural life that occurs in there".

This study was originally based on fieldwork carried out during a period of eight months between 2016 and 2017 in which we observed, listened, and registered the *musical praxis* of several musicians working in the streets and public plazas of Guanajuato. Nonetheless, the course of events comprised between 2019 and 2021, and the strategies of Guanajuato's inhabitants to cope with the COVID-19 pandemic in 2020–2021, revealed how street artists and citizens have advanced actions to reclaim the urban space, thus compelling us to expand the period initially considered. As a structure of the text, we first present the cultural legacies of Guanajuato and explain the history of the Guanajuato's estudiantinas by providing a detailed account of the *callejoneadas*. We then posit that the estudiantinas' dominance over the occupation of the public space is possible due to how their staged performance works in tandem with the urban setting. This creates a hierarchization of both urban spaces and musical practices. We close with a discussion of how such processes of hierarchization have been recently contested by Guanajuato's inhabitants, especially the younger members of the local artistic community.

Heritage, cultural legacies, and the streets of Guanajuato

The city of Guanajuato is settled in the middle of a valley that during the seventeenth and eighteenth centuries was one of the main mining trusts of the New Spain. With a current population of 80,000 and a modest extension of 996.7 km², Guanajuato displays a mix of cultural assets based on its historical trajectory. Due to its past as a rich mining area the city preserves a most distinctive colonial architecture. Declared World's Heritage site by the UNESCO in 1988, the urban layout of this city is characterized by twirling alleys, enthralling tunnels, and colourful houses that rise up the hills. It also features comfortable plazas, which are inviting as performing sites, to gather around or simply sit by the shade. Second, Guanajuato is considered "the cradle of Independence", a motto that arises from insurgent priest Miguel Hidalgo's incitement to take over the city to start the independence war. Although Guanajuato is not the only city in the region that in the nineteenth century started the independence movement, this anecdotic element has been successfully extolled by tourist agents. During the twentieth century, Guanajuato has added elements to its cultural image. It was precisely in one of Guanajuato's small squares – the Plaza de San Roque – where in the year 1953, University Professor Enrique Ruelas staged the baroque *Entremeses Cervantinos* with his student company. The public acceptance of the street performances of this set of plays by the famous baroque Spanish author Miguel de Cervantes Saavedra eventually led to the origins of the Cervantino Festival, an international arts event that since 1972 takes place each October. Guanajuato's colonial architecture has served tourist agents and local authorities to activate its "heritage discourses" around the imaginaries of the Golden Period of Spanish literature, and most specifically of Cervantes Saavedra's literature.[1] It is the successful association between the city, Cervantes, and of his celebrated character *El Quijote* that has given the city the motto of "Cervantino capital in the Americas". In fact, several statues commemorating scenes of his emblematic novel are scattered through the city.

The Guanajuato estudiantinas offer a clear example of music's capacity to build or reconstruct the cultural identities and authenticities of specific places. By reaffirming tunes, instruments, and sounds as "typical" of a place, music has proved to increase the desirability of an urban space while activating the economy around it (Connell and Gibson 2002, Gibson and Connell 2005; Cohen 2017; Fuarros 2013, 2016; Le Menestrel and Henry 2010; Sakakeeny 2006; Lashua et al. 2014; Guilbault 2017). Additionally, festivals and similar cultural events have also been identified as relevant factors in place branding a city (Bradly and Hall 2006; Wynn 2015; Wynn and Yetis-Bayraktar 2016). Indeed, the Cervantino Festival has served as the most important cultural event in the city which, along with Guanajuato's heritage discourses, acts as the most important element in attracting visitors. This festival has shaped Guanajuato's image as a cosmopolitan, liberal and "artistry" city, having a clear impact on other touristic industries (Barrera-Fernández and Hernández-Escampa 2017; Ovando-Trinidad 2015). This strategy of heritage and place making has taken recourse to the city's streets, public plazas, and theatres as main performing spaces, but also – as we will illustrate – as stages where the public performance of authenticity is further enhanced. Paradoxically, the local and well-entrenched tradition of spontaneously performing in the streets is being threatened: Over the past decade, the local government of Guanajuato has advanced severe rules to restrict common citizens' use of the public space. This tendency is somehow typical in places considered "heritage sites" and where authorities consider that the architecture, and the overall "heritage ambiance", needs to be protected through regulation, restriction, containment, and, in many cases, privatization and controlled commodification.[2]

Guanajuato's urban growth has extended outside of its historical centre, but the urban plan of the central area has not changed considerably in the recent years; rather, it has been preserved as existing buildings have been restored and adjusted to accommodate more tunnels, parking spaces, restaurants, boutique stores, hotels, and bars (Plan de Ordenamiento Territorial, Centro de Población, (POT-CP) Guanajuato 2011, 2; Cordero-Domínguez 2017, 2018; Cordero-Domínguez et al. 2017; Navarrete Escobedo 2017). This also implies that the regulations for space have also been adjusted to accommodate tourism (Álvarez de la Torre and Zubia 2017). If Guanajuato's convoluted geography, colonial plan, and alluring architecture are decidedly inviting for street music making – self-contained plazas, or picturesque portals that serve as semi-open forums – these very factors have led street music to be deeply institutionalized, highly competitive, and decreasingly diverse, at least in what are considered the most iconic areas of the city and where the estudiantinas take primacy.

Estudiantinas, callejoneadas, and the public space

The origins of these string and vocal ensembles date back to the Middle Ages in Spain, as a continuation of the Goliard traditions in which singing, playing, and joke-telling would allow young university-enrolled men to afford their alleged penchant for music, wine, good food, and travelling. By the seventeenth century, time of the Spanish Golden Age, literature had already crystalized the social imageries of the estudiantinas (Martínez and Ovies Alonso 2002).[3] In contemporary times, the term estudiantina is roughly used to refer to a group of musicians who play certain vocal repertories accompanied by instruments such as plucked strings (guitar, mandolin, double-bass), accordions, castanets, and tambourines. The term "tuno" is given to any member of the estudiantina who is also a student at the university. In Guanajuato, it was for a long time the University of Guanajuato (hence forth UG), the institution that played an important role in preserving and promoting the estudiantina tradition. This was in the interest of both, its institutional identity and the cultural identity of the city. The University's estudiantina was born from the interest of some students who in the early 1960s were part of the University's theater company and who, after listening a record by a Spanish estudiantina, wanted to emulate this ensemble in Mexico. They pursued the project with the support of Daniel Chowell Cázares, regent of the institution at the time, and of Enrique Ruelas, head of the University's theater company (Universidad de Guanajuato 2018). Founded by professor Juan Contreras in 1963, Guanajuato University's estudiantina became part of this institution's identity. Nowadays, as new cohorts enter the university, students are recruited to learn the *rondalla* repertoires. The ensemble regularly plays in internal events as well as in festivities that promote the city's historical interest. The estudiantinas' most characteristic performing event is precisely the *callejoneadas* (literally a "stroll through the streets"), a nightly walk-through Guanajuato's twirling alleys and hidden corners accompanied by the students' cheerful songs and jokes. According to the local tourism office, along with visiting the mines and the mummies museum, the *callejoneadas* are "one of the three things you should do when visiting Guanajuato" (Guanajuato's Tourism Office n.d.).

Most typically in Mexico, colonial cities have administrative and symbolic centres situated in an open square flanked by the government Palace, and the most important church. Most of these squares include an Odeon in the middle. However, Guanajuato's historical centre does not have such a central square. Instead, several buildings of symbolic importance are scattered through the convolute orography of the city. The historic governance building (Presidencia Municipal) and the cathedral (Basílica Colegiata de Nuestra Señora de Guanajuato) are steps ways from one another. As a rule of thumb, the central epicentre of the city is the Jardín de la Unión, located only few steps from the neoclassic styled Theater Juárez (see Fig. 2.1). It is in front of this garden, at the façade of the Museo del ex-convent Dieguino built on the remains of a seventeenth-century cloister, where the Estudiantina ensembles perform to convoke the crowd that will participate in the *callejoneada*. This is also the site where a tuno figure is memorialized with a bronze statue, hence reinforcing the association between this central square with the *rondalla* tradition.

The routes

According to the official regulation, only seven estudiantinas can work simultaneously; therefore, the spaces where they commercialize their musical tours are distributed in five official routes along the city and dispersed up to the hills. The five *callejoneada* routes authorized by the local authorities begin in five different points in Guanajuato's central area. The most popular of them, known as *Traditional Route*, starts nearby the Union Garden and next to the San Diego temple; next is the Route *Universitaria*, whose starting point is at the Grand Stairs of the University of Guanajuato's (UG's) main building. The Route *Plaza de La Paz* begins in the homonymous square while the Route *Reforma* normally begins next to the Hidalgo Market, and sometimes in the Reforma Garden, just across the street from the market. Finally, the *Alhóndiga* Route starts in one of the most

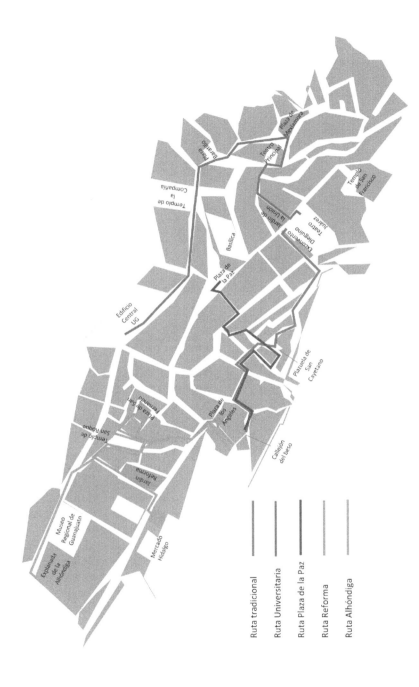

Map 3.1 Map of the five authorized routes for *callejoneadas*.

Source: Map created by Gustavo Gaván Cázares

Figure 3.1 El Callejón del Beso.
Photo: Gustavo Gaván Cázares

emblematic sites of Guanajuato: the square in front of the Grain Exchange Building, or the *Alhóndiga de Granaditas*, which nowadays hosts the State's History
Museum.

   To satisfy the ever-growing demand for *callejoneadas*, there are approximately
25 estudiantinas. While each estudiantina has its own way to start the event, it is
common that, as a starting number, one member of the estudiantina gathers its
crowd by playing the tambourine while doing a bombastic dance – cavorts and
capers included– while the rest of the members play cheerful welcoming songs.
The proper *callejoneada* starts when tunos play and escort a crowd through the
hills, alleys, and hidden corners of Guanajuato. Along the way, the musicians
explain the significance of different urban sites such as alleys, fountains, and
squares whose urban histories are connected to the repertory of local legends set
in in the seventeenth century. By so doing, the performers serve important social
roles: as touristic agents, as conveyors of the city chronicles, and as agents that
reinforce the literary imaginaries of the Golden Age, thus consolidating the city's
cultural identity as an architectural and living cultural monument. One of these
urban legends is that of *El Callejón del Beso* (the Kiss' alley), one of the most
iconic places in the city and which, as part of the normativity of the tradition,
serves as the peak point of the *callejoneada*. Following a tragic love legend, tradition dictates that all lovers who come to Guanajuato must step below the two
balconies that frame this narrow alley and kiss one another to bestow their love

with good fortune (see Figure 3.2). Not surprisingly, the lines of tourists awaiting their turn to lovingly kiss at the legendary passage, and surely take a photo while doing it, can be nerve-racking. Logically, the exceeded number of estudiantinas either clash with one another or await in nearby streets, prolonging the spectacle to entertain the enthusiastic visitors who finally spend one or two minutes under the auspicious balconies.

Because the estudiantinas are most closely tied to Guanajuato's cultural identity, one would expect that they enjoyed more freedom when it comes to using the city's public spaces, but that is not necessarily the case. In fact, the estudiantinas are strictly patrolled by the administrative authorities through the "Regulation of Spectacles and Public Festivities" first issued in 1994. According to this regulation, each estudiantina should request space allocation to the municipality and must issue tickets to their customers. Additionally, a 10% of their revenues are paid to the fiscal office (4th article). Each *callejoneada* can host a maximum of 90 people and they should take place between 8 and 11 pm (36th article), to avoid being an annoyance to locals. After the global pandemic caused by COVID-19, the allowed number was reduced to 50 people. The estudiantinas' musical praxis, however, is deeply influenced by the changing fluxes of tourists to Guanajuato over the year. Notwithstanding the regulatory measures, the allowed number of participants in each *callejoneada* is almost always exceeded. This is directly connected to the fact that Guanajuato's touristic carrying capacity is often surpassed

Figure 3.2 Callejoneada.
Photo: Gustavo Gaván Cázares

during weekends and in the high seasons which include Eastern Holidays, Christmas, and the summer months, with the highest tourist-income peak in October, during the Cervantino Festival.[4] As a result, more often than not, the *callejoneadas* are overcrowded to the point of making it impossible for the tourist to walk close enough to the ensemble so as listen to the songs or even enjoy the event. Likewise, the times allowed for performance are often violated causing the annoyance of neighbours.

The success of these musical events among tourist has had a strong impact on both locals and visitors in several realms. Selling the right to participate in a walk around the streets (with a fare of around US$5.5 per ticket) constitutes a case of privatization of the public space, or rather, as Georgina Born (2013, 25) puts it, of "nesting of the private within the public". This is particularly evident when the services of an estudiantina are hired to play for private ceremonies held in open public spaces such as engagements, birthdays, bachelor(ette) parties, or weddings.

One of our interlocutors, a tuno who requested to remain anonymous, told us that compliance with the established route and allowed times is often broken, especially during the Cervantino Festival and peak holidays:

> The authorities know that we must satisfy the tourists' demands for callejoneadas, so we must recruit more musicians. They [the municipal authorities] don't let us go after midnight, but they know that there are more estudiantinas than the number allowed. They just issue a fine, and because it is the high season, we can pay it. Sometimes the fine is not official, if you know what I mean . . . and that is how it works out. If not all the musicians can participate, we take turns.
>
> (Personal Interview, 20 July 2017)

Our interlocutor's assumption that "we knew what he meant" acknowledges the common practice of paying bribes to inspectors, who understand that the high demand for *callejoneadas* on the part of tourists must be satisfied.

Ethnographic research also showed that dwellers of Guanajuato have an appreciation for these ensembles given their contributions to the construction of identity, and their contribution to enlarge the economic gain to other areas that depend on tourism such as bars, restaurants, and museums. An interview done in 2017 suggests that some neighbours were rather tolerant to these spectacles for considering they were distinctive of their city's culture:

> We got used to it. They come, you wait, and they leave. Sometimes it is annoying, like in the high season, Cervantino or during vacation periods. But big crowds only happen then. The rest of the year is not so bad, and after midnight they stop. Besides, the *callejoneadas* are something nice you only find in Guanajuato. We like to show our culture and such things. Sometimes they play songs that are not the same as always and we even enjoy them.
>
> (Personal Interview, 4 August, 2017)

Separated by three to four years, the interviews we conducted suggested that the opinion of neighbours concerning the estudiantinas is divided: While some perceive the *callejoneadas* as part of the local identity and even take pride in them as an expression of the local culture, many coincide that these musical events are nowadays "pure business". In contrast, some neighbours who live in the streets of the estudiantina's routes, reported in 2016 and 2017 that they see the callejoneadas as necessary evil for the benefits that tourism leaves behind. But in 2021, after the respite of tourism that the COVID-19 pandemic gave to the city, people were more open to accept being annoyed by tourists and confessed that in fact, they avoid visiting the central spaces where tourist converge. As they said, along with mariachis and norteño ensembles the estudiantinas "make their city noisy and crowded and it is not a nice experience" (Personal Interview, 7 October 2021).

Space hierarchies and staged authenticity

As it can be inferred, the asymmetrical power distributed among the different musical ensembles and styles has contributed to create differential urban hierarchies. Guanajuato's estudiantinas – along with the mariachi and norteño bands – have not only taken advantage of the pre-existing spatial hierarchies of the city[5]; they have also contributed to further hierarchize urban spaces in Guanajuato. In the specific case of the tunas, this has been done by how their music crystallizes the cultural legacies of this colonial city by providing musical ambiances to specific spots. Concerning the relationship between street music making and territories, Micael Herschmann and Cinthia Fernandes (2014) assert that the new territorialities marked by musical practices in the street depend on the movement of musicians through the material space as well as the symbolic position that each musical genre or style occupies within the hierarchical order of the local culture. They propose the use of the term "sonic-musical territorialities" to those "territorialities promoted by bands, musicians and their fans, [that] encourage specific forms of territorialization" (Herschmann and Fernandes 2014, 13). As they explain, "the decision of the area that will be occupied with music, works not only against the circulation of social actors, but also along the directions and intensity of the sonic fluxes of the local" (2014, 13). Said sonic fluxes suggest that in Guanajuato, those musical expressions that contribute to branding it as a historical Cervantino city will occupy the central and privileged spaces. This includes art music, especially early music and – of course – the *rondalla* ensembles. Along with the mariachi – impervious and ubiquitous in most Mexico's touristic places – and the norteño bands, the estudiantinas are allocated in the symbolically most important squares of the city. The increasing demand for norteño bands, in turn, responds to the process called "norteñizacion"; namely the ongoing national tendency, started in the late 1980s and intensified in the decade of the 1990s, which refers to the expansion of this once local musical repertoires to all the national territory by effect of all, increased migration, the media and the growth of the narco culture (Alarcón 1988; Olvera Gudiño 2018). Over the past years, the successful norteño ensembles have territorialized the sonic spaces of Guanajuato and many other cities, even by using technologies of sound amplification. Logically, the superposition and competition for the control of this "sonic territory" cause an acoustic saturation that has made the aural urban experience of Jardín Unión somehow uncomfortable to some locals and frankly unbearable for those who reported to avoid it altogether (LaBelle 2010).

A significant aspect concerning the spatial distribution of the estudiantinas in Guanajuato's public space is closely connected with extant notions of authenticity. However, such appreciations of what is "authentic" are less attributed to the musical repertoires than to the ensemble's staged performance. The authenticity of the ensemble is thus conferred by the mandatory attire that the tuno wears: all in strict black velvet garment, with "bombachas", black tights, and log cape, as if coming from the Golden Age. The *beca*, is a distinctive ornamental band crossing the chest that only musicians who are students can wear.

The issue of staged authenticity in touristic settings was brought about since the 1970s by sociologist Dean MacCannell (1973), who claimed that tourism entailed a deliberate deception, mediated by local power dynamics. These dynamics are determined by tacit agreements that local agents pursue to "make believe" the tourists that what they are enjoying is in fact how their culture usually works. The intention is hiding that the act is actually staged. More recently, however, Mexican anthropologist Cristina Oeminchen-Bazán has explained a shift in the perception of authenticity stating that in Mexico, one of the effects of tourism on different cultural traditions means that performers do not expect audiences to believe that the act is authentic, but rather it promotes a tacit agreement in which both parties know that what is on front of their eyes is a "simulacrum as credible representation" (2013, 44). Such representation works hand in hand with the setting – urban or otherwise – whereby both, tourist and hosts, come to a tacit agreement concerning the veracity, or lack thereof, of the performance. In the case of Guanajuato, the city acts as the perfect scenery of a Spanish Golden age town, facilitating that said simulacrum, galvanized through the combination of heritage discourses and these musical acts, is put at the service of tourism. Since the notion of architectural heritage has been so internalized by audiences through official discourses, public policies, and touristic programmes, there is little questioning of the implications first, for the natural transformation of musical cultures, and second, for local citizen's use of public space.

Paradoxically, while the apparel and performative strategies of the estudiantinas may seem somehow fixed or stagnant, the musical repertories are not. Rather, they have been renewed or enriched to satisfy the visitors changing tastes. Many estudiantina members admit that besides performing songs considered "traditional" to the estudiantina repertory, they have also incorporated repertories they identify as "alien" to the tuna tradition. As they explain, repertoires should evolve and adjust to the people's taste, since ultimately their work depends on pleasing the people who attend to the callejoneadas. Referring to the role of sound and music in the lucrative business of tourism, Steven Feld explains:

> [M]usicians are ever and always workers as much as they are creative artists. They labor relationally not just to live audiences of local and visiting

listeners, but to managers and to corporate management invested in regimes of music and sound control, understood as integral to the industrialized hospitality business. From a management standpoint, music and sound are supply necessities as critical as ample and enticing food and drink, or beautiful ambiance and weather. Sound on the ears are thus as critical as sands on the toes in the making of a sensuous experiential zone for vacationers.

(in Prologue to Guilbault and Rommen 2019, 2–3)

Indeed, leaders of the estudiantinas are active agents in the making of the touristic experience. By commodifying the callejoneadas as a touristic product, they have contributed to legitimate practices that posit the streets of Guanajuato as privatizable outdoor space, causing multiple financial benefits throughout the years, but this has had a severe impact on how local's construe their urban experience. As explained earlier, this musical practice in the streets contributes to the making of the spatiality of the city both, materially and symbolically. Administratively, the special spaces and most iconic streets and plazas have been reserved for estudiantinas with the support of local authorities, which creates inequalities in the administration of power while also favouring some musical styles over others. Additionally, the centrality of the estudiantinas has contributed to assign economic and symbolic value to different urban spaces altering the pre-existing urban hierarches. The resulting territorializations have encouraged a greater vigilance and overcontrol of the touristic hotspots to institutionalize street music and to preserve such allocations of musicians in space.

The local authorities' tolerance towards and control of the estudiantinas have contributed to their dominant position as the legitimate music ensemble of Guanajuato. The centrality of these ensembles has caused both a reduction in the variety of music performed in the streets and the displacement of some other forms of street music to non-central areas. This is generally true with the exception of the "norteño" ensembles, a music style that has expanded in all the Mexican territory over the past few decades. In contrast with how estudiantinas are connected to the space and architecture of downtown Guanajuato, the norteño ensembles performing in the central Jardín Unión produce a sonority clearly decontextualized from the urban scenery, yet the public acceptance of this music style justifies their presence because, much like the estudiantinas, they too satisfy the musical demands of national tourism. The ultimate result is that the former local fluxes of music are structured by effect of both tourism and popular taste.

New spatial hierarchies and civil resistance

Due to the authorities' favouritism towards the estudiantinas, musicians representing other musical styles have struggled to remain in the central streets of Guanajuato. To increase their chances to remain in the central areas, they have developed a series of strategies to avoid conflict with authorities. The most common strategy is playing solo and only seasonally, for example during the Cervantino Festival or in Summer Holidays. Additionally, most of them are peripatetic musicians who do not remain in the same spot for more than 30 minutes. As we observed, increasingly musicians other than those working in estudiantinas, mariachis, and norteño bands have relocated their activities in areas considered "peripheral" by the local population. These include the Tepetapa Street – around the former train station – the Embajadores Garden, the Presa de la Olla, or outside of the Mummies Museum, since inspectors rarely supervise these sites. Musicians who pertain to more established musical scenes and ensembles, such as those who play norteño music but do not battle over the central spots, promote their music in the public space, in the hopes that people will hire them for private events or spaces. As one of them explained to us, to circumvent the regulation they take advantage of the inherent ambiguity of being in the public space:

> The regulation states that "any musician that invades the public space will be fined", so we just stand in the square without playing. We understand that any person a has the right to be in the public space, so we do it while carrying our musical instruments. Then we wait until someone from a private house, or a restaurant calls us.
>
> (Personal Interview, 11 August 2017)

Be it as a mere strategy to preserve a source of income, or as a gesture to defend the right of using the public space, the increasing restrictions for spontaneous musical activities in the central area have catalysed civic responses. Moreover, the dominance of the estudiantinas over the central touristic hotspots has inadvertently reformulated musicians, neighbours, and audience's positionality towards public space and towards the social sphere, prompting the emergence of a movement for the defence of their city.

Existing since 2019, the street art movement *Calle en Movimiento* has summoned young dancers, actors and actresses, street poets, and many more to reclaim their right to use the public space beyond permits or institutionalized initiatives. Its members – organized through Facebook, Instagram, and Twitter – advocate for the democratization of art through improvised interventions in the public space offered to general audiences for free and not as a consumption product targeted to the privileged. Therefore, most of their members do not support busking; instead, they produce artistic actions aimed to promote culture in the streets. The goal, however, is not only to provide the city of more cultural events. Rather, it is through such cultural activities that the city is recovered. This example demonstrates that street music is another cultural activity which renders audible cries for what both Henri Lefebvre ([1968] 2000) and David Harvey (2012) following him, named "the right to the city", which refers to citizen's actual opportunities to decide the course of their cities and of urban life.

Conclusions

As observed through this study, street music making in Guanajuato reveals the connections between cultural legacies, urban planning, cultural policy, and tourism. The combined study of these elements illustrates street music's impact on all, the forging of cultural identity, place marketing, sonic territorialization, and thus on hierarchization of the urban space. Due to Guanajuato's over-reliance on tourism for economic growth, the centrality of the estudiantinas as the indisputable form of street music has served to solidify the constructed cultural legacy of Guanajuato as a historical, legendary, fairy-tale baroque town, with a sonic ambiance put at the service of tourism. Consequently, a more rigid control and hierarchization of public spaces have ensued. Music making in the streets of Guanajuato is structured and it structures the imageries of the city, its culture, the social relations between and among inhabitants as well as with tourists. Additionally, street musicians also impact how public space is used and hence how locals socially construct their urban experience. The effects on the urban experience of Guanajuato's inhabitants are varied. First, local musicians are in a constant competition for the niches of employment, disputing the spaces that will bring them financial benefits. This has caused the displacement of other music genres to non-central parts of the city. While such displacement has helped to preserve the diversity of musical practices, it has also unofficially structured the city into different musical territories. For both the musicians and the inhabitants of Guanajuato, this has partly translated in more limiting conditions of use of the public spaces for musical expression.[6] Yet these effects may not be as negative as they seem at a first glance. The official measures to control music making in the public space have triggered Guanajuato's inhabitant's desire to defend a territory they consider their own. The emergence of new places for musical practice and initiatives to reclaim their city illustrates people's creative ability to reinvent their relationship with their city, their authorities, and with the community. This entails how contested urban hierarchies are re-created, accepted, and/or subverted by the people of Guanajuato. Ultimately, we believe that these musical practices and the social interactions they prompt contribute to renegotiate the relationship with authorities, and thus model how citizenship is exercised daily.

Notes

1 We borrow the idea of "activation of heritage discourses" as developed by Prats (1997) and applied to the process of commodification of cities for touristic purposes in the case of Spain.

2 For a discussion of how heritage has been transformed into a commodity by a combination of social agents, see González (2013).

3 Alejandro Mercado (2017) has provided an historical account regarding when the estudiantinas began performing in the central streets of downtown Guanajuato.

4 According to the United Nation's World Tourism Organization, a destination's carrying capacity is

> the maximum number of people that may visit a tourist destination at the same time, without causing destruction of the physical, economic, socio-cultural environment and an unacceptable decrease in the quality of visitors' satisfaction and the locals' quality of life.

> (UNWTO see website)

5 While the term "urban hierarchy" refers to a ranking of cities within the same national territory as informed by extension, population, services, interrelations among them, commerce, etc., spaces hierarchies within the same city emerge from a combination of material, experiential, and symbolic factors, that determine how locals assess the importance of one urban space versus another. See Tomko et al. (2008).
6 The case of four students detained by the police for having played music in the streets without a permit became famous, and it unleashed public indignation. For further information, see press articles written by Cohen (2017) and Segura 2017a y 2017b.

References

Alarcón, R. 1988. "El proceso de norteñización: impacto de la migración internacional en Chavinda, Michoacán." In *Movimientos de población en el Occidente de México*, edited by T. Calvo and G. López, 337–357. Zamora: Centro de Estudios Mexicanos y Centroamericanos/El Colegio de Michoacán.

Álvarez de la Torre, G., and V. O. Zubia. 2017. "Evolución urbana y poblacional del Centro Histórico de Guanajuato de 1990 al 2010." *Revista MEC-EDUPAZ* 2 (12): 27–52.

Argüello González, P. I. 2018. "Epicentros de revitalización en el centro histórico de la ciudad de México. Gentrificación, apropiaciones y conflictos en torno al trabajo de músicos callejeros." *Revista Latinoamericana de antropología del trabajo* 3: 1–28.

Barrera-Fernández, D., and L. Arista Castillo. 2016. "La tematización de la ciudad en torno a referentes patrimoniales materiales e inmateriales." *Academia XXII* 7 (13): 57–69.

Barrera-Fernández, D., and M. Hernández-Escampa. 2017. "Events and Placemaking: The Case of the Festival Internacional Cervantino in Guanajuato, Mexico." *International Journal of Event and Festival Management* 8 (1): 24–38.

Bennett, A., and I. Rogers. 2014. "Street Music, Technology and the Urban Sound-scape." *Continuum* 28 (4): 454–464.

Bennett, E., and G. Mckay. 2019. *From Brass Bands to Buskers: Street Music in the UK*. Norwich: AHRC/UEA.

Bevan-Baker, K. 2016. "Performativity and Place Making: Vernacular Fiddling on Canada's Prince Edward Island." *Landscape Values; Place and Practice* 31: 31–35.

Bieletto-Bueno, N. 2017. "Los músicos callejeros y sus aportes sociales." *Andares* 2 (11): 78–85.

Bieletto-Bueno, N. 2019. "Construcción de la marginalidad de los músicos callejeros. El caso del 'Rey Oh Beyve'." *Cultura y representaciones sociales* 14 (27): 309–347.

Bieletto-Bueno, N. 2021. *Ciudades vibrantes: Sonido y Experiencia Aural Urbana en América Latina*. Santiago de Chile: Ediciones UM.

Bieletto-Bueno, N. 2022. "Street Musicians in Early Mexican Photography and the Making of the Urban Experience." *Music in Art* 46 (1–2): 10–30.

Born, G., ed. 2013. *Music Sound and Space: Transformations of the Public and Private Experience*. Cambridge: Cambridge University Pres.

Bradly, A., and T. Hall. 2006. "The Festival Phenomenon: Festivals, Events and the Promotion of Small Urban Areas." In *Urban Experience Beyond the Metropolis*, edited by D. Bell and M. Jayne, 77–89. Oxon and New York: Routledge.

Cohen, K. 2017. "Detienen a estudiantes de la UG por Cantar en la Plaza el Baratillo." *Caracol en Movimiento*, July 10, 2017. www.caracolenmovimiento.com.mx/ver-noticia. php?idn=741.

Cohen, S. 1997. *More Than the Beatles: Popular Music, Tourism and Urban Regeneration*. Oxford: Berg.

Cohen, S. 2017. *Decline, Renewal and the City in Popular Music Culture: Beyond the Beatles*. Oxon: Routledge.

Connell, J., and C. Gibson. 2002. *Soundtracks: Popular Music, Identity and Place*. New York and London: Routledge.

Connell, J., and C. Gibson. 2017. *Outback Elvis: The Story of a Festival, Its Fans and a Town Called Parkes*. Montgomery: NewSouth Publishing.

Cordero-Domínguez, J. 2017. "La gentrificación y boutiquización en los centros históricos de Zacatecas, Zacatecas y Guanajuato capital." In *Campus Multidisciplinares del Arte IV. Espacio Música y Poética en México*, 35–50. Zacatecas: Taberna Libraria editores.

Cordero-Domínguez, J. 2018. "La piel y las venas urbanas en el Centro Histórico de Guanajuato, México." *Revista Cuestión Urbana* 2 (3): 167–178.

Cordero-Domínguez, J., C. Meneses, and C. Aguilar. 2017. "La producción cultural y artística en el Centro Histórico de Guanajuato, México." *Revista El Topo* 8: 38–67.

Doughty, K., and M. Lagerqvist. 2016. "The Ethical Potential of Sound in Public Space: Migrant Pan Flute Music and Its Potential to Create Moments of Conviviality in a 'Failed' Public Square." *Emotion, Space and Society* 20: 58–67.

Flores-Mercado, G., et al. 2016. *Identidades en Venta: Músicas tradicionales y turismo en México*. México: UNAM. Instituto de Investigaciones Sociales.

Fuarros, I. S. 2013. "Migration and Musical Practices in Multicultural Spain." In *Made in Spain Studies in Popular Music*, edited by S. Martinez and H. Fouce, 144–153. London: Routledge.

Gibson, C., and J. Connell. 2005. *Music & Tourism: On the Road Again*. Clevedon: Channel View.

Gibson, C., and J. Connell. 2007. "Music, Tourism and the Transformation of Memphis." *Tourism Geographies* 9(2): 160–190.

González, P. 2013. "From a Given to a Construct. Heritage as Commons." *Cultural Studies* 28 (3): 359–390.

Guanajuato's Tourism Office. n.d. "Guanajuato's SECTUR Website." https://sectur.guanajuato.gob.mx/

Guilbault, J. 2017. "Political Economy of Music and Sound in All-inclusive Hotels in Santa Lucia." Talk presented on October 3, 2017, as part of the MMaP Research Centre's 2017–2018 Lecture Series. www.youtube.com/watch?v=V4QcW6gMxGc.

Guilbault, J., and T. Rommen, eds. 2019. *Sounds of Vacation: Political Economies of Caribbean Tourism*. Durham, NC: Duke University Press.

Harvey, D. 2012. *Rebel Cities: From the Right to the City to the Urban Revolution*. New York: Verso.

Herschmann, M., and C. Fernandes. 2014. *Música Nas Ruas Do Rio De Janeiro*. São Paulo: Intercom.

Holt, F., and C. Wergin, eds. 2013. *Musical Performance and the Changing City: Post-industrial Contexts in Europe and the United States*. New York: Routledge.

INEGI – Instituto Nacional de Estadística y Geografía. "Indicador Trimestral de la Actividad Económica Estatal." Accessed January 30, 2018. www.inegi.org.mx/est/contenidos/proyectos/cn/itaee/default.aspx.

LaBelle, B. 2010. *Acoustic Territories: Sound Culture and Everyday Life*. New York and London: Continuum.

Lashua, B., K. Spracklen, and P. Long. 2014. "Introduction to the Special Issue: Music and Tourism." *Tourist Studies* 14 (1): 3–9.

Lefebvre, H. (1968) 2020. *El derecho a la Ciudad*. Madrid: Capitan Swing.

Le Menestrel, S., and J. Henry. 2010. "'Sing Us Back Home': Music, Place, and the Production of Locality in Post-Katrina New Orleans." *Popular Music and Society* 33 (2): 179–202.

MacCannell, D. 1973. "Staged Authenticity: Arrangements of Social Space in Tourist Settings." *American Journal of Sociology* 79 (3): 589–603.

Martínez, F., and J. M. Ovies Alonso. 2002. "Estudiantina." In *Diccionario de la Música Española e Hispanoamericana*, Vol. IV, edited by E. Casares Rodicio, 834–838. Madrid: Fundación Autor.

Mercado, A. 2017. *Música y fiesta en Guanajuato. Notas sobre la vida cotidiana en dos ciudades del bajío porfiriano*. Guanajuato: Forum Cultural Guanajuato.

Navarrete Escobedo, D. 2017. "Turismo gentrificador en ciudades patrimoniales. Exclusión y transformaciones urbano-arquitectónicas del patrimonio en Guanajuato, México." *Revista INVI* 32 (89): 61–83.

Oehmichen-Bazán, C., ed. 2013. *Enfoques Antropológicos sobre el turismo contemporáneo*. México: IIA-UNAM.

Olvera Gudiño, J. J. 2018. "La norteña: una historia desde los dos lados del río." *Desacatos* 58: 204–208.

Ovando-Trinidad, M. G. 2015. "Desarrollo de las industrias turísticas de Guanajuato en el marco del festival internacional Cervantino." *Jóvenes en la ciencia. Revista de Divulgación Científica* 1 (2): 941–945.

Plan de Ordenamiento Territorial, Centro de Población. (POT-CP) Guanajuato. 2011. Accessed January 30, 2018. http://seieg.iplaneg.net/seieg/doc/POT_CPGTO.pdf.

Prats, L. 1997. *Antropología y Patrimonio*. Barcelona: Ariel.

Presidencia Municipal de León Guanajuato. Periódico Oficial. "Reglamento de Mercados Públicos y Uso de la vía pública." Accessed October 25, 2017. http://ordenjuridico.gob. mx/Documentos/Estatal/Guanajuato/Todos%20los%20Municipios/wo52159.pdf.

Sakakeeny, M. 2006. "Resounding Silence in the Streets of a Musical City." *Space and Culture* 9 (1): 41–44.

Sakakeeny, M. 2013. *Roll with It. Brass Bands in the Street of New Orleans (Refiguring American Music)*. Durham: Duke University Press.

Sanchez-Fuarros, I. 2016. "'Ai, Mouraria!' Music, Tourism, and Urban Renewal in a Historic Lisbon Neighbourhood." *MUSICultures* 43 (2): 66–88.

Segura, T. 2017a. "Detienen a jóvenes en Guanajuato por cantar en la vía pública; les imponen mil pesos de multa." *Zona Franca*, June 9, 2017. http://zonafranca.mx/ abuso-policial-contra-cuarteto-de-jovenes-que-cantaban-en-la-via-publica/.

Segura, T. 2017b. "Condena estudiante arbitrariedad policial en Guanajuato y llama a protesta contra el abuso de poder." *Zona Franca*, June 10, 2017.

Tomko, M., S. Winter, and C. Claramunt. 2008. "Experiential Hierarchies of Streets." *Computers, Environment and Urban Systems* 32 (1): 41–52.

Truax, B. 2001. *Acoustic Communication*. Westport: Greenwood Publishing Group.

Universidad de Guanajuato. 2018. "Estudiantina UG Celebra 55 años. A callejonear!" www.ugto.mx/noticias/noticias/13320-estudiantina-de-la-ug-celebra-55-aniversa rio-con-a-callejonear

UNWTO, World Tourism Organization. Website. Accessed October 20, 2017. http:// www2.unwto.org/en.

Vargas-Cetina, G. 2009. "Through the Othering Gaze: Yucatecan Trova Music and 'the Tourist' in Yucatan, Mexico." In *Cultural Tourism in Latin America: The Politics of Space and Imagery*, edited by M. Baud and J. L. Ypeij, 69–92. Leiden: Brill.

Wynn, J. 2015. *Music/City: American Festivals and Placemaking in Austin, Nashville, and Newport*. Chicago: University of Chicago Press.

Wynn, J., and A. Yetis-Bayraktar. 2016. "The Sites and Sounds of Placemaking: Branding, Festivalization, and the Contemporary City." *Journal of Popular Music Studies* 28 (2): 204–223.

4 Graffiti tours and urban metamorphosis

The production of tourist ambiances in Comuna 13, Medellín

Maria Lindmäe

Introduction

In recent years, scholars from different fields have paid increasing attention to favela tourism (Freire-Medeiros 2011; Rodrigues Da Silva et al. 2014) and how it aestheticizes poverty (Roy 2011) and commodifies urban deprivation (Dürr and Jaffe 2012), some arguing slum tourism to be a continuation of the 150-year-old practice of othering that takes place in tourist encounters (Steinbrink 2012), which may be facilitated by the previous consumption of films and other audio-visual materials of deprived areas (Freire-Medeiros 2011). More optimistic stances have expressed that slum tourism can change elitist imaginations of the city and offer an alternative understanding of global urbanism (Sanyal 2015). This chapter, however, focuses its lens on how tourist ambiances are produced in Comuna 13 – a former slum area of Medellín – and how these spread to the rest of the city through atmospheric contagion.

Tourist places, just like other spaces of consumption, are often intervened with aims of producing authenticity for outsiders (Zukin 2008) through the provision of consumption sites that legitimize the area as a commercial attraction or turn it into a Disneyfied theme park (Sorkin 1992). The production of themed ambiances and atmospheres that provide a desired "feeling" of a place (Thibaud 2011, 2015) has a substantial role in drawing the attention of temporary visitors. The ambiances of tourism and consumption have been at the focus of different scholars who have studied the atmospheres of festival spaces (Edensor 2012), mobility infrastructures that facilitate traveling (Lin 2015) and touristified historic centres (Paiva and Sánchez-Fuarros 2021). Nevertheless, there is a gap in studies that look at how tourist ambiances are produced in peripheral urban areas that do not follow the urban development logic of city centres (Roy 2011) and are often abandoned by the state (Rozema 2007). For tourists who seek immersion in something new and exotic, urban peripheries can offer plenty of experiences of sensual alterity that is a fundamental aspect of touristic practices (Paiva and Sánchez-Fuarros 2021). Slums in particular have been argued to provide alternative visions of otherwise elitist imaginaries of the city (Sanyal 2015), precisely because they do not obey the development trajectory of the centre and thus maintain their vernacular atmospheres. But what happens to these alternative spatial imaginaries

DOI: 10.4324/9781003207207-6

if the state introduces urban regeneration practices, turning the periphery into a landmark attraction that represents the city's hegemonic development narrative? Is there space for multiple ambiances when the "premium atmosphere" (Paiva and Sánchez-Fuarros 2021) is economically most beneficial for an urban area that has otherwise suffered from decades of abandonment by the state? This chapter will provide answers to these questions by focusing on two aspects: first, the design of ambiances through major urban planning and architectural interventions, and second, the staging and performing of ambiances through tour guides' performativity.

The production of tourist ambiances: from design to performance

Literature on place ambiances (Ambriz 2013; Thibaud 2011, 2015) and atmospheres has been growing in the past decade (Anderson 2009; Albertsen 2019; Buser 2014; Böhme 2013; Edensor 2012). Nowadays, not only do architects use a vocabulary that describes the aura (Buser 2014) or the "genius loci" (Norberg-Schulz 1980) of places, but urban scholars and other social scientists too are showing increasing interest in understanding the more-than-physical and more-than-representational aspects of places. For conceptual clarity, in this chapter I mainly apply the concept of ambiance, but I will also be drawing on literature on urban atmospheres to conceptualize the case study.

One of the central themes in studies of place ambiances and atmospheres is their production (Albertsen 2019; Böhme 2013; Lin 2015; Thibaud 2015). In an extensive literature review, Paiva and Sánchez-Fuarros (2021) pointed out three ways in which atmospheres tend to be produced: first, the design of atmospheres, which involves urban planning and architecture and requires major resources and interventions in the built environment; secondly, the staging of atmospheres, which requires less resources and smaller interventions such as lighting, cleaning, and organizing space; and lastly, the performing of atmospheres, which involves their production through public events such as festivals, concerts, or artistic interventions. Drawing on this categorization, this chapter pays special attention to two of these categories: the power or urban planning and design to lay the material foundation for a new, regenerated place ambiance, and the role of tour guides' performativity in reinforcing and reproducing what I term the "tourist ambiance of urban metamorphosis".

Looking at the role of urban planning and architecture in producing atmospheres, Albertsen (2019) has argued that modernist town planning has tended to create functionally segregated cities with sterile buildings that can produce nothing but "sanitized atmospheres" (Albertsen 2019, 9). He adverted that these sanitized places could become sites of surveillance where a sense of institutional presence is always in the air, informing dwellers that they "must do things right" (Albertsen 2019, 10). Urban planning not only organizes space into practical functionalities but also arranges people's movement and behaviour in it. In this line, Ambriz (2013) has spoken about "hyper ambiances" in places where internationally renowned architects have been commissioned to design outstanding landmark buildings to draw attention to that specific urban area. She questioned the inhabitants' adaption to such ambiances without their own sense of self and belonging being suppressed. Similarly, Sorkin expressed his concern for the profession of urban design being almost wholly preoccupied with reproduction and creation of urban disguises, that is, of "stripping troubled urbanity of its sting, of the presence of the poor, of crime, of dirt, of work" (1992, XV). Architecture, urban planning, and design thus have a major potential of introducing large-scale changes in the built environment and in the ways that people behave and relate to the environment (and who can relate to it).

But how exactly can the "designers" of ambiances intervene in the way how people *feel* themselves in an environment? In his study on the staging of atmospheres in airplanes, Lin (2015) argued that beyond the interior design of the aircraft, the behaviour of its staff was also "meticulously choreographed" with the aim to provide travellers a determined experience and to achieve the strategic aims of the company. The air hostesses behaved as brand ambassadors who had to advocate the positive aspects of travelling with that airline, providing a pleasant social experience for the travellers. By so doing, they both staged and performed the ambiance that was aligned to the airline's commercial principles and aims.

As Lin's (2015) study indicated, travellers' experience is also largely influenced by their social reception. In travel plans that consist of recurring to organized tours, guides have a significant role in creating the atmospheric experiences of the place, establishing themselves as mediators between the built atmospheres of the place and the general public (Paiva and Sánchez-Fuarros 2021). This is even more so when the travel plan includes visits to areas that can be perceived as dangerous and unknown, such as (former) slums, which regular travellers rarely visit on their own. In those cases, the guide not only takes the role of a local ambassador who advocates the positive aspects of the place, but also becomes a guardian on whose place expertise (Jacobs 1961) the tourists rely on.

In what remains of the study, I will discuss how the ambiance of Comuna 13 that has been sanitized by urban interventions is reproduced on a daily basis through tourist practices, especially through the performativity of tour guides. But first, I will provide the methodological and historical contextualization of the study which explains the origins of the narrative of "urban metamorphosis" in Medellín.

Methodology

This chapter is based on the second stage of a three-month fieldwork in Medellín in 2018. During this time, I resided in the district of Comuna 13, in the neighbourhood of Las Independencias, which is the focus of this study, and paid regular visits to the touristified area that is described later in detail. As part of my PhD research that looked at the role of hip hop in the social transformation of Comuna 13, interviews were made with several social leaders, hip hop and graffiti artists, people involved in organizing tours in the district, the Secretary of Tourism of Medellín and the marketing manager of Medellín Convention Bureau. I also performed non-participant field observations and participant observations in graffiti tours that are regularly held in Comuna 13. The vignette used for this chapter is recreated from field notes and from the personal diary held during the fieldwork period. In addition, I made videos and photos of the area and recorded ambient sounds in order to complement the traditional ethnographic methods with more sensory data (Pink 2009). The field notes that were complemented by photos, videos, and sound recordings were used for catching both the textual layer of the ambiance, and the visual and aural aspects that play into the production of the ambiance. Since the interpretation of the material corresponds to my own subjective perception, I acknowledge that materials used in this chapter mainly describe moments when "hot data" (Ringrose and Renold 2014) occurred in the field and this perception depended largely on my condition as a white, female, European researcher to whom the fieldwork area was a relatively unfamiliar environment. I hence only aim to offer a version of the experienced reality that is as loyal as possible to the context in which the knowledge was produced (Pink 2009).

Setting the scene for urban metamorphosis in Comuna 13

In the last decade, Medellín has been making a name for its "miraculous" makeover (Maclean 2015) which refers to the sharp decline in crime rates which was followed by the implementation of social urbanism that has gained the city several awards for innovative urban development. Social urbanism has been used as an umbrella term for different urban policies that were implemented in Medellín in the late 1990s until mid-2010s. As part of it, investments in infrastructure, public transport and outstanding architectural projects in some marginal areas of the city were designed to overcome the decades' long oblivion these areas had been experiencing since the city's plummeting urban expansion from the 1950s onwards. The Medellín miracle thus refers to its transformation from being the world's most violent city in the early 1990-s to becoming the most innovative city on the planet in 2013 (Urban Land Institute 2013).

One of the most marginalized areas of Medellín used to be Comuna 13, which was connoted with a negative spatial imaginary related to crime and violence. It is a densely populated district that consists of 20 neighbourhoods and 140,000 inhabitants (Medellín Cómo Vamos 2016). Life conditions in the district are toughest in the hillside neighbourhoods with slope inclinations of over 50% which is where poorly resourced economic migrants and displaced families live. Poverty, exclusion, and the lack of state intervention have all favoured armed groups to install and remain in these neighbourhoods. Both leftist urban militias and right-wing paramilitary groups have been present in Comuna 13 also because of its geographic location that connects Medellín with the port of Antioquia and the coastal Urabá region, where the trafficking of drugs and weapons takes place.

In 2002, the Public Forces changed their presence and operational mode in Comuna 13, where they had merely been present up until then. Between February and October 2002, 11 military operations were carried out in the territories that were considered to be under the control of the guerrilla (Grupo de Memoria Histórica 2011). The so-called pacification process inaugurated the "democratic security" policy of the recently elected right-wing president Álvaro Uribe Vélez, who authorized the implementation of heavy warfare for what would become the biggest military operation ever carried out in an urban area of Colombia. The military attacks on Comuna 13 led to several civil deaths, numerous unfounded arrests, further displacements, and turbulence among the residents because of the disproportionate use of force. The dominant representations of Comuna 13 in the local media as a dangerous and derelict area legitimized the militarized acts of securitization which in turn allowed displacing unwanted people (those suspected of collaborating with the guerrilla) and preparing the territory for interventions in its urban tissue.

Designing the ambiance of urban metamorphosis in Comuna 13

In the years that succeeded the military operations, Comuna 13 became the recipient of the biggest public investments that paid for the implementation of social urbanism (Fierst 2012). This included the construction of San Javier Library Park, a new line of the Metrocable aerial transit system, new schools, sports fields, day-care centres, playgrounds, neighbourhood amenities, and other public infrastructures (Sotomayor 2017). In 2011, the most eye-catching element of the new urban design of Comuna 13 was inaugurated. This consisted of six sections of electric escalators that were to facilitate residents' mobility between the lower parts of the district that offer public transportation and other services, and the hillside neighbourhoods that are exclusively dedicated to housing. Shortly after the inauguration of the escalators and before the 2014 World Urban Forum took place in Medellín, the city council of Medellín also funded a project for painting the roofs of the houses that were located in the perimeter close to the escalators, substituting the dominating brown and grey bricks with colourful rooftops and façades (Alcaldía de Medellin 2015).

Just five years after their inauguration, the escalators were incorporated to the list of tourism attractions of Medellín as a result of the exponential growth of visitors exploring the area that had thus far lacked a wider interest. The construction of the escalators, the painted rooftops, and the subsequent creation of a new pedestrian street that takes people from the escalators to a long wall of graffiti have successfully created a "regeneration corridor" (Degen 2008) in which local entrepreneurs sell souvenirs and tourists take photos. By 2017, the escalators had become the third most popular tourist site in the whole city with a 100% annual increase in the number of visitors. During my visit in 2018, the regeneration corridor involved a few streets that surrounded the electric escalators where travellers could buy Comuna 13 T-shirts, locally made ice-creams, *micheladas*, chips, meat pies, or coffee with heavily inflated prices. While some of these businesses had an official locale, much of the sales was done with the help of cash-only mobile carts that allowed the entrepreneurs to follow the rhythm of tourist movement.

Architecture and design have had an important role in embellishing and initiating the tourist ambiance in the area because the new built structures create a strong visual contrast with the makeshift houses, making the landscape highly

Figure 4.1 Image of colourful hillside neighbourhood in Comuna 13 with three sections of modern escalators.

Photo: Maria Lindmäe

instagrammable. But it is also because elements like the escalators have been endowed with symbolically loaded meanings as a result of place branding and destination marketing efforts. The local and international media have framed the escalators as something that have "transformed lives" (El Economista 2019) and "brought peace" (CNN 2015) to Comuna 13. These ideas have been further reinforced by media coverage of the visits of delegates of international events and organizations (cf. El Colombiano 2019; El Mundo 2017) or extreme sport events like the International Downhill Challenge 2018 that took place on the slopes of Comuna 13. The effect of urban regeneration is so widely acknowledged that Comuna 13 is now promoted as a site that "surprises for its history of resilience and social transformation, for the colours of impressive murals and graffiti by mostly local artists" (Medellín Travel n.d.). The representative of the Convention Bureau of Medellín affirmed "the social transformation of Medellín as a key message for the promotion of the destination that attracts both MICE tourists and leisure tourists who come for an adventure to a city where others might not go" (Personal interview, 14 February 2018).

Together with the sanitizing effects that the military pacification had on Comuna 13, the aforementioned strategies of destination marketing also point towards intents of liberating urbanity of its unwanted sting, poverty, and crime (Sorkin 1992) to create a new, themed space where visitors can consume and reproduce the ambiance of urban metamorphosis. In the following sections, I will discuss how performativity related to tourism and street art uphold and reproduce the ambiance of urban metamorphosis. For this, I rely on descriptions of my own experience as a tourist in Comuna 13.

Performing and reproducing urban metamorphosis

We are sitting inside a small inner-city bus that climbs up the winding narrow streets at the sound of its worn-out motor. The slow bus ride gives us, travellers, time to get acquainted to the surroundings until we finally get to the starting point of the tour. I hear different kinds of Spanish being spoken around me, there are people from Bogotá, from Medellín's upscale areas, and from other parts of the continent. We are all white and below forty years of age, except for a couple who accompanies their 20-something children. In our first stop, the tour guide who teaches break dance at a local hip hop school, starts telling us some details of the neighbourhood's past – of how it used to be a hiding point for the members of the guerrilla. For now, we see little but the average, bricked houses mounted on top of one another, but as the tour evolves, we are introduced to a much more colourful side of Comuna 13. We are taken to a yellow slide that connects different levels of stairs that allow inhabitants to move through the steep landscape of the neighbourhood. Small children spontaneously join us and slide down the tube together with the visitors who are asked to leave behind their adulthood and experience the fun ride. We then arrive at the most picturesque spot of the neighbourhood which is situated at the joint of the electric escalators and a platform that offers views all across Medellín. One can barely finish taking selfies when our attention is drawn to a group of young men who start doing break dance, inviting our guide, too, to show his moves. They all earn a big applause and a round of tips before our group is taken further up the hill where the most impressive graffities are located. We learn that several of them talk about resilience, transformation and overcoming hardships. My fellow travellers activate their phones again to take photos, film and upload their images to social media.

Finally, on our way back we get a chance to ride the famous escalators. This triggers awe, as if none of us, middle-class travellers, had never used an escalator. Before the tour finishes in front of the hip hop school, each visitor is asked to use graffiti sprays to write something positive for the neighbourhood. Our guide drops a few lines of rap and then we are all asked to chip in and purchase some of their merchandising. Seconds after the last visitor has left, the wooden board on which we were asked to express our thoughts is washed up and repainted with black colour to make room for the following group's wishes.

(Fieldnotes, Comuna 13 Graffiti Tour, 4 February 2018)

Comuna 13 graffiti tours began more than a decade ago at the initiative of the leaders of a hip hop school who started taking people for walks in their neighbourhood. Today, there are more than 30 tour companies and independent guides who provide their services in the area. This includes businesses that combine the visit to Comuna 13 with that of discovering the vestiges of Pablo Escobar, Medellín's most famous drug lord whose fame through Netflix has attracted a lot of foreign interest despite local tourism authorities' rejection of using his figure for cultivating dark heritage tourism. Many of the tour guides present themselves as local

Figure 4.2 A tourist group getting prepared for a slide to experience Comuna 13's new infrastructures. The tour guide sits in the middle while sharing information about the neighbourhood.

Photo: Maria Lindmäe

inhabitants who experienced the hardships of the early 2000s on their own skin as a way to gain visitors' trust in them as local experts who can provide intrinsic knowledge of the place, its history, and current-day developments. When asking one of the tour guides what is the message that he shares on his tours, he responded me:

> We provide emotions and knowledge to people who ask us "what did you do to resurrect?" Do you know what resilience means here in the comuna? That [resilience] is what we show them.
>
> (Personal interview, 23 February 2018)

The "showing" of resilience was indeed an important element of the tourist practices on display in Comuna 13. It was visible in the graffiti, banners, and tour descriptions. Resilience was written into the historical narrative that tour guides retold with some critical notes of the past, especially regarding the military operations of 2002 which put Comuna 13 under extreme surveillance measures. But these narratives were also aligned to the idea of Medellín's miraculous makeover since this is what travellers were advertised and what they had come to see. As "local ambassadors" who could benefit the destination by advocating the positive aspects of it (Simpson and Siguaw 2008), the tour guides' critique only applied to past events to avoid damaging the current, predominantly positive image of Comuna 13. Consequently, the guides did not mention the ongoing conflicts between the different criminal groups, the increasing numbers of homicides, let alone the fact that tour companies and businesses that have established themselves along the regeneration corridor pay a *vaccine*[1] to the criminal groups that hold de facto control over the area. Instead, they adhered to the narrative of urban metamorphosis that has been legitimized by state institutions and the media.

Beyond the discursive practice that reinforced the narrative of resilience and resurrection, the guides also performed the tourist ambiance through their embodied actions and interactions with the place, the tourists, and the residents. By guiding tours that invited people to have a fun time cruising through one of the city's poorest areas, the guides affirmed and reproduced the ambiance of metamorphosis which told that crime and poverty were no longer part of the everydayness of Comuna 13. Finally, the feeling of overcoming the uncertainties of the past was also invoked by the festive spirit that reigned in the area throughout the day. The colourfully painted walls and rooftops, the break dance shows, and the artistic graffiti all composed an air of joy and festivity. Some guides who are hip hop artists themselves also painted, performed rap music, or showed (break) dance moves along the tour which further contributed to the carnivalesque ambiance and triggered smiles, positive affect, and applauses, making the sensory place experience even more intense. However, the artistic performances also helped drawing attention to this regenerated space while rendering others unnoticed (Paiva and Cachinho 2018). The concentration of colour and sounds thus contributed to the intensity of the ambiance in the limited tourist corridor, while leaving aside the nearby streets that have been left untouched by investments for regeneration.

While it is not in the scope of this chapter to speak of the sometimes controversial benefits that tourism has through its jammed streets and raising housing prices, I want to end this chapter with an excerpt from a conversation with another artist and social leader of Comuna 13 who saw the area's recent developments in tourism from a more critical perspective:

> The territories of Colombia are known through blood. Comuna 13, as many places in this country appeared because of a massacre or a victimizing act. By only naming the war, they [the tour guides] forget the cultural and historical past of the transformation of the territories, of people's struggles to construct their houses and their territories. What happens in Comuna 13 is that other, earlier things get nullified. . . . So people only focus on the victimizing events when the 29 military operations took place here in [Comuna] 13 but they don't talk about the cultural history. We think that in order to speak about memory, of course we need to speak about the men who have disappeared and about the homicides, but also about the cultural life, about the historical and cultural life of this territory.
>
> (Personal conversation, 11 April 2022)

While the opportunity of making an income through tourism has convinced many people from in- and outside of Comuna 13 to become tour guides who share their visions and experiences of the city with travellers, the aforementioned excerpt shows that the sudden changes in the social tissue and ambiance of the neighbourhood are not perceived in the same way by all of its inhabitants. Even if the premium ambiance of urban metamorphosis might be generating most tourist dollars, other visions and ambiances continue palpating in the back stages of the tourist setting, where fast-paced travellers are unlikely to have a gaze into (Mac-Cannell 1973).

Conclusions

In this chapter, I have argued that the production of the themed ambiance of urban metamorphosis in Comuna 13 has been a long process that began with the military pacification of the marginalized district which allowed state authorities to access the area and to carry out a series or urban interventions that have by now turned the area into a showcase of the city's transformation. In this process, the construction of a new built environment has been accompanied by destination marketing efforts which have helped establish the narrative of a new transformed Medellín after years of its stigmatization. The narrative has become especially predominant and effective in Comuna 13, thanks to its reproduction and embodiment by the tour guides as well and street artists who persistently express ideas such as resilience through their graffiti and murals.

The case study has also shown that despite the potential of peripheral (former) slum areas to provide alternative visions of otherwise elitist imaginaries of the city (Sanyal 2015), these too may become subject to development practices that commodify their differential traits and incorporate them to a larger, hegemonic vision of the city. In this case, it is the poverty and criminality of Comuna 13 that has been commodified and inscribed into a legitimized place narrative that attracts visitors. The intangible value of Medellín's disturbing history has thus become a heritage value that generates a new tourist economy and creates income opportunities in an area that has historically struggled with high unemployment rates. However, as earlier research has shown, tourist corridors also have the tendency not only to draw attention away from areas and issues that remain critical, but also to create new problems, such as gentrification and the expulsion of lower income inhabitants (Cócola-Gant 2018). Analysing the negative or positive effects of tourist ambiances in deprived areas has not been in the focus of this chapter, but it did aim to show that however intangible these ambiances might seem, their deliberate production and sanitization can have a big impact on the local economy and dwellers' everydayness, as well as for imposing hegemonic city imaginaries.

Note

1 In Spanish, *vacuna* – an illegal fee claimed by the power-holding criminal group in exchange for a supposed service of protection.

References

Albertsen. 2019. "Urban Atmospheres." *Ambiances*. https://doi.org/10.4000/ambiances.2433.

Alcaldía de Medellín. 2015. "Medellín se pinta de vida." Accessed November 5, 2021. www.edu.gov.co/images/publicaciones/Libro_Medellin_se_Pinta_de_Vida.pdf

Ambriz, C. C. 2013. "Urban Landscapes and Social Ambiences Under Mobility Dynamics: Barcelona City." In *Proceedings from the Conference on the Move: ACSIS Conference*, June 11–13, Sweden, 15–19. Linköping University Electronic Press. https://ep.liu.se/ecp/095/002/ecp13095002.pdf

Anderson, B. 2009. "Affective Atmospheres." *Emotion, Space and Society* 2: 77–81.

Böhme, G. 2013. "The Art of the Stage Set as a Paradigm of the Theory of Atmospheres." *Ambiances*. https://doi.org/10.4000/ambiances.315

Buser, M. 2014. "Thinking through Non-Representational and Affective Atmospheres in Planning Theory and Practice." *Planning Theory* 13 (3): 227–243.

CNN. 2015. "Las escaleras eléctricas que traen paz a la 'Comuna 13' de Medellín." Accessed October 29, 2021. https://cnnespanol.cnn.com/video/cnnee-imp-latam-medellin-comuna-13-escalators/.

Cócola-Gant, A. 2018. "Tourism Gentrification." In *Handbook of Gentrification Studies*, edited by L. Lees and M. Phillips, 281–293. Cheltenham, UK: Edward Elgar Publishing.

Degen, M. 2008. *Sensing Cities: Regenerating Public Life in Barcelona and Manchester*. Oxon, UK: Routledge.

Dürr, E., and R. Jaffe. 2012. "Theorizing Slum Tourism: Performing, Negotiating and Transforming Inequality." *European Review of Latin American and Caribbean Studies* (93): 113–123.

Edensor, T. 2012. "Illuminated Atmospheres: Anticipating and Reproducing the Flow of Affective Experience in Blackpool." *Environment and Planning D: Society and Space* 30 (6): 1103–1122.

El Colombiano. 2019. "La comuna 13 fue un carnaval para los alcaldes del mundo." Accessed October 29, 2021. www.elcolombiano.com/antioquia/grafitour-en-la-comuna-13-de-medellin-en-la-cumbre-de-alcaldes-DG11173176.

El Economista. 2019. "Comuna 13 y Las Escaleras Eléctricas Que Transforman Vidas." Accessed October 29, 2021. www.eleconomista.com.mx/sectorfinanciero/Comuna-13-y-las-escaleras-electricas-que-transforman-vidas-20190623-0014.html.

El Mundo. 2017. "¿Por qué Bill Clinton visitó la Comuna 13." Accessed October 29, 2021. www.elmundo.com/noticia/-Por-que-Bill-Clinton-visito-la-Comuna-13-/355443.

Fierst, S. 2012. "El presupuesto participativo en el contexto de los jóvenes de la Comuna 13 de Medellín." *Analecta Política* 3 (4): 113–137.

Freire-Medeiros, B. 2011. "'I Went to the City of God': Gringos, Guns and the Touristic Favela." *Journal of Latin American Cultural Studies* 20 (1): 21–34.

Grupo de Memoria Histórica. 2011. *La huella invisible de la guerra. Desplazamiento forzado en la comuna 13. Informe del grupo de memoria histórica de la comisión nacional de reparación y reconciliación*. Bogotá: Ediciones Semana.

Jacobs, J. 1961. *The Death and Life of Great American Cities*. Random House.

Lin, W. 2015. "'Cabin Pressure': Designing Affective Atmospheres in Airline Travel." *Transactions of the Institute of British Geographers* 40 (2): 287–299.

MacCannell, D. 1973. "Staged Authenticity: Arrangements of Social Space in Tourist Settings." *American Journal of Sociology* 79 (3): 589–603.

Maclean, K. 2015. *Social Urbanism and the Politics of Violence: The Medellín Miracle*. Basingstoke, Hampshire, UK: Palgrave Macmillan.

Medellín Cómo Vamos. 2016. *Informe de calidad de vida de Medellín 2012–2015*. Medellín. Colombia: Medellín Como Vamos.

Medellín Travel. n.d. "Comuna 13." Accessed October 29, 2021. www.medellin.travel/comuna-13/?lang=en.

Norberg-Schulz, C. 1980. *Genius Loci: Towards a Phenomenology of Architecture*. New York: Rizzoli.

Paiva, D., and H. Cachinho. 2018. "Artistic Practices and the Redistribution of the Sensible in Largo Do Chiado: Attention, Corporeal Isles, Visceral Politics." *Tijdschrift Voor Economische En Sociale Geografie* 109 (5): 597–612.

Paiva, D., and I. Sánchez-Fuarros. 2021. "The Territoriality of Atmosphere: Rethinking Affective Urbanism through the Collateral Atmospheres of Lisbon's Tourism." *Transactions of the Institute of British Geographers* 46 (2): 392–405.

Pink, S. 2009. *Doing Sensory Ethnography*. London: SAGE.

Ringrose, J., and E. Renold. 2014. "'F**k Rape!' Exploring Affective Intensities in a Feminist Research Assemblage." *Qualitative Inquiry* 20 (6): 772–780.

Rodrigues Da Silva, D., S. Dalila Corbari, C. Alberto Cioce Sampaio, and I. Jurema Grimm. 2014. "Turismo comunitario en favelas. Un estudio del Favela Inn Hostel, Chapéu Mangueira – Rio de Janeiro, Brasil." *Estudios y Perspectivas en Turismo* 23 (4): 786–804.

Roy, A. 2011. "Slumdog Cities: Rethinking Subaltern Urbanism." *International Journal of Urban and Regional Research* 35 (2): 223–238.

Rozema, R. 2007. "Paramilitares y violencia urbana en Medellín, Colombia." *Foro Internacional* XLVII (3): 535–550.

Sanyal, R. 2015. "Slum Tours as Politics: Global Urbanism and Representations of Poverty." *International Political Sociology* 9 (1): 93–96.

Simpson, P. M., and J. A. Siguaw. 2008. "Destination Word of Mouth: The Role of Traveler Type, Residents, and Identity Salience." *Journal of Travel Research* 47 (2): 167–182.

Sorkin, M. 1992. *Variations on a Theme Park: The New American City and the End of Public Space*. New York: Farrar, Straus and Giroux.

Sotomayor, L. 2017. "Dealing with Dangerous Spaces. The Construction of Urban Policy in Medellín." *Latin American Perspective* 213 (44–2): 71–90.

Steinbrink, M. 2012. "'We Did the Slum!' – Urban Poverty Tourism in Historical Perspective." *Tourism Geographies* 14 (2): 213–234.

Thibaud, J.-P. 2011. "The Three Dynamics of Urban Ambiances." In *Sites of Sound: Of Architecture and the Ear*, Vol. 2., edited by in B. LaBelle and C. Martinho, 43–53. New York: Errant Bodies Press.

Thibaud, J.-P. 2015. "The Backstage of Urban Ambiances: When Atmospheres Pervade Everyday Experience." *Emotion, Space and Society* 15: 39–46.

Urban Land Institute. 2013. "Medellín Voted City of the Year." Online resource. Accessed October 28, 2021. https://americas.uli.org/medellin-named-most-innovative-city/

Zukin, S. 2008. "Consuming Authenticity: From Outposts of Difference to Means of Exclusion." *Cultural Studies* 22 (5): 724–748.

Part II

Urbanism, architecture, and built ambiances

5 The visual spectacle of shopping malls as tourist destinations

Panizza Allmark

Introduction

For the last ten years, I have been photographing shopping malls in many cities across the world. My photographic documentation of shopping malls is of relevance in the early twenty-first century as a record of the physical and sensory spaces of consumption that are increasingly facing competition through online shopping. The use of the web for purchasing goods has engendered a questioning of the relevance of the shopping mall. Online shopping has meant a decline in pedestrian traffic. Dead malls, malls that have been left abandoned and decaying, are now well documented (Parlette and Cowen 2011; Techentin 2004; Ritzer 2011). As a response to the decline in the number of visitors, shopping malls are getting grander in scale and have increasingly focused on lifestyle and entertainment features, as well as stimulating visual displays, to lure shoppers and tourists as a way of ensuring their survival. Malls are advertised as "shopping destinations": "Mega-multi-malls have become the center of tourist attention for many countries and regions and, for millions of people, they are popular destinations" (Dallen 2005, 48). As a tourist and photographer, I have visited and documented some of these malls, such as the Dubai Mall in the United Arab Emirates, which is considered the world's largest shopping mall with a total area of 1,124,000 m^2 and 1,200 shops; Central World in Bangkok, Thailand, which is the largest shopping centre in Thailand and tenth largest mall in the world; and Cehavir, in Istanbul, the largest shopping mall in Turkey. I have also visited an array of shopping malls in other tourist city locations across the world such as Galerías Pacífico in Buenos Aires, Argentina; the Emporium in Melbourne, Australia; Centro Colombo in Lisbon, Portugal; Pacific Centre in Vancouver Canada; and the Discovery Mall in Kuta Bali, Indonesia. The allure of these malls for the tourist is that they provide a hedonistic experience which includes shopping and leisure facilities. It engages shopping tourism, which is "a contemporary form of tourism fostered by individuals for whom purchasing goods outside of their usual environment is a determining factor in their decision to travel" (UNWTO 2011, 13). It is important to consider that "shopping has been used in many places as a focus of tourism marketing and has featured prominently in tourism policy making and promotional campaigns" (Timothy 2018, 136). Moreover, after sightseeing, shopping

DOI: 10.4324/9781003207207-8

is the major activity that tourists engage in (Asadifard et al. 2015, 230). As such, increasingly shopping malls are tourist sites. In many cities, the shopping mall is the centre of tourist attention and has transformed destinations.

Methodology

The topography and aesthetics of shopping malls are specifically designed to invite the female consumer and her gaze (Ameen et al. 2021; Backes 1997; Fiske 1989; van Eeden 2006). As a documentary photographer, or *visualista*, photographing the mall spaces was an opportunity to provide commentary on the visual spectacle with which I was engaging. This chapter provides a small sample of my *oeuvre*. As a feminist photographer, I draw upon strategies from feminist cultural geography including reflecting upon a woman's sense of space and highlighting the role of the feminine in popular culture. In my approach, "like effective shopping, feminist criticism includes moments of sharpened focus, narrow gaze – of skeptical, if not paranoid assessment" (Morris 1999, 395). Meaghan Morris, in her much-cited feminist work, "Things to Do with Shopping Centres", states that shopping malls are

> like departments stores [which they now usually contain] . . . they are described as palaces of dreams, halls of mirrors, galleries of illusion . . . the fascinated analyst identified as a theatre critic, reviewing the spectacle, herself in the spectacle, and the spectacle in herself.
>
> (199, 397)

My photographs convey the spectacle, and some images also visually convey my reflection. They are informed by my experiences as a photographer and as an academic. Moreover:

> In order to get at these disparate structures that meet in and flow through a complex site like a shopping mall, the theorist (because this is never simply a *descriptive* activity) will have of necessity to draw upon, and to cross, the discourses of a number of different disciplines (and again, this cross-disciplinary perspective is characteristic of the working methods of cultural studies).
>
> (Frow and Morris Elizabeth 1993, xvi)

My photographs of shopping malls convey prevalent details of late capitalism in the twenty-first century. The significance of the shopping mall is that it is "an ensemble of material and social practices and their symbolic representation [that] . . . represents the architecture of social class, gender, and race relations imposed by powerful institutions" (Zukin 1991, 16). My work is illustrative of this, and further through my use of juxtaposition, the framing of seemingly incongruent elements draws attention to the cultural discourses in the mall.

In this chapter, I will consider the appeal of the shopping mall as a tourist destination and in particular focus on the shopping mall, as being more than just a retail space. The ambiance in the malls is an attraction. The mall functions as a cornucopia of visual and sensorial display, which encourages the tourist gaze, and in particular the female consumer. First, I will briefly discuss the history of the shopping mall considering the shopping mall as a destination location. I focus on the design elements of the shopping mall because it is these which designate the space as a sanctuary from the outside world. This involves the common features shared by malls in which the shops serve as a refuge from the outside world. They share the aesthetics of postmodern pastiches and promote transnational companies and brands. Then I will discuss the replica and recreation that abound in shopping malls. Most notably exploring the notion of "cathedrals of consumption", a term coined by George Ritzer (2010, 2011), which can be used to describe mega malls that entice and enchant the consumer through the grandiose blend of multipurpose venues. The mall serves as a recreation, simulacrum, and replica of natural and cultural landscapes. But it is not only products as commodities that are on offer, in the section "Culture on Display", I examine the cultural performances that are endorsed and enacted in shopping malls that provide a commodification of cultural identity as staged tourism. The final section further explores the experience of immersion, with a particular focus on the relationship between gender and malls.

A key concept considered throughout this chapter is the role of commodity fetishism and the shopping mall. Marx's concept of commodity fetishism is intricately linked to consumer capitalism, in which labour production is disavowed and the object, the commodity, is supra sensual. "The products of labour become commodities, sensuous things which are at the same time supra-sensible or social" (Marx 1976, 165). Furthermore, "the commodity fetish allows us to relate to commodities in such a way as to construct an idealized self" (Cluley and Dunne 2012, 10). My photographs reflect and comment on the mediated spectacle of the shopping mall, in which "the commodity is being produced and reproduced at a variety of different levels of reality and representation" (Böhm and Batta 2010, 354). Moreover, the work comments on the experience of the shopping mall as a sensory touristic experience through encouraging window shopping, the art of strolling through the arcades of the mall, and gazing and engaging in what's on display.

The shopping mall as a destination location

The European history of the shopping mall and shopping arcades dates back to the Paris Passages built in the early nineteenth century. "They were the first buildings to adopt new lighting and heating techniques and iron and glass coverings. Shops attracted and enchanted people with the help of large and brightly lit windows" (Bauman 1996, 86). There was an abundance of goods on offer, but this was also entwined with a supposedly enriching experience. The arcades were seen as the "hallmark of a modern metropolis (as well as Western imperial domination), and had been imitated throughout the world, from Cleveland to Istanbul, from Glasgow to Johannesburg, from Buenos Aires to Melbourne" (Buck-Morss 1991, 39–40). Although there may be a similar architectural design found in shopping malls in numerous geographical locations, such as grand cathedral domed ceilings or atriums with glass and metal contoured curved skylights, there is also a sense of place that engages in a postmodern eclectic harmony of the past and present, as well as a globalized display, which brings together transnational corporate marketing and international commodities. As Malcolm Voyce argues in his discussion of neoliberalism and the shopping mall, "the local loses its uniqueness and there is little space for notions of locality or local public opinion. When consumers are inside such places they could be anywhere in the world" (Voyce 2005, 539).

The shopping mall represents a microcosm of the world (though sanitized, heavily edited, climate controlled and commodity fetishized), but it can also be seen as "separated from the rest of the world, it possesses the characteristic both of a retreat, a place for spiritual enlightenment, and a resort, a place for secular refreshment" (Backes 1997, 6). The experience of the mall as a retreat is also evidenced in the sense of timelessness in the wandering through the mall with its absence of clocks, which may create a somewhat leisurely atmosphere. In its lack of clocks, the mall bears a resemblance to the Las Vegas consumption and entertainment sites where the visitor is encouraged to unwittingly stay longer and hence spend more. The shopping mall, for some of its visitors, may reflect an escape from the banal every day, and as Meaghan Morris suggests that "refuge or R&R, is one of the social functions of shopping centres, though women who just hate them may find them hard to accept" (1999, 400). Morris states "as Eden, or paradise: the shopping centre is figured as, if not exactly utopian, then a mirror to utopian desire, the desire of fallen creatures nostalgic for the primal garden, yet aware that their paradise is now an illusion" (1999, 397). Seen as paradise, it is "removed from the social relations of production" (Winchester et al. 2013, 80). It is important to note that the benefits of a retreat or leisurely space are certainly not shared by the many low-income workers employed to sell goods that they may not be able to afford to buy, or by those who labour intensively to maintain the sanitary conditions of the shopping mall's resort style facilities.

Places like Singapore are top shopping tourist destinations. "Singapore is thus, without a doubt, a space penetrated by the global marketing strategies of producers of consumer goods" (Chua 2003, 21). Like Hong Kong, it has been considered a shopping mecca (Hall 1994; Rahman 2017). In Singapore, which is a regional and world city, the "official ability to reduce class awareness is constantly being undermined by consumer culture" (Chua 2003, 9). Chua Beng Huat, in his aptly titled book *Life Is Not Complete Without Shopping*, presents cases on how late capitalism penetrates life experiences. He cites sociologist Mike Featherstone's comments that "walking through the heart of Singapore is like walking through a series of large shopping centres" (Chua 2003, 41). There is a culture of consumption, and visiting a shopping mall is part of the aesthetic experience.

Bangkok is also a key shopping destination, and the grand-scale shopping malls can be reached by passageways from the SkyTrain (a symbol of modernity), elevated above the heat, humidity, and city pollution and noise. It is also for the outside observer or middle-class patron far removed from the densely positioned street vendors who tout their trade beneath the transit lines. In this spatial segregation, "two separate patterns of use, almost different 'worlds' exist, one above and the other below" (Jenks 2003, 547). The shopping mall provides a sanitized refuge from the experience of everyday life and from the wider population. Generally, the mall may be seen as "a contemporary phantasmagoria, enforcing a blindness to a range of urban blights: the homeless, beggars, crime, traffic, even weather" (Friedberg 1993, 113). The notion of the removal of "urban blights" is a discriminatory view, but one also taken up by gated communities in order to create a middle-class enclave, safe from crime and undesirable urban disorders. They too, like the shopping mall, blur the line between private and public spaces.

Despite the somewhat bland exteriors, shopping malls have interiors that provide a spectacle for the gaze. There is a remarkable contrast between inside and outside. A sea of asphalt parking space surrounds many shopping malls and the mall looms above this stark exterior. There is a binary between the abundance and spectacle contained within the Mall of the Emirates, one of the largest shopping malls in Dubai, and the barren, arid landscape which is it is set against. The mall appears as a concrete oasis in the middle of the desert in which the mall's air conditioning provides a respite from the intense desert heat. Whereas the outside may be bland, the inside of the mall is strewn with palm trees and water features and filled with the spectacle of goods on offer. Similarly, The Mall Athens, one of the largest malls in South Eastern Europe, conveys a shopper's paradise. It is built near the edge of the city on what was once agricultural land. It is set high above the desolate landscape of road and rail infrastructure, and a bridge with an above-ground walkway from the train line leads consumers to the shopping centre. The interior, like many mega malls, displays transnational brands representing the triumph of late capitalism, and its ambience provides a retreat, an escape for the everyday reality of the urban context.

Recreation and replica

Most importantly, mega shopping malls, what George Ritzer calls "cathedrals of consumption" (2010, 2011), are designed to attract and enchant the consumer.

My photographs of the shopping malls depict appealing imagery and architecture that provides both solace and spectatorial appeal for the visitor. The photographs of the vaulted ceilings, which bestow light and, like iconic sacred imagery, the advertising signs either beckon the consumer towards an ideal state of being or present a glorified ideal to which to aspire.

The shopping mall is more than a retail space, and the notion of the "cathedral of consumption" relates to malls that are not only grandiose in size but also offer entertainment facilities, such as cinemas and gaming centres, and are sometimes linked to hotels, all of which encourage shopping. This can be found in malls in places such as Montevideo, Singapore, Surabaya, Bangkok, Hong Kong, and Dubai. Notably, the shopping malls linked to hotels are upscale luxury malls with designer brand shops and transnational corporations. With the seamless pedestrian link between hotel and shopping mall, the tourist need not venture out into the city space, as the mall provides a plethora of aesthetic experiences estranged from the exterior urban elements of the city, such as pollution, traffic, and crime. Within the mall, they can gaze at luxury goods, shop for pleasure, experience cultural events, such as art exhibitions, and enjoy an array of restaurants and eating venues in a safe controlled environment.

Many mega shopping malls present hybrid, eclectic displays of elements to simulate ideal touristic sites and create an ambience for the visitor. Shopping malls in major tourist cities compete to attract visitors, and as such provide elements and experiences of distinction. Moreover, applying John Urry's much-cited notion of the tourist gaze, the mall designers direct the "gaze to features of landscape and townscape which separate them off from everyday experience" (Urry 2002, 3). For example, within the Mall of the Emirates, in Dubai, there are Moorish arcades with diffused light filtering the space. This can be understood as reflecting a contemporary interpretation of an eastern bazaar with design elements that display an Arabic influence. Alongside this are design approaches that include International Modern, Classical Greek Revival and Italian Mediterranean. The mall also takes inspiration from the 19th century monumentality of the Galleria di Milano, with an eighteen metre glazed domed skylight. Hybrid styles and fusion abound in a postmodern mix of attractions.

There are many examples of a mall attempting to create a replica of the world, not only in visual simulacra but also in ways that it constructs a middle-class touristic experience. Replica of natural landscapes can be found in the Dubai Mall, considered the largest mall in the world. The general manager, commenting on the spectacular waterfall, has highlighted that its construction has an appeal for a family meeting place (The Dubai Mall 2009). Interestingly, as a tourist attraction, it is one of the most photographed features in the mall (Exploring Emirates 2022). Similarly, in the West End Plaza, Budapest, there is also a waterfall, which publicity material claims to be a replica of Niagara Falls (Broser 2011). In Eastern Europe, as Bodnar explains: "Malls are a novelty in the local culture of shopping" (2001, 147). Their presence signals a clearly Western turn towards a "more advanced, lifestyle and general sense of abundance to consumers whose appetites have been whet for quite a long time by a socialist shortage economy" (Bodnar 2001, 147). The urban spectacle of West End Plaza "was touted as [being as] splendid as Piccadilly Circus but more exciting" (Bodnar 2001, 148). As such, it aimed to recreate the energy and vitality of the public space in the corporately owned enclosed mall.

"Developers install nature like a sign to affluent middle-class shoppers, saying this is a real place, and it's for you" (Price 1995, 188). However, this real place does not necessarily replicate the land that the shopping mall is built on. The idea of "nature" in the shopping malls harks back to theories of the shopping mall being a retreat or an oasis, a place of respite. Palm trees are used to evoke an oasis or holiday destination in diverse places from Sheffield, England, to Melbourne, Australia. Palm trees are not native to these geographical locations. They are used to connote the notion of a tropical "paradise", or a desert oasis, yet they can be found in numerous disparate locations. It seems "all shopping malls contain elements of the Paradise myth, even if it is merely the use of palm trees, hanging baskets or water features to induce a feeling of calm and well-being" (Winchester et al. 2013, 79).

The illusion of the "ideal" outdoors is created in shopping malls; for example, simulated nature can also be found in wall murals of a dense forest, in Wollongong Central, New South Wales, Australia, as well as in the creation of an aquarium in Dubai, United Arab Emirates. It is important to consider that

> the mall itself is no longer is a buffer between the human and natural worlds, which was one function of a traditional city, it carves a fresh and ahistorical space from the drab monotony of contemporary life via the totalitarian opulence of its inside passageways.
>
> (Backes 1997, 4)

The Mall of the Emirates also reflects the contemporary trend of shopping malls blending shopping and recreational space. It features two international food courts, a ski slope, with 14 cinema screens, a Magic Plant family entertainment centre with an array of indoor rides and games. The Mall of the Emirates conveys the mall as a resort concept: palm trees, water features, and rest areas abound. There is a sense of immersion in the shopping expedition and a design focus on choreographing visitors' experiences in order to amplify the feeling of discovery and awe. The Mall of the Emirates contains a wide array of leisure sites that recreate nature or natural environments, such as a snow-covered terrain for skiing and as an opportunity to encounter penguins. The icy temperatures created in this space are in stark contrast to the natural, intense desert heat of the Middle East. Replica of natural landscapes can also be found in the Dubai Mall. It features a spectacular waterfall that runs through the considerable height of the mall. There are various vantage points and stylized sculptures of elegant divers poised in the cascading water. In addition to the spectacular waterfall, the Dubai Mall also has one of the world's largest aquariums, comprising over 140 aquatic species. My photograph of the aquarium at the Dubai Mall conveys allegorical imagery that reflects the spectacular incongruence in the mall (see Fig. 5.1). It combines what may be considered the perils of nature (the shark and ocean life) with the signifiers of consumption and cultural capital (the retail outlet). My reflection is also within this image, conveying my presence as photographer and consumer in the scene. I am part of the spectacle.

Shopping malls reflect cultural vestiges. For example, in the Galerías Pacífico, in Buenos Aires, Argentina, the 1889 Beaux Art building accommodated a copy of the Paris' *Le Bon Marché*, the first modern department store. Several years later, the Galerías Pacífico housed the Museo Nacional de Bellas Artes, the national art gallery. In 1945, 12 large-scale frescos on the vaulted ceilings of the building were painted by the most important Argentinian painters at the time. The frescos on the domed ceiling present a cathedral-like atmosphere in their richly painted grandeur. In 1991, after years of neglect, the area was transformed into a spectacular upmarket shopping mall, which bears the traces of its history of a celebration of art and commerce.

Figure 5.1   Dubai Mall, United Arab Emirates, 2014.

Photo: Panizza Allmark

On a different scale, the four-storey Discovery Mall in Kuta Bali also pays homage to its local history. On wide columns in the arcades, there are large black-and-white photographic murals depicting its original space as an outdoor local marketplace. Interestingly, the photographs of market women in traditional Balinese clothing are juxtaposed with commercial advertising of Western women in fashion posters on shop fronts. These images convey the past in the present and the local and the global. The black-and-white photographs on display serve nostalgically as reminders of how the space was used as a place of interaction and community, prior to commodification. Interestingly, the Discovery Mall is portrayed on numerous websites as a destination in the style of a "Western" shopping centre to attract the high number of tourists who visit Bali. Notably, "tourism is Bali's greatest economic source" and the homage to the traditional marketplace is of cultural interest (Collinson 2012). As you wander through the Discovery Mall, on display there is an eclectic mix of traditional imagery and advertising images, the latter promoting the transnational global commodities and western beauty ideals, such as blonde blue-eyed slender women (see Fig. 5.2).

As highlighted by a number of authors, the postmodern mix of attractions in shopping malls also reflects the identity of the area (Abaza 2001; Morris 1999). In the Mall of the Emirates, for example, a golden camel is illuminated at the entrance of the mall. Elevated on a podium, the camel conveys the cultural heritage of the area and its geographical positioning in the desert. In the United Arab

Figure 5.2   Galerías Pacífico, Buenos Aires Argentina, 2008.
Photo: Panizza Allmark

Emirates, the camel is on permanent display; it is a symbol of life and journeying in the desert space.

Culture on display

The shopping mall may provide respite from the harsh climate, and within these spaces, as I have seen in a number of locations, such as in Perth, Honolulu, Singapore, and Dubai, the shopping mall is also a space which brings the community together to witness cultural performances, visiting celebrities, and art exhibitions. As Don Slater argues in his work "Going Shopping: Markets, Crowds and Consumption", "the appearance of culture in the market indicates that autonomous civil activity has subordinated to the logic of the commodity and the planning principles of the firm; the cultural has been rationalized and functionalized" (Slater 1993, 189). As such, only art or cultural activities that will enhance the desired reputation and increase retail spending are sanctioned under the politics of late capitalism.

The hosting of a cultural experience or the display and promotion of aspects of the outside world within the confines of the shopping mall benefit the corporate owners by increasing visitor numbers and subsequent retail exposure. In the malls, there are also constructed or staged cultural events to attract more visitors and to support the notions of the mall being a place of escapism, leisure, and safety. Staged performances and fragmented spectacles of the colonized, the original inhabitants of the land, are carefully orchestrated to appeal to the middle-class visitors and become a commercial cultural display. "Performances are typically devised to titillate tourists without alienating them by sticking too closely to complicated cultural meanings" (Edensor 2001, 70). In Honolulu, for example, its role as a tourist destination is capitalized on with regular performances of a hula show at the Ala Moana Center. Hula performances also occur in most shopping malls in the city. Notably, the Hula performances mainly consist of young dark-skinned women performing for white tourists. This draws "upon the long visual history of the development of the 'hula girl' as a tourist icon" (Desmond 1999, xx). The hula girl "evokes the feminized lushness of the tropics: accessible, hospitable, beautiful, exotic and natural" (Desmond 1999, 12). On stage in the shopping mall, these racialized gender traits transfer to the cold corporate space, into a cultural marketplace in which feminine body display is sanctioned in performance and advertising.

The performance of Hula, like other Indigenous symbolic representation, may be understood as ensuring "cultural reproduction while participating in capitalist markets", but "it [the culture] is also appropriated and commodified by the tourist" and commercial industry (Imada 2004, 119). The shopping mall offers access to a cultural experience constructed as an expression of hyper-capitalism in which corporate interests are subsumed into all aspects of life, including entertainment and leisure activities (Rifkin 2001, 6). Indigenous performances as a controlled spectacle are permitted. However, Indigenous performance as a political gathering is not tolerated. An example of this is the case of the "Idle No More" movement, an Indigenous rights movement of Native Americans who applied to the Mall of America for permission to perform traditional dancing and drumming, on New Year's Eve 2014. They received "letters from the Mall of America threatening with arrest if the event took place" (Regan 2014). It seems that their cultural exhibition did not adhere to the heavily commodified (imperialist) notions of culture that reflect the image of the mall, and as significantly, the constructed image of the Mall of America. "Importantly, music, sound and dance in Idle No More gatherings were not simply the media by which political messages were conveyed, but performative forms of politics in and of themselves" (Robinson 2017, 225). There is the cultural paradox in relation to the transmission of culture in which material culture is seen as acceptable in the mall, and this is in the form of native made or inspired goods being available for purchase, whereas "political" displays of culture from Indigenous people are not acceptable. This is, perhaps, reflective of the ownership and the target audience for the shopping mall to which the mall caters. The shopping mall is not seen as a "political" space, and it seems that the mall should not serve as a reminder of the violent histories of imperialism. Indigenous culture is fashioned as commodity to be consumed for visitor/tourist consumption and this is to be consumed from a "safe" distance as staged artifice.

The appeal of the Other or the exotic is not just confined to staged performances but is also found in shop displays. For example, Australian Aboriginal artefacts such as didgeridoos can be found in Dubai, the United Arab Emirates, and there is a shop selling Native American merchandise, such as feathered head dresses, in a mall in Chiang Mai, Thailand. In the shopping malls, the stereotypical items manufactured as commodities in Dubai and Chiang Mai as well as native cultural performances, as in Honolulu, conceal the history of violence endured by Indigenous peoples and the complex relationship of present-day Indigenous subjects with colonial powers. These powers present certain aspects of culture that they consider non-threatening to be marketed as commodities. For example, the shops may be considered equivalent to an exhibition display in a museum with its nostalgia for the exotic pre-colonial past and the memorabilia of the "noble savage", the idealized or romanticized Western vision of the "primitive", considered closer to nature. The displays, perhaps, are distractions from the frenzied contemporary world and serve as reminders of a time before commodification and spaces outside the confines of a shopping mall. They are also recreations of the world from a colonial tourist privileged perspective. Cultural tourism in the form of endorsed "native" performances and the "exotic" merchandise described provide a Western European notion of a utopian elsewhere.

The experience of immersion: gender and the shopping mall

"Mall designers fashion ideological "dreamland spaces" that appeal to customers' senses" (Stillerman and Salcedo 2012, 311) and, I would add, sensibility. Within this sphere, advertising signs, billboards, televisual screens, and larger-than-life posters mediate our desires and are the signs of silent veneration to cultural ideals and global idols, such as supermodels and celebrity icons, who gaze outwards and reflect a higher order.

As I have highlighted earlier, there are quasi-religious aspects to the shopping mall. "Like cathedrals, they are places where people want to be awed, inspired, cheered and surrender themselves" (Siang 2010, 5). John Fiske argues that "religion may act as a helpful metaphor when our aim is to investigate the power of consumerism" (1989, 14), and he acknowledges that commodities may become icons of worship; nevertheless, he critiques the notion of the passive consumer, indoctrinated by the allure of consumption, instead asserting that individuals may challenge the dominant ideology. To Fiske, the shopping mall may be "seen as a terrain of guerrilla warfare" (against the strategic interests of corporations) and this "looks quite different from the one constructed by the metaphor of religion" in which a religious congregation is led to believe "truths" on offer (1989, 14). Academics (Chua 2003; Fiske 1989; Backes 1997; Morris 1999; Shields 1992) have argued that consumers are active, rather than passive; space is utilized to satisfy one's own needs or desires.

Drawing upon the history of shopping malls and arcades as "tracts for strolling" (Bauman 1996, 27), the images convey the idea of the *flâneur*, an individual who wanders and gazes at the sights. For Walter Benjamin, the process of *flânerie*, or gazing, "was a way of understanding the city as a site of struggle, as an unequal place, but also as an unpredictable place, precisely because it has always been a site for meetings of difference". Benjamin's analysis of the phenomenon of the arcade, a forerunner to the department store and shopping mall, is pertinent as he describes it as a space providing scintillating sights for the consumption of the gazer.

Of particular interest to me is the role of the *flâneuse*, the female stroller. Janet Wolff (1985) argues that the *flâneuse* was a "non-existent" role in the experience of modern life in the nineteenth century. "Women could not stroll alone in the city" (Wolff 1985, 41). However, Ruth Isken, drawing on Benjamin's theorization of consumer society, contends that the "department store became the promenade of the *flâneuse*" (Iskin 2003, 334). "Shopping offered an acceptable context for cultural and social relation to the metropolis that transcended buying goods" (Iskin 2003, 335). Anne Friedberg also asserts that "the shopping mall is a "ladies paradise" for the contemporary *flâneuse*" (1993, 118). Notably, the topography of shopping malls is specifically designed to invite the female consumer and her gaze. The appeal of shopping malls is that they provide a liminal space for women and girls; as such, they offer spaces, which straddle the public and the private. A dominant theme is the fantasy of fashioning the self. This is reflected in the photographs of advertising signs, screens, and billboards that are aimed at the female consumer.

The shopping mall serves as a space to draw a crowd to the carnival-like spectacle on show. Significantly, this crowd is made of individuals and groups of individuals (women, youth, etc.) who engage with the space in different ways. Chua, for example, asserts that "it is common knowledge that for many urbanites the actual buying of objects of desire or necessity is not the primary purpose of 'shopping'. Browsing is" (2003, 42). Julie Marshall contends that in the showcasing of products, the "cathedrals of consumption serve as locations for consumers to interact with products without the obligation of purchasing goods or services creating a revolutionized form of window-shopping" (2006, 1). As discussed previously, the practice of window-shopping is enriched by the alluring displays in arcades of the shopping mall and the displays are often designed to attract the female consumer or *flâneuse*.

According to Laermans (1993, 95), shopping malls could be seen as "female leisure centres": "Women were redefined as professional shoppers or consumers and their performance of their traditional roles was thoroughly commodified or redefined in terms of commodities". The "shopping mall positively influences hedonic shopping", though "many shoppers adopt a reflexive stance toward shopping, developing strategies to curtail impulse purchases" (Michon et al. 2008, 456; Stillerman and Salcedo 2012, 326). In this sense, "cathedrals of consumption serve as locations for consumers to interact with products without the obligation of purchasing goods or services creating a revolutionized form of window-shopping" (Marshall 2006, 1). Window-shopping is an opportunity to partake in pleasures of the gaze, of commodity fetishism. It involves looking, possibly desiring, but not necessarily purchasing. There is also a tactile sensuality in visiting shopping malls that cannot be achieved through online shopping. Certainly, the experience of being in a shopping mall is immersive and the pleasure of trying on outfits at will is a powerful one. Chua (2003, 51) describes the freedom of the body when shopping:

> Fingers, grease and all, feel the fabric, hands pick up the clothes, hold them against the body so as to imaging oneself in them, and if desired, take them to the changing room to try them on. Clothes are thus donned and doffed at will. As the intention to purchase is not a prerequisite, fantasies of image-change are free.

It is important to consider that "more than 60 percent of non-anchor stores in major shopping centres specialize in apparel, footwear, and accessories, and three-quarters of these stores specifically target female shoppers" (Michon et al. 2015, 4). For consumers, who are mainly women, the "moment of choice is an empowered one", and there is a pleasure of control in the selection of commodities that can enhance the context of everyday life (Fiske 1989, 26). John Fiske suggests that shopping malls can be a site for female empowerment in which the female subject can detach herself from patriarchal domesticity. The shopping mall may be seen as a liminal space that offers the possibility of transformation. There is the possibility of creative self-articulations through fashion; in other words, expression of self and status can occur through the sartorial realm.

Furthermore, acknowledging the patriarchal nature of society, for some women "to 'go out' and buy invokes a relative emancipation in women's active role as consumers" (Bowlby 1985, 22). The shopping mall may be considered an escape or retreat from the monotony of everyday life, a space where one can be alone, yet be with others to engage in the spectacle. Friedberg further highlights that "the shopping mall appears to be a historical endpoint of increasing female empowerment, female spending power and a 'Ladies Paradise' for the contemporary *flâneuse*" (1993, 118). The idea of a "ladies paradise" is certainly how shopping malls are marketed. The advertising and the array of fashion in the mall are designed to appeal to the female consumer and construction of their hegemonic femininity. Here, the notion of the lady, as in "ladies paradise", could be expanded on, as it is a certain type of femininity that seems to be prevalent in advertising around shopping malls. It is a femininity in which women are seen as empowered through constructed notions of an "ideal" gendered look and feminine deportment.

There is a highly constructed notion of female identity displayed, with eyebrows that are shaped, hair coiffed, and nails that are perfectly manicured. The numerous posters and advertising signs consist mainly of images of women, larger than life, empowered, confident, and engaging in fashion and a lifestyle that is deemed admirable. Various advertisements address the female consumer through the female voice and female representation. In shopping malls, there are images of particular types of women (predominantly young, slender, and white). These are presented in magnified proportions. In my photographs, I reframe the images of advertising in shopping malls to draw attention to the spectatorial gaze towards the "desirable body", and juxtapose this with the women who are traversing the space (Stratton 1996).

Figure 5.3   Langham Place, Hong Kong, 2010.
Photo: Panizza Allmark

John Fiske suggests that shopping malls can be a site for female empowerment in which the female subject can detach herself from patriarchal domesticity. Similar to the tourist experience, the shopping mall may be seen as a liminal space that offers the possibility of transformation. There is the possibility of creative self-articulations through fashion; in other words, expression of self and status can occur through the sartorial realm.

Women may also be empowered in such a space by having a wide array of choices and a heightened sense of security. There is an elevated perception of safety conveyed by shopping mall design techniques such as the use of skylights and the increased lighting of the mall, in contrast to shadowy city streets. As previously discussed, the mall's European origins are in the department store. In the nineteenth century, the department store provided a space which women could traverse un-chaperoned, away from the male gaze and possible threats of the street. The shopping mall is considered a safe space, whereas "the public streets were a male domain" (Stratton 1996, 94). Bauman's often cited quote that shopping malls make the world "carefully walled-off, electronically monitored and closely guarded" and safe for walking is applicable here (1996, 95). Certainly, in my experiences of travel, often I would visit a shopping mall to be in a female-centred environment. The mall carries with it the awareness and reassurance that the amenities would be clean and safe. Unlike the streets, which are a less predictable terrain, and where, as a woman I have been the object of the gaze, a visit to the local shopping mall provided me with relief from the unsettling aspects of the city streets. These can at times be engaging but they are also more stressful. In addition, the shopping mall is also a topography with which I am familiar. For example, most upscale shopping malls have anchor stores at either end of the mall. These stores are surrounded by numerous boutiques and retail outlets. The shopping mall provides an opportunity not only to be in a global space but also to have a taste of somewhat local differences which may appear in specific shops or displays in the mall. In Turkey, for example, I visited the Istanbul Cevahir Mall, which was the largest mall near the city centre. In a country unfamiliar to me, the visit to the mall was a welcome respite. I could see familiar international brand stores, but more importantly I felt a sense of safety being around women because the mall is a predominantly female space. I felt I could move around freely, away from the male gaze and physical limitations that I experienced on the city streets. Perhaps my enjoyment gained by visiting malls also stems from the experience that it is a welcoming space for women and no matter what city I travel to, I know that I can feel that same sense of security and familiarity in the various malls I visit, yet, still be visually stimulated by the attractions on offer.

Conclusion

I have focused on the ambiance of shopping malls: the spectacle of the space and the features that attempt to create a utopian paradise, a cathedral of consumption and a site of secular touristic pilgrimage. The mall is designed as an aesthetic experience. As van Eeden contends, "the mall as an autonomous oasis of time-lessness, perfect weather and statis, free from the constraints of history reinforces the impression that its space is gendered as female" (2006, 58). The mall provides an escape from the everyday monotony of the outside world and presents an opportunity to foray into a sanitized commodified world. The mall is presented as a "shoppers' paradise", a combination of an abundance of commodities and spectacular display of chosen elements of the external environment that strives to balance clinical consumption sites and outdoor leisure spaces. I have aimed my lens at the way gender is conveyed and the examples of malls attempting to create a replica of the world, not only in visual display but also in ways that it constructs a middle-class touristic experience, and a seemingly safe for women to engage in. Nonetheless, the pleasure of looking is also the act of seeing beneath the surface of the commodified spectacle.

References

Abaza, M. 2001. "Shopping Malls, Consumer Culture and the Reshaping of Public Space in Egypt." *Theory, Culture and Society* 18 (5): 97–122.

Ameen, N., A. Tarhini, M. Hussain Shah, and K. Nusair. 2021. "A Cross Cultural Study of Gender Differences in Omnichannel Retailing Contexts." *Journal of Retailing and Consumer Services* 58: 102265.

Asadifard, M., A. Abd Rahman, Y. Abdul Aziz, and H. Hashim. 2015. "A Review on Tourist Mall Patronage Determinant in Malaysia." *International Journal of Innovation, Management and Technology* 6 (3): 229–233.

Backes, N. 1997. "Reading the Shopping Mall City." *Journal of Popular Culture* 31 (3): 1–18.

Bauman, Z. 1996. "From Pilgrim to Tourist – Or A Short History of Identity." In *Questions of Cultural Identity*, edited by Stuart Hall and Paul du Gay, 18–56. London: SAGE.

Bodnar, J. 2001. *Fin de Millenaire Budapest*. Minneapolis: University of Minnesota Press.

Böhm, S., and A. Batta. 2010. "Just Doing It: Enjoying Commodity Fetishism with Lacan." *Organization* 17 (3): 345–361.

Bowlby, R. 1985. *Just Looking: Consumer Culture in Dreiser, Gissing and Zola*. London: Methuen.

Broser, A. 2011. "Let it Flow." *Across Magazine*, Accessed January 24, 2022. www.atp.ag/fileadmin/user_upload/Presseartikel/ATP_Across_VARENA_Ausg0111.pdf.

Buck-Morss, S. 1991. *The Dialectics of Seeing: Walter Benjamin and The Arcades Project*. Cambridge: MIT Press.

Chua, B. H. 2003. *Life is Not Complete Without Shopping: Consumption Culture in Singapore*. Singapore: Singapore University Press.

Cluley, R., and S. Dunne. 2012. "From Commodity Fetishism to Commodity Narcism." *Market Theory* 12 (3): 251–265.

Collinson, L. 2012. "Is Bali Doing as Well as it Should Be?" https://balilive.net/wp-content/uploads/2013/02/Bali-Article.pdf

Dallen, T. J. 2005. *Shopping Tourism, Retailing and Leisure*. Clevedon: Channel View Publications.

Desmond, Jane. 1999. *Staging Tourism. Bodies on Display from Waikiki to Sea World*. Chicago: The University of Chicago Press.

Edensor, T. 2001. "Performing Tourism, Staging Tourism: (Re)producing Tourist Space and Practice." *Tourist Studies* 1 (1): 59–81.

Exploring Emirates. 2022. "Dubai Mall Waterfall: All You Need to Know." https://exploringemirates.com/dubai-mall-waterfall/

Fiske, J. 1989. *Reading the Popular*. London: Routledge.

Friedberg, A. 1993. *Window Shopping: Cinema and the Postmodern*. Berkeley: University of California Press.

Frow, J., and M. Elizabeth Morris. 1993. *Australian Cultural Studies: A Reader*. Urbana: University of Illinois Press.

Hall, S. 1994. "Cultural Identity and Diaspora." In *Colonial Discourse and Post-Colonial Theory: A Reader*, edited by Patrick Williams and Laura Chrisman, 222–337. London: Harvester Wheatsheaf.

Imada, A. L. 2004. "Hawaiians on Tour: Hula Circuits Through the American Empire." *American Quarterly* 56 (1): 111–149.

Iskin, R. E. 2003. "The pan-european flâneuse in fin-de-siècle posters: Advertising modern women in the city", *Nineteenth-Century Contexts* 25 (4): 333–356.

Jenks, M. 2003. "Above and Below the Line: Globalization and Urban Form in Bangkok." *The Annals of Regional Science* 37 (3): 547–557.

Laermans, R. 1993. "Learning to Consume: Early Department Stores and Shaping of the Modern Consumer Culture." *Theory, Culture, and Society* 10: 79–102.

Marshall, J. 2006. "Interactive Window Shopping: Enchantment in a Rationalized World." *Electronic Journal of Sociology* 1: 1–12.

Marx, K. 1976. *Capital: A Critique of Political Economy*. Translated by Ben Fowkes, Vol. 1. London: Penguin.

Michon, R., J.-C. Chebat, H. Yu, and L. Lemarié. 2015. "Fashion Orientation, Shopping Mall Environment, and Patronage Intentions." *Journal of Fashion Marketing and Management* 19 (1): 3–21.

Michon, R., H. Yu, D. Smith, and J.-C. Chebat. 2008. "The Influence of Mall Environment on Female Fashion Shoppers' Value and Behavior." *Journal of Fashion Marketing and Management* 12: 456–468.

Morris, M. 1999. "Things To Do with Shopping Centres." In *The Cultural Studies Reader*, edited by Simon During, 2nd ed., 391–409. London: Routledge.

Parlette, V., and D. Cowen. 2011. "Dead Malls: Suburban Activism, Local Spaces, Global Logistics." *International Journal of Urban and Regional Research* 35 (4): 794–811.

Price, J. 1995. "Looking for Nature at the Mall: Field Guide to the Nature Company." In *Uncommon Ground: Toward Reinventing Nature*, edited by William Cronon, 186–203. Cambridge, MA: Harvard University Press.

Rahman, A. 2017. "Hong Kong: An Insiders' Guide to a Shopping Mecca." *The Hollywood Reporter*, March 13, 2017. www.hollywoodreporter.com/lifestyle/lifestyle-news/hong-kong-an-insiders-guide-a-shopping-mecca-985477/

Regan, S. 2014. " 'Mall of America' to Native Americans: Happy New Year: You Are Under Arrest." *The Uptake*, February 26, 2014. http://theuptake.org/2014/01/01/mall-of-america-to-native-americans-happy-new-year-you-are-under-arrest/

Rifkin, J. 2001. *The Age of Access: The New Culture of Hypercapitalism, Where All of Life Is a Paid-for Experience*. New York: J.P. Tarcher/Putnam.

Ritzer, G. 2010. *Enchanting a Disenchanted World: Revolutionizing the Means of Consumption*. 3rd ed. Thousand Oaks: SAGE Publications.

Ritzer, G. 2011. *The McDonaldization of Society 6*. Thousand Oaks: Pine Forge Press.

Robinson, D. 2017. "Enchantment's Irreconcilable Connection: Listening to Anger, Being Idle No More" In *Performance Studies in Canada*, edited by L. Levin and M. Schweitzer, 211–235. Montreal: McGill-Queen's University Press.

Shields, R. 1992. *Lifestyle Shopping: The Subject of Consumption*. London: Routledge.

Siang, T. L. 2010. "Preface." In *SPACE: Shopping Mall*, edited by Diane Tsang, 4–5. Hong Kong: Pace.

Slater, D. 1993. "Going Shopping: Markets, Crowds and Consumption." In *Cultural Reproduction*, edited by Chris Jenks, 188–209. New York: Routledge.

Stillerman, J., and R. Salcedo. 2012. "Transposing the Urban to the Mall: Routes, Relationships, and Resistance in Two Santiago, Chile, Shopping Centers." *Peer Reviewed Articles* 1. http://scholarworks.gvsu.edu/soc_articles/1.

Stratton, J. 1996. *The Desirable Body: Cultural Fetishism and the Erotics of Consumption*. Manchester: Manchester University Press.

Techentin, W. 2004. *Dead Malls*. Orange County: The Forum Press.

The Dubai Mall. 2009. "The Dubai Mall Opens the Waterfall: A Spectacular Water Feature and Vantage Meeting Point for Visitors." *The Dubai Mail*, January 9, 2009. www.thedubaimall.com/en/Events/2009/The-Dubai-Mall-opens-The-Waterfall – a-spectacular-water-feature-and-vantage-meeting-point-for-visitors.aspx.

Timothy, D. J. 2018. "Shopping Tourism." In *Special Interest Tourism: Concepts, Contexts and Case*, edited by S. Agarwal, G. Busby and R. Huang, 134–144. Wallingford, Oxfordshire: CABI.

United Nations World Tourism Organization. 2011. *Tourism Towards 2030/Global Overview – Advance Edition Presented at UNWTO 19th General Assembly – 10 October 2011*. Madrid: United Nations World Tourism Organization.

Urry, J. 2002. *The Tourist Gaze*. 2nd ed. London: SAGE.

van Eeden, Jeanne. 2006. "The Gender of Shopping Malls." *Communication: South African Journal for Communication Theory and Research* 32 (1): 38–64.

Voyce, M. 2005. "Neoliberalism, Shopping Malls and the End of 'Property'." In *Law and Popular Culture*, edited by Michael Freeman, 527–559. Oxford: Oxford University Press.

Winchester, H., L. Kong, and K. Dunn. 2013. *Landscapes: Ways of Imagining the World*. London: Routledge.

Wolff, J. 1985. "The Invisible Flâneuse. Women and the Literature of Modernity." *Theory, Culture & Society* 2 (3): 37–46.

Zukin, S. 1991. *Landscapes of Power: From Detroit to Disney World*. Berkeley: University of California Press.

6 Cyclical ruins

A videopoem on sun and sand tourism spaces in the low season

Pablo Arboleda

The teaser

During spring 2020, the strict lockdown measures that were globally adopted to mitigate the spread of COVID-19 pandemic revealed how a planet without humans would look like. In those days, the mass media circulated multiple online photo galleries that portrayed empty cities worldwide, and surely, within this eerie representation, the most shocking pictures were the ones taken at international though deserted touristic hotspots, whose imaginary is associated with visitor crowds (i.e. Kimmelman 2020; Hecimovic 2020; Expósito et al. 2020). Contrary to the idea popularized by Hollywood action movies, it became clear that the apocalypse does not necessarily require the sudden physical destruction of the built environment. As a matter of fact, before the pandemic, sun and sand tourism spaces were characterized by hosting visitor saturation over the summer followed by long periods of absence – something that, only now that the pandemic seems to be slowly under control, is starting to happen again in the quest for "normality". This cyclical, recurring form of apocalypse, of yearly lack of human life, takes place throughout the low season.

ON-OFF-ON-OFF-ON-OFF . . .

The Mediterranean coast of Spain is a paradigmatic case of cyclical abandonment for having entrusted, over decades, a considerable part of its economic model on sun and sand tourism. Back in the 1960s, Franco's regime advocated for this type of development as a regeneration strategy that aimed to counter Spain's idiosyncrasy so far – still connected to exotism, folklore, and backwardness – by presenting the country as a more modern and liberal society (Pack 2006). The progressive democratization of tourism at both national and international levels has done the rest, and thus the number of people enjoying Spain's sun and sand destinations has raised steadily, setting new consecutive records every year; not surprisingly, the majority of this tourism activity occurs during the Northern hemisphere summer, and more specifically, between the months of June and September (Banco de España 2019).

DOI: 10.4324/9781003207207-9

Today, according to macroeconomic data, tourism represents 12.4% of Spain's GDP, being a "golden egg" that appears to be beyond dispute. Political authorities, the mass media, and the general public consistently celebrate tourism's quantitative success, that has allowed Spain, with 83.7 million tourists in 2019, to retain its position as the second-most visited country in the world only after France (Instituto Nacional de Estadística 2019). Therefore, in a context of persisting economic shrinkage derived from the bursting of the property bubble in 2008 – where the construction sector lingered at a standstill – Spain is, now more than ever, re-embracing tourism, and specifically sun and sand tourism, to consolidate a national identity based on a series of assets (e.g. good weather, Mediterranean diet, relax and hospitality, and affordable prices) for what it's worth a visit (Domínguez 2015). However, when zooming in, it is observed that the sun and sand model does not rely on high professional qualification, and subsequently, precariousness is manifested in low wages and seasonal employment. In fact, those regions that are renowned for being important sun and sand destinations are not amongst the country's richest when compared to further financial and industrial nodes in Spain (Llaneras et al. 2020). Yet sun and sand tourism has been largely investigated within Tourism Studies, critically emphasizing the need of diversification and improvement as several case studies in Europe demonstrate (Assaker and Hallak 2012). Spain's reality follows the existing pattern, where researchers mainly focus on tourism management, seeking to provide assessed technical data and recommended policies (Alves et al. 2017).

Beyond these complexities, sun and sand tourism has an evident regional impact in terms of how localized urban developments are conceived, designed, and executed. The continuous growth of tourism figures has led to the massive and fast construction of new spaces (e.g. hotels, restaurants, leisure resorts, residential complexes, promenades, shops, water and amusement parks) that have radically transformed the Spanish coastline, which, only a few decades ago, was known for the coexistence between fisher's towns and untouched nature. Despite recent attempts that claim for the heritagization of sun and sand vacation sites (Royo 2014; García-Moreno et al. 2016), scholars have usually criticized the eclectic robotization of their architectures and urban fabrics, the disregard for landscape and environmental issues caused by the pouring of tons and tons of concrete, and the blind faith in a model that dramatically implies land privatization and the lack of public facilities (e.g. Aledo 2008; García 2014; Martínez-Medina 2016; Vázquez 2016). Said criticism is more or less explicit in multiple artistic manifestations that have contributed to create the "tacky" imaginary of sun and sand spaces when they are in full operation; such is the case of photography (Parr 1999; Salvans 2020), documentaries (Losada 2010; Natoli 2019, 2021), movies and TV shows (Berger 2003; Sánchez-Cabezudo 2011; Coixet 2020), and novels, graphic novels, and essays (Chirbes 2007; Carro 2019; Penyas 2021).

To these lines, the critical overview towards sun and sand tourism spaces is susceptible to be expanded considering that, when summer ends, they remain mostly empty, merely awaiting the next year, and within this vicious circle, it can be said that the increasingly occupied high season is paradoxically followed by an increasingly unoccupied low season (Millás and Clavera 2017). Following Lefebvre's rationale, these are absolute, concrete spaces provided that they are subjected to cyclical rhythms where, contrary to dominant linear temporalities, harmony emerges from the linkage between the sites' nature and their social appropriation patterns – despite the fact that there is no such thing unequivocally cyclical or linear but rather spaces that are closer than others to a certain opposing pole of the same scale (Paiva 2019). Hence, acknowledging that a ruin is an abandoned place where there was once an activity, and, similar to the way unfinished buildings have become Spain's ruined symbols after the 2008 crash (Schultz-Dornburg 2012), this chapter suggests that deserted sun and sand tourism spaces are "cyclical ruins", metaphorically representing the country's development model at present since, at all times, every society produces its own forms of spatial redundancy, emptiness, and ruination (DeSilvey and Edensor 2013). In what follows, I set out to engage with the phenomenon of cyclical abandonment by using ruin-related theories. This research approach will be two-folded as it deliberately aestheticizes the experience of being-in while implicitly puts into question the architectural and urban notions of progress promised by the tourism industry.

My conceptual point of departure is that sun and sand destinations are hermetic environments, architecturally impersonal and mundane, just like *non-places* whose yearly disposable character only exaggerates the "non-" (Augé 1995). Beyond this, during the low season, they are charged with a sense of absence that deprives the sites from existence in the collective imaginary even though, at the same time, absence is generative of a particular "urban ambiance" – understood as the sensorial awareness towards the surrounding space's tangibles and intangibles (Thibaud 2015). The originality of this theoretical proposal lies on the fact that, in principle, seasonally unoccupied tourism spaces are not meant to be ruins at all. The constructions are not deteriorated, they are not "ruined ruins"; however, when their deserted ambiance (which is characteristic over a considerable part of the year) is examined through the lens of temporality and subjectivity, sun and sand spaces truly feel like ruins. And though using the term "ruin" to refer to places that are not formally abandoned may well sound misguided, I have myself investigated this direction to demonstrate that ruin studies are not just useful to scrutinize past narratives, but it is also a suitable framework to reckon with current problematics (Arboleda 2017).

In December 2019, only a couple of months before the pandemic haunted our world, I conducted a three-day road trip through 500 km to explore the already ghostly highlights of sun and sand tourism throughout the Andalusian coastline, in Southern Spain. This region was chosen due to logistical and operational reasons, allowing me to maximize time and budget constrains while offering me the possibility to document multivariate space typologies. The conduction of fieldwork during the "full" low season consciously pursued, and afforded me, to reflect on a de-contextualized sense of place affected by intimate feelings and impressions – solitude, melancholia, sadness, etc. – that resulted just the opposite of those for which sun and sand tourism spaces are originally conceived. Through contemplation, video registration, and field notes gathering, my thoughts are encapsulated on a collaborative, eight-minute videopoem that has been uploaded to Vimeo, and which creatively questions the adequacy of continuing to develop and shape the seafront landscape. Prior to its playing, I deploy notions of liminality and spectrality within ruin literatures, and I extrapolate these to sun and sand tourism spaces conceptualized as "cyclical ruins". Further, I remark the potential of art-led, experimental forms of expression to translate affective knowledge and aesthetical experiences, and I suggest their suitability to enrich and advance (academic) writing on urban ambiances. The present contribution is relevant for both Spain and further societies whose economy partially depends on sun and sand tourism, where those emotions triggered by emptiness during the low season remain to be appraised.

Cyclical liminality

The ruin comes into being once its time of inhabitation ends. Temporality within "old" ruins is fixed, domesticated; here, their usual categorization as ordered heritage is manifested through formal conservation practices that constrain the sites' capacity to change and evolve, while for ruins of modernity, narratives are still under construction and open to interpretation (Orange 2008; Garrett 2010). This makes the heritagization of the latter a controversial process, in which the absence of conservation measures fosters entropy and the conceptualization of ruin-*ing* as a process is not ended (Pétursdóttir and Olsen 2014). Commonly seen as undesirable imprints causing discomfort or embarrassment, the sense of tragedy within modern ruins can be cushioned by prospects of hope through which multiple futures are offered (Dobraszczyk 2017), and yet ruination is a liminal phase walking the line between becoming rubble and awaiting a potential afterlife. However, the notion of "cyclical" opens a particular temporal spectrum, which is novel within ruinology literatures as it contests timely features from both old and modern ruins. Characterized by long-term rhythms, sun and sand tourism spaces are places of in-betweenness – where loneliness and solitude affections over the low season do not speak to any other fate than the certainty that, over the next year, they will be bustling in fun and amusement again. Their liminality is yet bounded: Cyclical ruins are not frozen in time, they are not melting, and they cannot rely on the possibility to become something different either.

Within the built space, liminality is often considered to be a physical attribute, and consequently, it is not uncommon to read the term as a synonym of Marion Shoard's "edgelands" (2002) to denote city margins and tangible urban thresholds. To this understanding, seashores and beaches are meant to be *the* archetypical expression of the liminal as they are not only located at the edge of land – literally – but they also comply with a temporal dimension of liminality, where transitions relate to seasonal periods and even a daily shifting status such as high and low tides (Andrews 2012). Indeed, in anthropology, liminality is the ambiguous affirmation taking place during a rite of passage, where "the initiands live outside their normal environment and are brought to question their self and the existing social order through a series of rituals that often involve acts of pain" (Thomassen 2006, 322). For sun and sand tourism spaces in the low season, these acts of pain manifest in closure, abandonment, desertion, public and private facilities at standstill, and the sudden raise of unemployment – cyclically embodying one of the main features of ruins, that of dual meanings and temporal paradoxes (Dillon 2011). And yet every winter becomes a reiterative rite of passage towards the pre-existing, affording a constant lucubration between rise and fall, triumph and drama, and rowdiness and silence.

If there is such thing as "liminal aesthetics", they are found in a space between two states of being (Brandt 2009). A gas station at night, a theatre hall once the play is over, a swimming-pool in New Year's Eve. Cyclical ruins are capable of triggering a series of feelings (i.e. eeriness, dislocation, derealization) when experienced outside of their planned dynamism, and yet the absence of life and movement creates unsettling ambiances in spaces that are usually identified by being full of life and movement. The assumption of normality is thus tilted, making room for the 'uncanny' in the Freudian sense as it involves *compulsive repetition* and its terror does not derive from "the unknown, but from something which is familiar and old-established in the mind and which has become alienated from it only through the process of repression" (Freud, as quoted in Allmark 2011, 141); a driving phenomenological notion, the uncanniness, with a long-standing trajectory within the (extra)ordinary sensing of industrial ruins, through which "the familiar and homely suddenly become strange" (Edensor 2005, 835). In this sense, it is worth noting that the growing concern towards ruin aesthetics is commonly associated with pleasing visuals, while less attention is paid to aesthetics as what can be felt and sensed through fully corporeal perceptions that are closer to affect and emotion (Pétursdóttir and Olsen 2014). Acknowledging the shortcomings of subjectivity – through which what appears solitude to one person may be actual serenity to another and even some may not express any sensibility at all (Arboleda 2021) – it is undisputable that the role of the self is crucial to the aesthetical formation of liminality, prioritizing and valuing embodied narratives that "care for personal experiences and convey moments of wonder" (Pétursdóttir 2016, 372).

Vibrant in summer, sun and sand tourism spaces somehow cease to exist in our collective consciousness once the high season ends, and it is only then when they emerge as cyclical ruins. The mere fact that they remain empty does not mean that they are meaningless, so quoting Susan Sontag one may well say that "[a]s long as a human eye is looking there is always something to see" (2002, 10). These spaces demand thus novel engagement, particularly because by being strangely familiar, they result exciting, attractive, and full of emotional possibilities that are useful to find *another* truth, opening them to fresh discussions that counter collective amnesia. Walking through liminal, cyclical ruins implies experiencing what others do not usually experience; it is a transgression "in search of a break from the normal" (Thomassen 2012, 21), highlighting qualities of fascination and discovery – and also fear, risk, and danger – that are inherent within urban exploration narratives and psychogeographic accounts on modern ruins (Fraser 2012). Said embodied journeys are productive to intimately reflect on the historical, political, and economic reasons and consequences behind the production of ambiances, placing the individual at the core of their connection with the inhabited world (Crouch 2012; Selwyn 2012). In the case of my encounter with cyclical ruins in Spain, it afforded a critical relation between my sense of self as a national, and how the coastline operates off season. Here, rumination in place served me, through an invaluable aesthetical experience, to metaphorically question, in urban terms, the price to pay for embracing the idea of a supposed success.

Spectrality and the videopoem

Amongst the myriad of resonating methods available, my approach to cyclical ruins draws from what Justin Armstrong (2010), after a series of short visits to several ghost towns in the North American High Plains, labels as "spectral ethnography". The author examines the material, environmental, and visual culture considerations that emerge when abandoned places *are left to speak for themselves and one is willing to listen*. To these lines, spectral ethnography documents

> fragments of time at a momentary standstill, a snapshot of humanness etched on the landscape and as an accumulation of time outside the realm of human influence. [Here,] it is necessary to embrace and cultivate the slowness and reflexivity of these spaces in order to effectively . . . offer a unique point of contact with the ephemeral nature of time and materiality through the lens of personal experience. [T]he ethnographer should explore and document the spaces and objects before engaging with the authors (the people who live, or have lived, in these places) directly to construct a personal and subjective reading of the space with limited outside influences. [In this practice,] I argue that the unseen is often as important as the seen and that emotions and individually perceived resonances can act as powerful analytic agents.
>
> (Armstrong 2010, 244–248)

In addition to this, Armstrong interestingly uses a beautiful poetic prose to describe his journeys, being this a clear sample of the writing creativity possibilities underlying at the intimate interactions with the liminal, spectral, and ruined space. Stylistically speaking, W.G. Sebald's novels, concerned with the themes of memory and decay, are considered to be a source of inspiration for a new generation of scholars building their contributions on first-person voices that emerge from displacement. In Sebaldian narratives, authors make places visible by their sole being-in, where it is not essential to travel from point A to point B but rather coming into terms with the sensorial effects of cumulative trajectories, and thus place "is in a sense what happens" (Wylie 2007, 181); not surprisingly, this form of writing also advocates for the de-construction of linear time, employing "a subtle form of literary montage that operates by a process of juxtaposition and discontinuity" (Hill 2013, 392). Challenging the standard scientific rationale, the result is not a quest for a single absolute truth but an invitation to critique – in other words, it consists of a *situated* perspective amongst many potential others, fuelling a notion of positionality that "does not claim objectivity and fixity, but emphasizes its own subjectivity and fluidity" (Weston 2011, 174). If said format and mission are no longer strangers in the realm of academic prose, I have attempted to achieve a supplementary degree of freedom creativity by verbalizing my approach to cyclical ruins through poetry. In this sense, poetry functions as a research method and valid mode of scholarly expression provided that the subject "is attuned to the way in which thinking and feeling are intertwined" (Paiva 2020), evidencing the conviction that experimental encounters with unobserved urban ambiances demand innovative forms of writing.

Nevertheless, despite text is the usual channel to disseminate academic findings, its capacity to communicate affect is occasionally limited – particularly at the time of facing sensorial moments that cannot be fully realized in language; thus, non-textual works come to fill this gap, facilitating knowledge translation as manifested in the growing body of art-led, scholarly contributions that employ alternative methods such as audio-visual creations, comics, and photo-essays alike (Philips and Kara 2021). Alongside the importance of photography, the use of video in ruin research is emerging as a hitherto unorthodox way to (re)present more effectively and affectively, not necessarily constrained to the formalisms of documentary making but prompting an artistic vision that provides value and credibility to subjective expressions (Arboleda 2021). Video's capacity to register movement, time, light changes, weather conditions, wanderlust, architectural scale, and depth of objects and textures lies in combination with the record of sounds and silences on site, activating wider impressions that are susceptible to amplify the haunting qualities of places through the strategic inclusion of music (Fletcher 2012). By revealing a closer sense of "I-was-there", these pieces pursue to share and cause reactions to the viewers (Garrett and Hawkins 2014), and thus, it is not unreasonable to state that, acknowledging that our era is dominated by visual culture, the use of video has the potential to democratize audiences, reaching a higher impact beyond the academia. Hence, though both poetry and video are increasingly popular as creative research methods, their combined power to fulfil academic purposes remains unexplored.

In his work *Videopoetry: A Manifesto*, poet and educator Tom Konyves (2012) coins videopoetry as a new genre that favours self-reflexive sequences and advocates for contrast, fragmentation, and the dissonant, differing it from other expressions where poetry and video coexist. Videopoetry is thus

> displayed on a screen, distinguished by its time-based, poetic juxtaposition of images with text and sound. In the measured blending of these three elements, it produces in the viewer the realization of a poetic experience. [Its function] is to demonstrate the process of thought and the simultaneity of experience, expressed in words – visible and/or audible – whose meaning is blended with, but not illustrated by, the images and the soundtrack. . . . As the work gradually unfolds, it is perceived that the visual (image and/or displayed text) and audible (sound and/or voiced text) elements are fragmented

expressions of the artist's imagination, suggestive of meaning, yet denying clarification of the purported meaning – a teasing, vertiginous exploration of desire. . . . Provided that the image-text-sound juxtapositions exhibit a pleasing balance between narrative and non-narrative moments – achieved through strategic, self-referential disruptions, a demonstration of awareness of the spatial and temporal relationships between elements, intentional repetitions, etc. – a viewer will experience their sense of time suspended or blurred.

(Konyves 2012)

Presented in the next section, the videopoem that accompanies this chapter follows the "how-to" provided by Konyves in his manifesto. First, it consists of a cooperative piece originally conceived by myself, filmed and montaged by Chema Aranda, and poetized by Pawel Jankiewicz – the latter two are usual collaborators of mine and acted according to my coordinating instructions, seeking what Konyves calls a *unified vision*. In the process of filming, Chema Aranda, who is the CEO of Humad® (a Malaga-based communication company), mostly employed still and fluid-motion shots, causing the engagement with the work in contrast to hand-held shots which, according Konyves, tend to be more disrupting and thus problematic. A first version of the videopoem was then edited through image-sound juxtapositions supplemented by a voiced-over sample poem, and presented to independent writer Pawel Jankiewicz, who did not join us on our journey though admitted that our assembling strategy caused him a surprising, mysterious effect in line with Konyves' vision towards *suggestive indirect relationships*. After sharing my field notes, thoughts, and conducting multiple online conversations with Pawel, he wrote an ad hoc poem that, similar to the drafted videopoem, lacked story-telling style though it provided a counterpoint, and yet the text, in Konyves' words, functions as "the essential catalyst in the transformation of a work from 'poetic' to poetry". From here, soundtrack arrangements – sound effects, music, and voiced text – constituted the penultimate phase to, paraphrasing Konyves, strengthen the sensorial capacity of the videopoem. The piece benefited from ambient soundings and silences to remark a syntactical structure, while the choice of music moved from soft and modulated to elegiac and epic. In order to recite the poem, a professional voice-over artist was hired, and he granted us with three versions that were multivariate in tone (affected; natural; passionate) so their combination enhances the whole work's internal rhythm. As such, all the elements of the soundtrack emphasize, accent, and support the emotional content of the videopoem, which was ultimately intensified by six daily sessions of colour adjustments. Last, with the purpose of optimising legibility, subtitles were accurately synchronized and added in "white, sans-serif font on a separate display below the screen" (Konyves 2012).

After nearly four years from conceptualization to execution, it is my hope that, by following Konyves' guidelines, the viewer is transported to my state of mind during the journeying, bringing closer, and triggering, a *poetic experience* for which it is only required to "press PLAY".

Press PLAY[1]

Figure 6.1 QR Code for Cyclical Ruins videopoem.

An invitation to critique

In essence, CYCLICAL RUINS is not a videopoem on sand and sun tourism spaces in the low season but on *what can be sensed* when exploring these in that particular time of the year. The piece was thought and elaborated under the premise of translating a similar degree of reflective complexity than the one found in the empirical section of a conventional academic writing; however, on this occasion, I opted for a creative, poetic language that dialogues with powerful visuals and soundings, forming altogether a suggestive assemblage that aims to result comprehensive beyond scholarship. Yet, this videopoem may well be embedded within the long-standing tradition of literacy and further artistic expressions carried out by travellers, writers, and researchers who, ruminating in and on ruination, placed their feelings at the core of their works. That being said, we would do wrong in perceiving CYCLICAL RUINS as a minor approach when compared to established academic formalisms, and thus the videopoem as a methodological output offers an added value over what it is solely meant to be read.

CYCLICAL RUINS was filmed in Andalusia, but it could have been filmed anywhere else: The portrayed spaces are not distinct from other sun and sand destinations. Intentionally, the videopoem does not show any information that could lead the viewer to identify exact locations because these are not considered relevant to understand the magnitude of seasonal abandonment. Indeed, the crucial here is that the spectator, regardless of their origin, recognizes and engages with those standard architectures and neutral spatial configurations prompted by massive forms of global urban planning. As such, since distances are huge and there is rarely a landmark, these spaces are made neither for walking nor for easing social encountering: They are not the city understood as a node of common life. On the contrary, fenced blocks dominate a landscape pierced by roads that pretend to be streets; unplanned, the public space tends to be the leftover from the private. And further, the sense of decontextualization is heightened by close-ups showing a symbolic material culture (i.e. colourful amusement rides; festive letterings; leaning umbrellas) that exemplifies the minimal expression of those contrasting emotions caused by entangled temporalities, where ruined ambiance is also composed by the particular weather of the winter season in which the fieldwork took place. Yet the cloudy skies and the dimmed light, the sound of the hitting wind, the goose bumps by cold, and the smell of the rain added up to the feeling of abandonment. Invisible to our collective imaginary once the summer is over, where do these spaces and objects go during the low season? The answer is that they remain, only to be taken by a faceless mannequin paralleling the witnessed anonymity while grounding a sense of human scale. An experimental observer who, in the land of hauntings, paradoxically becomes a ghost too.

The mannequin is a male one, also white, young, and bodily normative. He plays as a *persona*, a character taken on by myself (the resembling author) to speak in a first-person poem. This stylistic decision leaves the door open to think about different potential experiences that could have been felt in case the individual was other. In fact, the visiting of modern ruins is an activity criticized for its limitation to involve more diverse voices in terms of gender, race, and physical ability (Bennett 2013; Mott and Roberts 2013). This is important because though an implicit discrimination within the practice does not seem to exit (Garrett and Hawkins 2013), the truth is that masculine narratives are dominant to the extent of presenting the subject's imaginary as a sort of heroic conqueror of the space (Garrett 2013). This may well be the case of our mannequin, occasionally portrayed as a contemplative figure domesticating the horizon, however, as this chapter has shown, said placing is not at odds with words that, amongst further impressions, express vulnerability – something ultimately stressed by the mannequin's nude condition. Also, he speaks English with a distinctive British accent, a feature that could be reasonably linked to one of the main nationalities visiting Andalusia in summer thought this – once more – stylistic choice has more to do with the semiotics of language conventionalism in academia pursuing a global comprehension and authority that might have been at stake if I had voiced the poem by myself. In sum, the mannequin operates as a fictional being to channel and verbalize my reality, and his limitations must be understood, partly, as my own.

Be that as it may, sun and sand tourism destinations are places to be rediscovered. Moved by curiosity, my fieldwork responded to the desire of visiting these when they are stripped of their essence, enjoying the rare privilege of having nobody around. Yet I forced myself to be out of context (to the extent that my mere presence occasionally made me look suspicious) because one is not supposed to be there in December – it has no sense, somehow. As a result of observing the unobserved, CYCLICAL RUINS is a meticulous exercise of guilty pleasure whose visual and aural aesthetics aim to trick the audience through the employment of a careful, beautiful montage. Being-in was a two-folded experience and so it is its (re)presentation, where fascination sits at one side without undermining criticism. Hence, the videopoem's interest does not lie so much on what it shows but on what is left unsaid, raising a series of uncomfortable, elephant-in-the-room questions: How suitable and sustainable is to keep investing on the erection of places that are only used for a few months over the year? In which ways do abandoned architectures contest the actual economic system that fuelled them? What role does urban ambiance play in the collective identity of a given society when spaces are temporarily deserted?

In Spain, the categorization of a building as "a ruin" is a task reserved to technical experts formally denoting that a certain state of decay has no way back and is beyond help: The "ruin" is thus a pejorative label to be avoided. And despite recent academic approaches that seek the re-consecration of the modern ruin – mines included – this time I have played with the malleable meaning of ruin to stress its dual qualities. On one hand, cyclical ruins are celebrated for the phenomenological possibilities they offer, though on the other they serve to point towards a development scheme whose success is directly proportional to the territory it swallows. I cannot help thinking that ruins "exist by the gaze's effect through which we look at them" (Augé 2003, 50, own translation), and here, my usage of the term "ruin" may well sound exaggerated for it is a deliberate provocation. I am critical, but I am neither judgemental nor categorical. I understand that the sun and sand model must produce a benefit though questioning this sounds almost anti-patriotic in a country that rarely discuss the tourism dogma – especially, in a pandemic context where authorities made a huge effort to project Spain as a safe destination in a desperate plea to keep receiving visitors. But a society that insists on acting as a servant can hardly evolve, and yet CYCLICAL RUINS' ultimate goal is the employment of sensed ambiances to contest a dominant narrative around Spanish nationhood, guiding us to reflect on the not-always-true promises stated by the system. As seen in the videopoem's credits, the pouring of concrete over the country's coastline is far from ending, and perhaps, Spain would do well in re-thinking what it is at present and whether it is in a position to offer alternatives.

Acknowledgements

Thanks to everyone who contributed on the elaboration of the videopoem, particularly to Chema Aranda and Pawel Jankiewicz, with whom it is always a great pleasure to collaborate. My gratitude is extended to Daniel Donaire for accompanying us during the fieldwork, and to Rafael de Lacour for his assistance in the selection of shooting locations. I shout out to my mentors Hayden Lorimer and Lazaros Karaliotas for securing the necessary independence to tackle this research. Last but not least, thanks to Alfredo González-Ruibal, whose support was crucial to sketch a first conceptualization of "cyclical ruins".

Funding

This work has been originally funded through a Postdoctoral Research Fellowship granted by the Urban Studies Foundation. The writing's final materialization unfolded while the author was granted a "Juan de la Cierva-Incorporación"

Postdoctoral position; this contract is part of the fellowship IJC2020–042599-I, funded by MCIN/AEI/10.13039/501100011033, and by the European Union "NextGenerationEU/PRTR".

Note

1 Full access to the videopoem is available at https://vimeo.com/644278107.

References

Aledo, A. 2008. "From the Land to Ground: The Transformation of the Landscape and the New Residential Tourism." *Arbor: Ciencia, Pensamiento y Cultura* 184 (729): 99–113.

Allmark, P. 2011. "Safe Spectatorship? Photography, Space, Terrorism and the London Bombings." In *Environment, Space, Place* 3(1), edited by G. Backhaus, 140–162. Bucharest: Zeta Books.

Alves, B., R. Ballester, R. Rigall-I-Torrent, Ó. Ferreira, and J. Benavente. 2017. "How Feasible is Coastal Management? A Social Benefit Analysis of a Coastal Destination in SW Spain." *Tourism Management* 60: 188–200.

Andrews, H. 2012. "Another Place or Just Another Space? Liminality and Crosby Beach." In *Liminal Landscapes: Travel, Experience and Spaces In-between*, edited by H. Andrews and L. Roberts, 152–166. London: Routledge.

Arboleda, P. 2017. "Ruins Come What May: A Trip to the Capital of Spainistan." *Cultural Geographies* 25 (1): 221–228.

Arboleda, P. 2021. "A New Sensibility towards Unfinished Ruins: Affective Knowledge Translation through Experimental Video." *Space and Culture*. https://doi.org/10.1177/1206331221989962.

Armstrong, J. 2010. "On the Possibility of Spectral Ethnography." *Cultural Studies ↔ Critical Methodologies* 10 (3): 243–250.

Assaker, G., and R. Hallak. 2012. "European Travelers' Return Likelihood and Satisfaction with Mediterranean Sun-and-sand Destinations: A Chi-square Automatic Identification Detector–based Segmentation Approach." *Journal of Vacation Marketing* 18 (2): 105–120.

Augé, M. 1995. *Non-Places: Introduction to an Anthropology of Supermodernity*. London: Verso.

Augé, M. 2003. *El Tiempo en Ruinas*. Barcelona: Gedisa.

Banco de España. 2019. "Informe Anual 2019." Accessed April 7, 2021. https://repositorio.bde.es/bitstream/123456789/13053/1/InfAnual_2019-Rec4.1.pdf.

Bennett, L. 2013. "Who Goes There? Accounting for Gender in the Urge to Explore Abandoned Military Bunkers." *Gender, Place and Culture* 20 (5): 630–646.

Berger, P., dir. 2003. *Torremolinos 73*. Madrid: Estudios Picasso.

Brandt, S. L. 2009. "The City as Liminal Space: Urban Visuality and Aesthetic Experience in Postmodern U.S. Literature and Cinema." *Amerikastudien/American Studies* 54 (4): 553–581.

Carro, I. 2019. *Ensayo y error Benidorm*. Seville: Barrett.

Chirbes, R. 2007. *Crematorio*. Barcelona: Anagrama.

Coixet, I., dir. 2020. *Nieva en Benidorm*. Madrid: El Deseo.

Crouch, D. 2012. "Afterword." In *Liminal Landscapes: Travel, Experience and Spaces In-between*, edited by H. Andrews and L. Roberts, 234–241. London: Routledge.

DeSilvey, C., and T. Edensor. 2013. "Reckoning with Ruins." *Progress in Human Geography* 37 (4): 465–485.

Dillon, B. 2011. *Ruins*. Cambridge, MA: Whitechapel Gallery, MIT Press.

Dobraszczyk, P. 2017. *The Dead City: Urban Ruins and the Spectacle of Decay*. London: I.B. Tauris.

Domínguez, I. 2015. *Mediterráneo Descapotable: Un Viaje Ridículo por aquel País tan Feliz*. Madrid: Libros del K.O.

Edensor, T. 2005. "The Ghosts of Industrial Ruins: Ordering and Disordering Memory in Excessive Space." *Environment and Planning D: Society and Space* 23 (6): 829–849.

Expósito, D., J. Villanueva, J. Rojas, and V. Sainz. 2020. "Madrid se Vacía por el Coronavirus." *El País*, March 15, 2020. Accessed March 10, 2021. https://elpais.com/elpais/2020/03/14/album/1584179918_645596.html#foto_gal_1.

Fletcher, L. 2012. "The Sound of Ruins: Sigur Rós' Heima and the Post-rock Elegy for Place." *Interference: A Journal of Audio Cultures* 2. www.interferencejournal.org/the-sound-of-ruins/.

Fraser, E. 2012. "Urban Exploration as Adventure Tourism: Journeying beyond the Everyday." In *Liminal Landscapes: Travel, Experience and Spaces In-between*, edited by H. Andrews and L. Roberts, 136–151. London: Routledge.

García, H. 2014. "The Vicious Cycle of Residential Tourism: Analysis of Local Factors of Spanish Property Boom." *PASOS: Revista de Turismo y Patrimonio Cultural* 12 (2): 395–408.

García-Moreno, A. E., C. Rosa-Jiménez, and M. J. Márquez-Ballesteros. 2016. "The Banal as Heritage of Costa del Sol. Torremolinos (1959-1979)." *PASOS: Revista de Turismo y Patrimonio Cultural* 14 (1): 253–273.

Garrett, B. 2010. "Assaying History: Creating Temporal Junctions through Urban Exploration." *Environment and Planning D: Society and Space* 29 (6): 1048–1067.

Garrett, B. 2013. *Explore Everything: Place-Hacking the City*. London: Verso Books.

Garrett, B., and H. Hawkins. 2013. "And Now for Something Completely Different . . . Thinking through Explorer Subject-Bodies: A Response to Mott and Roberts." *Antipode*. https://radicalantipode.files.wordpress.com/2013/11/garrettand-hawkins-response.pdf.

Garrett, B., and H. Hawkins. 2014. "Creative Video Ethnographies: Video Methodologies of Urban Exploration." In *Video Methods: Social Science Research in Motion*, edited by C. Bates, 142–164. London: Routledge.

Hecimovic, A. 2020. "Europe Empties its Streets to Slow Coronavirus." *The Guardian*, March 15, 2020. Accessed March 10, 2021. www.theguardian.com/world/gallery/2020/mar/15/europe-empties-its-streets-to-slow-coronavirus-in-pictures.

Hill, L. 2013. "Archaeologies and Geographies of the Post-industrial Past: Landscape, Memory and the Spectral." *Cultural Geographies* 20 (3): 379–396.

Instituto Nacional de Estadística. 2019. "España en cifras 2019." Accessed April 8, 2021. www.ine.es/prodyser/espa_cifras/2019/51/.

Kimmelman, M. 2020. "The Great Empty." *The New York Times,* March 23, 2020. Accessed March 10, 2021. www.nytimes.com/interactive/2020/03/23/world/coronavirus-great-empty.html.

Konyves, T. 2012. "Videopoetry: A Manifesto." *Critical Inquiry*, October. https://critinq.wordpress.com/2012/10/13/videopoetry-a-manifesto-by-tom-konyves/.

Llaneras, K., B. Andrino, D. Grasso, and O. Medina. 2020. "¿Los Mejores y Peores Sitios para Crecer? En qué Barrios y Ciudades Prosperaron los Hijos de los Noventa." *El País*, July 17, 2020. Accessed April 8, 2021. https://elpais.com/sociedad/2020-07-16/

los-mejores-y-peores-sitios-para-crecer-en-que-barrios-y-ciudades-les-fue-mejor-a-los-hijos-de-los-noventa.html.

Losada, M. A., dir. 2010. *Las Riberas del Mar Océano*. Madrid: RTVE.

Martínez-Medina, A. 2016. "Arquitectura del Boom Turístico (1953–1979)." *Canelobre* 66: 166–185.

Millás, J. J., and O. Clavera. 2017. "Desiertos Urbanos: La Cara B del Turismo de Sol y Playa en España." *El País*, March 7, 2017. Accessed April 12, 2021. https://elpais.com/elpais/2017/03/07/eps/1488841506_148884.html.

Mott, C., and S. M. Roberts. 2013. "Not Everyone Has (the) Balls: Urban Exploration and the Persistence of Masculinist Geography." *Antipode* 46 (1): 229–245.

Natoli, D., dir. 2019. *A Costa del Sol*. Malaga: Peripheria Films.

Natoli, D., dir. 2021. *Se Vende*. Malaga: Peripheria Films.

Orange, H. 2008. "Industrial Archaeology: Its Place within the Academic Discipline, the Public Realm and the Heritage Industry." *Industrial Archaeology Review* 30 (2): 83–95.

Pack, S. D. 2006. *Tourism and Dictatorship: Europe's Peaceful Invasion of Franco's Spain*. New York: Palgrave Macmillan.

Paiva, D. 2019. "Transforming Nature through Cyclical Appropriation or Linear Dominance? Lefebvre's Contributions to Thinking about the Interaction between Human Activity and Nature." In *The Routledge Handbook of Henri Lefebvre, The City and Urban Society*, edited by M. E. Leary-Owhin and J. P. McCarthy, 318–326. London: Routledge.

Paiva, D. 2020. "Poetry as a Resonant Method for Multi-sensory Research." *Emotion, Space and Society* 34: 100655.

Parr, M. 1999. *Benidorm*. Hanover: Sprengel Museum.

Penyas, A. 2021. *Todo bajo el Sol*. Madrid: Salamandra Graphic.

Pétursdóttir, Þ. 2016. "For Love of Ruins." In *Elements of Architecture: Assembling Archaeology, Atmosphere and the Performance of Building Spaces*, edited by T. F. Sørensen and M. Bille, 365–386. London: Routledge.

Pétursdóttir, Þ., and B. Olsen. 2014. "An Archaeology of Ruins." In *Ruin Memories: Materiality, Aesthetics and the Archaeology of the Recent Past*, edited by Þ. Pétursdóttir and B. Olsen, 3–29. London: Routledge.

Philips, R., and H. Kara. 2021. *Creative Writing for Social Research: A Practical Guide*. Bristol: Policy Press.

Royo, L. 2014. "Landscape, Heritage and Architecture in Coastal Tourist Destinations: Notes on the *Costa del Sol*." *Anales de Historia del Arte* 24: 253–263.

Salvans, T. 2020. *Perfect Day*. London: Mack Books.

Sánchez-Cabezudo, J., dir. 2011. *Crematorio*. Madrid: Canal+ España.

Schultz-Dornburg, J. 2012. *Ruinas Modernas: Una Topografía de Lucro*. Barcelona: Àmbit.

Selwyn, T. 2012. "Shifting Borders and Dangerous Liminalities: The Case of Rye Bay." In *Liminal Landscapes: Travel, Experience and Spaces In-between*, edited by H. Andrews and L. Roberts, 169–184. London: Routledge.

Shoard, M. 2002. "Edgelands." In *Remaking the Landscape: The Changing Face of Britain*, edited by J. Jenkins, 117–146. London: Profile Books.

Sontag, S. 2002. *Styles of Radical Will*. New York: Picador.

Thibaud, J. P. 2015. "The Backstage of Urban Ambiances: When Atmospheres Pervade Everyday Experience." *Emotion, Space and Society* 15: 39–46.

Thomassen, B. 2006. "Liminality." In *Routledge Encyclopaedia of Social Theory*, edited by A. Harrington, B. I. Marshall and H. P. Muller, 322–323. London: Routledge.

Thomassen, B. 2012. "Revisiting Liminality: The Danger of Empty Spaces." In *Liminal Landscapes: Travel, Experience and Spaces In-between*, edited by H. Andrews and L. Roberts, 21–35. London: Routledge.

Vázquez, J. J. 2016. "Arquitectura y Fetiche en la Costa del Sol." In *Colección de Investigaciones del Departamento de Proyectos Arquitectónicos de la ETSA Sevilla*, edited by J. J. Vázquez, 313–328. Seville: RU Books.

Weston, D. 2011. "The Spatial Supplement: Landscape and Perspective in W.G. Sebald's *The Rings of Saturn*." *Cultural Geographies* 18 (2): 171–186.

Wylie, J. 2007. "The Spectral Geographies of W.G. Sebald." *Cultural Geographies* 14 (2): 171–188.

Part III

Walking, experiencing, and sensing

7 Commoning the touristic city

Urban pedestrian routes and the ambiguous politics of exploration

*Rachel Brahy, Luca Pattaroni and
Andrew S. Hoffman*

Introduction

At a moment when many Western cities are experiencing and defining themselves as being "in transition" – from former centres of industrial production to hubs of more creative and knowledge-based economies – specific discourses and imaginaries are being formed around the attractiveness of cities and the rise of an ambiguous urban aesthetic regime (Genard et al. 2016). These narratives have led to a bevy of new policies regarding the (re)development and maintenance of urban areas, as well as to a proliferation of socio-material devices that instantiate such policies.

In this chapter, we focus on urban pedestrian routes (henceforth referred to simply as "routes") as one such policy-backed device that is particularly demonstrative of the tensions running through the communal order of contemporary cities. Indeed, the number of these routes has multiplied in recent years, with the Liège Souffle Vert in Belgium, the "themed" routes of Geneva, Switzerland, and La Ligne Vert in Nantes, France, standing in as three hallmark examples.[1] These itineraries, designed and deployed in various urban centres to accompany tourists and residents in the (re)discovery of urban space, aim to highlight sites of ecological, historical, and commercial significance. Our own analysis, in turn, brings to the fore the ambiguous modalities of valorization and framings of exploratory urban experience which these routes instantiate.

In the case of La Ligne Verte,[2] the main focus of this chapter, we find that a thin green line painted on the asphalt and leading around the city of Nantes has an amazing capacity to connect individuals' personal explorations of the city with a whole host of other actors, institutions, devices, and issues: Urban policies, government institutions, carefully renovated industrial buildings, hurrying passers-by, hot button political topics, playing children, local parks, and public art installations, among many other entities dispersed across the urban fabric. Behind the painted line lies Voyage à Nantes (henceforth: VAN), the city's official bureau of tourism whose 300 employees are charged with developing and carrying out culture-based tourism policies in Nantes. The agency dedicates a significant portion of its resources to planning, designing, and maintaining La Ligne Verte, with each annual edition bringing further pieces of the urban landscape into its fold. In

DOI: 10.4324/9781003207207-11

many ways, VAN is itself one piece of a broader history of ambitious and incremental transformations of the postindustrial city dating back some 20 years.[3] Over this period, a number of policy directives have targeted the pedestrianization of the city's centre, counter-cultural and artistic initiatives, and the development of academic activities in Nantes.

Given this backdrop, we approach La Ligne Verte as an instance of what Lascoumes and Le Galès (2007, 4) call a "public policy instrument", and define as follow:

> a device that is both technical and social, that organizes specific social relations between the state and those it is addressed to, according to the representations and meanings it carries. It is . . . a technical device with the generic purpose of carrying a concrete concept of the politics/society relationship and sustained by a concept of regulation.

In our particular example, the device of La Ligne Verte is a socio-material enactment of this history of urban renewal efforts. As such, the route beckons visitors to explore the route and remain open to serendipitous discoveries; at the same time, it also regulates these very relations by way of its material inscriptions, bringing order to the myriad individual engagements with the route and providing a template for specific modes of commoning. Analysing the device in such a way allows us not only to explore the renewed role of experience in urban policies but also draws our attention to the anthropological conditions of public policy instruments and devices.

To do so, we ask several important questions: How is a given route thought out? How does it orient, or frame, the urban experience (Goffman 1991)? What phenomena do these routes privilege, and which things might they obscure? And in what ways do analyses of these routes promote a (re)thinking of questions pertaining to coordination, composition, and the makings of urban commonality (Thévenot 2006)?

The central *problématique* we address here, then, relates to the modes of exploration, experimentation, and sensory confrontation with the urban environment. It is linked to broader political questions concerning the conditions of possibility for individuals and groups to stand and express themselves in public space. The interest of socio-material devices like the aforementioned pedestrian routes lies from an analytical point of view in the possibility of thinking the contours of making commonality in the city, based on what Auray and Vétel (2013) refer to as engaging in a regime of *exploration*. Such a regime sits alongside and oftentimes in uneasy relation to several other so-called regimes of engagement and grammars of commonality in the plural as outlined in what sociologist Laurent Thévenot's calls a *sociology of engagements* (Thévenot 2006, 2014; Thévenot and Kareva 2018).

This opens up the study of an emerging "grammar of commonality in the plural" which we hypothesize is gaining in importance in the "aesthetic turn" of urban policies (Thévenot 2015; Blokker and Brighenti 2011). Indeed, when urban space is developed, for example by laying down a pedestrian route or installing large public artworks, and when the experience of that space is guided quite literally by lines, indications, and markings painted on the ground, the expression and coordination of a city's inhabitants and/or visitors occur vis-à-vis shared access to these socio-material elements. Moreover, these elements are equally capable of facilitating an experience of enjoyment for those who may simply opt to follow the route, as they are of prompting more (inter)active and sometimes transgressive engagements with the route, such as when users add to or redirect the route itself. Thus, new ways of being in the city – alone or together, organized or open – are invented and take shape in conversation with these devices.

In what follows, we introduce a theoretical framework that allows us to apprehend, in ideal-typical terms, the plurality of rationales for individuals' presence in urban space, and the different possibilities of composing them, or what Pattaroni (e.g. 2015) has previously referred to as constructing the "common of the city". Then, we will detail our case study of La Ligne Verte in Nantes, France, where we show by which characteristics, linked to this device, the "exploring experience" is framed and enrolled in enacting particular versions of commoning. The analysis continues with a discussion of the spectrum of users' engagements with La Ligne Verte we have observed – running from conformity to confrontation, with some uses deemed more legitimate and others less so – in terms of our notion of "composition". We then conclude with a reflection on the ambivalence carried by pedestrian routes such as La Ligne Verte and the emergence of contemporary urban policies supporting these devices. Before proceeding, however, we first offer a brief overview of the methods we have employed in conducting this study.

Methods

Empirically, our analysis is based on the study of the La Ligne Verte in Nantes, France, which has been designed, implemented, and maintained by a local organization called Voyage à Nantes (VAN) since the first installation in 2012. Our data consists of three main types: Field notes from participant observations conducted during two visits to La Ligne Verte; ethnographic interviews with those involved in managing the route and other similar initiatives; as well as content analysis of published materials about the route.

In the case of participant observation, we made two several-day research trips to visit La Ligne Verte, the first in 2017 and the second in 2018. On these spring and summer trips to Nantes, we walked the line several times over the course of each visit, taking care to experience it at different times of day, on both weekdays and weekends, sometimes doing so independently and other times in the company of two residents of Nantes (a man and his child, who were aware of our research ambitions). As we followed the route, we stopped to marvel at its many installations, taking periodic breaks at public benches or large flower pots along the way to make additional observations of the surroundings and to record these experiences in our book of field notes. In the evenings, we would reflect on each of the tours and the in vivo notes taken along the way, developing and structuring them and adding additional details where pertinent. The central questions guiding this auto-ethnographic praxis relate to what La Ligne Verte "does" to the urban experience: how it structures or accompanies the experiences, what supports or affordances it offers, and what forms of attention it directs. In line with Winkin's approach to auto-ethnography (2013), we used ourselves and our feelings as the "first instrument" of our research, paying deep reflective attention to these phenomena.[4]

In addition to these more experiential and auto-ethnographic modes of participant observation, between 2017 and 2020 we also conducted a few dozen semi-structured interviews with actors involved in various aspects of La Ligne Verte, some of which were conducted during our visits and others held remotely. Our respondents were primarily permanent employees of VAN, working in the functions of direction, communication, promotion, and curation of public artworks to be included in the route (the latter of which is beyond the scope of this chapter). However, two of our interviews were with actors in the cultural sector but not explicitly involved in VAN, with the objective of gathering perspectives of "outsiders" and understanding any counter-proposals to the route which had been put forth. A third and final source of data for our analysis consisted of both hard copy and digital texts about the route: published promotional brochures – targeted at both visitors and journalists – which were an excellent source for descriptions of the sites of interest, route maps, attendance figures, and narratives about the route aimed at attracting visitors; the official website for La Ligne Verte; digital news sites reporting on the city of Nantes, and whose coverage included pieces about La Ligne Verte; as well as other websites, such as TripAdvisor, where visitors' reviews of the route include details about their experiences following it.

On the plurality of registers of presence in the city and the composing of the common

There are many reasons why people may choose to visit or live in a given city. For residents, urban areas afford relatively easy access to economic and commercial hubs, and physical infrastructure such as public transportation supports this access. For visitors, it is often the draw of cultural celebrations, sports matches, or commercial events that motivates their presence. Inhabitants and visitors to cities have long been subject to regimes of urban governance, where policy determines the contours of the urban environment, setting out the conditions for stimulating or restricting the flow of human bodies and dictating the boundaries of legitimate presence in urban space. In this regard, there is clear political salience in the management of cities wherein urban policy becomes an indicator of democratic access and allowable forms of expression afforded to citizens. Lefebvre (1968) thought about this in terms of "the right to the city" (*le droite à la ville*), his critique of growing commodification of urban centres, the individualization of urban inhabitants' access to cities, and the inequalities thusly produced – all downstream effects of capitalism. This resolved in a call to reclaim urban centres as a type of commons whose visions and governance would be collectively decided, and where cultural life could proceed in ways that resist commodification.

From this brief description, it is quite easy to see that there exist many different registers or motives for being present in the city. Thought in a slightly different way, we can say that these different registers correspond to distinct modes of coordination such as those highlighted in more classical sociological theories of action, like Weber's (1921) distinction between rational action in purpose or value and affect-driven or tradition-driven action. Laurent Thévenot's *Sociology of Engagements* provides its own useful heuristic for thinking in this way, and his architecture of "regimes of engagement" outlines several different ways in which such presence might take shape (Thévenot 2006).

First, let us point out what the latter author refers to as a "regime of justification" (Thévenot 2006; Boltanski and Thévenot 2006), where coordination is oriented towards making one's voice heard in public. Political demonstrations, for instance, seek to constitute public space as a (temporary) forum for disputing and debating questions of justice; their often critical or denunciatory discursive inflections are indicative of this category of action. Next, let us note events of a more commercial or market-oriented nature, which correspond to a "regime of planned engagement" (Thévenot 1995), and are regularly studied as "vectors of urbanity" (*vecteurs de citadinité*) that trigger other forms of urban sociality (La Pradelle 2001). Discourses of strategy or planning immediately signal this regime, where what is at stake is nothing less than the practical realization of an activity or task. In our brief example, this consists of activities related to commercial exchange, but such a mode of coordination also extends to any goal-oriented presence or movement: going to the bakery to buy bread, visiting an acquaintance's house for a party, arranging a tennis match with a fellow club member, and the like.

In a third mode of coordination, dubbed the "regime of familiarity", we can consider the routine outings that residents of a city might make: those that lead them to play in the streets with kids from the neighbourhood, to take their dog for a walk along a familiar path, or to simply step out outside for a breath of fresh air. All of these also constitute a different modality of presence in the city, but one that relies on other attentional and affective modes of engagement that can be said to be "familiar" insofar as this presence in public space is based on situated knowledge of a place and on the routinization of activity that allows to orient oneself without thinking. The fourth and final regime of engagement we will discuss here is what Auray and Vétel (2013) have labelled the "regime of exploratory engagement". As its name may suggest, this regime presupposes curious, exploratory presences that remain open to adventure and to serendipity. A tourist who simply sets out for a walk in a new city, unguided by the map app on their mobile phone (which would be more of a planned engagement), or a city denizen taking a turn down a street they'd never noticed before: These are both instances of engaging in exploration, in letting oneself be guided by the unusual rather than planned or familiar modes of coordinating with oneself in space.

These different regimes of engagement are not only relevant as ideal-typical categories for understanding the diverse forms of being present in the city. Rather, they also serve to help us better understand the ways in which sharing and mutual engagements can be constituted, namely as grounds for establishing a common urban order. The regime of justification thus makes it possible to constitute sharing based on the valuation of common goods and the collective qualification of the importance of each person. In the regime of the plan, we find mutualization by way of a capacity to build collective projects ranging from informal agreements amongst neighbours to more formal contracts recognizing the interest and role of each of the participants. In the regime of familiarity, sharing and mutual coordination is done through a careful relation to the other, allowing fine adjustments and reciprocal sensitivity to one another's singularities (Thévenot 2015).

But the question now arises: What does mutualization look like in a regime of exploratory engagement? Would it be more resistant to sharing than what we find in other regimes? On what foundations would this mutualization be based? Returning to our case of urban pedestrian routes, we consider La Ligne Verte as enacting possibilities for a commoning of singular experiences. In doing so, it promises to make diverse forms of exploration communicate, ultimately resulting in the composition of new political form(s).

The course, a source of shared material support

While still allowing a sense of openness and freedom for those who might follow urban pedestrian routes, their material arrangements (indications, markings on the ground, etc.) nevertheless surface as a powerful tool for structuring experiences of presence in the city. Three aspects relating to this feature quickly appear to the observer. First, such routes *delimit*: They supply a thread of attention and interest, which works to frame a space that it defines. Thus, they also direct the gaze on certain objects within their space of circulation, rendering some things visible and others less so (e.g. Brighenti 2016). Second, urban pedestrian routes propose an *order*: Quite literally, they inform – indeed, determine – a path, a progression, a way of moving through an arranged space. Third, these routes mark out *discoveries*: They indicate the length of the itinerary, the places to stop (close to or far from each other, within or outwith the range of the eye) and suggest a cadence or, more fundamentally, a rhythm – yet one whose ultimate adoption is up to those who might visit a given route. These dimensions can be illustrated empirically, which we do here using the example of La Ligne Verte, one such cultural device located in the French city of Nantes.

In focusing on the explicitly material aspects of La Ligne Verte, a detailed history of the vast territorial cultural policies that have given rise to the route is beyond the scope of the present analysis. Suffice it to say that the route is the outcome of several decades of regional investments in culture and has, since its first edition in 2012, been designed and maintained by the aforementioned VAN. The organization is led by Jean Blaise, a very well-known and recognized cultural animator in the region and a close associate of former Nantes mayor Jean-Marc Ayrault, who held office from 1989 until 2012.[5]

In more concrete terms, La Ligne Verte is quite simply a green line (whence its name, translated into English as "The Green Line") painted on the ground, which extends for about 12 km around the city. As a public installation, the route is open year-round and leads visitors to a range of sites and designations aiming to reflect its "sensitive and poetic" essence. Its stops include "a work signed by a great artist" (*d'une œuvre signée par un grand artiste*); a "remarkable element of heritage" (*un élément remarquable du patrimoine*); "the must-see attractions of the destination" (*des incontournables de la destination*); and "little known treasures" (*des trésors méconnus*) of the region. Moreover, the route spans eras and periods – taking wanderers "from a historic alleyway to contemporary architecture" (*d'une ruelle historique à une architecture contemporaine*) – as well as nature-culture divides, leading them "from an amazing view of the city to an incredible sunset over the estuary" (*d'un point de vue étonnant sur la ville à un incroyable coucher de soleil sur l'estuaire*).[6] The route thusly presented serves to emphasize its role as both an arbiter of cultural significance for the city's inhabitants and as an attraction for tourists visiting Nantes from elsewhere. It continues to speak to both audiences in as much as further points of interest have been added in each of the route's subsequent annual iterations.

But how can we say that it delimits a thread of attention and interest for these visitors? In which ways does it order a path? And how does it give rhythm to a progression? It is to these questions which we now turn our attention.

Delineating spaces, triggering attention

Compared to printed guides like those published by Routard or Lonely Planet, which require the reading and appropriation of a map or a text through its correspondence to a physical space, the guidance offered by La Ligne Verte is much more accessible. The signage is clear, and by following the painted markings on the ground, it is possible to "do" the route at a lower cognitive cost, a point to which many visitors, including families, have testified in their online reviews of La Ligne Verte.[7] As researchers engaged in an auto-ethnographic study of the route, this was precisely our experience upon discovering and following it for the first time, during a visit to Nantes in Summer 2018. Consider, for example, the following note RB jotted down in her book of field notes[8]:

> I can stroll without the risk of getting lost. What is frequented is expected/ authorized, is signalled to me: I will not disturb anyone; nor will I surprise them. I am driven. The world to be discovered is marked out for me. What facilities! All I have to do is follow the line and go on a trip. I feel safer [than elsewhere in the same circumstances of time and unfamiliarity with the place]. I dare to walk in places that would have seemed unusual at times. I am not afraid.
>
> (First impressions, Monday, 9 July 2018)

Thus, by supporting orientation, as much as by signalling places of pause, zones of meeting possibilities (cafés, benches), and the like through the thread of its physical inscription in the urban terrain, the route produces a form of reassurance in those who visit it. We are thinking in particular of children and single women, who literally find themselves accompanied by the green line. The route thus contributes to a sense of authorization (a permission to circulate) and instils a sense of confidence (to carry on) amongst those who follow it. This reflects the manifold nature of presence, which is a physical capacity (to be there); a cognitive capacity (to know how to be there); and an embodied capacity (processing the emotional intensities of being there) (Brahy 2019, 2020). Moreover, presence is also related to legitimacy and hospitality (Stavo-Debauge 2017), where the concern about the validity of the presence (i.e. who has a right or warrant to be there) and, more broadly, the risk of an infringement (upon those for whom another's presence may have an impact) are at stake. With the route's painted line, these two conditions of possibility of a trusting presence seem guaranteed.

Beyond the question of presence, the route also serves to frame or (in)form the follower's gaze. Such is the case with the addition of pictograms during the Summer 2018 edition of La Ligne Verte, wherein images of eyes were painted on the ground alongside the green line itself, serving to indicate particular places of interest for visitors and thus intensifying the supports for attentional engagement (Fig. 7.1). Through these pictograms, the device contributes to the establishment

Figure 7.1 Legend for pictogram in brochures: "Remarkable site, nearby exhibition" (July 2018).

Photo: Rachel Brahy

of attentional zones, where followers' attentional efforts are channelled towards specific spatial points as if to say: "Look over *here!*"[9] Thinking with Goffman ([1974] 1991), the pictograms work as "frames" that (re)modalize attention, prompting a disruption of one's walking rhythm if not a lifting of eyeballs from the ground to a particular place on the horizon. The visitor is thus led to try and match the attentional signal of the pictogram (i.e. the prompt *to* look somewhere) with the particular phenomenon of interest (the *what* that is supposed to be seen). Importantly, these pictographic supports can only ever be suggestive insofar as they provide no further textual or visual clues for exactly what it is that should be seen from any given vantage point. The frame, then, is only partially complete and retains elements of uncertainty that invite exploration. The visitor to La Ligne Verte is thus never guaranteed to have seen what was to be seen, as it were.

Propose an order

While working to sustain uncertainty along certain axes, the device simultaneously works to reduce uncertainty along other axes. In this latter case, the route organizes the experience of walking in the city by ordering it.

Strictly speaking, La Ligne Verte is in fact a closed loop rather than a straight line, and there is nothing essential to the route in the way of a specific chronology: In theory, one can follow the route in any direction, and need not begin or end at any particular point along the way. However, a cursory glance at the route's official website or at its promotional materials (such as the brochures produced for the 2020–2021 season, which we consulted in our content analysis) reveals that the different "stops" along the route are numbered in a logical sequence and thus clearly suggest an "order" in which the route should be followed.

For instance, upon visiting the website for the 2018 edition of the route, we observed that visitors are offered the option of viewing the route "in images" (*voir en images*), "on the map" (*voir sur le plan*), or else viewing it "in order" (*voir le parcours dans l'ordre*).[10] When selecting this third option, we are informed that the first stop of the route is the central railway station in Nantes while the second stop is the nearby Le Lieu Unique: A jewel of Nantes, formerly the home of the LU cookie factory – famous throughout France for its Petit Beurre biscuits and sugary Boudoirs (similar to a "Lady Finger" cookie) – which, in January 2001, was converted into what is now branded as "an atypical and multidisciplinary arts centre" dedicated to "the spirit of discovery in different fields of art" (Le Lieu Unique, n.d.; c.f. [Carmo et al. 2022; Pattaroni 2020] on the inclusion of centres of alternative culture in the tourist landscape of European cities). Similarly, in the official La Ligne Verte guidebook from that same year, visitors are invited to follow "les 54 étapes *à découvrir dans l'ordre du parcours* . . . du Lieu Unique jusqu'au Jardin des plantes . . . ou inversement!" ("the 54 stops, *to be discovered in the order of the route* . . . from the Lieu Unique biscuit factory to the Botanical Garden . . . or in reverse" (Le Voyage à Nantes 2018, 75; italics ours)!

In short, punctuated by 52 stops (in the 2021 edition), the route suggests sequences and arrangements that can appear as micro-contexts for people who are enacted across the route's various stages as "visitors", "curious" explorers, "meditators", "clients", etc. In other words, at each step of the itinerary, a single register of action is favoured above others for visitors. So too does the suggested sequencing of stops along the route point to a privileging of certain phenomena: modes of transportation (e.g. train travel), local establishments (restaurants, bars, shops), cultural spectacles (public artworks and community arts centres), and even entire neighbourhoods (with pictograms encouraging visitors to stop often in certain neighbourhoods, while the route passes through others more quickly, or even bypasses them entirely).

Arranged in such a way, the route aims to foster a disposition of curiosity and open exploration among those who visit it. Yet this nevertheless rubs up against the delimited set of goals suggested by the many stops along the way and the manner in which they are sequenced. Do these bifurcated tendencies speak to setting some forms of equivalence between cultural, commercial, and patrimonial purposes? What articulations or correspondences seem to impose themselves between these aims? Is a precedence given to some of them over others? A whole series of questions that we will not be able to answer here but that the device raises, showing itself also as a "common place" open to multiple interpretative, cognitive, and even practical arrangements.

Pace the discovery

On the basis of our previous description, one can see how in maintaining openings and ambivalences in its design and its rhythms – recall the pictograms, which suggest the presence of notable spectacles but does not name them – La Ligne Verte delicately frames the experience of its visitors without completely overwhelming it with structure and detail. It says not simply what *should* happen along the route, but places great emphasis on what *could* happen there, remaining open to experiences that may overflow the prescribed frame and giving rise to novel compositions or situated contestations.

In sum, the material inscription of the route as a literal green line painted on the ground works to create continuity, a thread. And yet it also signals ruptures, breaks, openings in urban space: offering places to stop along the way, beckoning visitors to play next to shopping areas or to admire works of art, and in a more general sense, to let oneself be surprised. In its material construction and narrative style, the route invites diverse interpretations, heterogeneous uses, and rhythmic multiplicity; in the latter case, the rhythms tend to be decelerated, punctuated, thus placing them in tension with the seamless rapidity that is so characteristic of most comings and goings in urban public space. In this way, we noted on our own visits to La Ligne Verte that the route functions as device for resuming rhythmic control over urban itineraries, even while certain zones along the way occurred to us as being almost too dense with discoveries and stimuli, threatening to saturate the visitor to the point of exhaustion (Antonioli et al. 2021).

On the plurality of uses, expressions, and sharing

By offering a frame for visitors – suggesting an order, and a rhythm with which it may be followed – La Ligne Verte normalizes certain experiences, modes of presence, and formats of expressiveness in urban public space. As we have seen, the frames are themselves derived from the territorial cultural policies, which function as conditions of possibility for the existence of urban pedestrian routes in the first place. Uses and modes of participation that conform with the intention of such routes can be said to stick with the "script" as it were (Akrich 1992). However, there also exist uses and modes of participation that may sit tension with such expectations – or, indeed, oppose the script outright. In this section, we discuss several instances where visitors have engaged with the route, some that have been judged to be in alignment with the frame, and others that have sought to overflow it, opening a space for criticism through alteration.

Sidestepping questions of public attachment

In our interviews with employees of VAN, the organization that oversees La Ligne Verte, one line of questioning was about what were considered to be "legitimate" uses of the route. Among the responses, our interlocutors indicated that they take delight when visitors "take pictures of themselves", "take selfies in front of the works [of art]", "post [their photos on] Instagram", and when they "play on the playgrounds". The employees see these participative and playful behaviours as clear signals of their operation's success. Indeed, after a period of resistance and public scrutiny, some of the largest and most notable cultural institutions in the world now actively encourage the taking of selfies and use them as a tool for international promotion.[11]

In the case of La Ligne Verte, the scripted, playful engagements invoked by our respondents are a feature of what Breviglieri calls the "guaranteed city": an urban space which offers denizens a range of "certified options" (Breviglieri 2013, 227) whose predictability and comparability take precedence over other modes of evaluation, like those oriented towards feeling at home in one's surroundings, or upon qualifications of urban space oriented towards principles of solidarity or ecological sustainability (Blok 2015). The guarantee offered in this case is not intended to produce a homogenization of urban space, as was the case with the "functionalist" urban policies of the 1970s and 1980s (Cogato et al. 2013). Rather, it is more ambiguous in nature, engendering a regulated diversity aimed at aligning conduct, thereby reducing the possibility of disruptions to the political and commercial happenings within city limits. It is for this reason we argue that journeys which follow La Ligne Verte are, in the first instance, carried out according to what we earlier referred to as a regime *of planned engagement*, which strives for the achievement of a goal that has been mapped out in advance. What is more, Breviglieri goes on to suggest that one of the most notable characteristics of contemporary guaranteed cities is their capacity to render "excesses" as manageable events (Breviglieri 2018b, 5). Thus, the route-qua-device makes it possible – through its openness and flexibility – to (re)incorporate the unforeseen into the sphere of the planned, whereupon its organizers greet what they call "detours" (*détournements*) with great pleasure rather than with disdain.

To demonstrate this point, we turn to an example from the 2018 edition of La Ligne Verte, where adaptations to the route were welcomed as legitimate (and perhaps even expected) disturbances. Our vignette here concerns a work of art entitled, "Ode to sidestepping" (*L'Éloge du pas de côté*), a statue by artist Philippe Ramette who La Ligne Verte artistic director, Jean Blaise, invited to install this work as one of the stops along the route. Quite classical in its aesthetics, the bronze piece depicts a man standing atop a pedestal, with one foot firmly rooted to the pedestal, while his other foot dangles off the pedestal in open space (Fig. 7.2). The statue lacked any kind of barrier around it, as one might find in a museum, and so visitors were often inclined to rub its free leg – "like a gesture of superstition, to bring themselves luck" (*tel un geste de superstition, pour se porter chance*) (Rédaction Actu 2021).

This raises the question about "borderline" uses and behaviours and the legitimacy of certain engagements along the route. In this case, after several years of its free foot being handled by visitors, the bronze exterior of the statue began to deteriorate, a "victim of its own success" (*victim de son succès*), as one local news outlet put it (Cabanas 2021). The route's organizers were thus confronted with the decision whether to take some protective measures and keep the work in place, or to remove the statue from the route entirely. In justifying their decision to proceed with the former plan (carried out in Spring 2021), SPL VAN argued that this would allow "the work to experience the multiple signs of public attachment" (*permettant à l'œuvre de vivre les multiples marques d'attachement du public*) (Rédaction Actu 2021). Thus what could have been deemed an inappropriate interaction with the statue (caressing its free foot) is instead rendered legitimate by choosing to simply apply a more durable protective bonze wax coating to its exterior and re-opening the work up for continued contact.[12] Such (re)composition of uses and processes of legitimation (here in line with the idea of the appropriation of an artwork by its public) is not unique to Ramette's work alone, but extends to many other cases as well, leading us to new ways of conceptualizing urban commons vis-à-vis the alterations made to urban pedestrian routes.

Accommodating and (de)legitimating alterations

The very notion of alteration evokes an action that transforms, modifies, and deteriorates (more or less slightly or discreetly). What interests us here is the relationship between the device of the urban pedestrian route, the many different alterations that can be made to the route by its users and visitors, and the possibilities of forging an enlarged common of the city out of the alignment and sharing of these individual manipulations and explorations of the route. Another set of cases pertaining to "borderline" engagements with La Ligne Verte help surface the ways in which the device's materiality affords certain critiques of cultural and tourist

Figure 7.2 "L'Éloge du pas de côté" by Philippe Ramette, Nantes, pictured here during the period when it was closed to the public for the purposes of refurbishing its exterior.

Photo: Rachel Brahy

animation and works to channel legitimate forms of differentiation.[13] In the final analysis, this will allow us to outline the dynamics of composing a "commonality in the plural" (Thévenot 2014), equally capable of being mobilized by those who design and maintain the route as by its staunchest critics.

Selling pet supplies; selling one more beer

The draw of visitors to La Ligne Verte has meant that many of the proprietors and merchants of Nantes have expressed interest in the route passing in front of their shops, in the hopes of attracting new customers and boosting their revenues. In this respect, the VAN team is in continuous dialogue with these stakeholders. Of course, the route cannot possibly pass by every local business in each annual iteration, and so some businesses ultimately benefit from the increased foot traffic while others do not. In the past, this has sparked jealousy on the part of some shop-keepers about the advantages conferred upon others from the route's placement.

One way in which this former group has responded has been to actually change the trajectory of the line, which one respondent from VAN discussed with us in an interview: "there are some who divert [the route]", who retrace its path "during the night" to make it "pass in front of their stores". In one case, the owner of a pet supply boutique painted a trail of cat paws on the ground, leading off of the main green line in the direction of the shop entrance. In another, our interlocutor discussed the case of several pubs "that have really hijacked [the route] so that [the line] enters the bar . . . People enter the bar and come out, without having consumed [anything], to continue [onward]". Our interviewees describe these deviations as a "nice hijacking", as being "hyper funny" and "not mean", with the painting of detours being like "a game" that shopkeepers play with the route and its visitors. For those involved in organizing the route, these disruptions can indeed be "very funny" and so "we let it go".

In sum, these more commercially motivated detours of the course, in which merchants partake as a kind of "game", are rather accepted, and even appreciated, by the community of stakeholders concerned with La Ligne Verte. Indeed, those charged with maintaining the route by ensuring the green line remains visible to visitors throughout the summer season tend to leave the painted detours intact, rather than scrubbing them away.

Can we understand these engagements with the route as operating within the same frame, and according to the same grammar, espoused by the route's designers: one that aims to develop a sustainable form of cultural tourism, where commercial interests exist in harmonious relation to urban playfulness and cultural discovery? At first glance, we can relate such alterations to the enactment of a *regime of planned engagement* (Thévenot 1995). Here, there is a clear goal to increase foot traffic to local businesses, and thus to sell more products. This move could, from a certain critical vantage point, be "unveiled" as a market logic masquerading as cultural promotion. Nevertheless, it is interesting for our analysis to note that such commercial interventions respect the requirements for creative expression demanded by the route's frame of urban public space, thus reaching a more hybrid arrangement that brings together market-oriented activities and exploratory cultural experience. In the absence of any such creative flair, without the humour or carefully planned designs such as we have seen in the case of the cat paws vignette, interventions upon the route risk being deemed illegitimate and open themselves up to more corrective responses from the route's maintainers. In "composing" the commercial and the creative in the self-same bundle of practices, and arriving at a kind of compromise between these two objectives in framing the experiences of the route's many visitors, the aforementioned detours work in service of the version of commonality promoted by the policymakers and designers who support La Ligne Verte.

Yet not every detour has achieved such a delicate balance between the functional and commercial registers of the route's original and intended frame, revealing also the political ambiguities and even limits of a commoning through exploration and what are considered to be legitimate modes of expression within this register. In the next section, we present one such case where the route has instead been mobilized for the purposes of bringing public attention to politically charged issues and for denouncing the political positions held by local officials, thereby introducing elements of *public justification* (Boltanski and Thévenot 2006) into an already complex admixture of *planned* and *exploratory* engagements that drive commoning practices in the creative city.

Raising awareness about the situation of migrants (2018)

On 18 May 2018, students and faculty at L'Université Permanente de Nantes (Nantes Permanent University) had organized a conference entitled "Is the refugee crisis over?" The "refugees" in question, largely of Syrian origin (but also from Iraq, Sudan, Eritrea, and elsewhere) had begun arriving in Nantes – as to many other European cities – in 2015, in an attempt to escape political instability and civil war in their home countries. Popular media accounts would come to refer to this as Europe's "migrant crisis", which was felt across the European Union and led to a populist backlash in many of its member states.

Conference participants had decided, as part of their broader efforts to raise awareness about the situation of migrants living in Nantes, to set up what they called "The Other Canteen" (*L'Autre Cantine*) along La Ligne Verte, an alternative to the "official" canteen run by VAN. Opened on 4 July 2018, this former canteen was based on principles of solidarity, rather than purely commercial gain, and had a twofold mission: increasing the visibility of migrants in the city, and providing these communities with support, including offering them free food at the canteen.

During an interview with an employee of VAN in July 2018, our interlocutor described an additional intervention into the route which had been made earlier that summer where "the day after the line opened, it was diverted to go to the squat where the migrants live". This particular squat was one of several (illegally) occupied places where these newcomers to the city had taken up residence, with a number of other squats – under threat of eviction – and Jean-Baptiste-Daviais Square, in the city centre of Nantes, being other notable locations.

VAN did not meet this detour with the same openness as those discussed earlier, and the aforementioned interviewee expressed doubts that visitors to La Ligne Verte would be interested in going to see "the people who survive in such a space" (*d'aller voir les gens qui survivent dans un espace*). Despite any shared concern

for the unfolding humanitarian crisis, as instantiated by the conference participants' intervention into the route, the manoeuvre was frowned upon by VAN: "No . . .
no . . . to divert the line so that we go to lose ourselves in this place, in this
squat. It is ridiculous – *ridiculous!*" (*Non . . . non . . . de détourner la ligne pour
qu'on aille se perdre dans ce lieu, dans ce squat, c'est ridicule. Ridicule.*) They
continued:

> If [a detour to the route] brings visitors to a place of total debauchery, we will
> erase it. If it's to bring [visitors] to a place that can create danger, or as I said
> in relation to Daviais Square, that is to say, to this squat [where] migrants
> [are living], which therefore causes discomfort or uneasiness [for visitors],
> we will erase it. Period.[14]

In short, organizers of La Ligne Verte confront the hijackings of the route in one
of two ways. On the one hand, there are those that are amusing, funny – and thus
deemed legitimate – which are left in place or even maintained as part of the
overall trajectory. On the other hand, those which are deemed troublesome or
disturbing, or are thought to pose risks to visitors, are deemed illegitimate and
are subject to erasure. In comparing the situations described across the two fore-
going vignettes, we can see how VAN refocuses La Ligne Verte in terms of its
objectives: the development of the tourist economy and the promotion of sites of
cultural, artistic, and commercial importance. In the final analysis, tolerance for
uses and interventions upon the route that overflow this frame – and in particular
when the urban fabric becomes a site for critique, contestation, and the expression of political difference – is limited at best. Responses to these overflows are
accordingly quite severe: There is no possibility of leading visitors to sites of everyday life, and especially not to places that are revelatory of the seams of political
conflict, (un)livability, and (in)hospitality in the urban fabric. In this case, erasure
is the name of the game.

In this sense, the commoning at stake in La Ligne Verte as a *public policy
instrument* (Lascoumes and Le Galès 2007) implies a strong formatting of the
socio-material matrix which *is* the route (Thévenot 1984). In so doing, the route
channels particular imaginaries of the creative city that simultaneously reduce
the possibilities of urban sociality to a pre-given frame and engender particular
modes of commoning supported by that frame and its socio-material enactment.
The commonality constituted here on the basis of a *regime of exploration* extends
therefore only to a set of operators of enchantment (Winkin 2002; Brahy et al.
2022), largely artistic and commercial in scope. These operators come to sharpen
and feed what takes shape as a mode of commoning intimately bound up in the
"creative" and "guaranteed" city, founded on supporting a succession of experiences of cultural and commercial consumption.

Contrary to more "classical" approaches, including those rooted in functional-
ism, which consider only the "substance" of policies, an appreciation of urban
pedestrian routes as a type of public policy instrument helps surface the empirical
complexity of these phenomena as *devices*. Approaching them from this vantage

point is instructive insofar as it highlights the fact that such tools lack any "axiological neutrality", that they do not support all interventions or uses equally, and demonstrates the values they embody in shaping and performing the urban experience – as much for those who visit and follow the route, who design/maintain it, and who otherwise introduce this or that detour for their own interest or cause (be it commercial or political).

New critical ranges through the intermediation of public art

While the cases of detour we have discussed heretofore concern alterations made to the route – that is, redirections or extensions of the green line painted on the ground, which guides visitors to the route's many different sites around the city of Nantes – this does not exhaust the totality of interventions upon La Ligne Verte that we have observed in our studies of this device. In our final vignette here, we reflect upon a still further mode of hijacking that targets the artistic works situated along the route, but which leaves the route itself untouched. Despite the presence of more overtly political messaging (like those seen in the second vignette) in the present example, playing games with the artworks in this way lends an air of acceptability that the previous detours were not afforded. This suggests that they are somehow more aligned with the frame delimited by existing public policy, and by the green line which materially inscribes such policy objectives in public space.

Demanding accountability and action: from "Where is Steve?" to "Open the borders!" (2019)

On 21 June 2019, a group of local disc jockeys organized a free music festival on Quai President Wilson, part of the industrial port spanning the Southern portion of the Île de Nantes (Nantes Island) along the Loire River. The event, a large electronic music celebration to welcome the Summer solstice, was permitted by the city but only under the condition that the music would stop by 4 am on 22 June. While most of the sound systems at the festival complied with this order, a small group of DJs in one area of the quay decided to resist and continued to play music past the agreed deadline. This prompted a first intervention by the local police force, and the music was stopped at around 4.20 am. However, the DJs began playing music again, prompting a second police intervention – only this time, the police took more physical measures, charging at the partygoers and causing 14 of them to fall into the Loire River. Among this group was 24-year-old Nantes resident Steve Maia Caniço, who disappeared into the river's murky waters, his lifeless body only to be found over a month following the events.

Then, on 10 July, a few weeks after Caniço's disappearance but before his body had surfaced, a collective acting in solidarity with his family and friends descended upon an installation called "Reconstitute" by the French artist Stéphane Vigny – a collection of sculptures installed around the Place Royale plaza as part of La Ligne Verte's eighth edition – and affixed signs, banners, and posters to many of the some 700 pieces, asking the question: "Where is Steve?" (*Ou est Steve?*) In other words, they had taken one of the route's many stops, and repurposed it as a venue for bringing public awareness to Steve's disappearance and the questionable circumstances surrounding it. Faced with this provocation, VAN had arranged for all of the posters to be removed from the installation, whereupon concerned groups returned to the site several days later with a fresh batch of posters. This time, however, it was a group from The Other Cantine (discussed earlier) who hung signs around the statues' necks to raise awareness about the situation of migrants in Nantes, including demands to "Open the borders!" and calling for "Johanna, open your door!"[15] Christophe Jouin, co-founder of The Other Cantine, says in a newspaper interview: "In Nantes, it is not only tourists who come for the Voyage à Nantes. There is also another trip that ends more sadly" (Anne 2019).

Amidst this second intervention into the route, VAN Artistic Director Jean Blaise contacted the artist Vigny directly to inquire about his point of view on the matter. In his response, Vigny instructed VAN to leave the posters up. Speaking to the newspaper *Ouest-France*, the artist later declared:

> If I had wanted my work to be protected, I would have put it in a museum. Here, I install a "piece" that lasts two months on the Place Royale. People touch it, take selfies, and this relationship between the public and the work suits me very well. . . . I have no problem with that.
>
> (Biret 2019)

When asked about his views on the tragic events leading to Caniço's disappearance, Vigny went on to say:

> I can't say too much because I don't know much about it. Somehow, I am unknowingly implicated. Nevertheless, I accept to be, if it brings something to this collective. It seems to me to be a more than honorable cause.
>
> (Biret 2019)

And as Blaise himself recalled in an interview with a local newspaper:

> Our first instinct was to remove the messages. . . . Then they came back and we interviewed the artist, Stéphane Vigny. He thinks that this work is there to provoke and he doesn't see any problem with it being a support for messages. So we decided together to let it go. It is part of the issue of public space, which belongs to everyone.
>
> (Brenon 2019)

From this third vignette, about the interventions relating to Steve Caniço's disappearance and to the plight of migrants living in Nantes, we are able to grasp two levels of expression which La Ligne Verte affords, and which may sometimes sit in tension with one another. At the first level, the route appears as a kind of institutionalized, and thus durable and indisputable, support for commoning. It is a device, which is itself part of a broader public policy instrument, whose singular frame has been established at the outset – and which, as we have characterized earlier, aims to hybridize *planned* and *exploratory* engagements (Thévenot 1995), as any touristic policy is wont to do. At a second level, however, the stops along the route, including public art installations like Vigny's "Reconstitute", afford a more multivalent frame, supporting a broader plurality of expressive formats and sites of convergence where actors and collectives may publicly question the social and political status quo, adding dynamics of *public justification* (Boltanski and Thévenot 2006) to the commoning matrix.

Accordingly, we now turn to conclude our analysis with a comment on the specificity of urban pedestrian routes as devices for carrying and capturing expressions and tensions that cross the common order of contemporary cities. Supported by the vignettes presented earlier, our hypothesis has been that such routes contribute to the development of an exploratory mode of commoning. They do so by composing varied and partially opposed engagements with the urban environment, whose creative expressions leave open the possibility of forging new ways of sharing public space and of living together – both within and beyond what the narrow frames of policy dicta might otherwise imagine for city dwellers.

Conclusion

In the analysis of La Ligne Verte we have presented in this chapter, we have sought to highlight the complex, and often fraught, dynamics that urban pedestrian routes produce in the urban environment. On the one hand, these devices – as a component of public policy instruments working in service of an urban aesthetic regime (Genard et al. 2016; Brahy et al. 2018) – aim to frame experiences of the contemporary city in terms of openness, creativity, and exploration. They support a mode of commoning based on the sharing of individual expressive singularities. On the other hand, however, their very potential to frame experience at all suggests that urban pedestrian routes also have a certain regulatory capacity running in the opposite direction: towards control. In the present case, this amounts to control over the public image of the city of Nantes, policed as it were by the normative decisions about what spectacles the route reveals to visitors, and which it keeps out of public view. In this way, a certain dialectic of ambivalence between openness and regulation, exposure and erasure, emerges.

This dialectic is not limited to the framings of urban policy alone, however, but plays out in the socio-material arrangements of urban pedestrian routes as well. That is, the very same elements that support the frame – which give visitors new sites to visit, new public artworks to gaze upon, new boutiques to shop at – also become enrolled in still other practices of exploration and public expression. As we have seen in several of the vignettes discussed earlier, they overflow the intentions and expectations of the "engineers of enchantment" behind the route – whether this means introducing new detours to the green line itself, as in the case of the pet shop's cat prints painted on the ground; attempting other detours into spaces deemed uncomfortable for visitors, such as those displaying the plight of migrants living in Nantes; or fundamentally transforming what can be seen as one follows the route, as when Vigny's sculptures become clothed by political placards.

In looking at how these three hijackings were understood and treated differently by VAN, the contours of – and limits to – urban commoning become abundantly clear. Deviations and hijackings that fit with the commercial and creative spirit of the route are tolerated, if not altogether incorporated into La Ligne Verte. Conversely, those which are directed towards locations that are revealing of the socio-economic fault lines in the city – exposing poverty or the plight of those forced from their homeland – are forbidden and, if attempted, then quickly erased. And then there is this curious third type of hijacking, consisting of temporary moments of critical public expression, which are rejected at first but ultimately accepted as legitimate interventions upon the route.

From this, we can ascertain that urban pedestrian routes, as public policy devices, indeed delimit the modes of engaging with the urban environment, pushing forward a form of exploration that valorizes commercial and cultural exchange; favours spectacle and creativity over quotidian existence; and privileges recognizable demonstrations of public critique over emplaced demonstrations of injustice. The result of all of this is what we call a *liberalized commoning through exploration*, built upon a compromise between two distinct grammars of commonality: a *liberal* grammar (Thévenot 2014; Eranti 2018) where individual (or group) interests confront each other and are settled through negotiation and trade-offs; and an *exploratory* grammar (Auray 2013), where it is individuals' creative expressions and resonant experiences that confront one another in publicly visible venues. Whether its visitors' curious (and physical) interactions with public art installations, shopkeepers' attempts to redirect visitors into their places of business, appeals to an artist as to whether they accept that their installation should become a venue for political critique, or the sharing of any of these experiences on social media posts: each of these instances takes shape as confrontations of individual (or group) interests, and are settled through appeals to personal opinion – and yet they are all *also* evaluated in terms of their contribution to the creative intensification of urban experience.

Given this liberal mode of commoning through exploration and the centrality of creativity within it, it is no wonder that certain interventions upon the route are dismissed out of hand by its organizers. Here, we can think about attempts or proposals to divert the route into poor neighbourhoods, or through migrants' temporary housing. These gestures, which aim to instead intensify a more *emplaced* and *denunciatory* (Boltanski and Thévenot 2006) mode of exploration – bringing visitors into disadvantaged communities in order to expose them to societal inequities and incite them to political action – are beyond the remit of the device's frame. One may even go so far as to argue that preventing La Ligne Verte from traversing these latter locales works in service of the very communities in whose name the "hijackers" purport to speak. Under the current situation, allowing such a hijacking may in fact contribute to still further marginalization, either through gentrification of neighbourhoods and the pushing of residents further to the margins, or even through making a spectacle of disenfranchisement, or what Boltanski (1999) calls an "aestheticization of suffering" (Boltanski 1999) – which is likely a very different type of aesthetics than what the architects of the "aesthetic turn" in urban policy had in mind.

Considering the limits of this device, one could wonder in the end if it would be possible to build a more polyvocal, and even a more radical, mode of exploration that could accommodate other constructions of the political beyond the "liberal" ones we have identified herein. Following an alternative politics of exploration (or commoning through), it would indeed be possible to explore these other neighbourhoods but in such a way that fosters sustainable attachments (Breviglieri 2018a) over the touch-and-go aesthetic experiences which urban pedestrian routes tend to promote. What this could possibly look like is beyond the scope of this chapter, but presents an excellent opportunity for further research into urban commoning.

That said, even in the current absence of any such ideal manifestation of an exploratory commoning, the fact remains that in its annual iterations, La Ligne Verte nevertheless takes important steps towards producing new spaces that may contribute to the enrichment and intensification of democratic tendencies in public space. In particular, the commoning through exploration as formatted by the route produces a liberal political arena where the aesthetic and semantic dimensions of quotidian urban existence are opened up for debate and redefinition, if only fleetingly. It is creating more durable political arenas that are a central challenge for urban policymakers and residents alike, especially if one wishes to for cities to be not only "attractive", but also conducive to "attaching" residents and visitors to each other and to their physical environment.

Notes

1 These are but three examples drawn from the cities where the authors live, but there are many others. On the Geneva case, see "Genève à pied, 10 parcours à thèmes" (Éditions Slatkine 2008).

2 The English translation would be "The Green Line", but we have stuck with the original French name for the route throughout the chapter.

3 Among many predecessor instruments of a similar nature, one may recall the groundbreaking "Plan & Guide Map" of Alexandre Chemetoff, a kind of anti-"Master Plan" that allowed the progressive transformation of Nantes Island without planning the final result (Braae 2015, 225).

4 We had planned to return to La Ligne Verte for the 2020 season, where we hoped to conduct interviews with other implicated actors – such as tourists who had come to Nantes to walk the route, as well as local merchants and inhabitants whose businesses and/or residences were in close proximity to the route – in order to further supplement our corpus of data. Unfortunately, the COVID-19 pandemic made this additional fieldwork impracticable and so the current analysis is based only on the data sources discussed herein.

5 For more information on Jean Blaise, see Dossal (2015), among others.

6 We have drawn the original French language descriptions of the route's stops from the official website of La Ligne Verte, www.levoyageanantes.fr/le-voyage-a-nantes (Accessed April 2020).

7   For ethical reasons, we do not cite or quote from specific reviews, as contributors to websites such as Tripadvisor have not consented to having their writings used for research purposes however public they may be.
8   This passage is an English translation of the observation, initially written in French.
9   Beyond the scope of our analysis, the question arises as to whether this is a response to the almost generalized "zapping" of attention that we experience in our contemporary digitalized societies.
10   The routes can be accessed at www.levoyageanantes.fr
11   For example, the Louvre in Paris has organized a Museum Selfie Day, complete with a designated spot where visitors can take selfies with the Mona Lisa, the most famous painting in its collection, and a contest where visitors are invited to share their selfies on social media with the promise of winning prizes (20minutes.fr, 2018).
12   Although beyond the scope of the current analysis, media coverage of the municipality's decision to keep the sculpture beyond the 2018 season of La Ligne Verte shows not only how urban pedestrian routes transform the urban landscape along longer time horizons but also how installations that become "permanent" are imbued with very different meanings by the city's residents and become sites of contestation (see Augie & Grandet [2018] for an example of media reportage on this phenomenon).
13   On the idea that each grammar of "commonality in the plural" channels the "infinity of possible differences" in order to construct "a distinct mode of integrating differences", see Thévenot (2014, 17).
14   Si c'est pour amener dans un lieu de débauche total, on l'effacera. Si c'est pour amener dans un lieu qui peut créer du danger, ou comme je disais par rapport au square Daviais, c'est-à-dire à ce squat de migrants, donc, qui entraîne un malaise ou un mal-être, on l'efface. Point final.
15   In reference to Johanna Rolland, then mayor of the city of Nantes.

References

20minutes.fr. 2018. "#Louvre, #Beaubourg . . . Comment les musées gèrent vos photos sur Instagram?" November 18, 2018. Accessed May 25, 2022. www.20minutes.fr/high-tech/2373703–20181118-louvre-beaubourg-comment-musees-gerent-photos-instagram.
Akrich, M. 1992. "The De-scription of Technical Objects." In *Shaping Technology/building Society: Studies in Sociotechnical Change*, edited by Wiebe Bijker and John Law, 205–224. Cambridge, MA: Brooks/Cole.
Anne, M. 2019. "Statues place Royale: des pancartes interpellent sur le sort des migrants." *Ouest-France*, July 13, 2019. Accessed May 25, 2022. www.ouest-france.fr/pays-de-la-loire/nantes-44000/nantes-statues-place-royale-des-pancartes-interpellent-sur-le-sort-des-migrants-6443934.
Antonioli, M., G. Drevon, L. Gwiazdzinski, V. Kaufmann, and L. Pattaroni. 2021. *Manifeste pour une politique des rythmes*. Lausanne: EPFL Press.
Augie, A., and M. Grandet. 2018. "Nantes. Place du Bouffay, la statue ne bouge pas." *Ouest-France*, June 6, 2018. Accessed May 25, 2022. www.ouest-france.fr/pays-de-la-loire/nantes-44000/nantes-place-du-bouffay-la-statue-ne-bouge-pas-6004995.
Auray, N., and B. Vétel. 2013. "L'exploration comme modalité d'ouverture attentionnelle. Design et régulation d'un jeu freemium." *Réseaux* 182 (6): 153–186.
Biret, V. 2019. "Où est Steve? Une cause plus qu'honorable." *Ouest-France*, July 16, 2019. Accessed May 25, 2022. www.ouest-france.fr/pays-de-la-loire/nantes-44000/nantes-ou-est-steve-une-cause-plus-qu-honorable-6447478.

Blok, A. 2015. "Attachments to the Common-place: Pragmatic Sociology and the Aesthetic Cosmopolitics of Eco-house Design in Kyoto, Japan." *European Journal of Cultural and Political Sociology* 2 (2): 122–145.

Blokker P. and A. Brighenti. 2011. "An Interview with Laurent Thévenot: On Engagement, Critique, Commonality, and Power." *European Journal of Social Theory* 14 (3): 383–400.

Boltanski, L. 1999. *Distant Suffering: Morality, Media and Politics*. Cambridge: Cambridge University Press.

Braae, E. 2015. *Beauty Redeemed: Recycling Post-industrial Landscapes*. Aarhus: IKAROS Press.

Brahy, R. 2019. *S'engager dans un atelier-théâtre. À la recherche du sens de l'expérience*. Mons: Éditions du Cerisier.

Brahy, R. 2020. "Grand résumé de S'engager dans un atelier-théâtre. À la recherche du sens de l'expérience, Mons, Éditions du Cerisier, 2019." *SociologieS [En ligne]*. http://journals.openedition.org/sociologies/15481.

Brahy, R., É. Dumont., P. Fontaine, and C. Ruelle, dir. 2018. *Regards sur la ville. Échanges et réflexions à partir de Liège*. Liège: Les Presses universitaires de Liège.

Brahy, R., J.-P. Thibaud, N. Tixier, and N. Zaccaï-Reyners, dir. 2022. *L'enchantement qui revient*. Les Colloques Cerisy, Ed. Paris: Hermann.

Brenon, F. 2019. "Nantes: Le Voyage à Nantes ne s'opposera pas aux messages sur ses statues." *20 Minutes Nantes*, July 15, 2019. www.20minutes.fr/nantes/2564439-20190715-nantes-voyage-nantes-opposera-messages-statues.

Breviglieri, M. 2013. "Une brèche critique dans la "ville garantie" ? Espaces intercalaires et architectures d'usage." In *De la Différence urbaine. Le quartier des Grottes/Genève*, edited by E. Cogato-Lanza, L. Pattaroni, M. Piraud, and B. Tirone, 213–236. Genève: Mètis Press.

Breviglieri, M. 2018a. "L'affadissement des villes méditerranéennes et la désacralisation de la figure de l'hôte." *SociologieS [En ligne]*. https://doi.org/10.4000/sociologies.6821.

Breviglieri, M. 2018b. "The Guaranteed City. The Ruin of Urban Criticism?" In *Challenges of Communication in a Context of Crisis. Troubles, Misunderstandings and Discords*, edited by J. M. Resende, A. Cotovio Martins, C. Delaunay, and M. Breviglieri, 206–249. Cambridge: Cambridge Scholars Publishing.

Brighenti, A. M. 2016. "The Public and the Common: Some Approximations of Their Contemporary Articulation." *Critical Inquiry* 42 (2): 306–328.

Boltanski, L., and L. Thévenot. 2006. *On Justification. Economies of Worth*. Translated by Catherine Porter. Princeton: Princeton University Press.

Cabanas, E. 2021. "INSOLITE. À Nantes, le 'pas de la chance', victime de son succès et des esprits superstitieux." *Ouest-France*, April 4, 2021. Accessed May 25, 2022. www.ouest-france.fr/pays-de-la-loire/loire-atlantique/insolite-a-nantes-le-pas-de-la-chance-victime-de-son-succes-et-des-esprits-superstitieux-d14aacde-a1f6–11eb-a997-ae4b3c668f03.

Carmo, L., L. Pattaroni, and M. Piraud. 2022. "The Commodified Counterculture." LX Factory or the Making of a Lucrative Alternative Cultural Center. The Cultural Policy.

Cogato Lanza, E., L. Pattaroni, M. Piraud, and B. Tirone Chabert. 2013. *De la différence urbaine. Le quartier des Grottes/Genève*. Geneva: MētisPresses.

Dossal, P. 2015. *Réenchanteur de ville, Jean Blaise*. Paris: HD ateliers henry dougier.

Eranti, Veikko. 2018. "Engagements, Grammars, and the Public: From the Liberal Grammar to Individual Interests." *European Journal of Cultural and Political Sociology* 5 (1–2): 42–65.

Genard, J.-L., M. Berger, and L. Vanhellemont Linus. 2016. *L'architecture des débats: les imaginaires mobilisés*. Bruxelles: BSI-BCO.

Goffman, E. (1974) 1991. *Les cadres de l'expérience*. Paris: Les Èditions de Minuit.

La Pradelle, Michèle de. 2001. "Espaces publics, espaces marchands. Du marché forain au centre commercial." In *Réinventer le sens de la ville: les espaces publics à l'heure globale*, edited by Ghorra-Gobin Cynthia, 181–191. Paris: L'Harmattan.

Lascoumes, P., and P. Le Galès. 2007. "Introduction: Understanding Public Policy through Its Instruments? From the Nature of Instruments to the Sociology of Public Policy Instrumentation." *Governance* 20 (1): 1–21.

Le Lieu Unique. n.d. "Le lieu Unique – Center for Contemporary Culture." Accessed May 20, 2022. www.lelieuunique.com/en/lelieuunique/.

Le Voyage à Nantes. 2018. *Le Voyage à Nantes*. Le Voyage à Nantes – 30.06/26.08 2018 – Eloge du pas de côté. VAN.

Lefebvre, H. 1968. *Le Droit à la ville*. Paris: Anthropos.

Pattaroni, L. 2015. "Difference and the Common of the City: The Metamorphosis of the Political from the Urban Struggles of the 1970's to the Contemporary Urban Order." In *The Making of the Common in Social Relations*, edited by Alexandre Martin and José Resende, 141–172. Cambridge: Cambridge Scholars Publishing.

Pattaroni, L., dir. 2020. *La contreculture domestiquée: art, espace et politique dans la ville 'gentrifiée'*. Geneva: Metispresses.

Rédaction Actu. 2021. "Nantes: qu'arrive-t-il à la statue Éloge du pas de côté?" *Actu.fr*, April 28, 2021. Accessed May 25, 2022. https://actu.fr/pays-de-la-loire/nantes_44109/nantes-qu-arrive-t-il-a-la-statue-eloge-du-pas-de-cote_41231346.html.

Stavo-Debauge, J. 2017. *Qu'est-ce que l'hospitalité? recevoir l'étranger à la communauté*. Montréal, Québec, Canada: Liber.

Thévenot, L. 1984. "Rules and Implements: Investment in Forms." *Social Science Information* 23 (1): 1–45.

Thévenot, L. 1995. "L'action en plan." *Sociologie du Travail* 37 (3): 411–434.

Thévenot, L. 2006. *L'action au pluriel. Sociologie des régimes d'engagement*. Paris: Coll. Textes à l'appui/Politique et société, La Découverte.

Thévenot, L. 2014. "Voicing Concern and Difference: From Public Spaces to Common-Places." *European Journal of Cultural and Political Sociology* 1 (1): 7–34.

Thévenot, L. 2015. "Making Commonality in the Plural, on the Basis of Binding Engagements." In *Social Bonds as Freedom: Revising the Dichotomy of the Universal and the Particular*, edited by Paul Dumouchel and Reiko Gotoh, 82–108. New York: Berghahn.

Thévenot, L., and N. Kareva. 2018. "Le pain merveilleux de l'hospitalité. Malentendus éclairant les constructions du commun." *SociologieS [en ligne]*. https://journals.openedition.org/sociologies/6933.

Weber, M. (1921) 1995. *Économie et société*, 1: *Les catégories de la sociologie*, 2: *L'organisation et les puissances de la société dans leur rapport avec l'économie*. Translated by J. Chavy, E. de Dampierre, et al. Paris: Plon.

Winkin, Y. 2002. "De la pertinence de la notion d'enchantement: à propos du Pape à la Réunion." In *Communautés périphériques et espaces publics émergents. Les médias dans les îles de l'Océan Indien*, edited by Jacky Simonin, 177–186. Paris: L'Harmattan.

Winkin, Y. 2013. "Le dialogue de l'anthropologue avec lui-même: l'autoethnographie." In *Entre linguistique et anthropologie. Observations de terrain, modèles d'analyse et expériences d'écriture*, edited by D. Londei and L. Santone, 120–134. Bern: Peter Lang.

8 Sensoryfication of place

A sensobiographic approach to sensing transformations of urban atmospheres

Sandi Abram

Introduction

The article discusses how the contemporary production of an urban space of Ljubljana (Slovenia) is narrated through the lived sensory experiences of citizens affected by the daily changes.[1] I will examine how the urban transformation in the Old Town and the surrounding areas under the influence of touristification affects people's everyday practices and their sensory experiences from the perspective of sensory ethnography. My aim is to study how late-capitalist processes produced a specific sensory reorganization of the city, resulting in gentrified urban atmospheres as places of sensory-affective enticement. I will investigate how the contemporary production of new tourist- and lucrative-oriented urban atmospheres reflects in people's sensory experiences. In other words, I will address the question of how capital translates into human experience (Chari 2015): how the sensory, perceptual, and affective dimensions of subjective experiences in the urban space are incorporated into the post-postmodernist (Nealon 2012) processes of global hyper-aestheticization (Welsch 1997). I propose the term "sensoryfication of place" to refer to the contemporary deployment of commodity-oriented hyper-aestheticization and spectacularization techniques and technologies in public space that aim to shape gentrified urban atmospheres as places of sensory-affective enticement.

The article starts with a brief contextualization of the transformation of Ljubljana's urban space. Drawing on sensory (auto)ethnography (Pink 2015) and walking methods, I argue that the public space in the city centre is not becoming a space of controlled desensitization (cf. Sennett 1994), but turns into a space of sensory stimulation aimed at intensifying the human sensorium. In the empirical part, I therefore examine how some inhabitants of Ljubljana felt and verbalized the bodily inscribed "atmospheric transformations" (Abram and Bajič 2022).

Footpaths of urban touristification

After Slovenia entered the EU in 2004 and after the municipal elections in 2006, the gradual process of touristification in Ljubljana achieved its historic peak in 2019.[2] Following the 2008 recession (Slovenia felt the effects in February 2009), wherein the construction industry and real estate investment speculation left voids

DOI: 10.4324/9781003207207-12

on the grounds of the demolished old historical buildings, the accumulated capital did not hesitate to seize fresh re-investment opportunities. Investors presented new blueprints for urban voids, left after old historical buildings were demolished, encompassing largely blueprints for hotel complexes or luxurious residences. For instance, the first five-star hotel in Ljubljana opened up in 2017. Across the street, another luxurious five-star hotel was completed in 2022. The construction of at least seven four- and five-star hotel accommodation facilities in the city centre is planned in the near future. These facilities will provide a total of about 2,000 new hotel rooms (more than 37% rooms are planned in the five-star segment and 29% in the four-star segment) or a 67% increase in the existing number of hotel rooms in the city (Horwath HTL 2020, 26–28).[3]

The effect and significance of urban tourism were also reflected in economic figures. The total contribution of tourism to Slovenia's total Gross Domestic Product (GDP) accounted for 11.9% in 2017, 12.3% in 2018, and 9.9% in 2019, and it was predicted to reach 14.5% of GDP by 2028, but this was estimated before the COVID-19 pandemic (WTTC 2018, 2020). The number of overnight stays in Slovenia's capital increased by 55,000 annually in the period 2011–2016, and the number of overnight stays in the city tripled between 2002 and 2016. Since Slovenia joined the EU in 2004 until 2019, the number of foreign tourist arrivals in Ljubljana quadrupled – from 246,597 in 2004 to 1,070,904 in 2019 (Turizem Ljubljana 2020; MOL 2004, 2009, 2014).[4] Between 2010 and 2019 alone, tourist overnight stays in Ljubljana increased by 165% (Turizem Ljubljana 2020).

The statistics of short-term rentals, such as Airbnb, picture a drastic concentration of providers in the Old Town and steep increase of citywide short-term rentals. Between 2013 and 2018, the number of active providers on Airbnb increased by 1881% (from 99 to 1,961). Although the majority (68%) of active providers rent out one piece of real estate, 3.6% of professional tourist investors offer more than six properties on the Airbnb platform, with a total of 36% of all available rooms in Ljubljana (Horwath HTL 2020, 9, 14).

The effects of the drastic increase in short-term rentals, especially Airbnb accommodation, were questioned as well. As the economic conjecture powered the inflation of real estate investments and market prices, "over tourism" and "tourism phobia" not only became common terms in academia (see Ploštajner 2016; Kuščer and Mihalič 2019; Veríssimo et al. 2020), but have also gained popularity in the discourse of the civil society, mass media, and grassroots movements. As someone who has lived in Ljubljana for almost two decades, I found it difficult not to feel the gradual process of touristification, gentrification, and commodification of urban life in the Slovenian capital. For instance, a clear harbinger of the changes to come was the growing number of lockboxes on the outside of buildings used for self-check-in by guests of short-term holiday rentals.

Sensobiographic walking as a method of the urban sensory ethnography

The participants in the ethnographic study conducted between 2017 and 2020 also perceived these changes in the sensory experience of urban space. I now turn to outline the sensobiographic walking as an ethnographic method that helped to answer the question of how people in Ljubljana, individually and collectively, remember the transformed urban atmospheres in terms of sensory perception.

The sensobiographic walking method (Järviluoma 2015) is a method for researching transgenerational sensory transformations. It was implemented in three medium-sized European cities, namely Ljubljana (Slovenia), Brighton (UK), and Turku (Finland). More than two dozen pairs of participants from two different generations took part in this walking biographic study in each city. In Ljubljana, a medium-sized city with about 300,000 inhabitants, 20 walks were conducted in the city centre. Participants were invited to take part in the study together with a person from a different generation. Older participants born before the 1950s formed the first cluster and participants born between 1990 and 2009 formed the second cluster. The overall participation involved two urban walks: The first, where the participant took the person from another generation on a journey of their choosing and, the second, where the roles were reversed. During the transgenerational sensobiographic walks, participants were asked to talk freely about their own experiences, senses, memories, and other relevant topics[5] (Bajič and Abram 2019).

The production of urban sensory atmospheres

In the last 15 years, Ljubljana's development has moved in the direction of redesigning the sensory experience and urban atmosphere. In 2006, after municipal elections, a new urban planning policy was announced that rebranded the city as green and ecologically sustainable. This image largely enveloped the sensory dimensions of urban space, creating sensory atmospheres with a differentiating "sense appeal" (Howes and Classen 2014). Extensive restructuring work in Ljubljana, including streets, roads, embankments, and parks that affected public spaces, was carried out, especially in the Old Town, which has become a car-free zone since 2008. The pedestrianization of the city centre is in the process of giving way to the smooth space of newly paved streets and refurbished sidewalks. These remodelled spaces, on one hand, open up new ways of walking and, on the other hand, they reduce the walking space on behalf of private enterprises with permanent and mobile billboards, bar and restaurant terraces, and other street furniture. For example, embankments were converted into walkways. Viewing balconies rose above the surface of the river, and new boarding points made it possible to get on and off the tourist boats that ply the Ljubljanica River. Walking became the dominant mode of movement in the rearranged streets of the Old Town. Since March 2019, several new traffic signs on the edge of the Old Town indicate the priority of pedestrians and remind cyclists to give way to pedestrians.

Hence, the pace of movement in some parts of the Old Town had come to a complete standstill. The bar and restaurant terraces on rented public spaces are a case in point. These commercialized patches of urban space are now reserved, for most of the tourist season, as areas for gustatory, visual, and aural enjoyment (in some outdoor beer gardens of restaurants, the staff began to refuse to serve drinks unless they were consumed with food). Similarly, soon after the "regeneration" of a given public space had been completed and freed from motorized traffic, the space was redesigned and physically remodelled to accommodate cultural, sporting, and other types of events and "mega-events" (Salazar et al. 2017). The "revitalisation" not only promoted walking over motorized driving, but also moved events to streets previously used by vehicular traffic. This is called eventization, and "turns all forms of leisure and culture into events, stages in a series of projects, with profit margins and ideological, hegemonic status" (Spracklen and Lamond 2016, 110), ultimately leading to the transformation of public spaces into private and privatized spaces (Spracklen and Lamond 2016, 110).

This eventization and pedestrianization of public space in the city centre under the guise of "revitalisation" (Abram 2021; see also Thibaud 2006; Williamson 2016) actually conceals the particular language of an urbanism sensible to the somatic perception of everyday life and sensory properties of space. Such a shifting paradigm of urbanism, centred on multi-sensory design in urban planning and rooted in the ontological turn in architecture pioneered by Juhani Pallasmaa (see e.g. Pallasmaa 2012),[6] is known as sensory urbanism (Zardini 2005).[7] The implementation of sensory urbanism in Ljubljana eventually led to institute traffic-free places in the Old Town by banning motorized vehicles in order to establish pedestrian-only, experiential and eventful zones, thus creating *particular* urban atmospheres. The discourse of "revitalisation" not only points to a new wave of gentrification, but also signals that "the victory of this language in anesthetizing our critical understanding of gentrification in Europe represents a considerable ideological victory for neoliberal visions of the city" (Smith 2002, 99).

A representative implementation of sensory urbanism in Ljubljana was the renovation of Slovenska Street (former Titova Street). In 2015, four architectural firms were entrusted with the task of redeveloping 400 metres of road from a busy thoroughfare into a "shared space" for pedestrians, cyclists, and public transport. The discourse of these architectural firms on "revitalisation" is indicative. One firm saw the transformed Slovenska Street as a "manifest[ation] of the future of the city of Ljubljana, it is a visual transformation of the capital" (Dekleva Gregorič Architects 2020). In this discourse, the image of the future is not only built on sustainability, but also distinguishes itself from a bygone (post)socialist era, a city spirit contaminated by boredom. In the words of the second firm, Ljubljana: "has transformed itself from a sleepy post-socialist town into a contemporary European city, and a[n] ever more popular tourist destination" (Katušič Kocbek Architects 2020). In the discourse of sensory urbanism, Europeanism and the tourist industry thus symbolize progress, the transition from an industrial, post-socialist town to a post-industrial city in the global market of cities (see Harvey 1990). The historical centre of Ljubljana turns into a palpable manifestation of the discourse on tourism-led urban regeneration projects (see Uysal and Özden 2012). A third architectural firm described the new surface texture of the rearranged Slovenska Street, as a "horizontal a geometric pattern of the pavement, which creates the impression of a fine carpet and increases the optical dimension of the urban space" (Dekleva Gregorič Architects 2020). The architects involved in the renovation understood Slovenska Street as "a place of *becoming* – a place where the city shows what kind of future it strives for" (Katušič Kocbek Architects 2020; own emphasis).

We thus encounter a motorized public space turned into a shared space among pedestrians, cyclists, and public transport in the local adaptation of architectural Deleuzism (Spencer 2016), defined as a turn in architecture (and urbanism) towards the conceptualizations of the affect theory (Spencer 2016). The cohesive thread (and ideology!) of such sensory urbanism is that pedestrians participate on equal footing with their senses in the newly designed, classless urban atmospheres.

The perception of urban sensory atmospheres

Through the prism of sensory studies, the following empirical analysis ventures into an exploration of how the tourism industry shifted everyday sensory experiences in the Old Town and its adjacent areas. I will thus examine the perception of urban sensory atmospheres from an ethnographically informed approach, through sensobiographic walking.

Polona, a young architect in her late 20s, approached the issue of the tourism industry and urban planning with unease: "I only fear tourism. I'm afraid that the [city] will become too touristy". Her testimony indicates how the socio-cultural components of public space are being eroded in the name of economic profits driven by the tourism industry. She commented on the urban redevelopment of Slovenska Street from the perspective of a cyclist:

> I think it's nice that they renovated Slovenska [Street], but they could make the roadway just a bit wider. When two buses meet, it's extremely, extremely uncomfortable, because there's only half a metre between them. And then you are practically sandwiched between two buses.

"I think they exaggerated a bit with the width of the sidewalk" she said, pointing out the socio-spatial segregation of Slovenska Street in the name of profit, and added:

> It's all well and good that the street was renovated, but it's also very clear why it was [renovated]. Because they can charge so much for tables [on bar and restaurant terraces] that it pays better to have. . . . I mean, it pays more for the municipality to have bars than cars driving around.

Of note is her assurance that she almost never goes to such bars. The only exception was when a friend from abroad visited her and they went together to a pub in Slovenska Street, a situation she described as "a total tourist experience".

Katja was another younger participant, born and raised in Ljubljana. As someone who has spent her whole life near the central marketplace in the Old Town, she witnessed the touristification of Ljubljana. She observed how the city centre, being overcrowded with tourists, exacerbated the habituated movement:

> There are really more tourists. We already noticed that last year [in 2017]. You could quickly cycle through the city. In July, August, there was nobody. Today you cannot do that anymore. I mean, walking is the fastest way. You just can't get through by bike.

Katja complemented the description of the feeling of touristification through proprioception with other sensory modalities, starting with sound. She was optimistic when the Old Town was turned pedestrian, and expected that the demise of noise produced by motorized vehicles would change the urban soundscape for the better. "There was a bus stop at the end of this street", Katja pointed out in the direction of Vodnik Square, "and there was normal traffic, and you had to be extremely careful because there were cars and buses driving around. . . . After this [area] was closed, I thought it would become quieter". The noisemakers eventually shifted from the road traffic to the newly emerging restaurants on the ground floor of her residence. The entertainment industry in the form of the eventization of public space could also be heard from far away. After the pedestrianization of the Old Town,

> [b]ars and some street events started. For example, on the marketplace, on the Butchers' Bridge. There is such a corridor that [the sound] bounces off the walls. You hear these [events] as if they were happening right under your window. Every now and then it's very nice, there are some very nice concerts. But it can also be annoying when you have to study or you are ill.

Although she expressed an ambivalent attitude towards the eventization, it remains to be noted that the change in the urban sensorium followed the change in the production of urban atmospheres. This was similar to the change in Slovenska Street described earlier. Just as pedestrians occupied the new city surfaces, bars and restaurants had terraces at fronts of residential and other structures. The process leading to specialized public spaces intended for leisure, entertainment, and consumption, a process that Zukin calls "domestication by cappuccino" (Zukin 1995, xiv), however, profoundly affects the sensory experience of urban atmospheres; the experience penetrates the body in every sense. "I experienced the peacefulness as something completely normal", Katja said about a pre-turistified city, of a Ljubljana easy on the ear, "only when it [the peacefulness] was gone you did realise it was so quiet". Katja noticed a double source of noise, especially at night. If one came from external speakers from nearby bars or from distant events, the second came from inebriated guests far beyond the bars' opening hours. Specific ear-piercing indicators were memorable: "Suddenly, in the middle of the night, some started shouting, and then you couldn't sleep. Or there were concerts, and [the music] was pounding. Well, with this commotion, you notice that there used to be quietness".

At this point I would like to draw attention to what Katja has implicitly pointed out, namely the ambiguity in the consideration of touristification. She, as well as other participants, denounced unpleasant situations and the problematic influx of tourism and capitalist-oriented urban development. However, one can note that her argumentation bases on a negotiation of the effects of touristification, whether in spatial or temporal terms. The sensory nuisance caused by eventization only transforms into a disturbing perceptual overload after protracted repetition. For Katja, the experienced proximity of music events was not a priori unpleasant. Concerts only had a disturbing effect after prolonged repetition in liminal states.

In this context, Paiva and Sánchez-Fuarros' (2021) concept of collateral atmospheres should be mentioned, as it captures "other" atmospheres that arise at edges of dominant, gentrified atmospheres, leading to a deterioration of liveability (i.e. strained neighbourhood relations, well-being, and local identity). I could argue that this ambivalence, inherent in the processes of intensive touristification, is inscribed into the collateral atmospheres precisely because the collateral atmospheres emerge in a liminal state of in-betweenness. This in-betweenness allows ambivalence to emerge, as the process of negotiating the transformative effects on somatic experiences is not yet complete, that is it is still being processed, negotiated, and evaluated. Katja first addressed the issue of proprioceptive experiences. Next, she discussed the topic of acoustic stimuli, and finally, with an insightful example of a semi-basement bar, arrived at the question of thermoception. One might wonder how touristification influences the feeling of temperature. She felt the transformation in her own home, in a house that has belonged to her family for four generations. "I only recently found out how the Down Bar affects our house", she said with a smile on her face,

> [I]n fact our cellar is right next to Down [Bar]. My father keeps his wine bottles in the cellar. Since the bar has been up and running, they [the bar] heat up, so our cellar is no longer cold. And it's true that it will no longer be possible to cool [the wine bottles]. That's quite a problem [laughs].

Since the catering industry in the city centre works almost around the clock, some indoor bars and restaurants open and close as late as the law allows.

Katja's sensobiographic narrative of how the tourism industry has swamped the Old Town stems from her time as a local resident and, moreover, from her time as a temporary worker in tourism. In conversation with Pavla, an older co-walker born in the mid-1940s, Katja conveyed a multi-layered transformation of urban atmospheres:

KATJA: I think for some time now there has been a trend to drive residents out of the Old Town. . . . We have observed this because there were many older residents who used to live in Old Ljubljana. And after they closed the centre, it was not even possible to get there by car. And then, say, you cannot cross the entire Old Ljubljana [if] you have something to carry. An acquaintance of mine had a grandmother at Cyril Methodius Square. And whatever had to be taken or carried, that meant a whole coordination plan of how to get there by car, what to put in the car, or what to take with you.

PAVLA: Yeah, I really believe that. But that must be a torment for those residents!

KATJA: Uh-huh [affirmative]. And then there's that noise. Say, all summer long, if something happens on the street, [then] there's no peace anymore. For many people, it was then easier to move a bit away from the old [city] centre.

PAVLA: Yeah, that's right.

KATJA: I worked in some accommodation in Old Ljubljana. The company wanted to expand, and we were supposed to look for houses that were for rent or for sale, because they wanted to do viewings [of properties]. I think that practically all the houses in the Old Ljubljana are rented out as accommodation. Or to live in.

PAVLA: [with astonishment] Really?

KATJA: I mean, almost all of them. It's just interesting to see that [in the Old Ljubljana] there are no permanent residents anymore.

The relatively new staging of the urban sensory atmospheres resulted in gentrification: The revalorized and "re-sensoryficated" public spaces allowed the extraction of class monopoly rent, a rent extracted from an urban resource (Harvey 2002), ultimately leading to a re-composition of the local population. We see how the interplay between new urbanism, cultural politics, and urban touristification has led to a deterioration of long-term liveability for inner-city residents in terms of atmospheric transformations, which ultimately led to gentrified sensory atmospheres. The overall gentrification manifested itself as a general decline in the residential quality of the Old Town as "displacement pressure" (Marcuse after Cócola-Gant 2016) and as the "direct displacement" (Cócola-Gant 2016). As the wave of urban touristification in Ljubljana engulfed public spaces and private residences, it drove up rents, caused real estate prices to skyrocket, and reorchestrated urban sensory atmospheres.

For Nika, a young semi-professional violinist born in the early 1990s, the change of the sense of place, and the bodily estrangement to the new urban sensory atmospheres (see Abram and Bajič 2022), meant she simply decides to circumnavigate some parts of Ljubljana. Unlike her favourite place in summer that enables her to escape the unbearable city heat, "when it's terribly hot, and . . . you're lying on a couch until ten o'clock in the evening, so that you can go out to those [tolerable] 28 degrees", the Old Town represents an area that she avoids today:

In recent years, I simply can't go in the city centre in the summer to have a beer or a cup of coffee in peace. Because there are always so many people there that you don't feel like going there anyway . . . because of the tourists. Somehow, I really started to avoid the centre, which is a real pity. I've the feeling that in two years there will only be tourists in the centre. Everything will [then] be adapted to their needs.

The loss of a sense of place (Cócola-Gant 2016) is no longer a hackneyed metaphor for the process of uprooting residents from their living space. Instead, it becomes a concretization of how the physical creation of upscale and gentrified urban atmospheres that can generate a new "urban sensorium" (Goonewardena 2005), creating a new way of sensing urban atmospheres, and eventually exchanging poorer (long-term) residents for wealthier ones. To rephrase Steven Feld (1996, 91): As sense makes place, the sensory-enriched place makes profit.

Conclusion: sensoryfication of place and the production of gentrified urban atmospheres

In this article, I explored how the reorganization of perceptions and "ways of sensing" (Howes and Classen 2014) in touristified areas of the city are part of a broader strategy of neoliberal reorganization of the modes of production and exploitation of space within a new urban political economy. The mass tourism industry as a form of urban economy in the Old Town shifted the everyday urban atmospheres of a mid-sized city on the semi-periphery of late capitalism and created a new "urban sensorium" (Goonewardena 2005) that was experienced by participants as sensory alienation. I examined the ways in which hyper-aestheticization (Welsch 1997) reconfigured the urban landscape through an increase in practices and discourses of sensory and affective enticement in public space (see also Abram and Bajič 2022), such as the eventization and pedestrianization of the historic centre, or the proliferation of commercial semi-public spaces.

I proposed the concept of *sensoryfication of place*, by which I mean the deployment of commodity-oriented hyper-aestheticization and spectacularization techniques and technologies in public space that aim at engineering sensory gentrified urban atmospheres as sites of sensory-affective enticement. Both urban renewal and the tourism industry played a decisive role in ensuring that the historic district stages various mechanisms of animation. Drawing on sensory ethnography, the text showed the ways in which consequences of urban touristification not only reconfigured the historical quarter but also profoundly influenced the perception of public space in Ljubljana. A 28-year-old participant described this as "*the transformation of the vibe*" of a given locale, ranging from environmental sounds to human scents. "*People are perfumed even when they go running*", she concluded.

In sum, the materialization of "the art of enticement" (Harvey 2006, 26) was perceived through the production of the atmospheric *genius loci*, the spirit of a place, to cater to consumers of the tourism-led industry (Volgger 2019), and to appeal to affluent social groups in the refurbished historic area. "*Sometimes I don't feel like going there to drink beer*", Nika summarized her dislike of an upscale summer bar garden, whose atmosphere and menu prices cater to affluent classes: "*it's more [of a place] for a glass of wine*". Even though contemporary urban planning processes are in the post-political rhetoric often portrayed as depoliticized, thus neutralizing both social conflicts (Holgersson 2014) and the high degree of segregation in a homogeneous space (Lefebvre 1991, 151), the neoliberal senso-ryfication of place has another important trait. Enlivening public space not only means eliciting a variety of enticing sensory stimuli, but such designs of experiential urban landscapes and atmospheres also preclude other alternatives (Hajer and Reijndorp 2001; see also Degen 2014).

Notes

1 This chapter is part of the research project SENSOTRA funded by the European Research Council (ERC) under the European Union's Horizon 2020 Research and Innovation Program (Grant agreement No. 694893). The Finnish Cultural Foundation funded the author's additional research.
2 Two significant declines and a drastic drop in foreign tourist arrivals occurred in the period of nearly four decades: after Slovenia's independence (1991), after the global recession (2008–2009), and during the pandemic (2020).
3 These are only illustrative figures and do not cover the numerous boutique hotels under construction that evade statistics.
4 Parallel to this, the average annual price for apartments per square metre in Ljubljana increased from €1,887 in 2005 to €2,910 in 2019 (Surveying and Mapping Authority of the Republic of Slovenia 2020).
5 All verbatim quotations are transcribed from the sensobiographic walks and in-depth interviews. All participants were given an altered personal name to match their age group.
6 Another precursor to the phenomenological discussion about the sensory perception of places is represented in the "atmospheric turn" with the key figure Gernot Böhme (see Böhme 1993).
7 It is important to stress the growing body of literature on the engagement of (particular) sensory experience and designs (for a list, see Abram 2021).

References

Abram, S. 2021. "Sensory Capital: Sensing Transformations in Ljubljana, 1850s-2020." PhD diss., University of Eastern Finland.
Abram, S. and Bajič, B. 2022. Perception Against. Reflecting Ethnographically on the Sensory, Walking, and Atmospheric Turns. *Etnološka tribina*, 52 (45), 112–126.
Bajič, B., and S. Abram. 2019. "Čutnobiografski sprehodi: med antropologijo čutov in antropologijo digitalnih tehnologij." *Glasnik SED* 59 (1): 27–38.
Böhme, G. 1993. "Atmosphere as the Fundamental Concept of a New Aesthetics." *Thesis Eleven* 36 (1): 113–126.
Chari, A. 2015. *A Political Economy of the Senses. Neoliberalism, Reification, Critique.* New York: Columbia University Press.
Cócola-Gant, A. 2016. "Holiday Rentals: The New Gentrification Battlefront." *Sociological Research Online* 21 (3): 112–120.
Degen, M. 2014. "The Everyday City of the Senses." In *Cities and Social Change: Encounters with Contemporary Urbanism*, edited by R. Paddison and E. McCann, 92–111. London: SAGE.
Dekleva Gregorič Architects. 2020. "Slovenska Street Pedestrianisation." Accessed April 7, 2021. www.dekleva-gregoric.com/#/slovenska-street/.

Feld, S. 1996. "Waterfalls of Song. An Acoustemology of Place Resounding in Bosavi, Papua New Guinea." In *Senses of Place*, edited by S. Feld and K. Basso, 91–135. Santa Fe: School of American Research Press.

Goonewardena, K. 2005. "The Urban Sensorium. Space, Ideology and the Aestheticization of Politics." *Antipode* 37 (1): 46–71.

Hajer, M., and A. Reijndorp. 2001. *In Search of New Public Domain. Analysis and Strategy*. Rotterdam: NAi Publishers.

Harvey, D. 1990. *The Condition of Postmodernity. An Enquiry into the Origins of Cultural Change*. Cambridge and Oxford: Blackwell Publishers.

Harvey, D. 2002. "The Art of Rent: Globalization, Monopoly and the Commodification of Culture." *Socialist Register* 38 (1): 93–110.

Harvey, D. 2006. "The Political Economy of Public Space." In *The Politics of Public Space*, edited by Setha Low and Neil Smith, 17–34. London and New York: Routledge.

Holgersson, H. 2014. "Challenging the Hegemonic Gaze on Foot: Walk-Alongs as a Useful Method in Gentrification Research." In *Walking in the European City Quotidian Mobility and Urban Ethnography*, edited by T. Shortell and E. Brown, 207–224. Surrey and Burlington: Ashgate.

Horwath HTL. 2020. "Predlog Strategije razvoja turistične destinacije Ljubljana in ljubljanska regija 2021–2027." Accessed April 7, 2021. www.ljubljana.si/assets/Uploads/9.-tocka-strategija-razvoja-turizma-2021-2026.pdf.

Howes, D., and C. Classen. 2014. *Ways of Sensing. Understanding the Senses in Society*. London and New York: Routledge.

Järviluoma, H. 2015. "Sensory Transformations and Transgenerational Environmental Relationships in Europe, 1950–2020. SENSOTRA Research Plan B2. ERC-ADG – Advanced Grant." Accessed April 7, 2021. https://bit.ly/2DKxfTB.

Katušič Kocbek Architects. 2020. "Slovenska Street." Accessed April 7, 2021. http://katusickocbek.com/work-post/slovenska-cesta/.

Kuščer, K., and T. Mihalič. 2019. "Residents' Attitudes towards Overtourism from the Perspective of Tourism Impacts and Cooperation-The Case of Ljubljana." *Sustainability* 11: 1–16.

Lefebvre, H. 1991. *The Production of Space*. Translated by Donald Nicholson-Smith. Oxford and Cambridge: Blackwell.

MOL. 2004. "Statistični letopis Ljubljane 2004." Accessed April 7, 2021. www.ljubljana.si/assets/O-Ljubljani/ljubljana-v-stevilkah/letopis-2004.pdf.

MOL. 2009. "Statistični letopis Ljubljane 2009." Accessed April 7, 2021. www.ljubljana.si/assets/O-Ljubljani/ljubljana-v-stevilkah/letopis-2009.pdf.

MOL. 2014. "Statistični letopis Ljubljana 2013." Accessed April 7, 2021. www.ljubljana.si/assets/O-Ljubljani/ljubljana-v-stevilkah/statisticni-letopis-2013.pdf.

Nealon, J. 2012. *Post-Postmodernism: Or, the Cultural Logic of Just-in-Time Capitalism*. Stanford: Stanford University Press.

Paiva, D., and I. Sánchez-Fuarros. 2021. "The Territoriality of Atmosphere: Rethinking Affective Urbanism through the Collateral Atmospheres of Lisbon's Tourism." *Transactions of the Institute of British Geographers* 46 (2): 392–405.

Pallasmaa, J. 2012. *The Eyes of the Skin. Architecture and the Senses*. West Sussex: John Wiley & Sons Ltd.

Pink, S. 2015. *Doing Sensory Ethnography*. 2nd ed. London: Sage.

Ploštajner, K. 2016. "Iskanje urbanega v podjetniškem mestu." In *Novo urbano vprašanje*, edited by Andy Merrifield, 181–195. Ljubljana: Založba.

Salazar, N. B., et al. 2017. *Mega-Event Mobilities. A Critical Analysis*. London and New York: Routledge.

Sennett, R. 1994. *Flesh and Stone. The Body and the City in Western Civilization*. New York and London: W.W. Norton & Company.

Smith, N. 2002. "New Globalism, New Urbanism: Gentrification as Global Urban Strategy." In *Urban Restructuring in North America and Western Europe*, edited by N. Brenner and N. Theodore, 80–103. Malden, Oxford and Carlton: Blackwell Publishing.

Spencer, D. 2016. *The Architecture of Neoliberalism. How Contemporary Architecture Became an Instrument of Control and Compliance*. London, Oxford, New York, New Delhi and Sydney: Bloomsbury.

Spracklen, K., and I. R. Lamond. 2016. *Critical Event Studies*. London and New York: Routledge.

Surveying and Mapping Authority of the Republic of Slovenia. 2020. "Evidenca trga nepremičnin." Accessed April 7, 2021. http://prostor3.gov.si/ETN-JV/.

Thibaud, J.-P. 2006. "La fabrique de la rue en marche: essai sur l'altération des ambiances urbaines." *Flux* 66–67: 111–119.

Turizem Ljubljana. 2020. "Statistični podatki." Accessed April 7, 2021. www.visitljubljana.com/sl/mediji/statisticni-podatki/.

Uysal, Ü. E., and P. Özden. 2012. "Cultural Tourism as a Tool for Urban Regeneration in Istanbul." In *Sustainability Today*, edited by Carlos A. Brebbia, 389–400. Southampton: WIT Press.

Veríssimo, M., et al. 2020. "Overtourism and Tourismphobia: A Systematic Literature Review." *Tourism* 68 (2): 156–169.

Volgger, M. 2019. "Staging Genius Loci: Atmospheric Interventions in Tourism Destinations." In *Atmospheric Turn in Culture and Tourism: Place, Design and Process Impacts on Customer Behaviour, Marketing and Branding*, edited by Michael Volgger and Dieter Pfister, 139–151. Bingley: Emerald.

Welsch, W. 1997. *Undoing Aesthetics*. London, Thousand Oaks and New Delhi: SAGE.

Williamson, R. 2016. "Walking in the Multicultural City. The Production of Suburban Street Life in Sydney." In *Walking in Cities: Quotidian Mobility as Urban Theory, Method, and Practice*, edited by E. Brown and T. Shortell, 23–42. Philadelphia, Rome and Tokyo: Temple University Press.

WTTC. 2018. "Travel & Tourism Economic Impact 2018. Slovenia [Online]." Accessed April 7, 2021. www.slovenia.info/uploads/dokumenti/raziskave/slovenia2018.pdf.

WTTC. 2020. *Slovenia. 2020 Annual Research: Key Highlights*. London: WTTC.

Zardini, M., ed. 2005. *Sense of the City: An Alternate Approach to Urbanism*. Montréal: Canadian Centre for Architecture.

Zukin, S. 1995. *The Cultures of Cities*. Cambridge: Blackwell.

9 "Taman Tugu: Interference/ Resistance"

Using augmented reality and placed sound to engage audiences with an urban jungle soundscape

Yonatan Collier

Introduction

"Taman Tugu: Interference/Resistance" is performed through a GPS-enabled Smartphone and headphones. GPS technology allows for the mapping of a composition over a landscape so that the music is experienced within the context of a very specific geography. It is possible to achieve a fine alignment of sound with space that enables the structuring of a musical work around specific landmarks. In addition to hearing a musical piece that has been mapped on to the environment, the audience also hear the sounds of the surrounding ambiance in real time, a soundscape that has formed the basis for the musical composition itself. This work therefore combines the real and the virtual into an AAR experience.

The piece is a location-specific meditation on the importance of green spaces in the urban environment. Through the use of GPS mapping and AAR, it encourages listeners to reflect on changes in ambiance as they move from the edges of the park, where the city is still clearly audible, to the centre of the park where the sounds of the jungle dominate. This chapter explains how the author constructed "Taman Tugu: Interference/Resistance" to engage an audience more deeply with this incredibly unusual urban ambiance while also highlighting the importance of urban green spaces.

A jungle park in Kuala Lumpur

Taman Tugu is a jungle park in the centre of Kuala Lumpur. I had the opportunity in 2019 to spend six months in the city and had compiled a shortlist of potential locations at which to create an immersive musical work before arriving in Malaysia. I was intrigued by Taman Tugu from the moment I read about it; a 66-acre secondary forest right in the heart of a modern metropolis. It seemed that a location at which nature and the city could be experienced in juxtaposition could be useful for raising questions regarding the climate crisis and our response to it. Upon visiting the site, I found Taman Tugu to be a unique and fascinating place, and one that would lend itself extremely well to the kind of work that I had in mind to create.

DOI: 10.4324/9781003207207-13

The Taman Tugu site was once a city neighbourhood, home to British residences prior to Malaysian independence in 1957, and to Malaysian government officials after this date. More recently, the area had become an illegal dumping ground, although nature was thriving in certain parts of the site. The Taman Tugu site is a prime piece of real estate, situated extremely close to the Malaysian National Monument, and when it was earmarked for redevelopment, the sovereign wealth fund of the government of Malaysia (Khazanah Nasional Berhad, also known simply as Khazanah) was tasked with finding a use for the land. The initial plan was to turn the site into a for-profit theme park, primarily for tourist use, but several NGOs approached Khazanah and asked them to consider preserving it as a green space. Khazanah approached the government with this idea and, with the proposal being green lit in principle, an organizational structure was developed that would allow the park to be financially self-sustaining once redevelopment had taken place (BFM Media 2021).

This organizational structure took the form of a public trust, Amanah Warisan Negara (AWAN), based on the British National Trust model. Unlike many National Trust sites, however, Taman Tugu is free to enter and AWAN must therefore raise money through other means. Alongside donations and schemes for the public to adopt trees and benches in Taman Tugu, an important part of the financial strategy is to run events at the park and its adjoining nursery to attract residents and tourists alike. Driving footfall is key to the park's financial stability. Not only do park visitors often buy refreshments, bringing visitors to the park has another important effect; it has been shown that "high levels of connectedness to nature" tend to correspond with an individual's willingness to pay for forest conservation (Sato et al. 2021, 1). It is therefore thought that bringing more visitors to the park will increase the likelihood of receiving more donations in the future. Additionally, there is a further benefit to staging events such as yoga classes and educational programmes for children at Taman Tugu; the accompanying publicity spreads awareness of the park's existence both in Kuala Lumpur and further afield.

Taman Tugu opened in 2018, and some signs of the unusual history of the location are still evident; in places concrete ruins poke through the foliage, a reminder that this was once an urban area. More than 1,000 trees that were growing at the site were preserved, some of which are estimated to be over 100 years old. However, as the development of Taman Tugu began, the extent of illegal dumping at the site became evident. Calvin Jacob, executive director of the Taman Tugu Project, explains that the project transitioned from being one of "preservation and conservation" to one of the "rehabilitation of what had become an illegal dumping ground" (Jacob in BFM Media 2021). Almost 300 truckloads of waste were removed from the site by hand in order not to further damage the flora and fauna in the area, and a huge number of trees were brought in. More than 230 Indigenous Malaysian rainforest tree species have been planted, many of these species being selected due to the wide range of fauna they will attract, the overall aim being to encourage biodiversity. The park now contains more than 4,000 trees, including over 1,000 categorized as "endangered" or "critically endangered" by the International Union for Conservation of Nature (Taman Tugu Project 2021).

Figure 9.1 A pathway in Taman Tugu.

Photo: Yonatan Collier

Despite AWAN's understandable focus on generating local and domestic inter-est in Taman Tugu, the park quickly drew international attention too. Lonely Planet named the park one of the ten best new openings for travellers globally in 2019, and also added Taman Tugu to its suggested itineraries for travellers visiting Kuala Lumpur (McCarthy 2018; Lonely Planet 2021). To date, more than half a million visitors have been through the site.

While Jacob is realistic about the scale of the difference small sites such as Taman Tugu can make in the face of global heating, he believes that green spaces such as this can nonetheless be incredibly important both for educational purposes and as a refuge from urban life:

> It's a small space, 66 acres . . . Saving this green space is not going to make a big impact towards the climate reality agenda, but what we hope this does is create a lot more awareness. City folks and city kids, they come here and this is the first time they are in a forest environment and it's right smack in

the heart of the city – but in the depths of Taman Tugu you don't hear the city. And they get to experience what a forest is like. . . . You experience the serenity of the site. And the idea is that this will be an impetus to drive a mindset of conservation, preservation and really, saving planet earth.

(Jacob in BFM Media 2021)

Jacob's hope of instilling an interest in conservation is supported by the work of Dunn et al., who posit that "people with more exposure to nature are more interested in conserving it. Although interactions with nature are not the only route to interest in conservation . . . they are clearly an important and arguably necessary condition" (2006, 1814). The idea that the serenity of Taman Tugu can provide a refuge from the city is borne out by Hartig and Kahn's assertion that

theoretical claims, laboratory and field experiments have repeatedly shown that spending time in natural environments or viewing scenes of nature can quickly help people to lift their mood, improve their ability to direct attention, and reduce physiological arousal to a greater degree than do urban streets and other comparison conditions.

(Hartig and Kahn 2016, 939)

In this chapter, I will explain how I created an immersive musical experience that formed a part of the Taman Tugu outreach strategy. I will show how the piece uses Augmented Reality (AR) and *placed sound* to engage listeners with the Taman Tugu soundscape while also highlighting the importance of urban green spaces. I will first offer some grounding in AR and placed sound, before explaining how I attempted to combine musical and environmental sound. I will then show how the work was structured around the physical features of the site in order to deliver a specific environmental message.

"Taman Tugu: Interference/Resistance"

"Taman Tugu: Interference/Resistance" (TTIR) is an AR musical work which I created in response to this unique location. The work aims to encourage new visitors to come to Taman Tugu while offering regular visitors an opportunity to explore the park in a new way. The work premiered on 4 September 2019 as part of the international Soundwalk Sunday festival. The first public presentation of the piece occurred at a fully booked event at the park on 1 December 2019, and was covered on Malaysian national TV news channel Berita RTM.

Through use of GPS technology, TTIR aims to engage visitors to Taman Tugu with the realities of the climate crisis and the importance of preserving green spaces in response to this. Furthermore, through the use of AR, the work draws the attention of participants to the jungle soundscape – a collection of sounds that is rarely encountered within the city limits of a modern metropolis and one that is unique in Kuala Lumpur.

TTIR is performed through headphones via an app that can be downloaded for free onto GPS-enabled Smartphones. The vast majority of the music created for TTIR uses field recordings gathered in Taman Tugu as its raw material. I gathered these recordings from various locations within the park over the course of many visits in 2019. In some cases, these recordings have remained largely unprocessed; in others, they have been digitally manipulated to create software instruments. In places these field recordings are augmented by synthesized tones that have been designed to sympathize with the timbre of the Taman Tugu soundscape. As AR and GPS are so central to the success of TTIR, it is necessary to define certain terms related to these technologies before exploring the work itself in detail.

AR is often perceived to be in the visual domain; users can view digital content overlaid onto the real world by looking through a phone screen or smartglasses. However, AR experiences can be created for the other senses as well; Audio Augmented Reality (AAR) takes place when a real-world soundscape is overlaid with digital sound (Behringer 2001).

Van Krevelen and Poelman (2010) suggest that in order to be classified as AR, an experience must satisfy three conditions:

1. Combines real and virtual objects in a real environment.
2. Registers (aligns) real and virtual objects with each other.
3. Runs interactively, in three dimensions, and in real time.

Green (2013) relates these conditions specifically to AAR and expands upon them accordingly; a listener must be able to engage with the virtual sound layer and their surrounding, real environment concurrently. The virtual layer should also align contextually and/or spatially with aspects of the real environment. Therefore, virtual content should be included that "sympathises with reality" or that appears to "originate from a comparable point in space" to real objects (Green 2013, 1). This is the spatial alignment of real and virtual objects that is termed *audio-visual congruence* by Hazzard (2016) and is discussed in more detail later in this chapter. Finally, in order to be designated an AAR experience, the virtual sound layer must be delivered in real time and in three dimensions (the listener should feel immersed) while also responding in some way to the listener's activity.

The playback of recordings in the location of their capture allows an audience to listen to sound from the same location delivered in multiple layers. The sounds of the "real world" are audible to listeners, beneath a virtual sound layer. The interaction of real-time and recorded sound will guarantee a unique listening experience to every listener, but AAR offers the opportunity to do more than that. Behringer and Kastel assert that "Augmented Reality has significant potential for enhancing the human interaction with cultural contexts through enabling a deeper engagement" (2016, 197). The challenge is therefore to use this technology to encourage engagement with the wider context of a location: its history, its culture, its environmental context, and its soundscape.

GPS technology allows for the mapping of an audio composition over a landscape so that it is experienced within the context of a very specific geography. Passages of audio can be attached to specific locations so that as participants move through the landscape, they experience audio that is tailored to their journey. Behrendt has termed this type of work *placed sound*:

> Here, artists or designers curate the distribution of sounds in (outdoor) spaces, often – but not exclusively – by using GPS. The audience typically experiences these sounds via headphones and sometimes via mobile phone speakers or other mobile speakers. The audience does not contribute their own sounds or determine the location of sounds. . . . But each member of the audience creates their own version or remix of a "placed sound" piece, depending on their trajectory.
>
> (Behrendt 2015, 7)

A placed sound work is tied to a specific location by definition, and this offers the artist an opportunity to tap into deeper layers of meaning associated with that location. Indeed, in their Brief Bibliography and Taxonomy of GPS-Enabled Locative Media, Bleecker and Knowlton (2006, 1) show the greatest interest in "experiences that take into account the geographic locale of interest, typically by elevating that geographic locale beyond its instrumentalized status as a 'latitude longitude coordinated point on earth' to the level of existential, inhabited, experienced and lived place". Placed sound works can engage with the historical, cultural, or environmental context of their location of performance and can also engage directly with its ambiance. In addition, physical objects can be aligned very closely with virtual *sound objects*, creating audiovisual congruence.

There are compelling reasons for creating an AAR experience of this kind. In his writing on Kudsk Steensen's AR work "The Deep Listener", Obrist (2019, 6) proposes that

> digital world building can in fact entangle us with the natural world rather than separate us, training our attention on the details of how our actions create irreversible change to those environments and the biodiversity it plays host to – a necessity in light of our current environmental emergency.

With TTIR, I aim to "entangle" participants with nature in two distinct ways. First, the work uses AAR to draw attention to the ambiance of the park. Second, it uses placed sound to explore its key themes, drawing attention to the climate crisis while also inviting participants to reflect on the benefits of urban green spaces. Later in this chapter, the methodology behind the creation of this work is expounded, offering an explanation of how the piece was conceived and structured to deliver its message. However, first some thought must be given to the way in which musical and environmental sounds can be combined into a cohesive whole.

Combining musical and environmental sound

Participants in TTIR hear two layers of sound – one layer being the environmental sounds happening in real time around them, the second being the digital sound layer heard through headphones. The sounds coming through the headphones are a combination of field recordings that are of recognizable origin as well as more "musical" sounds constructed from manipulated field recordings or synthesized to match the timbre of the environmental sounds. Therefore, three sets of sounds must be integrated into the same experience; for the sake of clarity let us call them "recorded environmental sounds", "musical sounds", and "real world sounds". In reality, the picture is somewhat more complicated than this, as there is no clear boundary between the first two sets. In fact there is more of a continuum of sounds, some more processed than others, between the "recorded environmental" and the "musical". It is useful to group the sounds in this way, however, as it allows us to consider how other practitioners have attempted to integrate musical and environmental sound in their work. Some of these approaches are briefly discussed here, before an explanation is offered of how this integration is attempted in TTIR.

The attempt to integrate musical and environmental sound is nothing new. Writing in 1974, Maryanne Amacher set out her hope that "the split which now exists between these two worlds – that of musical language and of environmental sound – one day will be closed". Discussing his 1978 work "Dreamsong", Michael McNabb explained:

> The basic intent of the piece was to integrate a set of synthesised sounds with a set of digitally recorded sounds to such a degree that they would form a continuum of available sound material. The sounds thus range from easily recognisable to the totally new, or, more poetically, from the real world to the dream world of the imagination.
>
> (in Emmerson 1986, 31)

These examples are four decades old, but this is an area of music that is still very much in development (Vickery et al. 2016) and we must therefore consider carefully how we are to combine the different sets of sounds.

To begin with, we will discuss how recorded environmental sounds are combined with musical sounds into a cohesive whole. Vickery et al. (2016) contend that one can either place instrumental parts into a field recording's "sonic world", or position them in juxtaposition to it. TTIR takes the first approach, and therefore it is important that all musical sounds in the work are sympathetic to the recorded environmental sounds they are placed alongside. When considering how best to achieve this sympathy between the environmental and the musical, it may be instructive to consider John Dack's writing on collage. Dack draws parallels between the collage work of visual artists such as Picasso and Braque and the work in music and sound art of composers such as Pierre Henry. He describes the way in which "the early collages of Picasso and Braque introduced 'reality fragments' into the flat surface of the painting" (2013, 278). We could similarly describe the recognizable, recorded environmental sounds of TTIR as "reality fragments". It should therefore be possible to draw inspiration from the ways in which these visual artists integrated the two strands of their work into a whole, creating a musical "collage" of sorts:

> Artists often juxtaposed these real-world objects with painted cubist images where the artist's technique shifts from the insertion of a real-world object to a concentration on the abstraction of shape and multiple depictions of perspective. This is in many ways the most interesting aspect of such collages: the tension created between the "real" objects which are loaded with social and culturally derived meanings and the representations of objects like guitars or furniture which have their shapes simplified and features abstracted to be transformed into planes of colour. We see the subjective decisions of the painter relate sometimes at odds with, at other times in harmony with, the "reality fragment" placed on and occupying the painting's surface. . . . Can we detect attempts by the painter to relate colours and textures of the reality fragment to the purely painted sections? Does the painter in other words, abstract – as an active transitive verb – characteristics of the object and extend them into the painted surface in an attempt at assimilation?
>
> (Dack 2013, 279)

Of course, the third layer, real world sounds, also needs to be successfully assimilated into the whole. Thankfully, as the recorded environmental sounds were captured at Taman Tugu, there is a ready link to the timbre of the Taman Tugu soundscape. This integration is assisted further by a phenomenon described by Smalley as "source bonding", a term he coined to represent the "intrinsic-to-extrinsic link, from inside the work to the sounding world outside". He defines source bonding as "the natural tendency to relate sounds to supposed sources and causes, and to relate sounds to each other because they appear to have shared or associated origins" (1997, 110). In the case of TTIR, the sounds will in fact have associated origins, so this bond will only be stronger.

Schafer contends that "what the soundscape analyst must do first is to discover the significant features of the soundscape, those sounds which are important either because of their individuality, their numerousness or their domination" (1994, 9). The soundscape of Taman Tugu is rich and varied. Wind rustles the leaves of the diverse foliage, water runs in small streams and drips from plants. The park is home to many varieties of birds and to bands of monkeys who can be heard calling and swinging through the trees. In certain places, urban sounds can also be heard: construction work, motorbikes, trucks. The most dominant sound in the forest, however, is the ever-present roar of insect noise. Schafer terms this kind of sonic base layer a *keynote sound;* the sound of a landscape, dictated by its geography and climate, that acts as a kind of anchor or fundamental tone of the soundscape. Schafer borrows the term keynote from music theory; "it is the note that identifies the key or tonality of a particular composition" (1994, 9). The sound of insects is so fundamental to the Taman Tugu ambiance that it was essential to reference it in the composition of TTIR. Recordings of insect sounds captured at the park were therefore manipulated in the studio to create a set of tonal drones that retain the shifting timbres of the jungle soundscape. These drones were then used as the basis for TTIR, becoming the literal keynote for the musical composition. The intention is to provide the sense that each drone, and therefore the composition as a whole, is very much embedded in the Taman Tugu soundscape: blending with it, rising out of it, creating moments of interplay between the real and the virtual. The drones are supplemented by melodic parts played on separate software instruments, constructed using samples of other distinctive jungle sounds – chosen for their individuality or numerousness – such as bird and monkey calls or trickling streams. Where possible, these melodic parts were placed in locations at which their timbre would match the ambiance; for example, an instrument constructed from recordings of a stream in the north-eastern corner of the park is to be heard only in the vicinity of that stream.

Structuring a placed sound work to deliver a message

There are numerous factors that mark out Taman Tugu as a suitable site for a placed sound work that incorporates environmental sound. First, the site has good mobile phone network coverage meaning that apps triggered by GPS function well. Second, the park has an interesting and varied soundscape. Third, the park contains notable geographical features around which moments of audio-visual congruence can be constructed.

In total, 22 interlocking musical passages were created for TTIR, ranging from five seconds to six minutes in length. In total, just over 43 minutes of original music was created, although the length of the actual performance experienced by any individual is determined by the time they spend exploring the work in the park. I mapped these musical passages onto the Taman Tugu landscape using an app named Echoes. The Echoes app can be downloaded for free from the Apple App Store or the Google Play Store, with participants then able to stream TTIR within the app when physically present at the park. The barrier for entry to the work is deliberately low – the app is free and can be downloaded quickly. Other than a mobile phone, the only equipment needed in order to experience TTIR is a pair of headphones, an item owned by most people and one that many tourists visiting Kuala Lumpur would have brought with them. Each of the 22 musical passages that make up the work is mapped to a separate audio zone in Echoes. When participants enter a zone with the app running, the attached audio is triggered and playback begins. The behaviour of the audio playback within the Echoes app is dependent on several settings. The audio can start abruptly, or can fade in gradually as the participant approaches the centre of the zone. The audio can be looped until the participant leaves the zone, or can play once from start to finish before ending. TTIR makes use of all of these audio behaviours. The zones are mapped in such a way that they frequently overlap, and thus participants often hear playback of two or three musical passages simultaneously. The music has been designed to anticipate this, and TTIR is therefore experienced as one cohesive whole rather than a collection of musical fragments.

In the weeks I spent gathering field recordings for TTIR, I was struck by the dramatic shifts in ambiance that I often experienced while navigating the park. In certain places, the city of Kuala Lumpur feels entirely absent; neither seen nor heard. However, in other places a corner can be turned and through gaps in the foliage one is suddenly confronted by skyscrapers. Kuala Lumpur is a bustling city of 1.75 million inhabitants, with an estimated 5.8 million more living in the greater metropolitan area (Department of Statistics Malaysia 2021b; UN DESA 2018). The city has a population density of 7,188 people per square kilometre (Department of Statistics Malaysia 2021a), is often congested with traffic, and in 2019 was host to numerous large-scale building projects. The soundscape of urban Kuala Lumpur therefore has a completely different makeup to that which is experienced in the park. In the depths of the park, the thick vegetation serves to mask the sounds of the city, immersing the visitor in nature. In the parts of the park where the city can be seen, it also becomes audible and the complexion of the ambiance therefore changes. These liminal zones – in which one finds oneself between nature and the city – became key areas in TTIR. The changes in ambiance that occur when the sounds of the city infiltrate the park are digitally exaggerated in order to draw attention to them. Digitally distorted layers of jungle soundscape and field recordings of urban sounds are layered into the music at these points – a reminder that the city is not far away and that many green spaces are under continual threat from urban expansion.

A fruitful comparison can be made here with the work of Jordan Lacey, who has written at length on *translating ambiance*; "the ambient expressions of an environment (especially sound and light) can be considered to be moveable and transitory (in flux), which the field recording artist apprehends and translates into an alternative environment" (Lacey 2020). In his installation, COLD, he translates a natural ambiance – hydrophone recordings of a river environment – into an urban space. Lacey argues that "soundscapes of the urban are controlled by *functionalist imperatives*, and that art installations are able to rupture these controls by opening human experiences to the new" (2016). Rather than translate natural ambiances into an urban setting, TTIR does the reverse. The intention of COLD is to rupture the controls that are placed on urban spaces as a result of capitalism "programming" such spaces in order to reduce "human experience to activities centred around consumerism" (Lacey 2020). The aims of TTIR are very different, and yet this idea that one ambiance can be disrupted by another is central to the success of the work. COLD and TTIR both work on the understanding that new experiences are possible when ambiances are translated.

An important component of this device in TTIR is that the city is seen as well as heard in these moments. This creates moments of audio-visual congruence that are important to the success of the work for two reasons: one experiential and one narrative (Hazzard 2016). First, they make the work feel more immersive, and second, they can be used to evoke and reinforce themes explored by the TTIR. One of Green's requirements for AAR experiences is that virtual and real objects

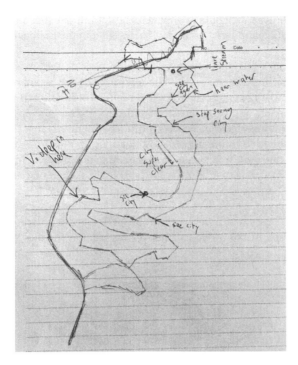

Map 9.1 Artist's map, hand drawn in the jungle. The map shows the points on the Taman Tugu trails at which the city becomes visible, and was used as a guide for audio mapping.

are aligned in space, but he goes on to say that "the contextual alignment of an augmentation with reality is of equal or greater importance than spatial alignment. For contextual alignment, a conceptual link between the virtual and real realms is needed" (Green 2013, 5). Reid et al. (2005) describe the physical-virtual collisions of audio-visual congruence as an example of *magic moments*; "those moments which are deemed to be both moving and memorable and thus are those that people really value". They deemed these moments to be of such importance to "situated mediascapes" that they identified a "need to design for coincidence; that is creating events which we know will happen synchronously in the real and virtual worlds".

Hazzard (2016) holds that there "is strong consensus that music shapes and drives an audiences referential and emotional interpretation of imagery" while Stevens (2021) demonstrates the impact of music on the interpretation of images, explaining that "when watching images and hearing music the viewer will form mental associations between the two, bringing the connotations of the music to bear on their understanding of a scene". TTIR makes use of the inclination of audiences to forge links between what they are seeing and the music that they are hearing in order to encourage engagement with the themes the work seeks to address. The final mapping of audio to Taman Tugu in the Echoes app can be seen in Map 9.2.

Participants in TTIR are free to wander the park as they wish – there is no prescribed route through the work. The audio zones are arranged such that the message of the work is unaffected by the direction or duration of travel, although the experience itself will be quite different depending on how any particular participant chooses to navigate it. A benefit of this structure is that the length of the walk can be tailored to fit the itinerary of tourists who may be in town for a short visit; however, the work was primarily designed in this way in order to encourage an approach to place that was known as *Topos* to the Ancient Greeks. In his paper on the subject, Parmar (2017, 234) defines Topos as being "less concerned with directed travel than peripatetic wanderings and the experiential nature of the journey". TTIR dispenses with a map, or a prescribed route, in order to foreground the experiential nature of the walk. This allows participants the mental space to fully

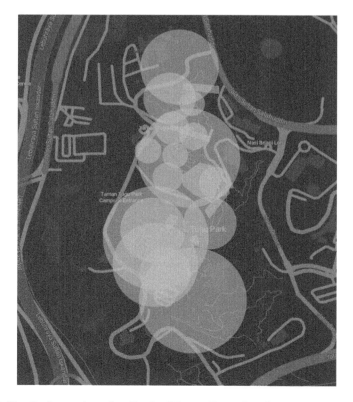

Map 9.2 The final mapping of audio for "Taman Tugu: Interference/Resistance" in the Echoes app. Screenshot by the author.

take in the rich landscape and ambiance of the jungle while leaving room for the themes of the work to gradually emerge.

Conclusion

In summary, TTIR has two aims: to engage participants with the Taman Tugu ambiance, and to highlight the importance of urban green spaces. While these aims could be seen as worthwhile ends in themselves, the hope is also to engage participants in thoughts of how these themes have a wider relevance. Let us tackle the aims one by one in order to explain how it is hoped that this is achieved.

TTIR draws attention to the Taman Tugu ambiance by inviting users to explore the park with their ears. Of course, by adding a digital sound layer to the park's real-time soundscape, certain real world sounds will be obfuscated. However, by performing a piece of music in which real world sounds are given prominence, an audience's attention can be drawn to those sounds and to soundscapes in general once the performance is over. There are certain parallels here to the work of Bill Fontana, whose Artists Statement explains his use of the natural environment as a sound source:

> My sound sculptures use the human and/or natural environment as a living source of musical information. I am assuming that at any given moment there will be something meaningful to hear and that music, in the sense of coherent sound patterns, is a process that is going on constantly.
>
> (Fontana 2017)

Any work attempting to incorporate the unpredictable noises of the real world into its structure owes a debt to John Cage, who in 1957 talked of "opening the doors of the music to the sounds that happen to be in the environment" (Cage 1958). As well as ensuring that each performance is unique, this kind of music can also encourage an audience to engage with the sonic world around them in a deeper way. Cage himself has said: "people have told me that, after hearing a concert in which noises are honoured as well as musical sounds, they listen to the sounds around them with more attention than they did previously" (Furlong 2012, 54). By "honouring" the Taman Tugu ambiance, TTIR encourages participants to engage with it more deeply, and to appreciate the extent to which it diverges from more common urban ambiances.

Hudson (2015) has written that musical composition that is strongly rooted in a specific location can help us to a greater understanding of landscape and our relationship to it, and indeed, Adorno suggested that sound and landscape can be used to "think with" (in DeNora 2003, 3). TTIR is an AAR musical experience that acts as site-specific discourse. It performs this function by aligning real and virtual objects; when the city is visible, the digital sound layer reflects this. This alignment, however, is contextual as well as physical, a factor that drives the message of the work; this green space provides a fragile refuge from the city and that requires consideration. Thus, Taman Tugu becomes a refraction point for a series of broader intersecting themes; it not only acts as a stark reminder of the climate crisis but also invites participants to reflect on the benefits of preserving urban green spaces.

References

Amacher, M. 1974. "Chicago Style." *Chicago Today*, May 10, 1974: 37.

Behrendt, F. 2015. "Locative Media as Sonic Interaction Design: Walking through Placed Sounds." *Wi: Journal of Mobile Media* 9 (2). https://pure.tue.nl/ws/portalfiles/portal/194772995/Behrendt2015LocativeMediaasSonicInteractionDesign.WalkingthroughPlacedSounds.pdf

Behringer. R. 2001. "Augmented Reality." In *Encyclopedia of Computer Science and Technology*, edited by A. Kent and J. Williams, 45–57. New York: Marcel Dekker.

Behringer. R., and T. Kastel. 2016. "Augmented Reality in Cultural Context." In *Kultur und Informatik: Augmented Reality*, edited by C. Busch and J. Sieck, 197–206. Berlin: Verlag Werner Hülsbusch.

BFM Media 2021. "Taman Tugu – From Dumping Ground to Public Park. BFM Earth Matters." *Podcast*. Accessed November 5, 2021. www.bfm.my/podcast/the-bigger-picture/earth-matters/taman-tugu-from-dumping-ground-to-public-park.

Bleecker, J., and J. Knowlton. 2006. "Locative Media: A Brief Bibliography and Taxonomy of GPS-Enabled Locative Media." *Leonardo Electronic Almanac* 14 (3) (June).

Cage, J. 1958. "Experimental Music." In *The 25-Year Retrospective Concert of the Music of John Cage*. George Avakian. No record label, vinyl. Liner notes.

Dack, J. 2013. "Collage, Montage and the Composer Pierre Henry: The Real, the Concrete, the Abstract in Sound Art and Music." *Journal of Music, Technology & Education* 6 (3): 275–284.

DeNora, T. 2003. *After Adorno: Rethinking Music Sociology*. Cambridge: Cambridge University Press.

Department of Statistics Malaysia. 2021a. "Current Population Estimates, Malaysia, 2021." Accessed April 28, 2022. www.dosm.gov.my/v1/index.php?r=column/cthemeByCat&cat=155&bul_id=ZjJOSnpJR21sQWVUcUp6ODRudm5JZz09&menu_id=L0pheU43NWJwRWVSZklWdzQ4TlhUUT09.

Department of Statistics Malaysia. 2021b. "Federal Territory of Kuala Lumpur." Accessed April 28, 2022. www.dosm.gov.my/v1/index.php?r=column/cone&menu_id=bjRlZXVGdnBueDJKY1BPWEFPRlhIdz09.

Dunn, R., M. Gavin, M. Sanchez, and J. Solomon. 2006. "The Pigeon Paradox: Dependence of Global Conservation on Urban Nature." *Conservation Biology* 20 (6): 1814–1816.

Emmerson, S. 1986. "The Relation of Language to Materials." In *The Language of Electroacoustic Music*, edited by S. Emmerson, 17–39. London: Macmillan.

Fontana, B. 2017. "Artists Statement." Accessed February 20, 2017. http://resoundings.org/Pages/Artists_Statement.html.

Furlong, W. 2012. *Speaking of Art: Four Decades of Art in Conversation*. 2nd ed. London: Phaidon Press.

Green, M. 2013. "Sounding Out Aural Augmented Reality." In *Proceedings of the 1st Fascinate Conference: Thoughtful Technology and Beautiful Interfaces, August 28–30, 2013, Falmouth*. Falmouth: Fascinate Conference.

Hartig, T., and P. H. Kahn. 2016. "Living in Cities, Naturally." *Science* 352 (6288): 938–940.

Hazzard, A. 2016. "Guidelines for Composing Locative Soundtracks." PhD diss., The University of Nottingham.

Hudson, M. 2015. "Archive, Sound and Landscape in Richard Skelton's Landings Sequence." *Landscapes* 16 (1): 63–78.

Lacey, J. 2016. *Sonic Rupture: A Practice-Led Approach to Urban Soundscape Design.* New York: Bloomsbury.

Lacey, J. 2020. "COLD: Translating the Ambiance of Rivulets Into Air-Conditioners." *Unlikely* 6. Accessed April 28, 2022. https://unlikely.net.au/issue-06/cold.

Lonely Planet. 2021. "Kuala Lumpur in Detail – Itineraries." Accessed November 10, 2021. www.lonelyplanet.com/malaysia/kuala-lumpur/narratives/planning/itineraries.

McCarthy, A. 2018. "Best New Opening for Travelers in 2019." Accessed November 10, 2021. www.lonelyplanet.com/articles/best-new-openings-for-travellers-in-2019.

Obrist, H. U. 2019. "Foreword." In *The Deep Listener*, edited by A. Boyes, A. Gad, E. Jäger, S. Netchaef, B. Vickers, and K. Watson, 4–7. Northampton: Belmont Press.

Parmar, R. 2017. "Geos, Topos, Choros." In *Proceedings of Invisible Places: Sound, Urbanism and Sense of Place, April 7–9, 2017 São Miguel Island.* São Miguel Island: Invisible Places.

Reid, J., R. Hull, K. Cater, and C. Fleuriot. 2005. "Magic Moments in Situated Mediascapes." In *Proceedings of the International Conference on Advances in Computer Entertainment Technology – ACE, June 15, 2005 Valencia.* New York: ACM Press. www.researchgate.net/publication/220982269_Magic_moments_in_situated_mediascamed.

Sato, M., I. Aoshima, and Y. Chang. 2021. "Connectedness to Nature and the Conservation of the Urban Ecosystem: Perspectives from the Valuation of Urban Forests." *Forest Policy and Economics* 125 (C): 1–11.

Schafer, R. M. 1994. *Our Sonic Environment and The Soundscape: The Tuning of the World.* 2nd ed. Rochester, VT: Destiny Books.

Smalley, D. 1997. "Spectromorphology: Explaining Sound-Shapes." *Organised Sound* 2 (2): 107–126.

Stevens, R. 2021. "The Inherent Conflicts of Musical Interactivity in Video Games." In *The Cambridge Companion to Video Game Music*, edited by M. Fritsch and T. Summers, 74–93. Cambridge: Cambridge University Press.

Taman Tugu Project. 2021. "Why The Taman Tugu Project?" Accessed September 15, 2021. http://tamantuguproject.com.my/en/.

UN DESA. 2019. "World Urbanisation Prospects, the 2018 Revision." New York: United Nations. Accessed April 29, 2022. https://population.un.org/wup/Publications/Files/WUP2018-Report.pdf.

Van Krevelen, D. W. F., and R. Poelman. 2010. "A Survey of Augmented Reality Technologies, Applications and Limitations." *International Journal of Virtual Reality* 9 (2): 1–20.

Vickery, L., M. Terren, S. Gillies, and J. Myburgh. 2016. "Between the Real and the Imaginary: Ecostructural Approaches to Composing with Field Recordings and Acoustic Instruments." In *Proceedings of Sonic Environments: The Australian Computer Music Conference, July 10–11, 2016, Brisbane.* Brisbane: Queensland Conservatorium.

Part IV

Neighbourhood life, sense of belonging, and place identity

10 Graffiti at the interface between tourism and the city we become

Plácido Muñoz Morán

Thinking at the interface of images: a literature review

> I like to think about the history and the hidden stories that encircle the walls of cities, the different architectures, its traces and layers left in the space over time . . . Our artworks are ephemeral and we paint on surfaces, which have their own stories . . . we integrate and add our art-works to those stories.
>
> (Personal interview, 12–04–2013)

Inspired by how the artworks of graffiti and street artists become part of the "stories" of urban landscapes, in my PhD research I approached the city as a "texture" or sensory vehicle that stimulated stories throughout my research. The properties of "textures" have been studied by anthropologists to explore how surfaces play an important role in the construction of knowledge and performances (Campbell 1993; Wassmann 1991; Morphy 1989). I argued in my previous works that graffiti artworks materialize from a relationship between surfaces, knowledge, and sensory relations in the city (Lefebvre 1991; Irving 2011; Borden 2001). For instance, the properties of a particular wall can stimulate creativity and memories that shape the actions of graffiti artists and the creation of images. But how do these images survive and stimulate further relations between people and the city space? Marilyn Strathern (2006) invites anthropologists to think about their worlds in terms of relations and encounters with other worlds so as not to remain tied to individual concepts and assumptions (2006, 199). In this chapter, I rethink the idea of "texture" beyond the boundaries of my own research to focus on the life of graffiti images and how they activate unfamiliar relations through new encounters. To rethink my textural approach beyond the practice of graffiti in the city of Barcelona, I begin by identifying graffiti images with the idea of an interface. Drawing from the multi-authored essay on interfaces between anthropology and STS (De la Cadena 2015), I understand the graffiti interface as a site for ethnographic practices shaped in my case by relations between cities and images. As Swanson points out, "taking seriously" should be extended to all sorts of things around us (in De La Cadena 2015, 459). It helps, Swanson adds, to think beyond our worlds, making the familiar strange. The graffiti interface, therefore, becomes

DOI: 10.4324/9781003207207-15

an interactional process in which I situate myself to explore how images, broadly understood, contribute to the production of urban ambiences and tourism. What do images do within this process?

I take a visual culture approach to study images as a broad field of critical practice; in accordance with what W.J.T. Mitchell (2005) proposes, images are analysed in terms of their "desires" rather than in relation to language and society. Here, I use Mitchell's idea of a "meta-picture", which refers to "pictures about pictures" (1994, 35), not only in terms of representation and aesthetics but also as part of "an entire system of knowledge/power relations" (1994, 58). This allows me to explore how images are embodied as part of different life processes. In this chapter, this implies looking not only at the creation and existence of the graffiti images in the city but also at how graffiti images are grounded in "ethical, political and aesthetics 'assemblages' that allow us to observe observers" (Mitchell 1994, 49). Doing ethnography at the graffiti interface is a way to discuss those "assemblages" within processes of transformation and meaning-making in cities. It also involves dialectic interactions between mental and material images and how these foster the production of "signs that culture weaves around itself" (Mitchell 1986, 43).

By themselves, images can activate imaginative spaces that are filled with spatiotemporal connections and possibilities forming narratives. Andrew Irving (2017) argues that these imaginative spaces do not exist in isolation but, rather, they are intertwined with everyday acts as well as multiple present and future events (Irving 2017, 25). I am interested in the dynamic nature of images in the city and how they become active entities within urban transformations and the production of urban ambiences. The role of tourism in these processes connects all of chapters in this edited book and will also act as a storyline between the case studies that I discuss in the cities of Barcelona and Berlin.

The city we become as a method

Dalakoglou suggests that the boundaries between spontaneous and non-spontaneous collective actions are blurred. He argues that the classification "provides a way of 'knowing' spontaneously acquired knowledge" as a way to domesticate an otherwise spontaneous world (Dalakoglou 2012, 540). The question, he suggests, should be focused not only on judging whether or not an action is authentically spontaneous but also on what happens after the spontaneous (or not) moments of revolt (Dalakoglou 2012, 541).

Brief historical context

On 9 November 1989, the dividing wall between West and East Berlin collapsed. Thousands of Berliners jumped over the wall that had imposed a separation on them for almost 30 years in the city and were able to move freely between the two cities. The images of people tearing apart the wall and the euphoria of the moment marked the end of the Cold War and shortly afterwards of the Soviet

Union. People who lived in Berlin at that time described their experiences of that moment as a roller coaster of emotions. One of my informants explained it as follows: "for a while there was a lot of interaction in the city between people, even between estrangers and what it was the physical reality of your city was radically transformed from one day to the other" (Personal interview, 25 September 2021). It could be said that during that time, the inhabitants of Berlin entered the realm of the mythical: a stage in which the temporality of events and the radical transformation of the city space ended up interconnected with the imagination of people. The symbols and signs of the two Berlins were interchanged or simply disappeared, opening up new narratives, which have remained until today. The fall of the wall transformed two familiar cities into an unfamiliar one fostering the production of new physical and sensorial ambiences. More than 30 years after that historical day, we could say that not only did the wall and the communist system in Germany collapse, but also that two cities became one.

Making an analogy between the collapse of the East and West cities into the current Berlin and my method of work in this chapter, I propose to overcome the distinction between space and time in which ethnographic events are usually located. This implies rethinking what the city is and how I can approach it as a "combination of past, present and future within a process of becoming" (Harrison 2011, 154). This also involves thinking about the city beyond its geographical and historical boundaries to move between spaces and times that exist here and now. How do the material and mental images of the city shape the imagination and sensory experiences of its inhabitants? The city in which I locate this discussion will be built out of my fieldwork practices in two cities: on the one hand, Barcelona, where I carried out research into its urban transformation in connection with the practice of graffiti and street art, and on the other hand, Berlin, where I conducted research on the transformation of the East Side Gallery as part of the urban transformation in East Berlin. In regard to both, I am interested in using the images of graffiti and murals in public spaces as a method to explore the production of narratives and urban ambiences in the city.

In Berlin, the historical narrative shaped by the Cold War and the Berlin Wall fits with the metaphor of the Iron Curtain; it is well established as a hegemonic Western narrative (Macwilliams 2020, 112). The dominance of this narrative, Macwilliams (2020) adds, is demonstrated by the commodification of the wall itself and how it has become a value for the tourist industry. The ambition of the tourist industry is to manufacture an "experience value" in cities (Löfgren 2008, 86); in the case of Berlin, this is widely inspired by the wall narrative and the conflict between communism and capitalism. But the wall and what it communicates is only one side of this process in which tourists, and what they demand, has a major power in terms of how the tourist sites are treated and transformed over time by local governments and industries. I will look at some of the stories that activate the wall to shed some light on their coexistence with the tourist consumption and the permanents inhabitants of cities.

In her book "The Naked City", Sharon Zukin (2010) portrays New York as a city that has lost its soul due to the mass construction and gentrification processes.

She connects the concept of authenticity with the idea of "origins": "a human right, that is cultivated by long-time residence, use and habit" (2010, 244). The rebuilding of Berlin after the fall of the Wall opened up spaces that the city is still trying to incorporate into its larger urban fabric. Looking at these processes from Zukin's perspective, Berlin could be searching for a lost soul and origins and trying to fill the void left by its multiple collapses over history with the cultivation of a new soul. But this is happening in a global world that is more interconnected than ever before, in which the image of contemporary Western cities has become a key element to attract flows of capital, labour, and tourists. I claim that the "global city" is built upon the overlapping of multiple images in which the material, digital, and mental dimensions are at play, whereby the images of the city rather than the use or habits of its population are the engine for its urban transformations (Sassen 2007). The city becomes a "meta-picture" formed by a compound of different images that stimulate perceptions and the transmission of meanings contributing to the existence of urban ambiences and their experiences.

Ambiences: stories of images and walls

To further illustrate my understanding of urban ambiences and their relationship with images and the city space, I will use an example from my ethnography on graffiti and street art in the city of Barcelona. I argue that the anti-tourist graffiti on the public space walls of the neighbourhood of Vallcarca are not only images but also signs of something else. The anti-tourist graffiti has contributed to the creation of a particular image of the neighbourhood that connects with local people and their community projects. Vallcarca's urban ambience emerges "in between"

Figure 10.1   Anti-tourism graffiti in Vallcarca (Barcelona).

Photo: Plácido Muñoz Morán

Figure 10.2   Teufelsberg (Berlin). Screenshot from Super 8 film by Plácido Muñoz Morán.

those material and mental images linked to present and future transformations of the neighbourhood. These different actors, including the anti-tourist graffiti, shape the lived ambience in Vallcarca. Within it, the idea of tourism is rejected as a source of displacement of local people and their ways of living. I argue that the current urban ambience in Vallcarca is experienced by close interactions over time between local inhabitants, images, and the space.

As I mentioned earlier, images have the ability to open up imaginative spaces, which are filled with narratives. The graffiti interface that I propose emerges from images and their capacity to create urban ambiences. Doing ethnography at the graffiti interface offers me the possibility to connect different worlds within the transformation of cities and the role of tourism within these processes. To explain what I mean by this, I ask the reader to look at the following images.

The images earlier are two clips captured from a super 8 video filmed by my friend in Teufelsberg during a Berlin holiday. At that time, I was starting my practice-based PhD research at the University of Manchester with the broad idea of filming a collaborative documentary on graffiti and street art in Barcelona. My friend gave me this footage in case I wanted to use it for my audio-visual work. Then this idea was transformed throughout my research into something else but I saved the footage on to one of my hard drives. The place that appears in the images was a listening spy station, during the Cold War, located on the highest mountain of West Berlin. In 2010, however, when these images were filmed the listening station was an abandoned compound of buildings and structures, which had been this way since the fall of the Berlin Wall. After that, the surfaces of the spy station started to be covered by graffiti and street artworks, becoming an attraction for urban explorers and the most adventurous tourists. Here, I have incorporated the images of Teufelsberg as a means to reflect on images in connection with different worlds, including my anthropological perspective. Although these images were almost forgotten inside my hard drive, later I encountered them in connection with other people, times, and materiality. Those interconnections shaped the basis of my interface idea to investigate what graffiti does and what it can become within tourist sites and the production of urban ambiences.

My second contact with the images of Teufelsberg and its geodesic domes took place during my fieldwork in Barcelona. During this time, I met the street artists Kenor and H101, who showed me a video[1] of their intervention on one of the dome surfaces in Teufelsberg, where they had painted a collaborative graffiti artwork. When I interviewed them as part of my PhD fieldwork, they used this example to describe how abandoned buildings offered them less restrictions and the possibility to experiment. In those cases, their artworks were more improvised and unpredictable due to the particular material and sensorial features of the space in which they had intervened. Together they shape ambiences that not only inspired them to paint but also dictated some of the terms of their own intervention. In similar ways, anthropologists move between the concrete and the abstract in their ethnographic encounters. "Thinking through things", anthropologists suggest experimenting with methods by which the material may itself illuminate unfamiliar realities and new concepts.

A couple of years after I completed my PhD research, I visited Berlin and the spy station in Teufelsberg for the first time. After I had taken a few photographs of the geodesic domes, I thought about their role as interfaces during the Cold War: on the one hand, as sonic interfaces to capture the waves of sounds linked to the secret conversations in East Berlin, and on the other as visual interfaces to capture visual attention at the top of the highest mountain in West Berlin. Both interfaces worked as sites of connections between different worlds, which were not only different but also related. In the end, it is the dynamic of how differences are created what is more intriguing.

The second of my ethnographic encounters at the graffiti interface was at the East Side Gallery in Berlin, where the urban ambience is strongly marked by mass tourism and narratives linked to the Cold War and the division of the city by the Berlin Wall.

Mass tourism can create a tension between the city imagined and promoted by urban planners, architects, and local governments and that experienced by the city's inhabitants. Tourist sites such as the Berlin Wall are charged with a mix of feelings, meanings, and memories, which tend to be simplified or erased by urban renewals. The East Side Gallery is not only one of the sites in Berlin that is visited by many tourists, but it has also become a contested arena of collective and individual actions regarding its conservation and the urban developments around it. This tourist site recreates the dominant historical narrative of the new city based on the division between East and West Berlin. The open-air gallery is not only an art gallery but also the longest remaining section of the Berlin Wall in the city. With more than 100 murals painted in 1990 on the East side of the wall, the gallery is visited by millions of tourists every year, who take photos of the most iconic murals as well as of themselves with the Berlin wall as a background. The sociologist John Urry (1990) states in his landmark work about mass tourism *The Tourist Gaze* that: "The gaze is constructed through signs, and tourism involves the collection of signs" (1990, 3). Following Urry's understanding of the tourist gaze in terms of signs, the photographs taken by tourists are not only images but also metaphors of something else. The photographs of the East Side Gallery, therefore, become visual signs, not only of a distinctive visual environment, in this case Berlin, but also of how and why tourists collect and consume it.

Before the fall of the Berlin Wall, painting on the West side of the wall was a common practice but it was completely forbidden on the East side. The visual interventions on walls of the East Side Gallery after the fall of the wall shifted that reality, as the wall facing East Berlin was filled with murals and graffiti. These actions produced a disruption of what Ranciére (2004) defines as the "distribution of the sensible" shaped by a dominant sensory order that conditions its transformation and the way in which people can participate in it. In this case the disruption of what was allowed to be painted and seen also symbolized the collapse of the East Germany government. The East Side Gallery became a political intervention and a symbol of that historical moment representing a new status quo in Germany. Shifting our way of thinking about the East Side Gallery and looking at it as a social and artistic movement uncovers a more static dynamic linked to its symbolic dimension. Around the same time, the New York subway graffiti movement transformed graffiti and muralism into a means of communication for people who had limited means of making their voice heard. This movement spread worldwide from locally "writing" names and symbols with spray cans and markers on any public space surface to creating artworks on trains and later in galleries. In contrast, the murals of the East Side Gallery, which were contemporaneous of the graffiti movement in New York, became a local heritage memorial, which has to be conserved and protected as it was originally painted.

The East Side Gallery encloses different views, styles, and painting skills and represents different ways of seeing the world around it. In an interview with Thomas Klingenstein, one of the artists who participated in the creation of the East Side Gallery, he said:

> I think that the artists who painted the murals tried to represent some personal experiences or views linked to the wall. For me the wall restricted my freedom to access other cultures such as the Japanese. This situation inspired me to paint my mural "Detour to the Japanese Sector".
>
> (Personal interview, 1 November 2021)

Margaret Hunter, a Scottish art student who also participated in the creation of the East Side Gallery, painted two murals: "Hands" and "Joint Venture". In the latter one, she explored the duality of the divided city in connection with her own personal life:

> There were two different worlds in Berlin which seemed to parallel my own life, split between home in Scotland and artistic life in Berlin, I tried to explore though my mural Joint Ventura the struggles and complexities of different realities.
>
> (Personal interview, 24 October 2021)

The East Side Gallery has ended up coexisting with the city and its transformation up until today. Thomas and Margaret never thought that what they painted would become part of a memorial of that time. In this sense, the murals have gone through different stages from being painted to almost being forgotten and erased by the passage of time, to being repainted and protected by the local government. Following the murals through their different temporalities allows us to explore how these images activate further relations in which personal stories, the image of the city and its narratives, are at play.

Thomas Klingenstein was born and lived in East Berlin until he was deported by the GDR government to the German Democratic Republic in 1981. Before he painted his mural, he remembered the area around the East Side Gallery as follows:

> grey and dark, a little bit destroyed, dirty with old buildings or ruins from the war. That was not an area to go because it was next to the wall and I could not imagine that it would become what it is today, crowded, full of buildings built with a lot of money to make money and tourists going up and down.
>
> (Personal interview, 1 November 2021)

At the time at which these murals where painted, the East side area around the wall was almost empty, a void. According to Huyssen (1997), the notion of Berlin as a void signifies more than a metaphor or a transitory condition, it carries historical connotations (1997, 62). The existence of empty spaces in Berlin and other cities can tell us more through their emptiness than through the new constructions in them. During the last stage of my ethnography in Barcelona, I was interested in the role of space and its material elements as non-human political agents. The neighbourhood of Vallcarca and its urban transformation became the main focus of my work. In it, the existence of empty building sites was preceded by evictions and the demolition of houses. The last stage of this process, however, coincided with the financial crisis of 2008, which stopped the construction of high-rise luxury blocks. This left a neighbourhood scattered with empty building sites. There, different collectives of the neighbourhood started to carry out interventions on the empty sites creating and an alternative political force. The empty sites became both places of meeting and resistance as well as political actors, which facilitated the flourishing of different projects such as community gardens, bike workshops, or graffiti creations.

Tim Ingold (2013) states that the properties of materials are not attributes but enclose stories regarding their ways to becoming something else (2013, 31). The ways in which we interact with them can activate those stories, empowering the people involved in the process. One of the issues that has activated an alternative political force in Vallcarca is linked to the transformation of its space. The empty building sites offer multiple possibilities that move between the ones imagined by architects, urban planners, and construction companies and the ones proposed by the inhabitants of the neighbourhood.

Making an analogy between the empty spaces in the city and the involvement of local collectives in the transformation of the city space, the question that arises is how these spaces and ways of making politics get incorporated into the larger urban fabric. Today, most of the empty areas around the East Side Gallery have become hotels, shopping malls, and luxury apartment blocks. Meanwhile, the East Side Gallery has gained official status as a "Denkmal", or heritage-protected landmark. Since then, the restoration and preservation of the murals has been the subject of some conflicts and copyright issues and some of the artists have refused to repaint their works. It is difficult to understand what the East Side Gallery is today outside of the tourist circuits and the dominant historical narrative linked to the Berlin Wall. As Margaret Hunter says: "the wall became more important than the murals painted on it" (Personal interview, 24 October 2021). But even if that is the case for many of the tourists who visit this site, Margaret also mentions that "it is not just a wall but memories kept alive, it represents the stories of people, their fears, hopes and dreams retained for future generation". However, the current ambience created between these images and the people who experience them is filled: on the one hand by the symbolic dimension of the Berlin Wall and the demand of mass tourism; on the other, it is identified with a particular image of the city and its global projection which has fuelled the urban transformation around the East Side Gallery into luxury hotels, holiday apartments, and buildings owned by international corporations. The mural images have become trapped in this process transforming themselves into part of the "metapicture" of the city and its system of knowledge and power.

Taking a different angle, in Barcelona, I followed the renewal of a mural on the façade of a community squatted centre called "La Carbonería". The old mural had ended up becoming a symbol for the collective members themselves and for most of the inhabitants of the neighbourhood, who accepted and recognized it as part of their urban landscape. However, some of the members of the collective also thought that the mural had become another of Barcelona's tourist attractions at which people stopped to take photographs. Eventually, the old mural was erased by a new mural, which became the symbol of their campaign and protest in the face of speculation and their eviction. They were aware of the potential of the new mural to make their claims visible and to give a voice to their cause. Like the murals in the East Side Gallery, once the mural in "La Carbonería" was produced, it achieved its own agency facing tourists and other inhabitants of the city. The interaction with people, however, stimulated not only narratives and memories but also contradictory interests and actions. In 2014 the eviction of "La Carbonería" was executed but the mural stayed on the façade until the building was sold again to a new construction company. Eventually in 2020, the mural, which was considered a symbol of the street art and the social movements in Barcelona, was removed by the construction company that got a licence from the local government to build luxury apartments.

Conclusion

The aforementioned examples show how images in the city activate multiple narratives as well as individual and collective actions between different worlds. Looking at them as part of the same city in which it is possible to combine spaces and past, present and future relations, I have explored unfamiliar connections between my research on graffiti and the transformation of the East Side Gallery into a tourist site. In this process, the material features of the urban environments such as walls, squatted buildings, or empty building sites and how they facilitate the existence of material and mental images have been incorporated as a method of study. Thus, my ethnography is not focused on studying the relations between hegemonic and resistance actors in the city but on searching for connections between the political roles of material and visual actors within the process of urban transformations.

I propose shifting and experimenting with social and material relations by taking seriously not only what people do and say but also what people become through their relations with the material elements of urban landscapes. The impact of mass tourism in cities offers a scenario to study how cities and their inhabitants are shaped by the tourist interests. Following images in the city such as murals and graffiti, I have questioned what they do and what they become over time as part of urban ambiences and research practices.

Note

1 https://vimeo.com/71673555.

References

Borden, I. 2001. *Skateboarding, Space and the City: Architecture and the Body*. Oxford: Berg.

Campbell, S. 1993. "Attaining Rank: A Classification of Kula Shell Valuables." In *The Kula: New Perspectives on Massim Exchange*, edited by Jerry W. Leach and E. Leach, 229–248. Cambridge: Cambridge University Press.

Dalakoglou, D. 2012. "Beyond Spontaneity: Crisis, Violence and Collective Action in Athens." *City* 16 (5): 535–545.

De la Cadena, M. 2015. "Anthropology and STS: Generative Interfaces, Multiple Location." *Journal of Ethnographic Theory* 5 (1): 437–475.

Harrison, R. 2011. "Surface Assemblages. Towards an Archaeology in and of the Present." *Archaeological Dialogues* 18 (2): 141–161.

Huyssen, A. 1997. "The Voids of Berlin." *Critical Inquiry* 24 (1): 57–81.

Ingold, T. 2013. *Making: Anthropology, Archaeology, Art and Architecture*. London: Routledge.

Irving, A. 2011. "Strange Distance: Towards an Anthropology of Interior Dialogue." *Medical Anthropology Quarterly* 25 (1): 22–44.

Irving, A. 2017. "The Art of Turning Left and Right." In *Anthropologies and Futures: Researching Emerging and Uncertain Worlds*, edited by Juan F. Salazar, S. Pink, A. Irving and J. Sjoberg, 23–42. London: Bloomsbury.

Lefebvre, H. (1971) 1991. *The Production of Space*. London: Blackwell Publishing.

Löfgren, O. 2008. "The Secret Lives of Tourists: Delays, Disappointments and Day-dreams." *Scandinavian Journal of Hospitality and Tourism* 8 (1): 85–101.

Macwilliams, A. 2020. "The Materiality of Metaphor: The Cold War and the Berlin Wall." In *Walling It and Walling Out. Why Are We Building New Barriers to Divide Us*, edited by L. McAtacney and R. H. McGuire, 111–130. Albuquerque: University New Mexico Press.

Mitchell, W. J. T. 1986. *Iconology: Image, Text, Ideology*. Chicago: University of Chicago Press.

Mitchell, W. J. T. 1994. *Picture Theory: Essays on Verbal and Visual Representation*. Chicago: University of Chicago Press.

Mitchell, W. J. T. 2005. *What do Pictures Want? The Lives and Loves of Images*. London: Chicago Press.

Morphy, H. 1989. "From Dull to Brilliant: The Aesthetics of Spiritual Power among the Yolngu." *Man NS* 24: 21–40.

Ranciére, J. 2004. *The Politics of Aesthetics: The Distribution of the Sensible*. Translated by Gabriel Rockhill. London: Bloomsbury Revelations.

Sassen, S. 2007. "The Global City." In *A Companion to the Anthropology of Politics*, edited by D. Nugent and J. Vincent, 168–178. London: Blackwell Publishing.

Strathern, M. 2006. "A Community of Critics? Thoughts on New Knowledge." *Journal of the Royal Anthropological Institute* 12 (1): 191–209.

Urry, J. 1990. *The Tourist Gaze*. London: Sage.

Wassmann, J. 1991. *The Song of the Flying Fox: The Public and Esoteric Knowledge of the Important Men of Kandingei about Totemic Songs, Names and Knotted Cords (Middle. Sepik, Papua New Guinea)*. Boroko, Papua New Guinea: Cultural Studies Division, National Research Institute.

Zukin, S. 2010. *Naked City: The Death and Life of Authentic Urban Places*. London: Oxford University Press.

11 Escaping the big box store

Examining change, gastrotourism, and provisioning at Findlay Market, Cincinnati, OH

Lisa Marie Beiswenger

Introduction

"An estimated 1.2 million shopping visits are made yearly to Findlay Market – making this historical landmark the 5th most visited place in Cincinnati (behind Cincinnati Zoo, Great American Ballpark, Museum Center & Casino)" (Economic Development 2019). This market, established in 1852 as a place for local producers to sell their wares, has evolved from exclusively a locus for provisioning to a site with a robust tourist trade. As this urban market evolved, management had to maintain a balance between features that will attract tourists while also selling products that remain true to this historic landmark's heritage as a place for neighbourhood residents to interact with producers and satisfy their food shopping needs. The public market represents a space where a welcoming and civil atmosphere is the background for social interactions; however, as the socioeconomic status of visitors has changed, the role of the market is shifting.

The examination of change at public markets and retail establishments has been of growing interest (Jones et al. 2007; Guimarães 2018, 2019; Gonzales and Waley 2013), and as these markets change, they are met with the twin challenges of appealing to new consumers while also maintaining relationships with existing clientele. Additionally, public markets, like Findlay Market in Cincinnati, Ohio, have significant logistical challenges compared to their grocery store and supermarket counterparts. These challenges range from residential decentralization, lack of sufficient parking, and issues of scale. Public markets are also competing against international big-box retailers which have increased power over suppliers and manufacturers, making it nearly impossible for public markets to compete on price and range of choice (Jones et al. 2007). This chapter will contribute to the growing body of literature about change at public markets. It includes an overview of the history of Findlay Market before examining the types of shopping that occur at the market and how the market has evolved to accommodate new clientele. Finally, it discusses how Findlay Market weathered one of its biggest challenges: the early months of the COVID-19 pandemic.

DOI: 10.4324/9781003207207-16

The history of Findlay Market and Over-the-Rhine

Findlay Market was not the first market founded in Cincinnati, but it is the longest lived. Over the course of the nineteenth and early twentieth centuries, Cincinnati established nine public/farmers' markets. Today, Findlay is the only surviving public market (Findlay Market: A Brief History 2019). Findlay Market was named after James Findlay, an early Cincinnati settler, retailer, civic leader, and mayor. Findlay purchased tracts of wooded land immediately north of the Cincinnati city line which he hoped to develop. He planned to use part of that tract for a general store and a market for local farmers to sell their wares but died before his grand plan could come to fruition. After his death in 1835, and the subsequent death of his wife in 1851, the executors of his estate donated a parcel of land to the city (Schweitzer and Gerbus 1974).

Meanwhile, a new neighbourhood, later named Over-the-Rhine, was forming on the outskirts of Cincinnati around the area that would become Findlay Market. Shortly after the market was completed in 1855, the area experienced a boom as German immigrants and German-Americans began to fill Over-the-Rhine with new businesses and residences. This era was the height of the neighbourhood with a flourishing population, strong businesses, and high employment rates. Findlay Market was a bustling part of this neighbourhood, and in 1902, it experienced its first major renovation when a masonry tower was added to the structure. A second renovation in 1915 enclosed the market and added refrigeration to alleviate public health concerns about pollution and disease contamination (Venison and Bear Meat 1961; Schweitzer and Gerbus 1974). These concerns were well founded; at its inception,

> the market house was of iron all right – sheet iron with no sides or ends, little more than an open-ended shed where meat hung on hooks exposed to the wind, dust and flies and whatever else came along to contaminate it.
>
> (Venison and Bear Meat 1961)

And while meat and produce were being stored adequately on days when the market was closed – vendors utilized the cool cellars beneath nearby breweries to keep perishables fresh – the public had begun demanding refrigeration to ensure higher standards of food safety.

In 1972, the market was listed on the National Register of Historic Places, but the market house and the neighbourhood around it had fallen into disrepair as the neighbourhood's population shrank.

> Like all the neighbourhood buildings around her, the old queen on the market square gradually grew older and became faded and shoddy. The wiring was ancient; the refrigeration dated back to 1915; the sanitation facilities were inadequate; there was no air-conditioning; what was modern in 1852 and 1902 was quaint, but utterly impossible if the historic Findlay Market was to survive.
>
> (Schweitzer and Gerbus 1974, 22)

The goal was not to eradicate the allure of the old market, but rather to freshen it up in a way that would "preserve the charm and flavor of her romantic past" (Schweitzer and Gerbus 1974, 22). In 1973–1974, the market was gutted, leaving the cast iron structure in place. The interior of the market was rebuilt, preserving the basic structure and feel of the market while giving it a much-needed update.

Three decades later, in 2006, the market underwent another renovation. Again, virtually everything was replaced, except for the market's historic iron frame. Electrical fixtures, plumbing, and refrigeration were updated, and stalls were expanded. In 2006, about a third of the market stalls were either empty or under construction. Findlay Market had passed out of consciousness for many Cincinnatians (Troy 2006), but still the market survived. As Mike Bender, owner of Mike's Meats stated in a 2006 interview, "We've weathered a lot of storms", he continues, "where else can you buy a good steak hoagie for $2?" (qtd. in Troy 2006).

The market persisted, but it took substantial assistance from the City of Cincinnati. In 2006, the Cincinnati government budgeted a subsidy of $632,000 to keep the market running, and while the subsidies have decreased in recent years, the city continues to cover some operation costs and improvements (Troy 2006; Fiscal Years 2016–2017 2016; Requested Consolidated Plan Budget Update 2013). There is value in the market for the city of Cincinnati, and even as the population

Figure 11.1 Approaching the Findlay Market House from the Farm Shed.

Photo: Lisa Marie Beiswenger

of Cincinnati plummeted through the second half of the twentieth century, they held on to this commercial institution where individuals could gather.

There are four major sections to today's Findlay Market: the market house, the farm shed, storefronts around the market, and the streets surrounding the market where temporary stalls are erected during weekends and special events. Aside from a few of the storefronts and the street itself, all of these areas are property owned by the Corporation for Findlay Market. Many of the storefronts are vacant, and Findlay Market has been slowly renovating them in an effort to expand the market and increase the goods available to the customers.

Currently, there are 50 permanent, full-time vendors. Twelve specialize in meats, fish, and cheeses, 12 offer prepared foods, 7 sell grocery items, 6 specialize in desserts/baked goods, 2 sell primarily produce, 5 sell beverages, and 10 sell other items such as pet food, candles, bags, flowers, and Findlay Market souvenirs. There are 70 seasonal and part-time vendors including over 40 local farmers and cottage producers. According to the Findlay Market website, about 300 people work at the market on a typical Saturday (Economic Development 2019). Along with these permanent vendors, there are temporary vendors who sell desserts, gift items, clothing, household goods, essential oils, prepared foods, baskets, and bread. On weekends, there is a farmer's market which includes the typical goods one might find at any farmer's market: fresh produce, cheese, meat, eggs, cookies, and other local products. The farm shed is most busy on Saturdays, but farmers and other vendors will occasionally come in off and on throughout the week to sell their wares.

Methodology

To gain an understanding of how customers utilize the market, self-administered surveys were utilized in this study. Surveys involve following a detailed schedule of questions and can be useful for generating quantitative data (Bernard 2006). A total of 180 surveys were distributed in self-addressed, stamped envelopes over seven visits to the market in the summer and fall of 2013. Surveys were distributed by myself and four undergraduate research assistants: Kayla Killoren, Meagan Jones, Maria Danna, and Evelyn Romeo. Seventy-five surveys were returned. The surveys consisted of 34 questions which inquired how customers use the market, how often they visit the market, what they purchase, and what they wish was available at the market. Basic biographical information – age, gender, marital status, adults/children living in the household, income, employment status, and zip code – was also collected. To support the survey results, six participant observation sessions were conducted at the market. All of these sessions were conducted from a customer's perspective and were recorded while seated inside the market house, walking around the perimeter of the market, walking through the farm shed, and seated in one of the two seating areas to the north and east of the market house. In other words, I moved through the market as a visitor or customer might, occasionally stopping to purchase an item or chat with some customers. These discussions with customers were noted in field notes. These observations were conducted with the goal of documenting movement around the market, what visitors discuss, how customers interact with each other and the vendors, and what customers buy at the market.

Provisioning, thrift, and treats at the public market

Daniel Miller models three dimensions of shopping – the treat, provisioning, and thrift – in *A Theory of Shopping* (1998). Provisioning encompasses the bulk of shopping. It includes the purchasing of clothes, personal care items, and general grocery items. Provisioning takes care of a shopper's immediate needs and is typically "highly routinized" and consists of regular trips to a local supermarket (Miller 1998, 44). While it may seem that provisioning is a calculated act, it is a social act as many customers are not only shopping for themselves but also shopping for their families. Provisioning forms connections between individuals. Miller's second category of shopping, thrift, takes into account the strategies that a shopper uses to save money and time as they provision. Many people balance concerns that include time, taste, value, and source as they make decisions over their purchases. Thrift is not always about price but is manifest in different ways individuals shop. A visitor may choose to go to the market as a leisure activity, but may purchase items for provisioning as a way to save time by avoiding a trip to the grocery store. Thrift encompasses short- and long-term strategies that are divided between a focus on immediate needs as well as the future (Miller 1998).

If personal provisioning covers the necessities of modern existence and thrift balances a shopper's time and energies, the treat is more complicated. Miller defines "the treat" as "any special purchase made with respect to a particular individual or group, often including the shopper" (Miller 1998, 5). A treat can be immediate, small, and simple like a cookie purchased to reward a well-behaved child. A treat can also be complicated and expensive and built around a trip to the market (Miller 1997). Ultimately, treats are a small portion of the actual shopping experience and are best understood as a personal indulgence which "help to define the rest of shopping as based around sacrifice and need" (Miller 1997). Most of the necessities of daily life can be found at the Findlay Market, including proteins, vegetables, fruit, eggs, flour, as well as assorted non-food items and kitchenware. As of April 2019, 21 vendors sell foods that must be prepared before they can be consumed, such as meat, fish, vegetables, and dry goods. A majority (83%) of customers surveyed for this project claimed that they purchase ingredients to prepare at home, and 75% state that they come for the farmer's market (Table 11.2).

Prepared food vendors add another dimension to the shopping experience at Findlay Market. These merchants sell meals to be eaten on the premises or to be carried-out. Prepared foods occupy a unique position in the study of shopping. They are provisioning because they replace the food and efforts consumers would make if they had to shop and cook, but prepared foods are also a treat because they save consumers time and effort while creating an opportunity to experience foods that are a break from the norm (Au and Law 2002; Chang and Hsieh 2006). They reside in the area between provisioning and the treat.

Thrift is also a factor in at least some of the shopping at Findlay Market. While many of the vendors do sell organic products that are more expensive than their conventionally produced counterparts, there are vendors who sell items that could be considered a bargain. For example, one of the produce vendors at the market sells "second-hand produce" that has been passed over by larger grocery stores and produce firms at distribution centres. This produce may be past its prime or it may have blemishes; nonetheless, it is just as edible as organic produce, and it is sold at a fraction of the price. Findlay Market also has internal competition, especially among the meat vendors. This means that a savvy bargain hunter may be able to find less expensive products if they compare prices between vendors before purchasing.

The treat is a little more difficult to quantify at Findlay Market. When asked if they purchased a dessert or snack during their last three visits to the market, 43% of survey participants responded in the affirmative and 37% claim that desserts/snacks are one of the reasons why they visit the market. Similarly, 53% of survey respondents state that they eat lunch at the market, but only 5% say that it is their primary reason for visiting the market. People like the environment and atmosphere of the market, and though only 21% of people listed it as their primary

Table 11.1 Why do you primarily visit Findlay Market?

Special events	0
Farmer's markets	15
To buy and eat lunch there	4
To buy and eat dinner there	0
To purchase lunch to take away	0
To purchase dinner to take away	1
To window shop	1
To purchase gifts	0
To purchase ingredients to prepare at home	27
To buy desserts/pastries/snacks	0
The environment/atmosphere of the market	16

Table 11.2 Why do you visit Findlay Market?

Special events	14
Farmer's markets	56
To buy and eat lunch there	40
To buy and eat dinner there	7
To purchase lunch to take away	14
To purchase dinner to take away	14
To window shop	31
To purchase gifts	18
To purchase ingredients to prepare at home	62
To buy desserts/pastries/snacks	28
The environment/atmosphere of the market	56

reason for visiting the market, 75% listed it as one of the reasons why they visit the market (Tables 11.1 and 11.2). This data, along with the shopping data, suggests that people are primarily visiting the market to provision; nevertheless, thrift and treats are also a factor.

Productive leisure and gastro-tourism

People shop for a variety of reasons. Personal motives for shopping include the fulfilment of socially expected roles (being a good spouse/parent and satisfying the needs of the family), diversion or entertainment, to alleviate boredom or loneliness, or for physical activity (Bardhi and Arnould 2005; Chang and Hsieh 2006; Miller 1997; Woodruffe-Burton 2002). There are social motives for shopping as well: Shopping may provide an opportunity to socialize with friends or strangers while browsing through the aisles and even a solitary shopper may be drawn to the attraction of a good bargain so they can brag about it with friends (Bardhi and Arnould 2005; Woodruffe-Burton 2002).

Productive provisional shopping fulfils basic needs; nevertheless, Miller's three elements of shopping are not discrete. As he notes, a person may buy a treat because it is a bargain or they may go to the high end store for provisional shopping as a treat because these types of purchases are something extraordinary or something beyond mere provisioning (Miller 1998). Building on Miller's ideas, one can argue that in some cases shopping becomes a leisure activity because it serves as a backdrop for exercise, the thrill of hunting for a bargain, and/or socializing with friends (Bäckström 2011; Bardhi and Arnould 2005; Beiswenger and Cohen 2017; Jansen-Verbeke 1987). Beiswenger and Cohen (2017) call this productive leisure. At Findlay Market, shopping at the farmer's market and shopping

Table 11.3 Comparison of the different types of shoppers at Findlay Market and North Market

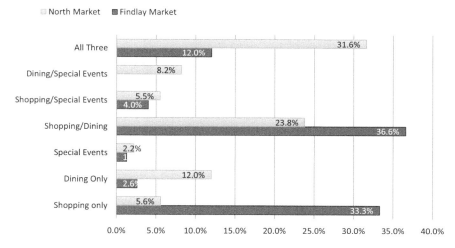

for ingredients to prepare at home are two of the primary reasons why customers visit the market. The market is crowded during special events, but these events are not the main reason why customers are drawn to the market: Findlay Market is the reason why people visit Findlay Market. They like the atmosphere and the environment, and they want to buy food there.

In a similar vein, productive leisure occurs while a person is traveling for business or leisure. Shopping ranks among the major categories of tourists' expenditure (Jansen-Verbeke 1998; Littrell et al. 2004), and over 33% of money spent by tourists is dedicated to food (Williams et al. 2014). Gastro-tourism captures the growing importance of food tourism and is "defined as the intentional pursuit of appealing, authentic, memorable, culinary experiences of all kinds, while travelling internationally, regionally or even locally" (Williams et al. 2014). Gastro-tourists seek more than fuel for the body: They seek unique food experiences. The search for food as both sustenance and an adventurous treat is an exceptional illustration of productive leisure and gastro-tourism is evident among visitors to Findlay Market. When asked what they wish was available at the market, customers emphasized a desire for unique shopping experiences that they cannot get in a regular grocery store. They not only want pawpaws[1] but also want locally produced lentils, beans, and meats. As Tim,[2] a customer at Findlay Market, explained, "I regularly cook for my family and friends. I like to cook. I come to the market for Amish poultry and fish because I like quality ingredients" (Personal interview, 28 June 2013). Jane, another customer, adds, "We live in Baltimore. When visiting son in Cincinnati, we always shop there for lunch and to get ingredients to cook. We visit two or three times a year" (Personal interview, 2 August 2013). There is a social aspect to the market. Jane is visiting the market with her family, but Tim is taking what he buys and using it to feed his family and friends.

Gastro-tourists do not have to come to the Findlay Market from far away. For those who live nearby, it serves as a destination spot. Indeed, 59% of survey respondents live in the Greater Cincinnati Area. Of these 44 respondents, three are from the same zip code as Findlay Market, eight live less than two miles away, and the remaining 33 have to travel 15–30 minutes to get to the market.

Generally, gastro-tourists will not visit frequently. Two-thirds of survey respondents visit the market fewer than 11 times per year. The market manager, Jennifer Hertwig, illuminates this assessment of Findlay Market as both a locus for provision and a locus for gastro-tourism. She explains:

> I call Saturday the "Cultural experience" for the suburbanite, and you see a lot of suburban people, even all the way from Dayton, from Louisville, people come from all over to experience a traditional European market. There are people that I know from Germany and from Europe they come and they're like "this is the closest thing I've seen that is part of home" which is cool. We've still embodied that. . . . And I hear, a lot of people complain about it, but really Sundays is where you have a lot of your serious shoppers. Saturdays, it looks busy. It is really busy, but Saturdays people want to buy a waffle and a coffee. Or take- get some street food and eat it, but they're not your

regular customers. On Sundays, you have the same people, you're going to see time and time again. Tuesday through Friday, same thing, same customers, you know, they might be your food stamps – mainly food stamp based, but they're going to be the same customers.

(Personal interview, 16 June 2013)

Just as the market adapts to its changing demographic, vendors must adjust their wares in order to establish and maintain lasting relationships with their customers (Plattner 1982; Jones et al. 2007). This is equally so for the market as a whole which plays a role in determining which types of vendors to include in their limited space. Over the past 20 years, there have been significant changes in the composition of the market. There has been a decrease in the quantity of permanent meat and produce vendors at the market and a rise in the number of prepared food vendors. This follows the general trend in my survey responses. People are shopping for meats and produce, but 55% state that they eat lunch while at the market. The market is transforming from a locus of provisioning to one where people seek prepared foods and other forms of entertainment.

Along with the changes in composition at the market, there has also been a shift in the hours and days that Findlay Market is open. In 1998, the market was only open three days per week. By 2005, those hours shifted to include two additional days, including Sunday hours. This addition of Sunday hours, which occurred in 2003, was not an easy transition for the vendors. Many vendors opposed Sunday hours because they wished to spend the day with family. While no vendor is obligated to be open on all the days that the market is open, some were concerned that they would lose business and might jeopardize the relationships that they had built with their customers. Some vendors believed that customers would not

Table 11.4 Types of permanent vendors at Findlay Market by year[3]

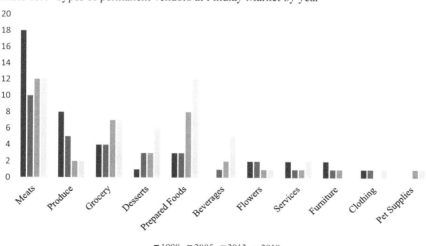

visit the market on Sundays, so they accepted the additional hours on a trial basis. According to vendor Charlotte Mathias, customers were indeed slow to accept the Sunday hours. Nonetheless, the market continues to be open six days per week (Tuesday through Sunday) as of this study, and Sunday is the second busiest day at the market.

The expansion of the hours attracted new visitors from outside of Over-the-Rhine (OTR). The population of OTR is declining due to a complex confluence of development plans, gentrification, and a history of violence in the neighbourhood. The neighbourhood is also poor. The median household income was $16,930 from 2009 to 2014. For decades, food stamps kept the market alive. In 1995, as much as 75% of the business at Findlay Market came from food stamp purchases (Barrett 1995, 4A). According to vendors interviewed at the market, this reliance on trade from food stamps continued up through about a decade ago, when development plans began to change the demographics of who was shopping at the market. As Richard George explained:

> I don't have to have chopped ham anymore. There's a guy with a credit card. He wants a $7, a $9 pound of salami. Let's put some of that in there. That's how, that's where my business has gone. I haven't pushed away the food stamp people. I still sell the stuff that they want that's available that I can put in my counter, but that portion of my business is shrinking, so is the space in my counter. Instead of Dutch loaf, jalapeno loaf, now there's peppered salami, Milano salami, sopressata. White guy with a credit card, black guy with a food stamp card. Less of them, more of these.[4]

As public markets gain popularity across the United States, many existing markets adjust to better suit the needs of their customers. Findlay Market is no exception. Over the past 20 years, it has made significant changes in what it offers to its customers and is striving to continue to solicit feedback in order to better serve its customers; however, there have also been changes in how the customers use the market. In 1998, there were relatively few prepared food and beverage vendors. Today, these numbers have increased significantly, and people are regularly stopping to eat at the market while they complete their shopping.

COVID-19 and the market

In March of 2020, an unexpected challenge hit the market: COVID-19. On 12 March 2020, just over a month after the first confirmed death from COVID-19 in the United States and three days after the first confirmed cases in Ohio, the state's governor, Mike DeWine, announced state-wide measures to combat the spread of the disease, including cancelling events of 100 or more participants (Ghose 2020; Ideastream Public Media 2021). Three days later, Governor DeWine announced the closure of all bars and restaurants with the exception of takeout or delivery orders (Brownfield 2020). While Findlay Market was deemed an essential business and remained largely open, tourism and visits to the market were curtailed

Findlay Market
March 20, 2020 · 🌐   •••

Major kudos to our fantastic Maintenance Staff who are ensuring that the Market District is safe, healthy and clean for our shoppers and employees. 👏🖤🧡

In addition to increasing the frequency in which our crew is cleaning common surfaces areas (like door handles), we want you to know some of the other measures we have taken to keep the market open and safe for the public:

*We are requiring all employees (Findlay Market and merchants) to comply with Governor DeWine's requirement to take their temperature before starting a shift - any employee with a fever will not be permitted to work
*A public hand washing station has been added inside of the market house (across from Luken's Seafood, Fish & Poultry & Mama Lo Hizo)
*Hand sanitizer dispensers have been added in the public restrooms (in addition to having sinks, soap and paper towels)
*Indoor seating has been removed
*Doors are being propped open on the north side, weather permitting, to allow for a hands-free entrance into the market house

Figure 11.2 A screenshot of a Facebook post from Findlay Market listing the strategies being implemented to limit the spread of COVID-19.

Source: www.facebook.com/98539886015/posts/10156989073246016/?d=n.

as the populace faced the uncertainty of a deadly pandemic. Events at the market, which usually draw large numbers of customers, were cancelled. On 20 March 2021, Findlay Market posted the following statement on their Facebook page, listing the various strategies they were implementing to limit the spread of COVID-19 (Findlay Market 2020).

These strategies included frequent cleaning of surfaces, hand sanitizer stations, removal of indoor seating, and improved ventilation. In May 2020, the market issued a statement encouraging shoppers to wear masks and practice safe distancing (Hansbauer 2020); masks were made mandatory in July, in line with the masking mandate instituted by the City of Cincinnati (COVID-19 Re-open Plan 2020).

The market itself also initiated a few programmes to alleviate the uncertainty its vendors were enduring. In April 2020, they launched a gift certificate programme so customers could financially support their favourite vendors (Fox19 2020). Additionally, they introduced delivery, pick-up, and carry-out options, as well as a phone application where customers could order groceries for pick-up

(COVID-19 Re-open Plan 2020). In January and February 2021, the market held a "Take-Out Tuesday" Contest. Even in the best years, these are the slowest months at the market, and facing the uncertainty of the pandemic, many vendors were struggling. Customers were encouraged to buy a take-out meal at the market and post a photo of that meal on social media. Each post counted as a separate chance to win a prize basket of goods from vendors at the market ("Take Out Tuesday"). As explained by the executive director of the Over-the-Rhine Chamber of Commerce Kelly Adamson, "Every day it's something new from marketing to getting out the stories of those businesses". Adamson further explains, "Ultimately, it really is up to the consumer. It's a citywide jump on and support thing. We're always calling on the consumer to help because it takes a village to save a village" (qtd. in Burke 2021).

Every change at the market brings its own risks and uncertainty. "In risky situations, decision makers can estimate the probabilities of different outcomes resulting from particular decisions. In uncertain situations, decision makers have no idea what the probabilities are of different outcomes" (Chibnik 2011, 61). Vendors negotiate risks with every decision they make (Guimarães 2019). If a vendor chooses to expand a product line, they must discontinue selling other products to make space. If a vendor chooses to invest in a new piece of equipment, they have to make sure that they have money in the budget during the lean months to repay loans.

Another challenge that vendors face is the changing customer base at the market. As the neighbourhood gentrifies and urban professionals take the place of poor African Americans, customers are demanding different products. Kenny Mason explains:

> It's becoming more – I don't want to use the word elitist – more gourmet. . . . The people who are cooking are cooking fancier dishes. For instance, three years ago, at Thanksgiving, I sold 300 cases of collard greens. . . . Bags of potatoes. Bags of onions. Specifically, black poor people bought all that stuff because they cooked huge meals for Thanksgiving and Christmas, now we don't do that anymore. I mean, I'll sell during the week, I might sell one or two- one case of collard greens. Thanksgiving, I might sell 20 collard greens, but not 300. . . . A lot of urban professionals don't cook. But when they do cook, they want special stuff. They don't want mashed potatoes, they want the creamers, and they want the ginger and the herbs. . . . And mushrooms, that kind of thing. But a poor black person who lived down here wouldn't know what to do with a shitake. They don't do that. That wasn't their food. They wanted turkey necks and collard greens. So it's a cultural shift in the food that's being bought.[5]

This means that vendors must stay informed about changes in their industry. They must be receptive to changes and willing to listen to customer suggestions. They cannot be stuck in the past because as the customers and market change they must change with it.

Conclusions

The primary function of a public market is to create a locus for economic activity and trade; however, "it plays a crucial and simultaneous role in presenting the residents' life and culture" (Silkes 2012, 327). Public markets connect visitors, vendors, and the local food and culture of a region (Silkes 2012; Smith and Xiao 2008). This chapter began with a discussion of the history of Findlay Market. It is ending with a discussion of the future of Findlay Market. In the past 20 years, the composition of Findlay Market has changed considerably. The quantity of produce and meat vendors has decreased while the number of prepared food and dessert/snack vendors has increased. As the neighbourhood continues to gentrify, these trends will probably continue; however, there are limitations to what will happen to the market in the next five years. Without major renovations, it is unlikely that more prepared food vendors will join those already selling in the market house because additional heat would put strain on the building's infrastructure; however, as the Corporation for Findlay Market continues to renovate the buildings surrounding the market, it is likely that at least some of those buildings will become restaurants.

Looking at the trajectory of another public market can shine additional light on the future of Findlay Market. Milwaukee Public Market, established in 2005, was modelled, in part, after Findlay Market. In 2012, Milwaukee Public Market had 20 vendors: Eight prepared food vendors, six grocery vendors, four sweets/pastry/snack vendors, one fish vendor, and one cheese/sausage vendor. They had no produce vendors. While the market was flourishing in 2012, its early years were not without strife. In 2007, it was within a month of closing as it struggled with high vendor turnover and lack of customers (Davis 2013). When the market was first established,

> Organizers wanted the market to focus on fresh ingredients in the tradition of European markets instead of prepared foods. But the market's current leaders and vendors say that model didn't work. Producers couldn't make enough margin on their products to pay the rent, and people didn't respond to the concept.
>
> (Davis 2013)

In 2007, the owners of the building transferred management of the market to the Historical Third Ward Association and changed the offerings at the market, namely the market added significantly more prepared foods, and that change made a difference in the success of the market. In 2013, vendor space was 100% leased and sales grew steadily between 2007 and 2013, reaching $9.75 million 2012 (Davis 2013). In 2013, fresh produce returned to the market when Commission Row Produce was added to the line-up at the market, and while the vendor was not making money "hand-over-fist", they were paying their bills (Davis 2013).

As Over-the-Rhine continues to gentrify, what customers expect of Findlay Market will change. This creates two possible futures for the market: (1) The market will become a food court. The Corporation for Findlay Market will buy out the legacy meat, poultry, fish, cheese, grocery, and produce vendors and install the infrastructure necessary for more prepared food vendors. A handful of fresh food vendors will remain as a nod to the market's history, but the market itself will be fundamentally altered. (2) The market will maintain the current number of meat, poultry, fish, cheese, grocery, and produce vendors, but the price points for those items will increase as the neighbourhoods' median income shifts. The low-income individuals and families who sustained the market for decades will no longer be able to afford to shop there. Examining the trajectory of the market and the neighbourhood, this second option is more likely. The market will remain a cosmopolitan canopy where everyone is welcome, but the market will be intangibly altered.

Acknowledgements

This chapter was produced with the immense support of the staff, vendors, and customers of Findlay Market. Thank you to Jeffrey H. Cohen, Douglas E. Crews, Anna J. Willow, and Dorothy Noyes. Financial support for this project was provided by the Food Innovation Center at The Ohio State University. Thank you to my undergraduate research assistants – Maria Danna, Kayla Killoren, Meagan Jones, and Evelyn Romeo – who diligently distributed surveys.

Notes

1 Scientific name *Asimina triloba*, a somewhat hard to find Indigenous fruit from the eastern United States.
2 Pseudonyms are utilized to protect the privacy of vendors, market management, and customers.
3 Information about the vendors available at Findlay Market in 1998, 2005, and 2013 were retrieved from the archive.org Wayback Machine, a service that archives intermittent snapshots of websites.
4 Personal interview, 26 October 2016.
5 Personal interview, 4 June 2016.

References

Au, N., and R. Law. 2002. "Categorical Classification of Tourism Dining." *Annals of Tourism Research* 29 (3): 819–833.

Bäckström, K. 2011. "Shopping as Leisure: An Exploration of Manifoldness and Dynamics in Consumers Shopping Experiences." *Journal of Retailing and Consumer Services* 18 (3): 200–209.

Bardhi, F., and E. J. Arnould. 2005. "Thrift Shopping: Combining Utilitarian Thrift and Hedonic Treat Benefits." *Journal of Consumer Behavior* 4 (4): 223–233.

Barrett, Amanda. 1995. "Food Stamp Reform Threatens Market." *Cincinnati Post*, January 9, 1995: 4A.

Beiswenger, Lisa M., and Jeffrey H. Cohen. 2017. "Provisioning, Shopping and Productive Leisure at North Market, Columbus, Ohio." In *Anthropological Considerations of*

Production, Exchange, Vending and Tourism, edited by Donald Wood, 137–154. Bingley, UK: Emerald Insight.

Bernard, H. Russell. 2006. *Research Methods in Anthropology: Qualitative and Quantitative Approaches*. 4th ed. Lanham, MD: Altamira Press.

Brownfield, Andy. 2020. "DeWine to Shutter All Bars, Restaurants in Ohio; to-go Food Permitted." *Cincinnati Business Courier,* March 15, 2020. www.bizjournals.com/cincinnati/news/2020/03/15/dewine-to-shutter-all-bars-restaurants-in-ohio.html.

Burke, Clancy. 2021. "Takeout Tuesday Contest Launched to Help Struggling OTR Businesses." *Local 12 News*, January 26, 2021. https://local12.com/news/local/takeout-tuesday-contest-launched-to-help-struggling-otr-businesses-cincinnati.

Chang, J., and A. T. Hsieh. 2006. "Leisure Motives of Eating Out in Night Markets." *Journal of Business Research* 59: 1276–1278.

Chibnik, Michael. 2011. *Anthropology, Economics, and Choice*. Austin: University of Texas Press.

Cincinnati Enquirer. 1961. "Venison and Bear Meat: Early Markets Had Wide Choice." *Cincinnati Enquirer*, March 4: 24.

City of Cincinnati. 2013. "Requested Consolidated Plan Budget Update." Accessed April 2, 2017. www.cincinnati-oh.gov/community-development/linkservid/E7A4B381-F28A-2CA0-F295D697EEADAE96/showMeta/0/.

City of Cincinnati. 2017. "Fiscal Years 2016–2017 All Funds Capital Budget City Manager's Recommended Biennial Capital Investment Program." Accessed April 2, 2017. www.cincinnati-oh.gov/cityofcincinnati/news/proposed-biennial-budget-for-2016-17-released1/fiscal-years-2016-2017-all-funds-capital-budget-city-manager-s-recommended-biennial-capital-investment-program-vol-2/.

Davis, Stacy Vogel. 2013. "Market Momentum: Milwaukee Public Market Thriving after Rough Start – Milwaukee Business Journal." *Milwaukee Business Journal*, September 27, 2013. www.bizjournals.com/milwaukee/print-edition/2013/09/27/milwaukee-public-market-thriving-after.html.

Findlay Market. n.d. a. "COVID-19 Re-open Plan." Accessed July 9, 2020. www.findlaymarket.org/covid-19.

Findlay Market. n.d. b. "Economic Development." Accessed May 8, 2019. www.findlaymarket.org/economic-development.

Findlay Market. n.d. c. "Findlay Market – A Brief History." Accessed January 28, 2019. www.findlaymarket.org/history.

Findlay Market. n.d. d. "Take Out Tuesday." Accessed January 26, 2021. www.findlaymarket.org/news/takeouttuesday.

Findlay Market. 2020. "Major Kudos to Our Fantastic Maintenance Staff." *Facebook*, March 20, 2020. www.facebook.com/98539886015/posts/10156989073246016/?d=n.

Fox19. 2020. "Findlay Market Launching Gift Certificate Program." April 16, 2020. www.fox19.com/2020/04/16/findlay-market-launching-gift-certificate-program/.

Ghose, Carrie. 2020. "Ohio Bans Gatherings of 100 or More, Impacting Sports, Theaters, Festivals." *Cincinnati Business Courier*, March 12, 2020. www.bizjournals.com/cincinnati/news/2020/03/12/ohio-bans-gatherings-of-100-or-more-impacting.html.

Gonzalez, Sara, and Paul Waley. 2013. "Traditional Retail Markets: The New Gentrification Frontier?" *Antipode* 45 (4): 965–983.

Guimarães, Pedro. 2018. "The Transformation of Retail Markets in Lisbon: An Analysis through the Lens of Retail Gentrification." *European Planning Studies* 26 (7): 1450–1470. https://doi.org/10.1080/09654313.2018.1474177.

Guimarães, Pedro. 2019. "Exploring the Impacts of Gentrified Traditional Retail Markets in Lisbon in Local Neighbourhoods." *Social Sciences* 8 (6): 190. https://doi.org/10.3390/socsci8060190.

Hansbauer, Joe. 2020. "A Letter from the CEO to Findlay Market Shoppers." *Twitter Post*, May 15, 2020. https://twitter.com/FindlayMarket/status/1261327416703795201?s=20.

Ideastream Public Media. 2021. "Ohio's Coronavirus Pandemic: A Timeline." Accessed November 12, 2021. www.ideastream.org/ohios-coronavirus-pandemic-a-timeline.

Jansen-Verbeke, M. 1987. "Women, Shopping and Leisure." *Leisure Studies* 6 (1): 71–86.

Jansen-Verbeke, M. 1998. "The Synergism Between Shopping and Tourism." In *Global Tourism: The Next Decade*, 2nd ed., edited by W. F. Theobal, 428–446. Oxford: Butterworth-Heinemann.

Jones, Peter, David Hillier, and Daphne Comfort. 2007. "Changing Times and Changing Places for Market Halls and Covered Markets." *International Journal of Retail & Distribution Management* 35 (3): 200–209.

Littrell, M. A., et. al. 2004. "Senior Travelers: Tourism Activities and Shopping Behaviors." *Journal of Vacation Marketing* 10 (4): 348–362.

Miller, Daniel. 1997. "Consumption and Its Consequences." In *Consumption and Everyday Life*, edited by H. McKay, 13–64. London: Sage.

Miller, Daniel. 1998. *A Theory of Shopping*. Ithaca: Cornell University Press.

Plattner, Stuart. 1982. "Economic Decision Making in a Public Marketplace." *American Ethnologist* 9 (2): 399–420.

Schweitzer, A., and H. Gerbus. 1974. *The History and the Story of Findlay Market and the Over the Rhine Community Center Dedication Day, June 9, 1974*. Cincinnati: Over-the-Rhine.

Silkes, Carol. A. 2012. "Farmers' Markets: A Case for Culinary Tourism." *Journal of Culinary Science & Technology* 10 (4): 326–336.

Smith, Stephen L. J., and Honggen Xiao. 2008. "Culinary Tourism Supply Chains: A Preliminary Examination." *Journal of Travel Research* 46 (3): 289–299.

Troy, Tom. 2006. "Cincinnati's 'Gem' of a Market Could Offer Lessons for Toledo – Over-the-Rhine Merchants Attract Both Neighbors, Tourists." *Toledo Blade*, March 13, 2006. www.toledoblade.com/local/2006/03/13/Cincinnati-s-gem-of-a-market-could-offer-lessons-for-Toledo.html.

Williams, H. A., et al. 2014. "Gastro-tourism as Destination Branding in Emerging Markets." *International Journal of Leisure and Tourism Marketing* 4 (1): 1–18.

Woodruffe-Burton, H., et al. 2002. "Towards a Theory of Shopping: A Holistic Framework." *Journal of Consumer Behavior* 1 (3): 256–266.

12 Queer cosmopolitan Barranquilla? Spatiality and temporality and the carnival's touristification

Sebastián Wanumen Jiménez

Along with Rio Carnival, the *Carnaval de Barranquilla* is one of the largest Afro-Latin American festivals. UNESCO declared it a Masterpiece of the Oral and Intangible Heritage of Humanity in 2003.[1] During the four days before, people from the Colombian city of Barranquilla parade with colourful costumes that represent the richness of their mixed-race culture. The *Carnaval de Barranquilla* is a tradition that was established during the nineteenth century, and today it is embraced by not only Barranquillans but also Colombians in general. Around 1970, a group of gay men started celebrating their own indoor version of the carnival in clandestine bars.[2] During the same decade, they took the carnival to the streets and started parading even though they were not authorized. As a result, and according to several informants in the field, the gay troupe was violently pursued by the police. Nonetheless, political reforms introduced in Colombia in the 1990s allowed the Gay Carnival to parade freely.[3] During the last two decades, the *Carnaval Gay de Barranquilla* has been institutionalized and recently structured as a cultural organization. Now, despite Barranquilla still being a city in which homophobia is a vast problem, the Gay Carnival is an event within the larger carnival (the "straight" carnival) for the LGBTIQ+ population to converge with its heteronormalized counterparts. Currently, inspired by the Gay Carnival, other LGBTIQ+ movements have created their own troupes to perform in the carnival. Despite being a major Afro-Latin American festival in the Caribbean, the *Carnaval de Barranquilla* and *El Carnaval Gay* have been understudied by Spanish-speaking scholars and English-speaking authors.[4]

Taking into account the spatial turn in the humanities and ethnomusicology, I suggest that the Gay Carnival has produced spaces that have been free from heteronormativity. I follow Peter Wade (1993), who rejects that space in Colombia is a "dimension that is either taken for granted or seen as a mirror or symbolic expression of certain social structures or concepts" (53) and Marié Abe's claim that "dynamic interrelations of sound, history, and sociality produce space" (Abe 2018, xxii). In other words, I consider space to be a product of social relations rather than a container. In this sense, space is not a final result – "never finished; never closed" – but a mutable product of ongoing relations, "always under construction" (Massey 1994, 9). Moreover, social geographer Doreen Massey (1994) refutes the idea of time/space as a binary in which one may be considered

DOI: 10.4324/9781003207207-17

more prevailing or independent than the other. Nonetheless, "the point here however is not to argue for an upgrading of the status of space within the terms of the old dualism" (260) but to understand that both are constructs that depend on each other and both on sociality. In describing relations that produce space is impossible to avoid the fact that the alteration of the producing forces results also in chronologies. Thus, "it is not that the interrelations between objects occur *in* space and time [my emphasis]; it is these relationships themselves which create/define space and time" (263). After these considerations, I suggest that the subversive intent of hosting an LGBTIQ+ version of the Barranquilla's Carnival permitted gay sociality and, therefore, less heteronormative space-times to be produced.

While I observe that some instances of the Gay Carnival and the Carnival are indeed liberatory and produce queer free space-times, I posit that they produce space-times that are not entirely free but that respond to economic neo-liberal principles, mostly by the effects of touristification and globalization. During the last two decades, national and local authorities, as well as private investors, have pushed the city to develop its tourist infrastructure. The construction of attractions such as the World's Window or the Golden Gate Convention Center is part of such development. The municipality has also branded the city as Colombia's Golden Gate appealing to the city's openness.[5] In the same vein, governors and mayors have promoted the city as a place full of ambiances[6] that are LGBTIQ+ friendly. For instance, during pride month, the esplanade is decorated with the rainbow flag and, during carnival time, the Gay Carnival is featured in media and marketing campaigns. I argue that these ambiances, however, are only a façade. Displaying the gay of the carnival, more than a liberation from heteronormativity is a strategic exception allowed by Barranquilla's neoliberal tendencies to contribute to the development of capitalist enterprises in the city.

Barranquilla's heteronormativity is one of those formations that have been somehow transformed by neoliberalism by means of touristification. In the attempt to represent Barranquilla as global, cosmopolitan, and modern, the local government has promoted, branded, and marketed the Gay Carnival as evidence of tolerance for the LGBTIQ+ people. Cities like Madrid (with Chueca) or New York (with Greenwich Village) have exploited the existence of LGBTIQ+ physical places for touristic gain. Proudness of these areas can be taken as a symptom of modernity (Adam et al. 1999), and displaying them shows a "shared historicity with other modern, liberal democracies" (Massey 1994). Some scholars have also indicated that public funds "are spent identifying and circulating the distinctive elements of a city's identity as 'gay friendly'" (Waitt and Markwell 2006, 54). Cities like Sidney, for instance, have analogously used its largest queer event (the Mardi Gras) to display "gay friendliness" (Johnston 2007, 9; Markwell 2002, 81). As other "wannabe world cities" (Rushbrook 2002, 188), Barranquilla is using the Gay Carnival to market allegedly ambiances of tolerant and diverse contemporaneity. This trend constitutes a "homonormativity" (Johnston 2007, 1) that does not only regulate queer bodies but that also regulate the way heteronormalized subjects relate to them.

In analysing the Barranquilla's Gay Carnival from a queer spatial-temporal perspective, I am also refuting some theories on carnivals. First, I do not consider that the carnival is necessarily a momentary and permissible rupture of hegemony (Eagleton 2009, 148), a moment of complete freedom (Bakhtin 1984, 7) or that has anomic nature that represents the obliteration of social norms (Reyes Morris 2011, 104). Similarly, I contest the idea that the Carnival produces an "egalitarian moment" (Da Matta 2002, 157). Instead, I pose that the Barranquilla's Gay Carnival (and also the non-gay Carnival) lodges relations that are not entirely free but are ruled by heteronormativity, neoliberalism, touristification, homonormativity, and queer identity all combined. This does not mean that the carnival is a space-time in which transgressions do not happen. My goal is not to state that the carnival is transgressive or not[7]; such a statement would reinforce a binary opposition (Lewis and Pile 1996, 37) that is contrary to queer theory. Rather, I consider that the relations that occur within the Carnival have relative levels of transgressive-ness and are contingent not only upon a comparison of carnival and non-carnival space-times but also within different manifestations and aspects of the carnival itself.

To illustrate this, I make two arguments in this text. First, I show how the predominance of heteronormativity and the novel neoliberal homonormativity could be noticed through the representation of soundscapes in the Carnival marketing campaigns. Second, I argue that capitalism via spectacularization and touristification made the gay carnival acceptable to Barranquilla's society because of its aesthetic contributions to Barranquilla as a touristic destination, hence, constituting the abovementioned homonormativity. In this way, the relation of gay men in Barranquilla to the carnival is one of creative contributions; they are ruled by principles of production. Instead of living a queer freedom, they are conditioned by a homonormativity that regulates the way they participate in the carnival, including their exclusion from musical practices.

Discriminatory representations of the soundscape

Representations of diversity in Barranquilla's and its Carnival's space-times (both gay and non-gay) are a frequent marketing strategy. The 2016 advertisement campaign, designed by Carnival S.A. (the administrative organizing institution of the carnival), had as an official motto "*Carnaval somos todos*" [we are all Carnival]. Similarly, the 2018 advertisements, designed and promoted by the office of the major, had as a motto "*La fiesta es de todos*" [the celebration is for everyone] (Fig. 12.1). These campaigns are aimed to show how Barranquilla's society is inclusive. Simultaneously, they reveal the introduction of homonormativity through the neoliberalization of the festivity. The homonormalization, for instance, is observed in a 2015 promotional video produced for national television. The video opens with King Momo (an emblematic character of the Carnival that is performed every year by a different person) as a street vendor at a *plaza*. King Momo starts chanting "*El Carnaval somos todos, todos somos carnaval*" [The Carnival is all of us, we are all Carnival] (Caracol Televisión 2015). Then, the Queen of the

Figure 12.1 2018 Barranquilla's Carnival advertisement motto's "La fiesta es de todos" [The celebration is for everyone].

Source: www.youtube.com/watch?v=8oT1jqXeKF4

Carnival starts dancing and invites everyone at the *plaza* to dance: street vendors, tourists, children, youngsters, and seniors. Similarly, the Queen of the Gay Carnival (Linda Yepes), a transgender woman, appears dancing next to the Queen of the Carnival. Thus, Linda Yepes, as a representative of the LGBTIQ+ community, symbolizes the sexual and gender "everyone" (*todos*) from the motto (Fig. 12.2).

These kinds of representations, as Rushbrook would argue (2002, 187), have favourable effects for the commodification of the city as offering it as a touristic destination. It reflects its cosmopolitanism attracting the LGBTIQ+ "niche tourism" (Hughes 2006, 8). Procolombia, the agency in charge of "the positioning of the country as a tourist destination for vacations and meetings and Colombia Country Brand" (PROCOLOMBIA 2017), has taken the Barranquilla's Gay Carnival as an exemplary model of an "LGBT+ attraction". For instance, the *Professional Guide for the Development of LGBT Tourism in Colombia* (FONTUR and PROCOLOMBIA 2018) depicts Barranquilla's Gay Carnival as a "public event of interest" (34).

However, in analysing the soundscape of some of these videos, one can see the tensions caused by heteronormativity. This is the case of a video (Barranquillacpt 2018) produced by Barranquilla's Council for Culture, Patrimony, and Tourism (*Secretaría de Cultura, Turismo y Patromonio*) in 2018. In this video, the soundscape is manipulated such that the sonic utterances of the audience are either emphasized or muted. In this way, drumming, clapping, calls, and screams of approval keep their volume. However, at some points, there are lapsus linguae, slips of the tongue, or, maybe more pertinent, *lapsus sonorum*. These are sounds

Figure 12.2   Linda Yepes (right), Gay Carnival Queen, dancing next to Marcela García
(left), Queen of Barranquilla's Carnival.

Source: www.youtube.com/watch?v=DOQ0JN9vLlI

that are not part of this "tolerant" soundscape: for instance, soft mocking whistles
and hooting. At other points, the soundscape of tolerance and openness does not
coincide with the image. When the camera focuses on a crowd that is cheering
the parade, some of the people stop chanting. Nonetheless, the volume of the ones
that keep chanting is turned up in the video. Similarly, many of the people who
stopped chanting start to cover their faces so they could not be captured by the
camera. Additionally, the intentionality of the manipulation of the soundscape is
evident throughout the video. For instance, when the director of the Gay Carnival
is interviewed (and while he asserts once more the motto in stating "we are all one
in our carnival"), the volume of the soundscape is notably reduced between the
first and the second sentences of his statement (QR code 1).

Moreover, in observing *amateur* videos that do not have alterations in their
soundscape, one can notice that there are plenty of moments in which sonic state-
ments of disapproval are uttered by the audience. In the amateur video *Guacherna
Gay de Soledad 2018*, one sees that the cameraperson is located in a fixed position (Omarvill Oe 2018). The cameraperson is next to a person who is scornfully
screaming to and mocking the gay troupe. The mockery increases every time a
member of the troupe engages visually or addresses the people (blowing kisses or
greeting) who are located next to the camera. Such incompatibility seen and heard

Figure 12.3 QR codes to watch Barranquilla's Carnival videos. QR Code 1 (left): Clip of Barranquilla's Council for Culture, Heritage, and Tourism video on the Gay Carnival; QR Code 2 (right): Clip of an amateur video of a Gay Carnival Parade.

in the videos shows the tensions between neoliberal-homonormative and heteronormative relations and demonstrates that queer freedom within the carnival is only ephemeral (QR code 2).

Homonormativity, the creative gay, and their absence in musical practices

Despite some attempts to represent Barranquilla as a "gay-friendly" city, discrimination towards the LGBTIQ+ people, and closeness about one's sexual and gender identity, is still the dominant feature of the city. Although there are some spatial-temporal exceptions (some public clubs and a couple of LGBTIQ+ events that are held publicly), Barranquilla is governed by heteronormative relations. In this way, LGBTIQ+ everyday relations are constricted to private places. The Colombian press has extensively covered cases of discrimination in Barranquilla's public places. It is easy to retrieve online sources reporting LGTBIQ+ couples being thrown out of business (malls or restaurants) for holding hands, kissing or hugging, and how people around did not prevent it to happen. Nevertheless, the NGO *Caribe Afirmativo* (Affirmative Caribbean) offers legal advice to LGBTIQ+ people who have been discriminated against. While the article 16 of the Colombian Constitution states that "All persons are entitled to their free personal development without limitations other than those imposed by the rights of others and those which are prescribed by the legal system", many people from Barranquilla and their judicial system still struggle to acknowledge and respect such right when it is related to sexuality. Many of the cases supported by Caribe Afirmativo end up in the *Corte Constitucional de Colombia* (the Supreme Constitutional Court). For instance, in July 2018, a business owner mistreated a lesbian couple because of their sexuality. After the couple initiated a writ for protection of their fundamental rights, two local judges from Barranquilla failed to sentence the owner. The couple appealed and the case made it to the Supreme Constitutional Court, which finally ruled against the business owner (Decision T-335, 29 July 2019). The intervention of local judges and the Supreme Court in these cases is common in Barranquilla. Furthermore, *Caribe Afirmativo* has published several reports in which Barranquilla is described as a patriarchal society "based in gender violence which is legitimated through unequal and dominant relations of power in which masculinity is reinforced by the performativity of manliness (aggressiveness, physical strength, and authoritarianism)" (Pérez Álvarez 2017, 23). As a result, *Caribe Afirmativo* keeps reporting that this patriarchal society allows diverse forms of violence that can be inflicted on the LGBTIQ+ population, in settings such as home or school, and extending through all the social life of the individual (Pérez Álvarez 2017, 14).

In conducting fieldwork, I could observe and hear about both the representation of Barranquilla as gay friendly and its discriminatory ambiance. I asked my interlocutors not only about living as a gay person in Barranquilla but also about being part of the Gay Carnival. More interestingly, both aspects were present in the discourse of a single person. While interviewing my friend, a Gay Carnival's King, a cisgender homosexual man in his earlier twenties, I asked how was to be gay there. He commented that "there is a lot of support for us. Barranquilla is not so much of a homophobic city". Nonetheless, I felt the meaning of this statement was not clear enough to me (as I was already realizing some homophobic traits of the city's population), so I formulated two other questions. I asked him first about his personal experience as a gay man. He responded:

[M]y mom accepted me after a while, she even admires me now because of my talents . . . my father now accepts me and is proud of me. But for my mother's family, I am "the faggot" [*marica*] who came to damn the family, the black spot. I am not close to them. When I am around them, they criticize gays. They speak badly about "faggots", forgetting that there is one at home.

Then, I told him that my partner was going to visit me during my field trip and if it was "o.k." to hold hands in public. He advised against it:

If you do so, there is going to be a scandal, especially in some places. . . . If you do it in this street, *mototaxistas* [motorcycle taxi drivers] are going to see you and will shout at you; "you faggot." It is better that you don't do it because this is a problem in Barranquilla.

I also met a show's producer, a gay man in his early forties, who has worked with the Barranquilla Carnival several times. He thinks that one can have a gay life in Barranquilla if "you don't show off your sexuality". When I asked him if he was part of the Gay Carnival troupe, he told me that he is not involved and that he does not parade because he has self-esteem: "I love myself too much, I don't want to go out on the streets and being shouted horrible things". In this sense, his statement echoed how Barranquilla's everyday life public space-times are predominantly heteronormalized. He mentioned that clandestine gay locations are not novel. At the time he came out "there were a lot of secret places to meet other gays", he mentioned. Then he continued,

> [E]ight days before marrying a woman, I told my family that I was not going to do it because I was in love with a man. And despite my family have stopped talking to me, I am happy . . . but I have gained prestige and respect.

When I asked him about how he earned such respectability, he commented that not showing off "gay mannerisms" and that his artistic productions were essential. He added that "If you don't include gays in the carnival, there is no carnival. Almost every artist and dancer is gay. In fact, I don't know straight dancers, neither directors or producers". Thus, he concluded that being a respected openly gay man in Barranquilla depended on acting "straight" and having a well-established career in the creative industry.

Thanks to another interview, I could see a pattern emerging. I met with a *cumbiamba* (a carnival dancing troupe) director, a heterosexual cisgender woman in her sixties, who said that gays "were mistreated frequently, especially if they are flamboyant". However, she added that they have gained recognition and respect because of their creative and artistic skills: "they have built up a good reputation for themselves, in being designers, hairdressers, pageant coaches or event organizers". She acknowledges that she respects them because they are hard to compete with:

> their costumes are very luxurious, they have feathers and ornaments, and can cost a lot. They are very clever and borrow their costumes to each other, they adapt them and make them even richer. That makes their carnival extremely popular.

Besides from showing that sexual and gender exclusion operates intensively in Barranquilla, all these three interviews agreed that being credited as a valuable person for society and despite sexuality was due to creative skills. This pattern reminds me of Alison Kafer's discussion on the supercrip: "the stereotypical disabled person who garners media attention for accomplishing some feat considered too difficult for disabled people (depending on the kind of impairment under discussion, supercrip acts can include anything from rock climbing to driving a car)" (Kafer 2013, 141). Kafer argues that disability is "to be overcome through hard work and perseverance . . . and by individual feats of strength and will" (ibid.), this is how supercrips gain their position in society. In the case of Barranquilla, the public space-times are produced mostly by heterosexual relations (or its enactment) leaving out the chances for openly gay men to be part of them. Nevertheless, once they become important actors in Carnival's creative industry (or of shows in general), the *creative queers* (á la Kafer) have the opportunity to interact in the public space-time. In other words, while there is discrimination towards people of diverse gender and sexuality, the respectability of an LGBTIQ+ person in Barranquilla is to be achieved through being artistically productive.

Nonetheless, creative queers are still confined to the production of visual expressions. Because of the UNESCO's declaration of the Barranquilla's Carnival as a "masterpiece of the oral and intangible heritage of humanity", many of the Carnival's performances are policed by cultural institutions, the tourism industry, and society in general to prevent the violation of traditional practices and its alleged authenticity.

The Gay Carnival's King (the same I mentioned before) told me that the Gay Carnival has always in its parades the traditional characters, but that they also add characters of the "gay mythology". He mentions that in the last decade many dancers are using lavish feather dresses that are not part of the traditions of the Colombian Caribbean. When the Gay Carnival was created in the seventies, men and women cross-dressing was seen as transgressive. Due to the introduction of contemporary neoliberal values (but also because of the improvement of gender and sexual rights in Colombia), LGBTIQ+ people now parade freely. Parading now as an LGBTIQ+ crossdresser is not any more transgressive. That is why expanding the costume's themes is a way of marking the LGBTIQ+ community distinctiveness. However, this distinctiveness comes with a discriminatory price. As one policy maker told me once: "an anthropologist that knows about the carnival and our traditions should tell them what to do".

Regarding musical practices, it is important to mention that musicians who participate in the Gay Carnival are not part of the LGBTIQ+ community. While there are dancers, choreographers, parade organizers, paraders, and staff who are openly LGBTIQ+ and active members of the LGBTIQ+ movements, musicians are hired and do not identify at all as part of this community, or as a member of the Gay Carnival suggested, "there are no gay musicians". As Peter Wade has widely commented, one of the ways in which Colombia constructed its modern racialized identity was through highlighting the music of its Caribbean. Thus, the homonormativity constructed by neo-liberalization, globalization, and touristification includes establishing musical gatekeepers to prevent LGBTIQ+ people to participate in music making and, subsequently, to modify it. Although feminist and younger movements are beginning to challenge this exclusion (and discrimination at large), this topic deserves a whole other place to be discussed.

Conclusion

As I have seen in Barranquilla, the Gay Carnival has allowed some LGBTIQ+ people to socialize openly not only during carnival time but also in preparation for it. Such sociality has produced free spaces for queerness. Nevertheless, this free space-time is violently intersected by hetero- and homonormativity and homophobic trajectories. In scrutinizing how local authorities and the tourism industry in Barranquilla represent sexual and gender diversity, one could see that the efforts for inclusion are merely cosmetic and promotional while structural problems remain anchored as observed in the different tensions lived in the city's everyday life. Globalization and neoliberalism have made marketing campaigns, and promotional videos represent Barranquilla as a city full of relational space-times that accept and respect the LGBTIQ+ people. Similarly, the discourses of the Gay Carnival's paraders, whose rights have indeed improved in the last decades, demonstrate that there is a perception that Barranquilla is now more inclusive. One could think that Barranquilla has a culture of acceptance towards queer subjects. The perception, however, that there is a "gay-friendly" ambiance is not entirely accurate. The attempt to touristify the city has galvanized such representations and obscured the homophobic and heteronormative reality. Queer people in Barranquilla still have to accommodate to certain norms if they want to be accepted. The creative queer, for instance, is one of those homonormative configurations that allow LGBTIQ+ people to gain respectability. In this chapter, I analysed how some forces produce relations while disregarding others. While class, race, political filiations, and ableism are also essential to understand the spatial temporal configuration of Barranquilla and its carnival, I focus on gender and sexuality as an integral part that shape relations. I also narrowed my chapter and discussed gay men's cases leaving aside other queer bodies. However, these remaining aspects need to be studied to gain a better understanding of Barranquilla. Meanwhile, in observing apparently positive relations of heteronormalized and queer subjects emerging, another big question that deserves attention is how neoliberalism is forcing these subjects to accept homonormativities that obstruct the actualization of queer utopias.

Notes

1 I would like to thank Marié Abe, Michael Birenbaum Quintero, and Gregory Barz for reading/listening, and commenting on this paper. Similarly, I wish to show my appreciation to Benjamín Juárez Echenique, and Adela Pineda who supported this project in its initial stage. I want also to acknowledge the sponsorship given by the "Graduate Arts Research Grant from the BU Arts Initiative and the Associate Provost for Graduate Affairs – Office of the Provost" to conduct fieldwork. Writing assistance provided by Brita Heimarck and Rachana Vajjhala was also greatly appreciated. Finally, thanks to my dear friend in Barranquilla, Roodnye Alberto Carrillo Palomino, who generously helped me to navigate Barranquilla and the Carnival.
2 Many practitioners say that the Gay Carnival started in the 1970s while others in the 1980s. In 2022, the *Corporación Autónoma del Carnaval Gay de Barranquilla* the official organizing institution of the Gay Carnaval declared that in that year the carnival was celebrating its 40th anniversary. Historical research of the *Carnaval Gay de Barranquilla* has not yet been done.
3 I am using the term "gay" since it is the way most practitioners have identified themselves and have, therefore, named the carnival (using the actual English word untranslated). However, this does not mean that there are no conflicts about this. Transgender, feminist, and other LGBTIQ+ movements have pleaded that the name does not represent gender and sexual diversity and Barranquilla's non-heteronormative population.
4 Among the scarce but relevant texts, the literature has concentrated in the anthropological, hermeneutical, and sociological side of the carnival in relationship to the African Diaspora: González Cueto and Lizcano Angarita (2010), Miranda Freitas (2013), Reyes Morris (2011), Ochoa Escobar (2017).

5 Barranquilla's openness reputation was acquired because during the last decade of the nineteenth- and the first half of the twentieth-century immigration from Europe and the Middle East grew up dramatically and was the city with the largest number of immigrants.

6 Here, ambiance is understood as the experiences and perceptions produced by the physical and lived spaces combined, or as Piga et al. (2016) describe it, "a combination of different stimuli coming from the environment to someone's attention" (371). Moreover, as shown in Chelkoff et al. (2004), the complexity of ambiance is given by its several components that can be scrutinized. Among these components is the effect that personal and collective experiences have on ambiances "which are influenced by the historical, social and cultural dimensions" (371). Therefore, in this paper, I am focusing on how lived experiences of place constitute part of the perceptions of LGBTIQ+ people in Barranquilla and, consequently, shape the ambiance while simultaneously comparing such perceptions with the marketed ambiances.

7 While there is cross-dressing and enactments that could not coincide with the gender, sex, or sexuality of the performer within the Carnaval de Barranquilla (and outside the Carnaval Gay de Barranquilla), most of these performances are parodies of specific characters. Similarly, these performances are normalized by the Carnival's traditions and are not performed to challenge normativity nor are they meant to be queer.

References

Abe, M. 2018. *Resonances of Chindon-Ya: Sounding Space and Sociality in Contemporary Japan*. Music/Culture. Middletown, CT: Wesleyan University Press.

Adam, B. D., J. W. Duyvendak, and A. Krouwel. 1999. "Introduction." In *Global Emergence Of Gay & Lesbian Politics: National Imprints of a Worldwide Movement*, edited by B. D. Adam, J. W. Duyvendak and A. Krouwel. Temple University Press. www.jstor.org/stable/j.ctt14bs8hv.

Bakhtin, M. 1984. *Rabelais and His World*. Translated by Helene Isvolsky. Bloomington, IN: Indiana University Press.

Barranquillacpt. 2018. "Guacherna y Coronación Del Carnaval Gay, La Fiesta Es de Todos." *YouTube*, May 2, 2018. www.youtube.com/watch?v=8oT1jqXeKF4.

Caracol Televisión. 2015. "¡Se Prendió La Fiesta! En El Carnaval de Barranquilla Se Vivirá 'Una Sola Gozadera'." *YouTube*, December 18, 2015. www.youtube.com/watch?v=DOQ0JN9vLlI.

Chelkoff, G., P. Amphoux, and J.-P. Thibaud. 2004. "Ambiances En Débats. A la croisée." https://halshs.archives-ouvertes.fr/halshs-01295544.

Da Matta, R. 2002. *Carnavales, malandros y héroes: hacia una sociología del dilema brasileño*. Mexico DF: Fondo de Cultura Económica.

Eagleton, T. 2009. *Walter Benjamin or towards a Revolutionary Criticism*. Reprint of the 1981 edition. London: Verso.

FONTUR and PROCOLOMBIA. 2018. *Guía Profesional Para El Desarrollo Del Turismo LGBT En Colombia*. Bogotá: Ministerio de Comercio, Industria y Turismo.

González Cueto, D. A., and M. Lizcano Angarita. 2010. "El aporte afrocolombiano al Carnaval de Barranquilla: su valoración e inventario en los estudios históricos, antropológicos y etnográficos (1829–2005)." *Revista Brasileira do Caribe* X (20): 447–474.

Hughes, H. L. 2006. *Pink Tourism: Holidays of Gay Men and Lesbians*. Wallingford, UK and Cambridge, MA: CABI.

Johnston, L. 2007. *Queering Tourism: Paradoxical Performances of Gay Pride Parades*. London: Routledge.

Kafer, A. 2013. *Feminist, Queer, Crip*. Bloomington, IN: Indiana University Press.

Lewis, C., and S. Pile. 1996. "Woman, Body, Space: Rio Carnival and the Politics of Performance." *Gender, Place & Culture* 3 (1): 23–42.

Markwell, K. 2002. "Mardi Gras Tourism and the Construction of Sydney as an International Gay and Lesbian City." *GLQ: A Journal of Lesbian and Gay Studies* 8 (1–2): 81–99.

Massey, D. B. 1994. *Space, Place, and Gender*. Minneapolis: University of Minnesota Press.

Miranda Freitas, J. 2013. "Las Raíces Africanas Del Carnaval de Barranquilla." In *Leyendo El Carnaval: Miradas Desde Barranquilla, Bahía y Barcelona*, edited by J. Mojica Madera, M. Lizcano Angarita, and D. González Cueto, 13–36. Barranquilla: Editorial Universidad del Norte.

Ochoa Escobar, F. 2017. "La cumbia en el carnaval de Barranquilla: construcción de un metarrelato." *Journal Encuentros* 15 (3). https://doi.org/10.15665/re.v15i3.1097.

Omarvill Oe. 2018. "Guacherna Gay de Soledad 2018 by Omarvill." www.youtube.com/watch?v=TSo5Gp-ti4E&t.

Pérez Álvarez, A. 2017. *Arco Iris En Blanco y Negro*. Barranquilla: Caribe Afirmativo.

Piga, B., C. Chiarini, I. Vegetti, M. Boffi, N. Rainisio, A. Bonnet, V. Signorelli, V. Tourre, and M. Servières. 2016. "Mapping Ambiance: A Synopsis of Theory and Practices in an Interdisciplinary Perspective." In *Proceedings of Third International Congress on Ambiances*, edited by N. Rémy and N. Tixier, 367–372. Volos, Greece: International Network Ambiances, University of Thessaly. www.ambiances.net/congresses/volos-2016-international-congress-future-of-ambiances.html.

PROCOLOMBIA. 2017. "About PROCOLOMBIA." August 1, 2017. https://procolombia.co/en/procolombia/about-procolombia.

Reyes Morris, V. 2011. "Tiempo anómico: el carnaval de Barranquilla." *Revista Colombiana de Sociología* 34 (1): 103–126.

Rushbrook, D. 2002. "Cities, Queer Space, and the Cosmopolitan Tourist." *GLQ: A Journal of Lesbian and Gay Studies* 8 (1–2): 183–206.

Wade, P. 1993. *Blackness and Race Mixture: Dynamics of Racial Identity in Colombia*. Johns Hopkins Studies in Atlantic History & Culture. Baltimore: Johns Hopkins University Press.

Waitt, G., and K. Markwell. 2006. *Gay Tourism: Culture and Context*. New York: Haworth Hospitality Press.

Part V
Creating authenticity for tourist consumption

13 Sounds like an authentic tourist experience! Listening to tourism-led transformations in the atmosphere of a Southern Mediterranean city

Nicola Di Croce

> Reinventing authenticity begins with creating an image to connect an aesthetic view of origins and a social view of new beginnings.
>
> (Zukin 2010, 234)

Introduction

In the last decades, the growth of tourism industry has affected urban neighbourhoods and entire towns worldwide as a consequence of the increasing international competitiveness among cities and regions (Ojeda and Kieffer 2020). This is particularly evident in Southern Mediterranean cities where, as suggested by Sequera and Nofre (2018, 843–844), the rise of investments in the touristic sector has been associated with the geo-political instability of Middle Eastern countries and their tourist destinations, and with the increase in low-cost flights and sharing economy platforms (Cocola-Gant 2016).

But what is at stake when a Southern Mediterranean city becomes the object of tourist consumption? Investigating the tourism-led impacts on the everyday life of the city of Palermo (Italy), I introduce in this chapter the notion of *affective tonality* (Goodman 2009; Thibaud 2015) as a key determinant of the atmosphere of a place (Böhme 2016), and one of the tourists' most-wanted object of desire. In particular, I explore the tourism-led transformations on urban atmosphere by taking into account tourists' and city users' sensory perception (Gaudin 2018), and more precisely by critically engaging with the urban sonic environment (Gallagher et al. 2016). Building on urban studies and sound studies literature, I give special prominence to the characteristic sounds of Palermo's traditional street markets as to analyse their role in the formation of a distinctive and attractive urban atmosphere for tourist consumption. This approach is also consistent with recent trajectories in tourist studies that are moving "away from the traditional focus on vision, towards multi-sensual analysis including the role of taste, smell, touch and sound" (Everingham et al. 2021, 70).

DOI: 10.4324/9781003207207-19

By inquiring into the process of tourism-led urban transformation through the "lens" of the sonic environment, I intend to show how tourists' quest for an authentic experience (Urry 1990) exposes contemporary tourist cities to a pervasive extraction of value from their most distinctive urban atmosphere. I claim therefore that such distinctive atmosphere, although shaped by the ever-changing relations between people and the built environment (Gandy 2017), is nevertheless deeply rooted in traditional human activities (as for traditional markets in the case of Palermo), which are often threatened by the impacts of tourism as well as by broader urban transformations (Paiva and Sánchez-Fuarros 2021).

What happens, then, when tourism interferes in the fragile relations underpinning a distinctive urban atmosphere and a characteristic sonic environment? And to what extent such atmosphere can continue, under the impacts of tourism, to be attractive towards tourists? Seeking to answer these questions, I support the idea that sonic inquiry into urban atmosphere can meaningfully inform the urban policy response to some of the most detrimental impacts of tourism (Ribeiro de Almeida et al. 2020). Reflecting on those urban areas affected by tourist-led transformations – especially within Southern Mediterranean cities such as Palermo – I mobilize the notion of *authenticity* (Zukin 2010) as a crucial factor influencing touristic attractiveness. I'm therefore interested to challenge to what degree a distinctive urban atmosphere can change under the burden of tourist consumption, and to what extent it can engage visitors in its continuous – and profoundly interactive – process of adaptation, domestication, or potential disruption.

In the case study developed in Palermo, I explore the sonic environment of the traditional street markets located within the historic centre of the city, and more precisely I focus on the traders' everyday cries and sales pitch: a sing-like typical practice in Mediterranean cities (namely *abbanniata* in Palermo's local dialect) performed by vendors to work the crowd and better sell their goods. Analysing the main findings from two research-creation projects (Loveless 2019) realized in 2014 and 2018, respectively, I investigate the presence of *abbanniata* over the different markets. I then examine the way in which street cries change or tend to disappear over the years as the city is facing in the meantime a significant growth in tourist presence. From this basis, I discuss the tourism-led impacts on Palermo's street markets and their distinctive sonic environment, and I argue for a politics of urban atmosphere that challenges how authenticity is, and can be, negotiated among visitors, residents, city users, and other public and private stakeholders.

The chapter is organized as follows: In the first section, I present a literature review where I focus on urban atmosphere and the sonic environment as to investigate the role of authenticity in tourist experience. In the following section, I introduce the case study area and describe the methodology used for the two projects. In the third section, I describe the main findings from the two studies, and finally in the last section I discuss the outcomes of the research in the light of the theoretical framework proposed in the literature review.

Literature review

To investigate what factors shape the tourist experience, I introduce the concept of urban atmosphere as a powerful connecting factor between people and the build environment they inhabit or visit. Urban atmosphere has been defined as "a concept and experience of the in-betweenness of subject and object in which the emotional and sensory experience are central" (Bille et al. 2015, 32). In regard to its relational character, atmosphere has also been described as "something peculiar to the city, what makes it individual and therefore cannot be communicated in general concepts" (Böhme 2016, 128). While being affected by people's activities and uses of space, urban atmosphere has at the same time the capacity to repel or attract people to a certain place (a neighbourhood, a square, a street); it affects them in a pervasive yet elusive way. For this reason, a number of scholars have referred to "affective atmosphere" (Anderson 2009, 78; Buser 2014; Gandy 2017) to underline the affective intensity that emerges from the relation between urban areas and city users.

In the wake of the growing attention given to sensory perception in urban studies (Gaudin 2018), I focus on the experience of everyday sounds and more broadly on the role of the sonic environment in the formation of atmosphere and in its affective intensity. Sound is affective as it does not limit to connect things, rather it actively changes them (Kanngieser 2015, 81), for example modulating a dance floor, repulsing bodies from sirens and alarms, or inducing muscle contractions after an intense movie scene (Gallagher et al. 2016, 8). In this sense "The affective aspect of sound comes precisely from the relations, exchanges and movements between bodies and environments" (8), which is an extremely relevant aspect to be considered when focusing on the experience of a (tourist) area. In fact, if sounds affect the experience of the build environment, the *tonality* they bring to the atmosphere is a key factor that shapes such experience; as stated by Thibaud (2015, 44): "an affective tonality colours the whole of the current situation by conferring it with a certain physiognomy". Describing affective tonalities, other authors have further argued that, while colouring a situation, sounds operate even beyond the formation of emotions; Goodman (2009, 189) in this regard claims that "unlike an emotional state, affective tonality possesses, abducts, or envelops a subject rather than being possessed by one".

Drawing from these formulations, affective tonality can be described as a prominent feature of atmosphere: one that modulates the affective responses to a situation (Ash 2012), thus deeply influencing the experience of the built environment and its transformations overtime. Investigating the transformations of affective tonality – the way atmosphere is designed, staged or performed (Paiva and Sánchez-Fuarros 2021) – stands for a meaningful entry point for better framing how tourism-led transformations impact urban everyday life. This is because, as suggested by Paiva and Sánchez-Fuarros (2021, 10), the "production of atmosphere not only generates territories but also collides with the production of territories of everyday life". The affective tonality of a place plays a crucial part in the formation of people's (and particularly tourists') preferences: It is a pull factor influencing their actions and behaviours – their feelings, emotions, and affects. For this reason, I argue that the concept affective tonality, by connecting the notion of urban atmosphere with the sonic environment (as perceived by people), can be effectively mobilized and operationalized in the framework of urban and tourist studies as to clarify the mechanisms through which specific sounds operate in the context of cities undergoing tourism-led transformations.

Here, the attention of this chapter falls, more specifically, on vendors' street cries, given the musicality and unique character embedded in their practice (Riedel and Torvinen 2019; Molina 2020), which strongly contributes to the formation of a distinctive atmosphere within the market areas. In this line, following Kreutzfeldt (2012, 62), street cries "testify [...] ways in which audible practices shape and structure urban spaces" pointing at "the dynamics of space-making, through which the social and territorial construction of urban space is performed". Inquiring how street cries modulate the affective tonality of street markets, I'm interested in exploring the role of audible practices (Di Croce 2016) in shaping the atmosphere of tourist consumption, their peculiar *rhythm*. Drawing from the urban sociological tradition focusing on urban rhythms – what Lefebvre (2004, 89) introduced as rhythmanalysis – through this chapter I aim at further understanding how "the rhythmanalyst . . . knows how to listen to a square, a market, an avenue".

Building on the abovementioned body of literature, it is possible now to draw attention to a central question formulated by Kourtit and her colleagues (2020, 1), which is absolutely relevant for urban areas undergoing tourism-led transformations: "what makes the city a 'real' and attractive city?". The distinctive (yet ever-changing) affective tonalities marking the atmosphere of a place are at the core of the "bodily and sensual" tourist experience (Terkenli 2002, 229) as they contribute to orientate visitors towards those destinations where they can have "a 'real authentic' experience based on eating, dining, consuming and being accommodated-like-a-local" (Sequera and Nofre 2018, 849). In so doing, tourists are often attracted by those unspoiled places that can be found within (sometimes just apparently) non-tourist areas of a city (2018, 851), as they consider these areas the most authentic and thus worth visiting. Hence, drawing tourists' attention towards "unspoiled" urban atmosphere, affective tonalities participate in what has been defined as "experience economy" (Oh et al. 2007), where "consumers seek unique experiences beyond merely consuming products and service" (119).

Tourists' constant search for authentic places to "consume" (Urry 1990) due to their unique atmosphere demonstrates that authenticity – the capacity of a city or neighbourhood to "create the *experience* of origins" (Zukin 2010, 3) – is often considered as an endangered product of the social and cultural history of an urban area. In this regard Zukin argues that, although "we think authenticity refers to a neighborhood's innate qualities, it really expresses our own anxieties about how places change" (2010, 220). This anxiety of change also challenges the distinctive yet fluid character of an atmosphere (and its affective tonalities), as its alleged invariability is at odds with what Zukin (2010, preface, xi) describes as the continuous "tension between origins and new beginnings". Through this expression, the scholar points out that the understanding of authenticity is constantly negotiated among those older generations interested in preserving the "original" character of a place, and those younger generations that constantly re-invent their own version of it. For this reason, an authentic atmosphere embraces the desire to experience at the same time the "origins" – a special, almost nostalgic immutability overtime – and the "new beginnings": the social, cultural, and economic relations that endlessly re-shape the character of a place, its aesthetics and tonalities.

Mobilizing the notion of authenticity in urban and tourism studies (for a review, see Noy 2009), I'm interested in highlighting how affective tonalities of touristic urban areas are exploited by the modern forms of capitalism in a very peculiar fashion. In fact, quoting Lamla (2009, 180), while capitalism is "making authenticity an object of desire to be consumed, corresponding commodities or services nonetheless depend on consumer's coproduction of value". Here, paradoxically, a distinctive urban atmosphere, while becoming the object of tourist consumption, needs at the same time to involve consumers (visitors) in the coproduction of the social, cultural, or economic relations which create that very atmosphere. However, such involvement is not simply based on visitors' consumption (i.e. mediated by tourists' spending power); instead, it challenges their role – and accordingly their responsibility – in the transformation, domestication, or potential disruption of the same atmosphere they are eager to experience.

What happens, within a tourist area, if urban atmosphere is changing "too much", its authenticity moving too fast, its tonality not affecting visitors the same way they were expecting? This question resonates with the long tradition of political economy critique; most precisely it challenges the notion of capitalism as a force "capable of conferring identity and meaning on all it consumes" (Brouder 2018, 916; see also Gibson-Graham 1997). Considering how much (and how fast) a distinctive atmosphere can change overtime under the burden of tourist consumption, I question to what extent new forms of authenticity can successfully "satisfy" tourists as much as "original" forms of authenticity used to do. Here two scenarios arise: the first is that of new forms of authenticity co-produced and well-received by tourists, the second is that provocatively described by Brouder (2018) as the "end of tourism".

The uncertain dynamics of authenticity is particularly evident in traditional cities, especially within public spaces that have become popular tourist destinations in reason of their characteristic everyday activities (their affective tonalities). This is the case of traditional street markets in Southern Mediterranean cities like Barcelona or Palermo.[1] In this regard, in his essay titled *The Rhythmanalysis of Mediterranean Cities*, Lefebvre argues:

> [T]he most traditional towns accept modern tourism; they adapt themselves by resisting the loss of identity that these invasions could entail. Wouldn't this be the case, not only for Venice, but also for Syracuse, Barcelona, Palermo,

> Naples and Marseille, cities delivered over to tourism that fiercely resist
> homogenisation, linearity and the rhythms "of the other"?
>
> (Lefebvre 2004, 98)

Interestingly, according to Lefebvre, the historic and cultural facets of Mediterranean cities should help prevent them to suffer under the burden of tourism-led transformations; yet modern mass tourism has proven to deeply affect (and often homogenize) these cities and most precisely their traditional retail landscape (Sequera and Nofre 2018, 848).

Building on this theoretical background, as the understanding of authenticity constantly changes overtime, how the affective tonalities shaping urban atmosphere impact (and potentially limit) the overall tourist experience? I claim, in this regard, that investigating the sonic environment can provide meaningful information to answer (or to better frame) such question, given that the acoustic dimension of the city strongly contributes to shape the authenticity of urban atmosphere, hence to orientate tourist experience. Urban sounds reflect the role of residents, city users, and tourists in the creation of shared living environments: "acoustic territories" (Labelle 2010) where their combined actions unfold the constant political process of negotiating and reconfiguring common spaces. In this sense, I recall the notion of "sonic commons" introduced by Odland and Auinger (2009, 64) to describe "any space where many people share an acoustic environment and can hear the results of each other's activities".

Building on the idea that a sonic commons is the result of a shared sonic environment, I argue that the future of tourist destinations depends, among other factors, on the way authenticity is (and will be) negotiated among residents, visitors, and other urban actors. This implies further investigating how affective tonalities are modulated by tourism-led transformations and how they contribute to shape the atmosphere of tourist cities. Here, in order to make sense of such modulations and transformations, I call for a broader understanding of "listening" practice within urban and tourist studies. I therefore argue for a listening practice not only intended as the capability to enter into contact with other people – as framed in urban planning and policy design literature (Forester 1989, 107–118) – rather as the ability to investigate urban atmosphere and resonate with affective tonalities. In this regard, I support the idea that further developing a sonic perspective to investigate on affective tonalities can provide meaningful policy responses to address the new challenges of tourism-led urban transformations (see in this regard Ribeiro de Almeida et al. 2020).

Methodology

Palermo's traditional and most popular street markets, namely "Capo", "Ballarò", and "Vucciria", are located in three of the four main neighbourhoods of the city's historic centre (see Map 13.1). Palermo has always been a famous tourist destination due to its architectures that combine elements of Western, Islamic, and Byzantine cultures, and in 2015 the site "Arab-Norman Palermo and the Cathedral

Map 13.1 Location of the three markets within the historic centre of Palermo. The higher or lower presence of the *abbanniata* among the markets is illustrated through a greater or lesser number of concentric circles. The dashed line follows the soundwalk path.

Map: Nicola Di Croce

Churches of Cefalú and Monreale" was listed as world heritage by UNESCO.[2] Later in 2018, the city has hosted the 12th edition of Manifesta European Nomadic Biennial, a major international art event that took place all over the city throughout the summer and fall. Especially from 2016 to 2019, these factors contributed, among others, to a significant growth of the number of visitors.[3] For the aim of this study, these facts and dates are significant as the two case studies were developed in September 2014 and November 2018, respectively, therefore covering a period of great change for the city.

I was involved in the two projects as urban researcher and sound artist. Both project fall under the category of Research-Creation (Loveless 2019), as a set of methods was used to produce artistic outputs and to generate academic research results (Chapman and Sawchuk 2012), with the ultimate aim to inform urban studies literature (Di Croce 2020). For the first project (2014), during an artist residency at the contemporary art centre Dimora OZ, I took field recordings in the three traditional markets at various moments of the day and the week, and I informally interviewed vendors, asking them to talk about their street cries. Field recording is a method used to capture through microphones the features of the sonic environment; it is widely employed in sound art practices (Lane and Carlyle 2013), as well as in social science and urban research (Gallagher and Prior 2014; Fong 2016). Once collected, I analysed the recordings to gather qualitative information about the presence of *abbanniata* within the different markets; I finally used selected fragments of the recordings to compose two sound installations, later presented as the main outcome of the residency.[4]

For the second project (2018), supported by the local cultural association Sguardi Urbani, I involved a group of 20 participants through an open call – circulated via the Manifesta 12 website – to take part in a soundwalk. A soundwalk is a guided walk where participants are invited to concentrate on the sonic environment they explore, and to later talk about their experience during a group discussion. Soundwalk practice was first experimented in the early 1970s of the twentieth century in Northern America urban contexts (Westerkamp 2007) with the aim of rising participants' sonic awareness. Since then, the practice has been used in different research fields and not least in urban studies (Drever 2020). Drawing from the experience of the previous project from 2014, I traced the route of the Palermo soundwalk as to link the three markets of Ballarò, Capo, and Vucciria in a unique path. During the soundwalk I invited participants to focus on the street cries they could hear throughout the walk; I then asked them to stop after each market for a brief group discussion. The end of the participatory event, which lasted about two hours, was finally followed by a longer group discussion where we addressed the issues emerging from each participant's experience.[5] I later analysed the outcomes of the event through notes and recordings taken during the walk and discussions; this way I could focus on the presence and use of the street cries among the markets and compare it to the previous experience from 2014.

Findings: listening to Palermo's traditional markets (2014–2018)

Analysing the data collected in 2014 and 2018, I present here the main outcomes of the projects through two main findings. The first illustrates the general presence of street cries in the three markets and is based on the results from both the two projects developed in 2014 and 2018. The second focuses on the tourism-led impacts on the sonic environment of Ballarò, Capo, and Vucciria, and is based on the results from the 2018 soundwalk as compared to the previous project from 2014.

First, the three markets present very different sonic environments due to their spatial distribution in the neighbourhoods, the everyday uses of the public spaces in which they are located, and ultimately the presence of street cries. In Ballarò the *abbanniata* is usually very present, especially during the day, while in Capo the street cries are generally less intense, and they almost disappear in Vucciria. Especially during the morning hours, the sonic environment in Ballarò is lively and vibrant, the street cries colouring the atmosphere of the streets and big public spaces in a very engaging manner. In the same hours, the sound environment in Capo is more subtle, as the market develops over narrow streets and small open spaces, while the vendors' cries chase each other from time to time to draw passers-by's attention. Ultimately, Vucciria presents over the day a very quiet sonic environment rarely animated by street cries as only few market stalls are operating in the area; the absence of human activities triggers here a sense of loss and melancholia.

The reason of the inconsistent pattern among the three markets lies in the city's trend in traditional retail, whereas the different fortunes of the neighbourhoods where the markets are located profoundly contributed to shape their atmosphere over the past decades. In fact, Ballarò is one of the most lively and multi-cultural areas of the historic centre while Capo remains more rooted in Sicilian traditions as it is primarily home to locals, and Vucciria turned to be a nightlife destination for both residents and visitors, thus slowly leaving aside its retail tradition.

The diversified presence of street cries illustrates how such a traditional practice is most evidently disappearing where street markets are threatened by broader urban transformations, and not least by the impacts of tourism. Interestingly, many vendors (especially from Vucciria and Capo) argue in this regard that performing the *abbanniata* is something they've learned from their fathers and grandfathers, yet they would have difficulties to teach it to their sons as they generally consider street trade to be endangered; they don't envision a long-term future for their business. Also, street vendors claim that, even if their cries are made as a good omen for their sales, they also need the presence of other sellers and customers to start performing the vocal practice; in fact they point out that *abbanniata* is deeply interactive as vendors are chasing each other through their cries, and customers need to understand them in order to react to their calls. Therefore, a lower number of local vendors and a growing number of customers who are not able to understand the local dialect (above all tourists) are among the main factors affecting the continuity of *abbanniata*.

The second finding concerns the recent evolution of the street cries (2014 to 2018), and more precisely the extent to which they are disappearing or are domesticated under the influence of tourism. In particular, the soundwalk unveils how street markets are affected by an increasing number of visitors compared to the past, and confirms that street vendors react in different ways according to the market they belong.

In Ballarò the *abbanniata* is still very present as for the high number of local customers. Participants to the soundwalk yet highlight that traders' use of language often changes in an effort to engage tourists and ultimately be understood by them; hence the Italian and sometimes English language is usually preferred over the local dialect. The overall atmosphere is however very attractive and the sonic environment maintains a diversified nature, which reveals how the market is still capable of perpetuating its traditional character under the presence of tourists by adjusting its communication codes.[6]

In the market of Capo, the atmosphere is enlivened by fewer street cries; the impression shared by the soundwalk's participants is that vendors are mostly interested in engaging tourists rather than local customers. Also, the presence of guided tours is more evident here and their impact on the retail landscape is visible: On their stalls vendors show a number of goods that are evidently oriented

Figure 13.1   A tour guide leading a group of tourists in the narrow streets of Capo's market.

Source: Photo Nicola Di Croce

to tourist consumption while vendors are rarely engaging passers-by through *abbanniata*. The atmosphere in Capo is in fact missing a fully engaging tonality, its sonic environment poorly contributing to the expected experience of a Mediterranean traditional market.[7]

Finally, in Vucciria the *abbanniata* seems to be almost disappeared as the number of stalls has dramatically dropped over the last years. The few street vendors still working during the day are rarely trying to engage passers-by, while people working in restaurants and cafes invite visitors to stop by their venues. Especially during the morning and throughout the afternoon, the presence of tourists is more evident due to the absence of locals, and the layering of foreign languages is among the most distinctive feature of the sonic environment. Here, soundwalk's participants agree that the quiet sonic environment is unlikely belonging to a traditional market; also, participants who are more familiar with the city highlight how, over the evening and night-time, the atmosphere in Vucciria suddenly changes as the market area has become a popular hangout for younger generations.[8]

Discussion and conclusions

The outcomes of the projects illustrate how the growing amount of tourists has deeply affected Palermo's traditional retail landscape (Sequera and Nofre 2018).

While the number of visitors is increasing, their impact on Palermo's traditional markets challenges, to some extent, Lefebvre's (2004, 98) assumption that Southern Mediterranean cities can "fiercely resist homogenisation". The case studies show, in this regard, how the three markets are exploring different avenues to adapt to tourism-led transformations, which not necessarily entail keeping traditional street cries alive. In fact, the two projects illustrate how tourism is impacting an affective tonality – the performance of *abbanniata* – that shapes the historic centre's atmosphere (Thibaud 2015). It is a tonality that fashion a peculiar acoustic territory (LaBelle 2010; Kreutzfeldt 2012), marking the tourist experience of Palermo's historic centre and contributing to the attractiveness of those neighbourhoods where traditional markets are located. In this sense, street cries are the perfect example of an audible everyday practice (Di Croce 2016) echoing the "origins" (Zukin 2010, 234) of Palermo, a practice now transformed, domesticated, or endangered by the impacts of tourism.

The domestication or potential disruption of street cries' practice raises a question on the dynamics of exploitation of authentic affective tonalities on the future of traditional urban areas such as street markets. Within this framework, I have pointed out that street markets' experience is strongly mediated by the pervasive mechanism of experience economy (Oh et al. 2007), and more broadly by the exploiting dynamics of capitalism (Gibson-Graham 1997). In this regard, the results from the two projects have illustrated how the three markets are facing different situations, and have shown how street vendors are experimenting different approaches to cope with the increasing number of visitors.

I have highlighted how such differences can be investigated by critically listening to the presence, intensity, and use of *abbanniata* throughout the three street markets. In Ballarò, the vendors performing the street cries are generally adapting to the presence of tourists and are often interacting with them as well as with locals; their creatively evolved version of *abbanniata* thus contributes to a perceived lively and vibrant atmosphere within the market. In Capo the *abbanniata* is being more evidently domesticated by the presence of tourists and is partially losing its "original" character; as a result, a less engaging atmosphere is perceived throughout the market. Finally, street cries in Vucciria are almost disappearing as the area attracts tourists and locals mostly for its nightlife; this situation deeply influences the humble atmosphere felt over the morning and afternoon in the area. On the basis of this scenario, the different trajectories followed by the three markets offer two interesting perspectives to critically reflect on the evolution of authenticity within Southern Mediterranean tourist cities.

First, those markets already suffering from the decline of their retail landscape (see Vucciria) are the ones where the affective tonality of their "origins" is more quickly disappearing, as the limited number of vendors don't seem to use street cries, not even in alternative ways, to engage clients and visitors. Drawing from the example of Vucciria, where vendors' stalls are slowly disappearing, the "new" authenticity of the market does not include anymore the performance of *abbanniata*; as a result, Vucciria waives the very character that had previously contributed to the tourist attractiveness of the district while investing on other forms of (likely more viable) economies. In such a situation, however, it is an open question whether: (i) tourists' reaction to an atmosphere that is missing a sense of "origins" – that have lost its (once) distinctive affective tonality – would lead to the "end of tourism" (Brouder 2018) within the area; or (ii) if the neighbourhood is eventually able or willing, through its new form of authenticity (i.e. nightlife economy), to reorient tourists' attractiveness towards the area.

In this regard, the case of Vucciria suggests that, under economic pressure and tourism-led transformations, the loss of an affective tonality belonging to the "origins" contributes to completely change the atmosphere of a popular destination for city users and visitors (see in this regard Paiva and Sánchez-Fuarros 2021 for the case of Lisbon). In fact, the "new beginning" of Vucciria, while quickly discarding the tradition of street cries, is also impacting the area's everyday life (especially its lack of perceived liveliness during the day) as well as vendors' traditional economy. Here, a negotiation among all the urban actors who co-produce the atmosphere of the market would be needed for the future of the city's economy, as well as for the sustainability of those precarious workers (vendors) whose activity was once strongly contributing to shape the affective tonality of the area.

The second point of discussion refers to those markets that show a stronger capacity to adapt to tourism-led transformations (see above all Ballarò); these are the ones where street cries still contribute (although in a different way compared to the past) to shape the affective tonality of the neighbourhoods' atmosphere. Here, the "new beginning" of authenticity (the new character of the markets) is still rooted in the traditional practice of *abbanniata*, which is certainly reinvented yet not abandoned by vendors. Interestingly, Ballarò is the most multi-cultural market of Palermo's historic centre: this aspect highlighting how the re-invention of authenticity is not exclusively a prerogative of native communities; on the contrary, it entails a shared attitude towards cultural construction. Ballarò ultimately shows a "new" authentic character anchored in its "origins", which demonstrates that a combination of tourism development, local economies, and cultural traditions can be possible, and that the gradual transition towards new forms of authenticity could benefit from the re-invention of traditional affective tonalities. Yet, other examples, such as the one from Capo, also highlight that the balance between tourism, local economies, and cultural traditions is fragile, and thus needs to be monitored and assessed collaboratively among urban actors.

How to monitor such a fragile balance? Building on the outcomes of this study and following discussion, I support the idea that engaging affective tonalities can help tourist cities exploring new avenues to challenge the most problematic tourism-led urban transformations, and ultimately contribute to a more resilient community of residents, city users, tourists, grassroots organization, or local institutions. To better engage affective tonalities, I recall here the need to broaden the understanding of listening practice, especially within urban planning research (Forester 1989, 107–118). In fact, I argue for listening practice as a tool to attune to those distinctive elements of the sonic environment that, by deeply contributing to the experience of the everyday built environment, ultimately shape urban atmosphere and fashion authenticity. Drawing from the concept of "sonic commons"

(Odland and Auinger 2009) as a shared space where people's attentiveness to the sonic environment is key, I emphasize the importance of a negotiation of authenticity among all those urban actors who contribute to the "coproduction of value" (Lamla 2009) in tourist areas. As each urban actor plays a part in the formation and transformation of authenticity, I finally suggest that fostering a critical listening culture among institutions residents, city users and visitors can represent a meaningful step towards such negotiation: It can inform policy-making and eventually inspire new forms of collaborative assessment of the impacts of tourism in Southern Mediterranean cities.

Notes

1 An example on how Mediterranean markets have become tourist destinations can be found in tourist platforms such as EDreams Travel stories. Quoting from the website page: "Hundreds of years ago, the cities beside the sea where the merchant ships docked became true hubs of trade. Markets were at the heart of these exchanges. These days they're also a tourist attraction." Further information are available at the following link: www.edreams.com/blog/10-mediterranean-markets-you-should-know-about/#
2 For further information see the related UNESCO webpage, available at https://whc.unesco.org/en/list/1487/
3 For further information see the report from the City of Palermo, available online at www.comune.palermo.it/js/server/uploads/_14082020170729.pdf
4 Audio excerpts of two sound installations are available online at https://nicoladicroce.cargo.site/urban-sampling
5 For further information on the project are available online at https://nicoladicroce.cargo.site/looking-for-abbanniata
6 A field recording of the soundwalk in Ballarò is available at the following link: https://soundcloud.com/ricerche-sonore/looking-for-abbanniata-ballaro
7 A field recording of the soundwalk in Capo is available at the following link: https://soundcloud.com/ricerche-sonore/looking-for-abbanniata-capo
8 A field recording of the soundwalk in Vucciria is available at the following link: https://soundcloud.com/ricerche-sonore/looking-for-abbanniata-vucciria

References

Anderson, B. 2009. "Affective Atmospheres." *Emotion, Space and Society* 2 (2): 77–81.
Ash, J. 2012. "Rethinking Affective Atmospheres: Technology, Perturbation and Space Times of the Non-Human." *Geoforum* 49: 20–28.
Bille, M., P. Bjerregaard, and T. F. Sørensen. 2015. "Staging Atmospheres: Materiality, Culture, and the Texture of the in-Between." *Emotion, Space and Society* 15: 31–38.
Böhme, G. 2016. *The Aesthetics of Atmospheres*. London and New York: Routledge.
Brouder, P. 2018. "The End of Tourism? A Gibson-Graham Inspired Reflection on the Tourism Economy." *Tourism Geographies* 20 (5): 916–918.
Buser, M. 2014. "Thinking through Non-representational and Affective Atmospheres in Planning Theory and Practice." *Planning Theory* 13 (3): 227–243.
Chapman, O., and K. Sawchuk. 2012. "Research-Creation: Intervention, Analysis and 'Family Resemblances'." *Canadian Journal of Communication* 37 (1): 5–26.
Cocola-Gant, A. 2016. "Holiday Rentals: The New Gentrification Battlefront." *Sociological Research Online* 21 (3): 10.

Di Croce, N. 2016. "Audible Everyday Practices as Listening Education." *Interference Journal* 5: 25–37. www.interferencejournal.org/audible-everyday-practices-as-listening-education/

Di Croce, N. 2020. "La politica degli affetti nell'atmosfera urbana. Ambiente sonoro e autenticità nei mercati storici di Palermo." *Sociologia e Ricerca Sociale* 122: 130–150.

Drever, J. L. 2020. "Listening as Methodological Tool: Sounding Soundwalking Methods." In *The Bloomsbury Handbook of Sonic Methodologies*, edited by M. Bull and M. Cobussen, 599–613. London: Bloomsbury Academic.

Everingham, P., P. Obrador, and H. Tucker. 2021. "Trajectories of Embodiment in Tourist Studies." *Tourist Studies* 21 (1): 70–83.

Fong, J. 2016. "Making Operative Concepts from Murray Schafer's Soundscapes Typology: A Qualitative and Comparative Analysis of Noise Pollution in Bangkok, Thailand and Los Angeles, California." *Urban Studies* 53 (1): 173–192.

Forester, J. 1989. "Listening: The Social Policy of Everyday Life." In *Planning in the Face of Power*, edited by J. Forester, 107–118. Oakland: University of California Press.

Gallagher, M., A. Kanngieser, and J. Prior. 2016. "Listening Geographies: Landscape, Affect and Geotechnologies." *Progress in Human Geography* 41 (5): 618–637.

Gallagher, M., and J. Prior. 2014. "Sonic Geographies: Exploring Phonographic Methods." *Progress in Human Geography* 38 (2): 267–284.

Gandy, M. 2017. "Urban Atmospheres." *Cultural Geographies* 24 (3): 353–374.

Gaudin, O. 2018. "Pragmatist View of Urban Experience: Sensorial Perception in Urban Studies." *Pragmatism Today* 9 (1): 173–188.

Gibson-Graham, J. K. 1997. *The End of Capitalism (as We Knew It): A Feminist Critique of Political Economy*. Oxford: Wiley-Blackwell.

Goodman, S. 2009. *Sonic Warfare: Sound Affect and the Ecology of Fear*. Cambridge, MA: MIT Press.

Kanngieser, A. 2015. "Geopolitics and the Anthropocene: Five Propositions for Sound." *GeoHumanities* 1 (1): 80–85.

Kourtit, K., P. Nijkamp, and M. Hårsman Wahlström. 2020. "How to Make Cities the Home of People – a 'Soul and Body' Analysis of Urban Attractiveness." *Land Use Policy* 111: 104734.

Kreutzfeldt, J. 2012. "Street Cries and the Urban Refrain. A Methodological Investigation of Street Cries." *Sound Effects* 2 (1): 62–80.

LaBelle, B. 2010. *Acoustic Territories. Sound Culture and Everyday Life*. New York and London: Continuum.

Lamla, J. 2009. "Consuming Authenticity: A Paradoxical Dynamic in Contemporary Capitalism." In *Authenticity in Culture, Self, and Society*, edited by P. Vannini and J. P. Williams, 171–185. London: Routledge.

Lane, C., and A. Carlyle. 2013. *In the Field: The Art of Field Recording*. Axminster, Devon: Uniformbooks.

Lefebvre, H. 2004. *Rhythmanalysis: Space, Time and Everyday Life*. London and New York: Continuum.

Loveless, N. 2019. *How to Make Art at the End of the World. A Manifesto for Research-Creation*. Durham: Duke University Press.

Molina, A. G. 2020. "Nostalgia, Internal Migration and the Return of Cuban Street-vendor Songs." *Culture, Theory and Critique* 61 (2–3): 229–245.

Noy, C. 2009. "Embodying Ideologies in Tourism: A Commemorative Visitor Book in Israel as a Site of Authenticity." In *Authenticity in Culture, Self, and Society*, edited by P. Vannini and J. P. Williams, 291–239. London: Routledge.

Odland, B., and S. Auinger. 2009. "Reflections on the Sonic Commons." *Leonardo Music Journal* 19: 63–68.

Oh, H., A. M. Fiore, and M. Jeoung. 2007. "Measuring Experience Economy Concepts: Tourism Applications." *Journal of Travel Research* 46 (2): 119–132.

Ojeda, Antonio B., and Maxime Kieffer. 2020. "Touristification. Empty Concept or Element of Analysis in Tourism Geography?" *Geoforum* 115: 143–145.

Paiva, D., and I. Sánchez-Fuarros. 2021. "The Territoriality of Atmosphere: Rethinking Affective Urbanism through the Collateral Atmospheres of Lisbon's Tourism." *Transactions of the Institute of British Geographers* 46 (2): 392–405.

Ribeiro de Almeida, C., A. Quintano, M. Simancas, R. Huete, and Z. Breda, eds. 2020. *Handbook of Research on the Impacts, Challenges, and Policy Responses to Overtourism*. Hershey: IGI Global.

Riedel, F., and J. Torvinen, eds. 2019. *Music as Atmosphere: Collective Feelings and Affective Sounds*. London: Routledge.

Sequera, J., and J. Nofre. 2018. "Debates Shaken, Not Stirred New Debates on Touristification and the Limits of Gentrification." *City* 22 (5–6): 843–855.

Terkenli, T. S. 2002. "Landscapes of Tourism: Towards a Global Cultural Economy of Space?" *Tourism Geographies* 4 (3): 227–254.

Thibaud, J-P. 2015. "The Backstage of Urban Ambiances: When Atmospheres Pervade Everyday Experience." *Emotions, Space and Society* 15: 39–46.

Urry, J. 1990. "The 'Consumption' of Tourism." *Sociology* 24 (1): 23–35.

Westerkamp, H. 2007. "Soundwalking." In *Autumn Leaves, Sound and the Environment in Artistic Practice*, edited by A. Carlyle, 49–54. Paris: Double Entendre.

Zukin, S. 2010. *Naked City: The Death and Life of Authentic Urban Places*. New York: Oxford University Press.

14 Sound and the moving tourist bubble in Harlem tourism

William Trevor Jamerson and Anthony Kwame Harrison

Introduction

A Sunday morning with Neal Shoemaker and Harlem Heritage Tours (HHT) is never spent the same way, but there is a rhythm to the activities, and each tour offers a unique experience for participants while hitting on the same beats and stops. The first stop on these tours is New Canaan Baptist Church, where HHT customers, along with hundreds of other invited visitors, congregate to view the musical segment of Sunday services and listen to the Gospel choir. After church, the civil rights-heritage themed tour continues through the streets of Harlem. Tour participants gather around Neal as he cues up music from an iPad connected to speakers he carries around in a backpack – sometimes it's Mavin Gaye's "What's Going On", other times it's Ella Fitzgerald's "Drop Me off in Harlem" – and heads towards the courtyard of the Martin Luther King public housing towers nearby. But as groups cross the north-south running Lenox Boulevard, Neal stops them on the raised concrete median and plays Bobby Womack's R&B ode to Harlem, "Across 110th Street". He plays this song, starts to sing along, and begins discussing negative media representations of the community, explaining how for a long time 110th Street was the dividing line separating Black from White New York, bad from good, poor from rich. While this is fundamentally a song about racial division, Neal uses it here as a tool of potential integration to create a link between the tour's mostly white participants and Harlem.

The location seems carefully chosen. From this position, one has sightlines to the South. where the glittering and towering Midtown skyline rises, while to the North stretches Harlem – with its broad, tree-lined avenues fronting the older, squatter, brick buildings. In this "moment", Neal combines music, visual cues, storytelling, history, and the symbolic power of the boulevard itself (traffic is whizzing by loudly as all this takes place) to connect rather than to divide: connecting parts of New York; connecting outsiders to the city; connecting tour participants to Harlem; and connecting Whiteness to Blackness. Neal then moves groups from the median into the courtyard of the Martin Luther King housing towers – the "projects" – a distinct and visceral symbol of the segregation and inequality imposed on African Americans. While there, Neal switches from speaking with a more standard and whitened New York accent to a fast-paced African American

DOI: 10.4324/9781003207207-20

vernacular while narrating an imaginary pickup basketball game between tour participants. His voice can be heard echoing up the walls of the towers while a maintenance worker waves and shouts "'Welcome to Harlem!'" across the courtyard. The presence of the tour group in the courtyard, typically quiet at this time of day, signals – as Neal says – that Harlem has put its darker and more dangerous past behind it and is moving towards a more prosperous future.

On Tripadvisor, reviewers writing about HHT discuss many of the moments described earlier. They discuss how they liked the architecture, or seeing New Canaan Baptist Church, or how friendly the people were. They praise Neal's actions and the authenticity of the experience. For these reviewers, visuality is the privileged medium of understanding, just as race is generally thought to be visually based (Smith 2006). In conducting ethnographic research on HHT, Jamerson thought the same until he revisited his field notes and realized how important sound was to his understandings and descriptions. In this chapter, we investigate how sound helps to create a moving tourist bubble that envelops mostly white tour participants in Harlem's sonic environment – a tourist bubble bounded by sound but one that also uses sound to stretch itself and its inhabitants across time and space – and the sonic environments of race and Blackness by proxy. Drawing from ethnographic research conducted by Jamerson between 2014 and 2018, we examine three sonic dimensions of the tour – music, voices, and ambient sounds – to understand how sound is incorporated into the tour experience and how tourism helps reveal the sonic tensions of gentrification and racial inequality in the community.

Data for this research is drawn from observations of eight HHT in conjunction with discourse analysis of the company's reviews on Tripadvisor. Jamerson's fieldwork approach was modelled on Soyini Madison's concept of "critical ethnography", or ethnography that "resists domestication and moves from 'what is' to 'what could be'" (Madison 2011, 5). While participating in tours and writing field notes, Harlem's sonic environment was not Jamerson's primary focus. In writing this chapter, we therefore observe Harrison's (2018) position that considerations of ethnographic data collection should not be defined by "bounded sets of practice, but rather by openness and appreciation for where our experiences with 'data' take us" (2018, 80). The process for this work, then, involved the two authors re-analysing Jamerson's accumulated data from a sound studies perspective. We also refer at times to online discourse analysis of HHT's Tripadvisor reviews, primarily to provide a context for how particular presentational strategies are received by audiences.

First, we situate our work theoretically in between racial sound studies and studies of racial commodification. The numerous references to sound in Jamerson's field notes illustrate how HHT guides make use of audible dimensions of the tour experience to produce value for their customers. Accordingly, we argue that the sonic environment produced through HHT serves as a major reason for why the company is consistently one of the highest rated Harlem cultural tourism companies on Tripadvisor (based on regular monitoring of Harlem-based attraction rankings on the website over an eight-year period). HHT offers a multidimensional immersiveness perceived by tourists as "real" and authentic to which sound is critical. Next, we provide context for the tourism industry in Harlem, which tends to emphasize the Harlem Renaissance of the 1920s but is also a key part of Harlem's 2nd – state sponsored – Renaissance that began in the 1990s (Hoffman 2003; Zukin 2011). We then analyse the role of three types of sound – musical, verbal, and ambient. We argue that, while each sonic element adds value in the context of a given tour, the ambient sounds of Harlem – because of how it combines unfamiliarity with immersiveness to the average tour participant – contain a mixture of "danger and pleasure" that, following bell hooks, serves as a key feature in contemporary processes of racial commodification (1994).

Literature and theory review

Our work issues from the premise that sound serves as an important signifier of both race and urban space. Despite the prevailing notion that race is primarily seen, increasingly scholars have recognized how ideologies and indicators of racial identity involve more than vision alone. Indeed, some of the most meaningful and emotional investments in race draw from nonvisual senses (Smith 2006). Such affective associations continue to shape our thinking and feeling about race. Building on these ideas, Stoever explains how "sound frequently appears to be visuality's doppelganger in U.S. racial history, unacknowledged but ever present in the construction of race and the performance of racial oppression" (2016, 4). Stoever's concept of the *sonic colour line* is directly influenced by W.E.B. Du Bois' original conception of the visual colour line and its articulation through the imagery of the veil, a material barrier that does not permit visual transmission across it but does, however, permit sonic ones. Sound's "invisibility", then, hides the fact that norms of listening developed apace with norms of gazing during the formation of US racial hierarchies and are very much a part of how they are enforced. As Stoever elaborates:

> The [sonic colour line] enables listeners to construct and discern racial identities based on voices, sounds, and particular soundscapes – the clang and rumble of urban life versus suburban "peace and quiet", for instance – and, in turn, to mobilize racially coded batteries of sounds as discrimination by assigning them differential cultural, social, and political value.
>
> (2016, 11)

Stoever's formulation obviously includes music, which has a long history of being deployed as an instrument of segregation through the efforts of lawmakers, scholars, and artists, as well as through transformations in the technologies of production and distribution (Miller 2010).

In explaining how urban environments are increasingly saturated by the sounds of new communications technologies, Bull (2016) reasons that our ability to hear is less focused, less tangible, and less discriminating than our ability to see. He thus posits that the audibility of the city serves as a primary vector through which city-dwellers' experiential horizons take shape. Stoever, however, cautions against such as passive understanding of listening. Through a concept that she calls *the listening ear*, she implores researchers to pay greater attention to the ways that "dominant culture exerts pressure on individual listening practices to conform" (2016, 7). It is therefore prudent to consider people's different socially, historically, and experientially positioned listening practices – or what Stoever calls *the embodied ear*.

Tourists visiting Harlem choose to take tours with community-based companies like HHT in order to get an "insider" or authentic experience with Harlem's Blackness. Whereas each tour in some way engages all five senses, sound seems to be especially privileged in tours led by Neal Shoemaker – the founder of HHT and its most written about tour guide on its online reviews. When leading groups though the streets of Harlem, Neal used his voice, audio technologies, and community connections to navigate the relationship between Harlem residents and the inquisitive visitors he shepherds, as well as between the district's iconic Blackness and its transforming racial identity. In this way, he organizes and conducts his tours as vehicles for both acknowledging and transgressing racial boundaries. Sound, we argue, gives the tours added and necessary elements of realism for these complex negotiations to occur.

Context: Harlem

The New York City neighbourhood of Harlem has been a majority African American community for about 100 years. However, due to insidious processes of gentrification and more benign diversification, Harlem is now less Black than it has been since the late 1910s. The past century has been bookended by two periods of increased tourism celebrating the community's Blackness, most particularly its Black music. The first tourist boom occurred during the Harlem Renaissance of the 1920s and was centred on Harlem's jazz venues. These were spaces where wealthy whites living downtown could go "slumming" and experience some of the "real" New York (Dowling 2007). During the Harlem Renaissance, Black culture, for the first time, became popular culture, and musical consumption by white tourists was one of the driving forces behind it. Thus, the sonic colour line has developed not only as a source of racial separation but of racial mixture as well, existing within what Pratt describes as "contact zones", or, "social spaces where disparate cultures meet, clash, and grapple with each other, often in highly asymmetrical relations of domination and subordination" (1992, 7).

As the Harlem Renaissance ended, outsider perceptions of the community shifted from that of a contact zone to a "no-go" zone: a poor, decrepit, and crime ridden space where it was exceedingly dangerous for well-meaning and law-abiding locals, to say nothing of the danger a white outsider might face upon entry. As Harlem became louder with the sounds of gunshots and police sirens, the plight of the community became increasingly invisible to the outside world and came to symbolize, for many outsiders, links between Blackness and criminality (Jackson 2001). In the 1990s, however, Harlem experienced a new " 2nd" – and state sponsored – Renaissance (Hoffman 2003; Zukin 2011). Harlem became a new frontier for investment, particularly in the retail, banking, and tourist industries, which in turn spurred increases in investment in residential real estate. Tourism, then, may act as an agent of gentrification at the same time that it is resistant to it, thus contributing to a general sense of ambivalence among Harlemites towards the presence of mass tourism in the community (Maurrasse 2006).

Analysis of musical sounds

All three types of sound (musical, verbal, and ambient) serve as attractions during HHT, but of the three, music – its sounds, spatiality, and history – is the most anticipatory from many tourists' perspectives. HHT reviewers, for example commonly write about how they were looking forward to experiencing or "getting closer" to some of their favourite music. Music is at once tethered to our deepest held beliefs about identity and difference, while also available as a pathway for transcending rigid social divisions ascribed on the basis of identity. Miller (2010, 2) has outlined how, in support of Jim Crow segregation, between the 1880s and 1920s, "a fluid complex of sounds and styles in practice" was codified into "distinct genres associated with particular racial and ethnic identities." This "musical color line", which can be heard as a subset of Stoever's sonic colour line, was perpetuated through the establishment of categories such as race records, jazz, rhythm and blues, soul, funk, hip hop, and a host of other music that naturalized the connection between Black people and specific musical styles.

Yet categories of Black music have never been as stable as Stoever's *listening ea*r would compel people to believe. Indeed, two prominent themes in twentieth-century popular music are, one, the changing nomenclature used to reference music associated with Black people (Brackett 2016) and, two, what Simon Frith describes as "the *intensity* of musical experience that [Black] music forms have made possible" (1987, 145, emphasis in original). Frith proposes musical experience as an experience of s*elf-in-process*: "the issue is not how a particular piece of music or a performance reflects people, but how it produces them" and how it facilitates "experiencing *ourselves* (not just the world) in a different way" (Frith 1996, 109, emphasis in original). Music should therefore be thought of as a social force that, among other things, serves as a resource for composing, making sense of, and moving through different social situations (DeNora 2000).

Music is a Harlem attraction unto itself. The Sunday morning musical services in Harlem's churches and the Apollo Theater – two musically driven sources of value and desire for tourists – are the community's most popular tourist attractions by a wide margin. The area's jazz clubs are also very popular. Like many other tour companies in Harlem, HHT recognizes tourists' desires to get closer to music and therefore strives to make musical spatiality and history central to the tour experience. Spatially, this involves stopping at former residences of famous Harlem musicians, such as Duke Ellington or Etta Fitzgerald, during the walking tour, where guides share stories about their lives. The Harlem Renaissance tour takes groups to the sites of the integrated – and fondly remembered – Savoy Ballroom and the segregated Cotton Club – which is not. All HHT tours end at the Apollo Theater, where Neal seems to have an arrangement with staff to let his groups in for a few minutes when the theatre is nominally closed to the public.

Arguably the most immersive means of integrating musical sound into the tour occurs when Neal plays Harlem-centric music through a pair of speakers in his backpack as groups walk around the community. The opening section's account of playing "Across 110th Street" is an illustrative example. Many reviewers comment on this practice as a highlight of their tour. Thus, Neal astutely builds off a key selling point of the Black experience, using his agency in making musical decisions to contribute to the story of Harlem he presents.

Many local residents also appear to appreciate the music Neal plays, often dancing along to James Brown or Cab Calloway as groups walk past on 116th Street leaving New Canaan Baptist. Similarly, tourists writing on Tripadvisor frequently describe the positive interactions they have with community members, with several references to locals dancing to Neal's music as evidence of this. This sort of interaction – instigated by musical sound – is probably most apparent during the finale of almost all tours featuring a promenade down 125th street that ends at the Apollo Theater. Clearly such interactions add value to the tourist experience by facilitating connections with local Harlemites. Drawing on the work of Lauren Berlant, Barry Shank (2014) theorizes the ability of musical anthems to create fleeting sentiments of *intimate publics* (see Berlant 2008). For Shank, shared recognitions of musical beauty confirm for listeners "the sense that this moment of listening has within it the promise of things being right" (2014, 2). While we should be cautious in characterizing the complex responses of Harlem residents to these guided tours, for tourists eager to have an authentic Harlem experience, these favourable responses by locals to musical sound generate a sense of harmony with the community.

The addition of musical sound to the act of walking around the neighbourhood produces, paradoxically, something akin to a televisual or cinematic experience. It helps to create a moving tourist bubble sealing tour participants inside Neal's carefully crafted route, itinerary, and presentation, thereby creating the "immersive" experience many tourists are seeking. Writing about personal stereo use, Bull (2006, 155) comments on music's role in generating filmic-type experiences of being in urban space: "the aesthetic recreation or repatriation of the urban through the act of looking is mediated through the subjects' desires, stimulated both by desire and music". Whereas Neal's backpack speakers are not individual, rather serving as a group stereo, the presence of music moving through the city helps to bind the tour members creating a sense of collective identity that is both internally and externally recognized.

The sounds of Neal's music also alert locals to the tour group's presence. As far as we're aware, he is one of the only tour guides in Harlem who engages in this practice. Perhaps not coincidentally, HHT has consistently been Tripadvisor's highest ranked tourism company operating in Harlem for 15 years.

Analysis of vocal sounds

Tour members' verbal encounters with Harlem residents take two forms. The first includes spoken interactions with community members both formal – such as greeting church congregants inside the lobby of New Canaan Baptist – and unscripted – such as more random shout-outs and greetings on the street. The second, and primary source of vocal sound, are the voices of HHT tour guides. Studies focusing on race often ignore the central role that language plays in constructing, affirming, and delineating racialized groups. Responding to this oversight, Alim encourages more researchers to attend to how language and race, as social processes, "mediate and mutually constitute each other" (2016, 3). Throughout any HHT, the voices of Harlem are an important part of an authentic, *raciolinguistic* experience (Alim 2016). Simultaneously, in conveying information to a general and often international group of tourists, tour guides frequently draw on the authority and legitimacy associated with standard English-speaking varieties.

As mediators between tourists and Harlem residents, HHT guides periodically code switch – that is, utilize different language varieties in the course of a single speech event – using their voices as *linguistic resources* through which to create multiple identifications with tourists and between tourists and the greater community (Alim 2016). Neal's verbal presentation shifts depending on the topic of conversation. We identify at least three different speech varieties or presentational strategies used in the course of a tour: *Harlem-talk*, *immersive historical narration*, and *community spokesperson*.

Harlem-talk

By *Harlem-talk*, we mean forms of speaking that are oriented towards African-American Vernacular English (AAVE). In using this voice, Neal projects sentiments and sensibilities historically associated with Harlem's Black residents. When Neal discusses his life as a Harlemite, for example, he adopts a more informal tone infused with higher levels of emotion as well as humour. At times, especially when recounting a story with multiple characters, he will draw directly from AAVE speech varieties and stylize his voice with a heavy "Harlem accent". The most notable time this occurs is when Neal brings groups into the courtyard of the Martin Luther King public housing towers and asks them to imagine themselves playing a game of pickup basketball with a large crowd of onlookers and a hype-man bestowing basketball nicknames for all the players. Neal transfers this practice verbally to the group, for example, a young boy from Australia named Charles becomes "Aussie C", a point guard who's really good at "passing and shooting the rock". Like the musical walking, Neal's "Harlem voice" creates real-time immersion, intimacy, and connection for tourists. For historical intimacy, however, Neal does more asking of tourists than imitating, particularly in how he constantly asks tour participants to "imagine" the content of historically based narratives so that they are able to "see" in their minds what Harlem used to be like in earlier eras.

Immersive historical narration

Several times during tours, Neal provides information about the history of Harlem through a distinct type of historical narration that toggles between AAVE-oriented speech varieties and those that sound more like Standard English. A key element of this voice is a verbal invitation to "imagine" scenes from Harlem's history and culture. One time, under the shade of a tree on West 114th Street, he began with a prompt for the group to "imagine", as he does this he sometimes closes his eyes, what it was when the Dutch arrived in 1626 and bought the island from "the Native Americans" [Lenape] – which he referred to as a "bad deal" for them. When the Dutch came to the North part of the island, it was all forested and there was "no Motown" then. Neal continues this narrative, which was included in all the tours Jamerson participated in, up to the period of the Great Migration and the beginnings of Black Harlem in the early twentieth century. The group is asked to imagine that scene, and their presence in it: "On a Sunday like this we're all dressed in our best. You ladies are wearing beautiful hats with feathers in them. And the guys? Your shoes are so shiny I can see my reflection". Neal employs similar narration strategies when talking about the history of famous jazz clubs or the Apollo Theater, in each instance offering thickly descriptive (Geertz 1973) invitations to imagine. These stories serve to connect tour participants to the community on a deeper intellectual level than the connections found from listening to music while walking down the street or engaging in verbal pleasantries with church congregants. They also serve as a way to produce a sort of temporal immersion connected to the immediate sonic and spatial settings.

Community spokesperson voice

Neal uses his voice in yet another way when speaking about community issues such as civil rights, poverty, community safety, and gentrification. This voice typically emerges in non-narrative situations and is explanatory in nature. It contains increased clarity of speech, using more precise grammar that would be appropriate in a business or educational setting, thus adding expert credibility and authority to the verbal presentation. In these moments, it often seems as if Neal is speaking – or claiming to speak – for the community. He uses this voice, for example, to explain how gentrification works and what it looks like. On one tour he stopped at two identical, small, brick apartment buildings near Abyssinian Baptist Church on 135th Street and discussed how one building had fixed rent tenants while the other was being renovated to make condominiums that would sell on the private market for over $500,000. "How long", he asked the group, "do you think the folks in the first building will be able to live there?" He explains that the possibility of displacement is a significant problem for Harlemites, but at the same time many locals prefer the era of gentrification to that of ghettoization, because it is safer for them. Neal's verbal delivery is generally informal during walking segments of tours when groups are moving from one location to another: making jokes and humorous small talk with tour participants, and saying hello to locals. But in these situations he adopts a more serious expression and speaks at a slightly slower pace with precise enunciation. In this particular speaking voice, most traces of AAVE or Harlem-talk are absent. Neal's speaking is more in line with a standard "professional" or white-normative cadence and verbal delivery.

The Community Spokesperson voice, then, conveys not a "higher" kind of authority, but one that is distinct from the authority derived by using Harlem-talk. It is complementary to Neal's other voices, while at the same time amplifying his ability to speak about pressing issues by drawing on norms of professional public speaking that many tour participants are likely to recognize. The professionalism in this voice may, perhaps, lend his other verbal styles more credibly to outsiders. Such amplification is useful when Neal uses the community spokesperson voice in conjunction with his other voices to discuss negative, outsider-based portrayals of Harlem.

Neal's voices, taken in aggregate, convey authority from multiple cultural and social sources. He appears to carefully manage these verbal presentations – shifting between strategic professionalization and strategic racialization (Alim 2016) – to create different moods and to underscore different informational points for the tourists he guides. Online reviewers of HHT often write about being pleasantly surprised at Neal's storytelling skills or how he serves as an authority on Harlem's culture and history. Reviewers also, interestingly, comment on how "alive" Harlem seemed to them, which is a term inclusive of the area's sonic ambience, or the "sounds of the city".

Analysis of ambient sounds

In the context of HHT, we define ambient sound as any sound that is not directly produced through tour presentations and in-group interactions. Accordingly, this does not include verbal interactions between group participants, between Neal and tour participants, and between Neal and local residents. It also excludes the music Neal plays while walking and the musical performances and church services that tour participants pay to see. Still, ambient sound encompasses everything from random noise occurrences to deliberate human-produced sounds. For HHT, such sound helps to round out the tour participants' sonic immersion into the life and history of Harlem.

The raised concrete median crossing Lenox Boulevard, referenced in the chapter's opening passage, marks more than a division of sightlines between Midtown and Harlem. The latter's specific architectural layout – shorter buildings with plenty of trees allowing for a quieter, more intimate street-level experience – creates a distinct sonic geography sounding unlike other parts of Manhattan (LaBelle 2010). As tours wind through Harlem, there is a marked difference between the ambient sound of the wider, busier, and louder North-South-oriented Avenues and the narrower, less-trafficked and quieter East-West-oriented Streets. Within this acoustic environment, the sounds of cars and traffic, horns and sirens, of wind rustling tree-lined streets and avenues, of vendors hawking wares on 125th street, of people greeting each other across the street, or of stroller wheels clattering along the sidewalk. all work to create a feeling of urban reality and the aforementioned sense that Harlem is "alive".

The most dominant source of ambient sound during tours, in terms of both loudness and frequency, are the sounds made from various motorized vehicles: cars, trucks, motorcycles, mopeds, and buses. Tours usually take place either on Sunday mornings or in the middle of a weekday. Since neither of these times is characterized by heavy traffic, vehicles generally move with relative ease, creating a layered and repetitive series of Doppler effects, as traffic continuously "whizzes" by. This is especially the case on the avenues. The effect can be disorienting to people who don't spend a lot of time on busy city streets. The ambient sounds found closer to tour groups on the sidewalk may include sounds from rolling suitcases, strollers, and the sounds of shoes on the sidewalk.

Notably, Jamerson did not notice much street conversation between locals as tour groups walked past – a contrast from when he conducted an individual self-guided tour, where the sounds of street conversation were much more frequent and audible. Brandon LaBelle conceptualizes urban sidewalks as gathering spaces and "primary site[s] of modern public life" (2010, 88). It is likely that the bubble of sound created by the tour group as it moves around Harlem momentarily suspends common community interactions. As such, Neal's use of music simultaneously prompts while also magnifying the social distance between tour-takers and residents. For example as Neal was playing Marvin Gaye's "What's Going On?" one Sunday morning we passed by a street vendor – grooving to the music in his chair – who was selling used vinyl records and framed pictures of famous Black musicians and luminaries. Neal stopped the music, perused his selection, and purchased a framed photograph of Malcolm X. The vendor asked Neal (not the group) if any of us were interested in buying something and Neal said we weren't, and the vendor responded by smiling and saying, "Well why not? They rich [sic.]".

Neal appears to intentionally use this topography of ambient sound as part of his tour presentations. He's more likely to stop groups to tell stories or provide historical narration on the side streets, for example, while more likely to play music when walking through avenues up and down. Storytelling is a much quieter activity than musical walking, and would presumably be less distracting or intrusive to residents on streets. Thus even Neal's staged presentations are calibrated through his awareness of the acoustics of Harlem's urban design.

Today, the streets of central Harlem are generally quiet places but it was not always like this. On most tours, Neal takes time to explain that Harlem's residential areas were once home to a thriving "stoop culture" where residents would spend time sitting on their front porches to visit with each other, with their neighbours, and with people just passing through. Now, however, as the area has become gentrified, these activities have become a thing of the past; Neal uses the expression "death of stoop culture". On one occasion, Neal was explaining this outside a brownstone, and the front door opened and a white man in a suit walked out. Neal joked, "Well in my head that guy is Black and migrated here from South Carolina and he lives in this house with other members of his extended family who have made the move". The newer quietness of the side streets is an effect of the area's gentrification.

Biguenet (2015) points out that silence is now a commodity, paid for in such things like air travel, luxury automobiles, and the neighbourhoods people live in. Changes in the class and racial demographics of a neighbourhood are accompanied by changes in the norms regarding sound in public. As Bull and Back explain:

> Sensitivity to the urban auditory is often class-based and culturally influenced. Cultures with strong notions of "private space" as a form of entitlement are more prone to complain about the noise of others.
>
> (2016, 10)

As Harlem increasingly gentrifies, the sounds of the city and the enforcement (or lack thereof) of noise ordinances have emerged as issues of public debate between older and newer residents. For example, Neal has shared a story about a compromise between public housing residents and gentrifiers living in luxury condominiums across the street regarding the crowd sounds generated by late-night basketball games in the courtyard of the Martin Luther King Towers: no games after 10 pm (see also Tempey 2017).

Neal additionally uses ambient sound as a reservoir of potential interventions to explain or highlight aspects of Harlem's cultural, historical, and social life to tour participants. For example, during an explanation of Harlem's demographic history, he drew the group's attention to loud salsa music, with heavy bass, coming from an upper floor apartment window of a nearby building. As he pointed out the music, he explained that Harlem is an extremely diverse place beyond its significance as a Black community – thus ambient musical sounds created an opportunity to speak about East, or Spanish, Harlem. On most tours Neal would reference Spanish Harlem once or twice as a way to make a point about Harlem's diversity beyond its Black heritage. If the salsa music had not been there at that moment he likely would have noticed, at another point in the tour, another marker of Harlem's Latinx influences and mentioned them in conjunction with that cue. In this moment Neal becomes an aural bricoleur, drawing from an available cultural element and weaving this sonic observation into a larger narrative of community history and demographics. Thus, salsa music ceases to be part of the ambient sonic environment and is officially transcribed onto the HHT soundtrack through auditory monitoring. In this sense, all ambient sounds surrounding the tour are candidates for inclusion in the tour presentation, although most of it remains in the background.

Discussion and conclusion

Stoever (2016) has provided an overarching theoretical framework for understanding how sound works to create racial categories and inequalities. As we consider the role of sound during HHT, we are reminded of bell hooks' (1994) ideas regarding the desire for racially dominant groups to transgress the sensory colour lines previous generations worked hard to create. hooks is far from the only theorist to engage with the relationship between race and capitalism, but her approach remains insightful in that she sees racial denigration as a primary source of racial commodification, or as she puts it, "the lure [of racial Otherness] is the combination of danger and pleasure" (1994, 370). The "danger" she mentions may be considered a stand in for how racial Others have been cast as enemies or threats to white supremacist capitalist patriarchy.

In this sense, it is telling that tour guides spend so much time discussing how Harlem is a safe community today. The influence of criminalizing discourse concerning Harlem, coming from state policy and popular culture, remains strong. They create a durable stereotype that tour guides are constantly working to dispel. Tourists collaborate in this "positive" rearticulation (see Omi and Winant 1994) of Harlem's Blackness through their validations of tour guide claims on Tripadvisor. Thus, by facilitating transgressions of these imagined boundaries of danger, in "friendly" or "supportive" ways, the tour becomes a conduit through which racial oppression seems diminished and trivialized: merely a means to narrowly defined economic ends that results in "communities of resistance becoming communities of consumption" (hooks 1994, 376). From these perspectives, the tours may be viewed as helping to maintain the sonic colour line in order to facilitate the experience of its transgression in the service of racial commodification. The online reviews of HHT, in particular, work to disconnect themes of Black Triumph from the oppression necessitating them, a development that could be partly influenced by the more "professional" and white normative voice used to explain many community issues.

During an HHT tour, musical, verbal, and ambient sound comes together to create a "moving tourist bubble" that works to suture tour participants inside the Harlem acoustic environment at the same time creating a sonic barrier between tour groups and the community as they move around the neighbourhood. This is especially the case with Neal's musical walking, which alerts residents to the tour group's presence while at the same time drawing them into the group's orbit through the distinct interactions music engenders. Similarly, Neal's different voices contain a mixture of insider and outsider speech patterns containing just enough authenticity and authority to please tour participants. But in conjunction with musical sound, Neal's talking also strengthens the sonic warning of the tour's approach to locals. As Bull and Back explain, "sonic defense often consists of producing a compensatory auditory envelope – not silence, but more noise" (2016, 11). Musical and verbal sound, carefully mediated by Neal throughout the tour, act as more controlled sonic elements of the tour's presentation, and allow him to maintain a balance between tourist immersion and community intrusion.

LaBelle remarks on how the "temporal and evanescent nature of sound" can destabilize urban spaces in both productive and unsettling ways (2010, xxi). Ambient sound, which is largely out of Neal's control, acts independently from the sounds of the "official" tour as a potential reservoir for inclusion in the tour's sonic presentation, imparting immersive qualities desired by tourists. Yet the unpredictability of such sound also provides a "lure" of imagined Otherness for tour participants, combining elements of uncertainty and danger, which hooks explains are central to racial commodification (1994). Sound directs visual attention to its source but, within urban contexts, it also has the capability of producing what Jean-François Augoyard calls the "ubiquity effect" – that is, the "disruptive and dislocating" appearance of coming "from everywhere" (cited in LaBelle 2010, xxii). Within the context of Harlem, which is both visually perceived and racially imagined as Black, primarily white tourists' *embodied ears* (Stoever 2016) hear the ubiquitous and, at times, disorienting sounds of the city as indexing Blackness and therefore potentially perilous.

Of the three types of sound analysed here, ambient sounds engender the largest sonic disconnect between tourists and locals. Thus, to HHT, ambient sounds create pleasurable and unsettling sensations in ways that musical and verbal sound do not (even as they are each coded as Black and "Other"). Ambient sound is also likely to change the most as the community further gentrifies, meaning that Neal and other guides may need to become more resourceful in linking community-based sounds to their tour presentations. Following Bull, we maintain that "an auditory investigation of experience produces a very different picture of urban experience" (2016, 74). Through analysing the sounds of Harlem cultural tours through three distinct yet integrated qualities of sound, we are able to better understand how tour guides negotiate tensions between racial commodification and gentrification as well as the sonic colour line in their efforts to provide tour participants with an authentic Harlem experience.

References

Alim, H. S. 2016. "Introducing Raciolinguistics: Racing Language and Languaging Race in Hyperracial Times." In *Raciolinguistics: How Language Shapes Our Ideas About Race*, edited by H. S. Alim, J. R. Rickford and A. F. Ball, 1–30. New York: Oxford University Press.

Berlant, L. 2008. *The Female Complaint: The Unfinished Business of Sentimentality in American Culture*. Durham, NC: Duke University Press.

Biguenet, J. 2015. *Silence*. New York: Bloomsbury.

Brackett, D. 2016. *Categorizing Sound: Genre and Twentieth-Century Popular Music*. Oakland: University of California Press.

Bull, M. 2006. "Filmic Cities: The Aesthetic Experience of the Personal-Stereo User." In *The Popular Music Studies Reader*, edited by A. Bennett, B. Shank, and J. Toynbee, 148–155. New York: Routledge.

Bull, M. 2016. "Sounding Out the City: The Auditory Epistemology of Urban Experience." In *The Auditory Culture Reader*, 2nd ed., edited by M. Bull and L. Back, 73–86. London: Bloomsbury.

Bull, M., and L. Back. 2016. "Introduction: Intro Sound . . . Once More with Feeling." In *The Auditory Culture Reader*, 2nd ed., edited by M. Bull and L. Back, 1–20. London: Bloomsbury.

DeNora, T. 2000. *Music in Everyday Life*. Cambridge, UK: Cambridge University Press.

Dowling, R. M. 2007. *Slumming in New York: From the Waterfront to Mythic Harlem*. Urbana, IL: University of Illinois Press.

Frith, S. 1987. "Towards an Aesthetics of Popular Music." In *Music and Society: The Politics of Composition, Performance and Reception*, edited by R. Leppert and S. McClary, 133–150. Cambridge, UK: Cambridge University Press.

Frith, S. 1996. "Music and Identity." In *Questions of Cultural Identity*, edited by S. Hall and P. du Gay, 108–127. London: Sage.

Geertz, C. 1973. *The Interpretation of Cultures*. New York: Basic Books.

Harrison, A. K. 2018. *Ethnography: Understanding Qualitative Research*. New York: Oxford University Press.

Hoffman, L. M. 2003. "The Marketing of Diversity in the Inner City: Tourism and Regulation in Harlem." *International Journal of Urban and Regional Research* 27 (13): 286–299.

hooks, b. 1994. *Black Looks: Race and Representation*. Boston: Beacon Press.

Jackson, J. L. 2001. *Harlem World: Doing Race and Class in Contemporary Black America*. Chicago: University of Chicago Press.

LaBelle, B. 2010. *Acoustic Territories: Sound Culture and Everyday Life*. New York: Continuum.

Madison, D. S. 2011. *Critical Ethnography: Method, Ethics, and Performance*. Thousand Oaks, CA: Sage.

Maurrasse, D. 2006. *Listening to Harlem: Gentrification, Community, and Business*. New York: Routledge.

Miller, K. H. 2010. *Segregating Sound: Inventing Folk and Pop Music in the Age of Jim Crow*. Durham, NC: Duke University Press.

Omi, M., and H. Winant. 1994. *Racial Formation in the United States: From the 1960s to the 1990s*. New York: Routledge.

Pratt, M. L. 1992. *Imperial Eyes: Travel Writing and Transculturation*. New York: Routledge.

Shank, B. 2014. *The Political Force of Musical Beauty*. Durham, NC: Duke University Press.

Smith, M. M. 2006. *How Race is Made: Slavery, Segregation and the Senses*. Chapel Hill, NC: University of North Carolina Press.

Stoever, J. L. 2016. *The Sonic Color Line: Race and the Cultural Politics of Listening*. New York: New York University Press.

Tempey, N. 2017. "New Harlem Resident Declares War on Jingle-Happy Mister Softee Man." *Gothamist*, July 21, 2017. Accessed May 8, 2022. https://gothamist.com/news/new-harlem-resident-declares-war-on-jingle-happy-mister-softee-man#comments.

Zukin, S. 2011. "Harlem Between Ghetto and Renaissance." In *New Blackwell Companion to the City*, edited by G. Bridge and S. Watson, 561–570. Chichester, West Sussex: Wiley Blackwell.

15 Creating ambiance through music in Dublin's cultural quarter

Temple Bar TradFest

Aileen Dillane and Sarah Raine

Even before the band begins to tune up, their uniforms of kilts and jackets, and their large bagpipes and impressive drums attract the attention of crowds on the cobbled grey streets of a wintery Temple Bar. The reeds of the pipes are notoriously hard to tune outdoors in such weather and the wail of multiple bagpipes preparing for a performance draws even more crowds in. Another group passes by, grooving and gyrating to the music in their silent disco headphones. Once ready, the band leader gets his troupe into formation, and with the drum roll the first tune is played and the band is off, marching around the streets of Temple Bar, ritually demarking the space of this Dublin district, and announcing the start of Temple Bar TradFest, a festival of music that takes over the area for five days and nights at the end of a northern-hemisphere January. The musical parade delights and enthrals. Like the pied piper, the band leader sets the pace, followed by his musicians, and with them a glut of tourists, busily taking phone footage and exclaiming in a multiplicity of languages at the unexpected pleasure of this experience. By the time the band circumnavigates Temple Bar, more people know about this festival. Afterward, people drift towards the many pubs in the area from which the sound of Irish music is emanating; cosy interiors and the sound of laughter and clinking glasses inviting participation in the conviviality, extending the moment they've just experienced.

(Temple Bar fieldwork observations, January 2020)

Music, festivals, and the tourist city

Temple Bar is both a historic district and a relatively new tourist playground in Dublin, Ireland's capital (Curtis 2016). Comprising a small grid of streets with old and new buildings, this state-designated "cultural quarter" is found in the heart of the city, in the shadow of major historic institutions such as Trinity College, City Hall, and Dublin Castle, and within walking distance of Ireland's leading tourist experience at The Guinness Factory, a multinational brewing company. With tourists now visiting year-round, Temple Bar is particularly famed for its pub culture and "craic" (social conviviality). Recorded and, especially, live music form a critical part of the Temple Bar experience, and music spills out onto the cobbled streets from "traditional" pubs, intermingling with buskers and the sounds of throngs of international tourists and locals moving through the space.

DOI: 10.4324/9781003207207-21

Temple Bar emerged from a regeneration project that initially almost saw the area razed to the ground and turned into an oversized bus depot in the 1980s. A last-minute intervention by government officials resulted in the establishment of a limited company to instead develop the area as a tourist destination and economic generator for the city centre. Since then, Temple Bar has largely thrived as a tourist destination, where kitsch tourist shops are juxtaposed with national cultural venues, and second-hand clothing stores sit comfortably between old pubs, new hotels, and chain or independent restaurants. Like many such urban tourist destinations found in capital cities across the globe, this resultant bricolage of buildings and business is heavily mediated by neo-liberal infused gentrification (Zukin 2010). At the same time, Temple Bar evidences older layers of habitation yet to be fully revived in a city whose porosity (Benjamin 1986) is understood as a key draw to tourists (ironically, often being erased by profit-driven developers). This dance between old and new, perceived "authentic" and "inauthentic", real and projected, is so often at the centre of any discussion of the tourist experience in an urban destination (Grazian 2003; Sarkissian 1998). It is our contention, however, that such binaries deflect from meaningful discussion of the plurality of experience of tourists, and while this book examines ambiences in tourist cities, we emphasize the complex ways in which ambient experience rests on layers of codes and meaning not always apparent, and particularly tied to the material and immateriality of music. Moreover, we insist on differentiating types of tourists as many come to the area specifically for cultural events and therefore have nuanced and multifaceted tastes and aesthetic expectations.

The initial *raison d'etre* for Temple Bar TradFest, which has run for 17 years, was quite literally to bring visitors into this part of the city to keep the local economy moving. In that time, the festival has become a keystone in the city's calendar, attracting a substantial number of visitors to the city and generating a not-for-profit event that in turn supports the local and national economy, the number of overnight stays in tourist accommodations and food and drink sales, but by also offering musicians paid gigs and networking opportunities. We examine the relationship between the festival and Temple Bar, the manner in which music becomes central to ambient experiences.

Music – specifically Irish music – not only animates the city centre built environment of Temple Bar, leading to heightened experiences by tourists and locals alike, but it is also powerfully symbolic in this context, enfolding place and time and a sense of authenticity in its own sound world and attendant significations (which we discuss shortly). The multiple layers of signification embedded in Irish folk and traditional music something the festival organizers are aware of and skilfully deploy in their regular festival offerings (and during the pandemic period of 2020–2021). Ultimately, our understanding of experiencing ambiance in the tourist city in this festival period proves contingent and plural, shaped by prior experiences and ideas of what constitutes an authentic Irish experience. Moreover, discourses of authenticity in relation to place/space and music (Kaul 2009; De Nora 2000) and the kind of centrifugal energy music performances bring to a city (Peterson 2010) are explored in this study.

Lacking the scope to address all types of venues offered at the festival, our analysis instead focuses on the Irish pub (Kneafsey 1994; McGovern 2002), the ubiquitous signifier of Irishness in the global experience, and one that is invariably accompanied by music. In pub spaces, music – along with food, Guinness, and other Irish materials – creates a sense of an intimate and shared experience. There were stark contrasts between the online experiences of the festival during lockdown in 2021 and the post festivals of 2022 (as well as the early 2020 festival referred to in the opening). We argue that the music bore the brunt of signification and ambiance generation. This "enfolding" experience of space into sound (Krims 2007) pervades the sense of community or being part of a participatory crowd (Turino 2008) that is essential to the in-person pub-based conviviality experience. Moreover, in the absence of live music during the lockdown, our own ethnographic techniques adapted, and these new ways of thinking about meaning-making and digital intimacies coalesced for us as ethnographers (see Raine and Dillane forthcoming), allowing us to come to new insights on how discourses are operationalized and sensuousness, grounded materiality is experienced.

In order to understand the role that music plays in creating an ambiance to satisfy touristic (and other) desires, it is necessary to understand both the role that Irish music holds in signifying Irishness in the first place, and what we mean by ambiance in this context. This is not about ambient music as a category or genre. Rather, we deploy ambiance here to refer to "atmospheres" as generated in festival spaces (Alves et al. 2021) and specifically those where music itself is a primary driver of this atmosphere (Brown 2021). The connection in the Irish music performance context and tourist experience in relation to conviviality is core to such notions of ambiance and directly relates to historical and current discourses and practices that tie Irishness and music together in very specific ways.

In the remainder of this chapter, we set the scene of a closer reading of the festival space of Temple Bar and, in particular, of the Irish pub experience. We then introduce the festival and its relationship with Irish governmental and tourist organizations, outline how it has developed into a flagship event for Irish cultural production in a network of music festivals, and use TradFest as a particular case study for considering the complexities of "authenticity" discourses and practices (Stokes 1994; Zukin 2010). Next, we look at what happened to Temple Bar Trad-Fest during the COVID-19 lockdown in Ireland and consider how the virtual festival acted as a holding place for tourists, creating a desire to return/visit, in part through the sophisticated mobilizing of practices that allowed for the holding onto a sense of ambiance and place in the virtual experience. Through both streamed events and a sophisticated TV production routed through the Temple Bar area, music itself became the temporary destination and a promise for future experiences in situ. A brief reflection on the 2022 in-person iteration of the festival illustrates the relief felt by attendees, including tourists, with the return to in-person concerts and events, animated by grateful audiences and performers as well as the city emerging from its hibernation.

In our conclusion, we return briefly to the need for nuanced, ethnographically informed research into touristic urban space where a range of contingent experiences are possible. Ultimately, we seek to problematize any singular under-standing of what constitutes ambiance in tourist destinations. Music, we argue, is far from a neutral sound component in the ambient mix of place. In times of crisis, it transfers – alongside interconnected discourses and practices – into the digital realm, bringing many intimacies. Yet ultimately, it is in the crush of people and bodies that music operates most affectively in the city space.

Irish music, identity, and discourses of authenticity

Irish music is replete with deeper meanings that are part of a broader discourse about Irish conviviality inflected with a post-colonial awareness (see Woods 2018 who both articulates and problematizes this). A sincere engagement with or more shallow consumption of these affects, particularly through music, are central to the experience of many tourists and constitute a considerable draw to Ireland in the first place. Understanding the complex dynamics involved in this process in part forms a critique of oversimplified ideas about the Disney-fication of touristic cultural quarters and makes claim for a space within music performances to engage at multiple levels for tourists and musicians alike. Far-rell (2014) discusses how much traditional music performances happens in 'in-between' spaces, such as historic buildings. These 'authentic' yet liminal spaces are porous (Benjamin 1986), in that the social activity and performances interact with the building and animate and remake historical, cultural, and the political memories through music. In turn, this interactive and iterative process ampli-fies the broader ambience, creating 'new authenticities' (Graham 1999) that are multimodal and contradictory. To this end, we critique Zukin's assertion that "authenticity" and "realness" are lost within historic neighbourhoods that have been transformed into spaces for tourism consumption (2010), instead offer-ing an alternative way of thinking about what happens within multi-modal and multi-signifying musical contexts. Furthermore, through our research, it is clear that these textures of place are not just evident in the built or material envi-ronment but also in the sound and powerful musical associations (Tuan 1973; Adams et al. 2001).

Irish Traditional Music is a genre of music/song that encompasses the instru-mental dance music, airs, harping tradition, and traditional singing practices with roots in the eighteenth century and earlier in some repertoires. Irish music has his-torically been heavily implicated in the struggle for nationhood following the con-quest and colonization of Ireland and subsequent absorption to the British Empire and Union in 1801. Instruments such as the harp long represented the ancient Gaelic order and were burned during colonization (White 1998). Old songs in Irish often spoke to the colonial cause and travelled with exiles to other parts of the world, informing music practices and perceptions of Irishness elsewhere. This is particularly true for migrants of the Great Hunger of 1845–1847, who took their cultural practice them and went on, in many cases, to inform the song and record-ing industries of, in particular the United State (O'Shea 2011; Murphy and Rog-ers 2023). The connection between music and Irishness is something that is well established in the discourse and practice of many Irish music genres (O'Flynn 2009; Smyth 2016; Mangaoang et al. 2020).

Traditional music has represented the Irish nation for centuries and was key to cementing cultural difference and uniqueness from Britain in the arts and politics of the Irish Free State when it came into existence in 1922. The mobilization of the music and other forms of culture to represent the nation-state, especially on festive platforms, is a particular characteristic of the nineteenth- and twentieth-century postcolonial nations (Guss 2000). Events such as the Irish Race Congress in Paris in 1922 and subsequent Irish cultural diplomatic missions throughout the twentieth century have placed Irish music front-and-centre of cultural, political, and economic platforms (Dillane 2022). At the same time, outside official state-sanctioned activities, Irish Republicans seeking the unification of Ireland and Northern Ireland (which is part of the United Kingdom) have long used music as a means of expressing and circulating their desires and ideologies. In the 1970s, certain Irish songs were banned from being aired on radio due to "The Troubles" in Northern Ireland, a period when sectarian policies and growing awareness of Civil Rights movements resulted in considerable unrest. Even as such political instability resulted in the loss of life, audiences could consume the rebellious sentiment at a safer distance; from the mid-to-late twentieth century in particular, European and North American audiences experienced nationalist ideals through sound recordings and tours by Irish band, and that same rebel spirit is in part what draws musical tourists to Ireland. The traditional dance music of Ireland (jigs and reels) and slow airs capture the stereotypical convivial, energetic, erratic, and sentimental Irish (Dillane 2013; Williams 1996). While recordings have proven important in the dissemination of Irish music across the globe (Motherway 2013; Mangaoang et al. 2020), the key place in which to encounter Irish music beyond the Internet and airwaves is the Irish pub. In the following section, we explore how the pub in general and the pubs of Temple Bar specifically are key to a rich and ambient experience of Dublin and, by extension, TradFest.

The Irish pub experience

No phenomenon has been more implicated in delivering Irish music culture across the world than the "Irish Pub" (Kneafsey 1994; Malcolm 1998; McGovern 2002). The pub, arguably, occupies as primary a position in the dissemination of Irish music as perhaps recording technology, and maybe even more so. By virtue of their decontextualized forms, CDs of Irish music are unable to convey what many believe to be the defining characteristic of Irish music – its social context, in the form of the pub session or gig. In looking at any representation of Irish culture – from books and films, to tourist infomercials – Irish dance music and ballad singing would be inconceivable without some reference to the pub and the idea of merriment or having great "craic" (Carson 1996; Hudson 2019).

Today's "Irish pub" can be characterized as a global phenomenon and its popularity is attested to by the plethora of local manifestations from Bournemouth to Bangkok, Melbourne to Moscow, and so many places in between (Carson 1996;

Kaul 2009). This is often the first experience people have of Irish culture. Many such pubs are formed by real materials from Ireland, imported (much via the Dublin-based Irish pub company) to their new destinations where they are put together to create an "authentic" Irish pub. Such fabrications might be seen as part of a process of musealization, where the cultural tradition or experience is made into a kind of museum through the deployment of old, authentic bric-à-brac. These pubs can, on one hand, generate what Appadurai (1996) calls an "ersatz nostalgia", a longing for something one never had. Appadurai links this phenomenon to consumer culture of the twentieth century, often achieved through a connection to something that never actually existed. While this type of postmodern critique is valid in many ways, engagement with visitors, tourists, and locals to the Irish pub worldwide reveals other kinds of experiences. Some "Irish pubs" are run by Irish diaspora, particularly in places such as the United Kingdom and the United States, and are instrumental in the development of diasporic Irish identities, acting as a hub of community activity, some of which is music focused. This Irish experience may represent something caught in a particular moment, reflective of the individual or family who run the pub and their personal emigrant history, and a notion of Ireland which may no longer exist "back home". Equally, newer pubs run by "ex pats" elsewhere mean that there is a historically broad and deep lexicon of Irishness in material and sonic culture from which to draw in the creation of a specific ambiance and experience locally that is in dialogue with global flows and generating a contemporaneous experience of sorts (Augé 1996).

When those who frequent pubs "elsewhere" do come to Ireland, their global pub experiences find resonance with local pubs in Dublin to varying degrees. Tourists and locals alike can generally tell the difference, but the "lie" is less important than the conviviality and context for social engagement (De Nora 2000; Turino 2008) provided. Therefore, the pub lies at the centre of experiencing Irish culture from a tourist perspective, in part because the pub also lies at the centre of Irish conviviality on a more general and local level. Not only is the pub the primary location for socialization in Irish life today, but also has provided much fodder for the stereotyping surrounding the Irish (Kaul 2009; Hudson 2019; Vallely 2011). The pub exists as a place to meet and the type of socializing concerned here centres on the consumption of alcohol. In this respect, many of the ideas surrounding "Irishness", particularly as historicized in song lyrics and cinematic representation of the Irish in America, manifest in the context of the pub, just as they do in Irish and Celtic music festivals. What is "real" or not is not the point in so much as how social relations are animated in these spaces and how ambiance can still be enjoyed at various levels, particularly where music is involved. The tourist that arrives in Dublin is already attuned to the pub experience, through their own in-person experiences or via mediated experiences, and the expectation is not just for good pints but great ambiance (and craic) generated by the heady mix of building materials and decor, social relations, and Irish music-infused conviviality. Temple Bar TradFest knows this and thus offers a range of musical experience, for a price and free, so that the festival generates this expected ambiance for the tourist who has made a choice to come for those very specific reasons.

These tourists, we argue, tend to be music tourists keen to experience a good Irish music festival. The festival may also pick up accidental audience members from visitors, as the opening ethnographic vignette suggests, but by and large most of the concerts and paid gigs are from visitors coming specifically for the music and the ambiance of Temple Bar and the surrounding venues.

Aileen engaged in informal ethnography in 2020, just before the Irish lockdown in March. As a practicing traditional musician from Ireland and ethnomusicologist, she has long been familiar with pub sessions and also has played in venues across the Irish Diaspora, most notably in Australia and the United States. Wandering the streets of Temple Bar in 2020, she gathered impressions, observed crowds and the sharing of spaces (with buskers; silent disco participants; tourists; locals), and observed those who went into pubs for more tradition or more techno-inspired sets of Irish music. While all the pubs in Temple Bar are largely made up of warren-like rooms or sections – with dark wood, ephemera, memorabilia, and other material layers to set the tone of oldness and "authenticity" – the music operates to underpin the experience, while simultaneously contextualizing and giving meaning, in spite of repertoire, simply by being performed in the physical setting. Layers of porosity accreted. One was conscious of being in a pub in an old part of town. From the seasoned performer and punter to the newly arrived tourist, space, textures, time, history, and signification at different levels created different ambient experiences. The conviviality of having a pint, chatting while listening to Irish music was the ultimate goal. Untutored tourists might not have appreciated the working/gig aspect of the performance by sometimes jaded performers, but even so, in their professionalism, the context did "enough" to smooth out those points of potential tension or utopian rupture. The degree to which these elements could translate online during lockdown will be discussed later in the chapter.

Mobilizing authenticity discourses and creating ambiance in the festive city

Starting out 17 years ago as a festival to bring tourism footfall into the area, Temple Bar TradFest has always openly embraced tourism as a vital part of its success. In terms of programming, then, the TradFest programming team maintains a balance between what might be understood as very traditional music, more commercially mediated traditional music, singer-songwriters and popular bands that are Irish, and musicians from proximate genres that include English folk, Bluegrass, Americana, and related "Celtic" genres. For the Irish music aficionado, local or tourist, the artists are a blend of established and emerging acts and the curation of seated concerts, informal sessions, formal pub gigs, and free front bar acts means that the experience is wide and varied with something for everyone. Sites for the festival include local churches, halls, and cultural centres with pubs in the Temple Bar area providing the critical centripetal force for the festival's identity and free music experiences. Highly priced gigs are for aficionados of the music whilst beverage and hospitality sponsors of the Temple Bar Company fund free music sessions over the five days of the festival.

Temple Bar TradFest is funded in a variety of ways, and this open relationship with tourism is an important dimension of the festival. This relationship is a pragmatic one. For the festival to run, funders (and, indeed, audiences) are needed. In terms of the festival funding model, while ticket sales are a part of the annual income, sponsorship is crucial and the predominant entities that partner with TradFest include: Dublin City Council (which provides grants as well as benefits in kind with access to venues under the council's control); Tourism Ireland (the agency responsible for marketing the island of Ireland overseas as a holiday and business tourism destination); Fáilte Ireland (the national tourism development authority); and commercial sponsors, such as the drinks company Diageo (associated with Guinness, whose original brewery is just down the quays from Temple Bar). These relationships exist in a mutually beneficial way, and the festival experience is not diminished by this financial model as top class musicians are hired in spaces that work for musician and audiences alike. Equally, in their use of space within Temple Bar and Dublin city more widely, the TradFest team consciously engages with the musical heritage of the city and emplaces their events within hallowed musical halls, offering emerging and established musicians an opportunity to play on renowned stages and more informal spaces, garnering new audiences while contributing to the overall atmosphere of a city festival.

Attending a TradFest event in one of the many pubs in the area during the festival, the ambiance is created by performers in their specific context and by audience members interacting within this particular space and the consciously constructed frame of the festival, demarcated by signage and the intervention of individual members of the festival team. The immersive and sensory experiences resist sweeping generalizations about the "realness" of a performance moment. As with Grazian's *Blue Chicago* (2003), these discussions of "realness" by those present at and absent from the event reflect instead (contested) discourses of authenticity, and attempts by individuals and groups to draw boundaries and make claims. It is within these discourses that the TradFest team attempts to narrate the cultural value of the festival for traditionalist genre gatekeepers and arts funders alike. In relation to our engagement as researchers, we argue that the notion of ambiance offers a different and more useful means through which to frame and understand the performance moment that of authenticity.

The COVID-19 pandemic, virtual place, and audio-visual ambience

Like many cities across the world during the COVID-19 pandemic, Dublin's Temple Bar was a place transformed. Eerie images of the normally bustling tourist centre of the city were shared on social media platforms by remaining residents, abruptly left alone in a much changed city. Live music, and the tourism and leisure activities within which it is entangled, was suddenly disrupted, the melange of city soundscapes that individualize cities so often animated by music (Jurková 2014; Shelemay 2015) brutishly stripped back to their bare bones as people were told by the Irish government to "stay at home". As in so many other places, the interconnected spaces and practices fundamental to established ways of producing and consuming music in Dublin and Temple Bar were abruptly removed, necessitating the rapid development of new processes and practices, and the construction of new places, on- and offline (see also Taylor et al. 2020, 2021 with a focus on the United Kingdom).

Temple Bar's TradFest team scrambled to rethink its mission and economic model. Given that the flows of international tourists were paused by global travel bans and border closures, it might be expected that the festival would be cancelled. But the team wanted to sustain the many musicians and support professionals reliant upon festival performances, while simultaneously keeping the Temple Bar brand visible and relevant within a very different and difficult time. In its response to the situation, TradFest consciously engaged with authenticating discourses and considered how to use place and the discourses at play within traditional music to their advantage in the online offerings. Focussing on conviviality and the hope to return to Dublin again in the future, the team generated a *TogetherInMusic* hashtag as the festival pivoted online to offer pre-recorded sessions from Dublin Castle, broadcast on social media at specific times during the usual festival period in late January. These events were priced from €2.99 upwards allowing easy access for audiences while also ensuring some income. During this period, over 20,000 people viewed the concerts, many of whom had never visited the city before (as evidenced in chat boxes) and who promised to visit next year. Performing in Dublin Castle, the site of handing over power from the British Government to the Irish Free State, was symbolic, as was the deployment of traditional various musicians whose informal banter and conviviality seemed all the more special, underpinned by very high production values. The team also commissioned a TV special, *Ireland in Music*, funded by various city and county councils (keen to bring tourism to their region), along with Culture Ireland (the body responsible for promotion cultural tourism abroad) and broadcast by RTÉ, the national public service media to a national (Irish) audience. The commissioned artists, a mixture of international stars of pop, folk, and traditional music, were filmed in iconic locations, such as the Cliffs of Moher in County Clare – arguably the most recognized tourist destination for the North American market – to a variety of sites with old castles and more natural landscapes on mountains and by seas. Crucially, Dublin remained at the centre, with the visual narrative of the programme routed through Temple Bar where musicians played outside a pub on the cobblestones or on the iconic Ha'penny Bridge in Dublin that marks the entrance to Temple Bar, and suggesting that it is also a gateway to the rest of Dublin and the wider world beyond. If material intimacy was absent in the virtual audience experience, this carefully constructed sonic and visual intimacy more than made up for it, and those who watched expressed on social media a longing to visit or return "when it was all over". Anchored into indisputable Irish place – the cobblestones of Dublin, the Cliffs of Moher – *Ireland in Music* sought to create ambiance through place-making animated by music. Music became place and mapped out a sonic geography (Krims 2007).

In-person fieldwork and navigating the pub

While there were many sites used for the 2022 TradFest festival – from churches to arts spaces, national arenas to castles – for the purposes of this chapter, we focus on our experiences of the pubs in Temple Bar during the festival period. During fieldwork in 2022, we split up to cover as much ground as possible and given her previous work in the area of gender and equality in music festivals, Sarah focused on gigs dominated by women and minorities, while Aileen visited pubs on the festival circuit that stages predominantly male performers. For us both, the sheer joy of being in these spaces resonated with the celebratory atmospheres generated through in-person access to live music. We both observed how audiences were quickly forgiving of any technical challenges (there were very few) and hugely appreciative of simply being in a room together (confirmed by our informal chats with audience members and musicians). The wearing of masks by many older attendees did not seem to deter people from speaking with each other, imbibing drink, and moving around. TradFest kept its capacity for seated sessions to between 50% and 70%, but pubs were not under the same level of control since many of the gigs did not require an entry fee. COVID-19 immunization passes were examined for paid tickets and, given that vaccination passports were a requirement for crossing the border into Ireland, any tourists who braved the city also had these passes. The city centre of Dublin had not returned to its usual tourist destination intensity and so most of the tourists at the event were in some way connected with TradFest's music partners in Europe or the United States and Canada. The pubs were full, the spaces were shared with other punters not connected to the festival, and the tendrils of hope for a full return to 100% capacity gigs lingered like a promise in the air. What the 2022 TradFest did, as far as we were concerned, was endeavour to make good on the promise of the 2021 online iterations, getting people back together in safe spaces and generating new ambient soundscapes for those both inside and out of the venues.

Musical, social, and spatial reflections

Ambiance, specifically in the convivial context of an Irish pub, is heavily reliant on music as both sonic ambiance and signifier of "authentic" experience. Our understanding of authenticity in this regard has not been definitive or singular but rather a liminal moment of experience of social relations generated by the music, the social context, and the a priori experience, at whatever level, that the musical tourist brings to the context. It is worth reasserting that the relationship between musicians, consumers, and cultural providers need not necessarily be tainted by commercial interests. If anything, the support to ensure that performance takes place in a festival like TradFest ensures that any encounter in the capital's cultural quarter will provide a range of experiences that should, ideally, benefit the consumer, the music industry, and the larger economic ecology of the tourist destination city. Professional musicians understand and appreciate only too well the business of music festivals. Equally, the TradFest team understand the layers of genre- and scene-specific meaning, and successfully generate meaning and meaningful experience with considerable success through the festival and associated mediations.

TradFest was initially created to boost visitor numbers, not to promote "authentic" Irish culture. The festival has since evolved to work at two distinct levels. First, it provides a heightened, definitively Irish, ambient pub culture experience for general tourists as well as locals as part of its festive offering. Second, the festival creates a rich, multimodal, experience for Irish traditional music aficionados and performers coming *specifically* to Dublin for TradFest, with the team acting as both a tastemaker and the festival as a genre-specific showcase for national and international industry professionals. Rather than considering locals and tourists in opposition and, by extension, authentic and inauthentic cultural production, we argue for a more nuanced understanding of tourist (and, indeed, local) engagement in music-focused events, where music plays a central role generating ambiance and a desirable, convivial experience. Irish music in the context of music tourism in the cultural quarter of Dublin is revealed to operate at multiple levels, relying on the music's signification in its material context and within the built heritage of the area. In problematizing ideas around dyads such as realness/fakeness that continue to inform discourse of tourism experiences in Ireland in particular, and from the consumer's perspective, we hope we have illustrated the nuanced ways in which the musical experience in situ can be understood. As Adam Kaul notes:

> [T]ourism creates ever changing connections between diverse individuals and diverse places. Individual and groups from all over the world travel to the same area but along different routes, and the totality of movement begins to evoke metaphors of webs, corridors, highways and byways rather than simplistic dichotomies between destinations and homeland.
>
> (2009, 82)

Thinking about ambiance as something which is negotiated and in flux provides a better and more useful frame through which to understand the relationship between places, people, and music. To do this, it is vital to engage in site-specific fieldwork and ethnographic practice. As we have learnt through partnership work, entities like Temple Bar TradFest evidence a sophisticated understanding of what is at stake for all concerned in the generation and experience of a musical tourist city.

References

Adams, P. C., S. Hoelscher, and K. E. Till, eds. 2001. *Textures of Place: Exploring Humanist Geography*. Minneapolis: University of Minnesota.

Alves, S., M. Gabriele, S. Carillo, M. Massulo, and L. Maffei. 2021. "Exploring the Soundscape and the Atmosphere of the Gigli di Nola Cultural Festival in Italy." *Emotion, Space and Society* 41.

Appadurai, A. 1996. *Modernity at Large: Cultural Dimensions of Globalization.* Minneapolis: University of Minnesota Press.

Augé, M. 1996. *An Anthropology for Contemporaneous Worlds.* Translated by Amy Jacobs. Stanford, CA: University of Stanford Press.

Benjamin, W. 1986. *Illuminations: Essays and Reflections.* Edited by H. Arendt. New York: Schocken Books.

Brown, A. 2021. "Is It Just the Music? Understanding the Atmosphere in FESTIVALGO-ERS' Experience at British Rock Music Festivals." In *Routledge Handbook of the Tourist Experience,* edited by R. Sharpley, 301–314. London: Routledge.

Carson, C. 1996. *Last Night's Fun: In and Out of Time with the World of Irish Music.* New York: North Point Press.

Curtis, M. 2016. *Temple Bar: A History.* London: Blackwell Press.

De Nora, T. 2000. *Music in Everyday Life.* Cambridge: Cambridge University Press.

Dillane, A. 2013. "Irish Nostalgic Song and the Performance of Identity." In *Béaloideas Journal of the Folklore Society of Ireland,* Vol. 81, 19–36. Dublin: An Cumann le Béaloideas Éireann.

Dillane, A. 2022. "Sounding Out Irish Identity: Music, Art, and Social Life (Then and Now)." In *Who Do We Say We Are? Irish Art 1922|2022,* Exhibition Catalog, 54–67. Notre Dame, Indiana: Snite Museum of Art, University of Notre Dame.

Farrell, R. 2014. "'In-Between' Spaces." MA Diss., Queens University Belfast.

Graham, C. 1999. ". . . Maybe That's Just Blarney': Irish Culture and the Persistence of Authenticity." In *Ireland and Cultural Theory: The Mechanics of Authenticity,* edited by C. Graham and R Kirkland, 7–28. London: Palgrave Macmillan.

Grazian, D. 2003. *Blues Chicago: The Search for Authenticity in Urban Blues Clubs.* Chicago: University of Chicago Press.

Guss, D. M. 2000. *The Festive State: Race, Ethnicity, and Nationalism as Cultural Performance.* Berkeley, CA: University of California Press.

Hudson, C. 2019. "The 'Craic' Goes Global: Irish Pubs and the Global Imaginary." In *Revisiting the Global Imaginary,* edited by C. Hudson and E. Wilson, 155–173. Cham: Springer International.

Jurková, Z. 2014. *Prague Soundscapes.* Prague: Karolinum Press.

Kaul, Adam. 2009. *Turning the Tune: Traditional Music, Tourism, and Social Change in an Irish Village.* New York: Berghahn Books.

Kneafsey, M. 1994. "The Cultural Tourist: Patron Saint of Ireland?" In *Culture, Tourism, and Development The Case of Ireland,* edited by Ullrich Kockel. Liverpool: Liverpool University Press.

Krims, A. 2007. *Music and Urban Geography.* New York: Routledge.

Malcolm, E. 1998. "The Rise of the Pub: A Study in the Disciplining of Popular Culture." In *Irish Popular Culture I 1650–1850,* edited by J. Donnelly and K. Miller. Dublin: Irish Academic Press.

Mangaoang, Á., J. O'Flynn, and L. Ó Brian, eds. 2020. *Made in Ireland: Studies in Popular Music.* London: Routledge.

McGovern, M. 2002. "The 'Craic' Marked: Irish Theme Bars and the Commodification of Irishness in Contemporary Britain." *Irish Journal of Sociology* 11 (2): 77–98.

Motherway, S. 2013. *The Globalisation of Irish Traditional Song Performance.* Farnham: Ashgate.

Murphy, M., and J. Rogers. 2023. *Sounds Irish, Acts Global: Explaining the success of Ireland's popular music industry.* Sheffield: Equinox Publishing.

O'Flynn, J. 2009. *The Irishness of Irish Music.* Farnham: Ashgate.

O'Shea, H. 2011. *The Making of Irish Traditional Music*. Cork: Cork University Press.

Peterson, M. 2010. *Sound Space and the City: Civic Performance in Downtown Los Angeles*. Philadelphia: University of Pennsylvania Press.

Raine, S., and A. Dillane. Forthcoming. "In Support of a Sustainable and Hopeful Popular Music Ethnography: Examples from Lockdown Ireland." In *Popular Music Ethnography: Practice, Place and Identity*, edited by Raine, Blackman, McPherson and Taylor. Bristol: Intellect Books.

Sarkissian, M. 1998. "Tradition, Tourism, and the Cultural Show: Malaysia's Diversity on Display." *Journal of Musicological Research* 17: 87–112.

Shelemay, K. K. 2015. *Soundscapes: Exploring Music in a Changing World*. 3rd ed. New York: W.W. Norton.

Smyth, G. 2016. *Music and Irish Identity; Celtic Tiger Blues*. London: Routledge.

Stokes, Martin, ed. 1994. *Ethnicity, Identity, Music: The Musical Construction of Space*. Oxford: Berg.

Taylor, I. A., S. Raine, and C. Hamilton. 2020. "COVID-19 and the UK Live Music Industry: A Crisis of Spatial Materiality." *Media Art Study and Theory* 1 (2): 219–241.

Taylor, I. A., S. Raine, and C. Hamilton. 2021. "Crisis as a Catalyst for Change: COVID-19, Spatiality and the UK Live Music Industries." *IASPM@Journal* 10 (3): 6–21.

Tuan, Y.-F. 1973. *Space and Place: The Perspective of Experience*. Minneapolis: University of Minnesota Press.

Turino, T. 2008. *Music as Social Life: The Politics of Participation*. Chicago: University of Chicago Press.

Vallely, F., ed. 2011. *The Companion to Irish Traditional Music*. 2nd ed. Cork: Cork University Press.

White, H. 1998. *The Keeper's Recital: Music and Cultural History in Ireland*. Cork: Cork University Press.

Williams, W. H. A. 1996. *'Twas Only an Irishman's Dream: The Image of Ireland and Irish-Americans in American Popular Song Lyrics, 1800–1920*. Champaign, IL: University of Illinois Press.

Woods, M. 2018. "Precarious Rural Cosmopolitanism: Negotiating Globalization, Migration and Diversity in Irish Small Towns." *Journal of Rural Studies* 64: 164–176.

Zukin, S. 2010. *Naked City: The Death and Life of Authentic Urban Places*. Oxford: Oxford University Press.

Afterword

16 Urban correspondences

Manuel Delgado

One of Charles Baudelaire's most significant sonnets – that which opens *The Flowers of Evil* ([1857] 2015) – is entitled "Correspondences". The poet therein describes the world as a unit as "vast as the dark of night and as the light of day", in which the "perfumes, sounds, and colours correspond". The poem expresses the fundamental premise of the symbolist movement, inherited from Swedenborg's enlightened mysticism: the universe as an order of synergies, a colossal echo chamber in which each perception reverberates in others until, incorporating them all, this constitutes a harmonious concert of the inputs obtained by each of the different sensory organs in a network of interwoven analogies perceived as a whole. The theory implicit to these verses is that of the sensed experience of the world as an objective correlation of tangible stimuli, whose final precipitate is a unitary contraction of reality that intermixes and confuses the subjective and the objective, thought and the cosmos, the intelligible and the sensible.[1]

Baudelaire constructs his view of experiencing urban modernity on the basis of the very premise that "Correspondences" summarizes: that of an immersion in a special and unprecedented microclimate that captures the immediate sensory information obtained on the streets in synthesized form. It is this appreciation of what Henri Lefebvre ([1970] 2003, 47–53) would later call the urban – urban society – a sensory totality through which Baudelaire calls for a new and different kind of poetry, a language capable of bearing faithful witness to the flâneur's experience in environmental terms. This new dialect for expressing urbanity as a way of life was also advocated by Baudelaire ([1867] 2021, 3) in his letter to publisher Arsène Houssaye with which he prefaces his *Paris Spleen*:

> Who has not, in bouts of ambition, dreamt this miracle, a poetic prose, musical without rhythm or rhyme, supple and choppy enough to accommodate the lyrical movement of the soul, the undulations of reverie, the bump and lurch of consciousness?
>
> It is above all in the habits of huge cities, the endless meeting of their ways, that this obsessive ideal originates. You have yourself wished to put into song the glazier's grating cry, and render in lyrical prose its heart breaking resonances, carried up to attic rooms higher than the mist in the Street.

DOI: 10.4324/9781003207207-23

The volume that we now close brings together a series of studies on the dynamics of touristification – one of the means of capitalist appropriation of our cities – that requires the provision of environments able to ensure comfort, security but, above all, the comprehension of values of monumental truth or identity. This is what the recreation – hence, the falsification – of historic centres or neighbourhoods considered unique consists of within the scope of endowing them with an ambience attractive in commercial terms, a key stage in a process that marketing calls "product presentation". The book contains a collection of examples of dealing with environments that satisfy what we not in vain refer to as tourist "tastes" in the dual sense of leisure activities and palates. This involves producing what we here term "local flavour", the environmental capture of a given setting through deploying a gustatory code but which might equally apply sonic, glottal, olfactory, or tactile analogies.

These research findings contribute towards the growing interest in the environmental conditions that accompany and undoubtedly define spatial practices while also contributing to different neoliberal forms of producing environments. Such attention interrelates with, but should not be confused with, perspectives that have addressed social relations in/with the immediate physical context. Environmental social science and psychology already existed. In fact, all the perspectives applied in geography, anthropology, or sociology to approach the interaction of social formations within their respective ecological niches were environmental in origin. This emphasis on the conditions of the environment as a medium has only intensified following the confirmation of the worst predictions about the planet's future as a consequence of the climate crisis.

However, here, in this same volume and in other works in its thematic field, we speak of ambiance as perceptual prevalence, thus as the capacity of the sensitive forms incorporated into any physical environment to capture the attention of human sensors through the balance or stability breathed into the environment. It is this unifying virtue that obtains the synergies of the sensitive qualities referred to by the symbolists and Baudelaire in his "Correspondences". Remember: Not a sum of sensations but rather a precipitate from which results a single trace. What this book conveys is how this impression of unity derives from programmed procedures that seek to create microclimates of both comfort and authenticity for tourists.

Furthermore, there should be due recognition that this deliberate design of a specific urban environment to generate prefabricated global sensations is inherent not only to the manufacture of tourist atmospheres but also, in general, to the architectural and urban planning projects that, above all, accompany the fierce dynamics driving the spatial turn of capitalism. In fact, the design of urban exteriors aims to generate atmospheres – that is, synergic patterns – suitable for promoting spaces subject to the law of supply and demand, rendering them comfortable, recognizable, and comprehensible. The aim is to avoid or keep at bay the perceptive saturation potentially caused by uncontrolled social reality and any perceptive signs of insecurity, disorder or conflict, everything that generates a "bad atmosphere" whether physically or morally.

It is in this function of literally producing packaging for the commodification of urban space – and not only for tourism – that a new application of the environment concept is under consideration, now understood as a complement to the training of architects and urban planners. This is deployed in delivering the commissions received by urban designers that incorporate the preparation of physical devices, which provide lighting, tactical, acoustic, optical, olfactory, thermal, or chromatic effects that "fill" a place with something resembling the special sensory effects that underpin its attractiveness as well as ensuring comfort and safety. In order to contribute to this task of environmental prefabrication, interdisciplinary and transversal lines have been drawn up, bringing together, in addition to the city council's own technical staff, sociologists, anthropologists, psychologists, engineers, and artists. They have provided their inputs with a view to modelling the sensorial decorations that endow congruence and homogeneity to highly complex urban spaces. Their task: To make them not only globally perceptible but also representable and memorable, capable of arousing not only sensations but also suitable actions and emotions. The recent mushrooming of core categories in the aesthetic production of the capitalist city – including *landscape, public space, imaginary,* and *heritage* – is inseparable from the promotion of this other type of environment as an amalgam of the apprehensions that fill the empty spaces of any territory.

This sensorial ecology, integrated into the training of architects and urban planners, was first formalized by CRESSON – the centre de recherche sur l'espace sonore et l'environnement urbain – founded in 1979 at the École National d'Architecture de Grenoble, under the leadership of Jean-François Augoyard. CRESSON was launched with a focus on sensitive and situated approaches to public places, built spaces, and infrastructural facilities, applying original multidisciplinary methods at the crossroads of architecture, human and social sciences, and engineering (Chelkoff and Thibaud 1993; Augoyard and Torgue 1995; Amphoux et al. 2004). CRESSON holds the particular merit of having pioneered a line of research experimentation attentive to the multiple dimensions of in situ perceptions of the urban reality, addressing light, sonic, thermal, olfactory, tactile, and kinaesthetic phenomena coupled with their relationships with ordinary practices but above all with the professional activities of architects and urban planners.

Hence, concerns over the sensory properties of the immediate surroundings – the environment – became incorporated into the training plans for urban designers in order to produce clear and predictable contexts for their initiatives. The sensorial domestication of the surrounding space was thus added to the strategies for controlling and appeasing real urban life deployed by city "specialists", themselves victims of what Henri Lefebvre ([1970] 2003, 151–164) deigned "the urbanistic illusion", a self-deception that makes them believe it possible to impose the holy trinity of modern urbanism, legibility, visibility, intelligibility, on intervened spaces – now also including the environment.

However, this obsessive desire to homogenize territories environmentally in order to endow them with an "air" appropriate to their economic and/or institutional profitability – the subject of this compilation, which focuses on the tourist business – is not always guaranteed success. Not in every case does it manage to implement its simplifying vocation. Urban realities continue to unfold as never-ending complexities in spaces that never cease evolving. In cities, social events, neither systematized nor scrutinized, continue to take place in the same scenarios that had once given rise to them and which taste, smell, sound, and felt through the skin.

The isomorphism between spatial forms and social forms is furthermore constantly repeated and translated into sensorial forms. Applied to urban contexts, this gaze has recognized its everyday activities as immersed in sensations coming from the immediate environment. Contrary to the simple linearity of programmed ambiences, which extends to the entirety of the senses provided by the ambient music model of shopping centres, unplanned urban life undergoes an uninterrupted discharge of physical stimuli that act as a low sensorial continuum, except for the opportunities generated by parties or riots, hyperaesthetic moments par excellence.

A sensitive ecology of urban space would include not only the more permanent morphological elements – the façades of buildings, street furniture, monuments, etcetera – but also the changeable factors such as the time of day, weather conditions, should the particular day be a public holiday or a normal working day and, in addition, the infinite number of events that give rise to the immense versatility of the uses – often unexpected – by those who are either there or passing through there. All this makes up a changing environment, fed by sensitive emanations of different natures: instantaneous visions, sounds that suddenly burst forth or resemble some kind of background murmur, smells, colours, etc. which are themselves organized into configurations that seem condemned to spend time making and unmaking their own selves. Of course, this sensory magma contains traces of the always prevailing social reality "in the atmosphere". Inequality, misery, marginalization, and poverty are "felt"; they give forth their own aromas and darken the world in their very own ways. There have been abundant attempts at ethnological approaches to the ordinary atmospheres in which planning has not managed to impose itself and where the live prevalences produced by passers-by and neighbours, including those associated with conflict, take precedence. To set out a couple of examples provided by researchers at OACU – the Observatori d'Antropologia del Conflicte Urbà in Barcelona – there are the studies by Caterina Borelli (2011) and Diana Mata (2018) on the atmospheres in two popular neighbourhoods in that city, Raval and Carmel.

However, while considering this sociology of environments valid and pertinent, it might be a matter of moving towards another that would also see them as serving the operations of human thought that, even in contemporary cities, requires contrasts and figurations in order to be exercised. To this end, let us return to Charles Baudelaire's poem "Correspondances". His influence on French ethnology is well known, with such explicit examples as Marcel Griaule's *Dieu d'eau* ([1948] 1975), which is a transference of the symbolist algebra of connections and analogies to the Dogon ritual system. Indeed, we should also recall how Victor Turner (1967) adopted Baudelaire's sonnet for the title of his best-known work, *The Forest of Symbols*, on the Ndembu symbolic universe, and reproduces the piece as the preface to his book. However, the poem's clearest heritage lies in the field of structural anthropology, within the scope of Claude Lévi-Strauss' acknowledged debt to nineteenth-century symbolism and to Baudelaire in particular (Boon 1970; Geertz 1988, 25–48).

This represents the origin of the Lévi-Strauss' ([1964] 1983) theory on the logic of sensible qualities and their laws, set out in the first volume of his *Mythologiques, The Raw & the Cooked*. The theory states that mythical thought functions in the manner of a science of the concrete, working by means of direct appreciation of the contiguous and the primary – luminosities, touches, tastes, colours, etcetera – as a means of bringing about a congruous apprehension of the world not out of abstract propositions – such as so-called rational thought – but from the most superficial impressions. Wild Thought (*La Pensée Sauvage*) organizes these perceptual materials in such a way that the final product as a whole, in the manner sought after by symbolist pantheism, does not establish a radical distinction between these subjective states and the properties of the environment. As James Boon (1970, 14) writes, referring to Lévi-Strauss' ascendant symbolism, "space has values peculiar to itself, just as sounds and smells have their colours and feelings their weight".

What if we were to apply this logic of sensitive qualities to the urban experience? How about conceiving the city not as a text – as architects and urban planners obsessed with directing its intelligibility claim – but as a texture? What if citizens were not only the inhabitants of a conglomerate of volumes and hollows, but also the inhabitants of a myth, a *mythozen*? What if they were also strangers in cities strange to them, just like tourists themselves whenever allowed to escape from the circuits into which they are confined? Just as Lévi-Strauss suggests, it is not we humans who tell the myths but rather the myths that use us to communicate with each other. Therefore, we might well imagine cities as orders of the places that mutually make social life through deploying our everyday practices and the sensitive attributes of the environment in which they are located or traversed.

From such a perspective, the urban would be constructed as a primordial and shifting ground whose direct experience would not establish sharp distinctions between states of mind and the luminous, tactile, chromatic, odoriferous, and gustatory properties of whatever surrounds the human body. This papillary perception of the city would identify it with what Deleuze and Guattari ([1976] 2015) refer to as a smooth space, an expansion made up of forces and intensities, of distances rather than sizes, an amorphous and informal space, as opposed to the striated space that is neither quantifiable nor measurable, constantly traversed by winds and noises, a space of "sonorous and tactile qualities" (479). In *Thousand Plateaus*, this smooth space is located both in the steppe and the desert, but also in the city, a tireless producer of spaces in which the striated is added to the smooth (481).

The real urban – not the planned – would then, in effect, come to be recognized as an amorphous and informal amniotic liquid which we agitate by producing it and within which we may discover ourselves traversing that jungle of symbols which, after having been rediscovered by Victor Turner in a remote territory of north-western Zambia, we may then return to the modernity of the cities in which and for which Charles Baudelaire conceived his theory nearly two centuries ago. Thus, either before or after serving as the seat of ephemeral and restless social structures, we may then think of each city, each neighbourhood, or each street as an order of profound coincidences, at once clear and lush, in which colours, smells, patterns, lights, and sounds dialogue and merge with each other until engendering something we are unable to either define or describe but which we should also end up calling atmosphere, even though this is not what the "experts" impose, but rather the work that thought and the social relentlessly produce in themselves.

Note

1 This chapter was originally written in Spanish and translated into English by Kevin Rose.

References

Amphoux, P., G. Chelkoff, and J.-P. Thibaud. 2004. *Ambiances en débats*. Grenoble: À la croisée.

Augoyard, J.-F., and H. Torgue. 1995. *À l'écoute de l'environnement: répertoire des effets sonores*. Paris: Editions Parenthèses.

Baudelaire, C. (1857) 2015. *The Flowers of Evil*. Translated by William Aggeler. Lawrence: Digireads.Com Pu.

Baudelaire, C. (1867) 2021. *Paris Spleen*. Translated by Martin Sorrelln. London: Alma Books.

Boon, J. A. 1970. *From Symbolism to Structuralism: Lévi-Strauss in a Literary Tradition*. Oxford: Blackwell.

Borelli, C. 2011. "Création d'une ambiance-Le cas du Raval de Barcelone." In *Faire une ambiance: Actes du colloque international, Grenoble, septembre 2008 (Ambiances, Ambiance)*, edited by J.-F. Augoyard, 423–428. Grenoble: A la Croisée.

Chelkoff, G., and J.-P. Thibaud. 1993. "L'espace public, modes sensibles: le regard sur la ville." *Les Annales de la recherche urbaine* 57–58: 7–16.

Deleuze, G., and F. Guattari. (1976) 2015. *A Thousand Plateaus Capitalism and Schizophrenia* Translated by Brian Massumi. Minneapolis: University of Minnesota Press.

Geertz, C. 1988. *Worizs and Lives. The Anthropologist as Author*. Stanford: Stanford University Press.

Griaule, M. (1948) 1975. *Conversations with Ogotemmêli: An Introduction to Dogon Religious Ideas*. London: International African Institute.

Lefebvre, H. (1970) 2003. *The Urban Revolution*. Translated by Robert Bononno. Minneapolis: University of Minnesota Press.

Lévi-Strauss, C. (1964) 1983. *The Raw & the Cooked: Mythologiques, Volume 1*. Chicago: University of Chicago Press.

Mata, D. 2018. "El olor del cuerpo migrante en la ciudad desodorizada. Simbolismo olfativo en los procesos de clasificación social." *AIBR: Revista de Antropología Iberoamericana* 13 (1): 23–43.

Turner, V. (1967). *The Forest of Symbols: Aspects of Ndembu Ritual*. New York: Ithaca.

Index

Note: Page numbers in *italics* indicate a figure or map and page numbers in **bold** indicate a table on the corresponding page.